OF PLANTING
AND PLANNING

JOIN US ON THE INTERNET VIA WWW, GOPHER, FTP OR EMAIL:

WWW: http://www.thomson.com
GOPHER: gopher.thomson.com
FTP: ftp.thomson.com
EMAIL: findit@kiosk.thomson.com

A service of

STUDIES IN HISTORY, PLANNING AND THE ENVIRONMENT

Series editors   **The late Professor Gordon E. Cherry**
Professor Anthony Sutcliffe, *University of Leicester*

OF PLANTING AND PLANNING

The making of British colonial cities

ROBERT HOME

E & FN SPON
An Imprint of Chapman & Hall

London · Weinheim · New York · Tokyo · Melbourne · Madras

Published by
E & FN Spon, an imprint of Chapman & Hall, 2–6 Boundary Row, London SE1 8HN, UK

Chapman & Hall, 2–6 Boundary Row, London SE1 8HN, UK

Chapman & Hall GmbH, Pappelallee 3, 69469 Weinheim, Germany

Chapman & Hall USA, 115 Fifth Avenue, New York, NY 10003, USA

Chapman & Hall Japan, ITP-Japan, Kyowa Building, 3F, 2-2-1 Hirakawacho, Chiyoda-ku, Tokyo 102, Japan

Chapman & Hall Australia, 102 Dodds Street, South Melbourne, Victoria 3205, Australia

Chapman & Hall India, R. Seshadri, 32 Second Main Road, CIT East, Madras 600 035, India

First edition 1997

© 1997 Robert Home

This book was commissioned and edited by Alexandrine Press, Oxford

Typeset in Great Britain by Cambrian Typesetters, Frimley, Surrey

Printed in Great Britain by The Alden Press, Oxford

ISBN 0 419 20230 7

A catalogue record for this book is available from the British Library

Library of Congress catalog card number 96–70426

∞ Printed on acid-free text paper, manufactured in accordance with ANSI/NISO Z39.48-1992 (Permanence of Paper).

CONTENTS

PREFACE

The history of towns and town planning in the most rapidly urbanizing parts of the world is still a relatively neglected topic. The growing body of academic work on planning history, nourished by networks such as the International Planning History Society, still deals mostly with Europe and North America. This book is an attempt to widen the area of inquiry, and explore the role of colonialism in forming Third World cities.

One's personal history often influences the choice of a research topic. In my case, I was brought up in the then British colonies of the Gold Coast, Nigeria and Cyprus around the time that they became independent, in the 1950s and 1960s. I trained as a town planner and my doctorate was on the influence of colonial government upon Nigerian urbanization, with fieldwork undertaken soon after the Nigerian civil war. Since then I have taught planning and land management to many students from the so-called 'New Commonwealth', as well as British students with backgrounds in the multi-cultural societies created by colonialism in the Caribbean and elsewhere. The growing internationalism of the planning history academic network has encouraged me to persevere with the research in spite of the daunting scale of the enterprise, and I was fortunate to make short study visits to some of the countries in the story, particularly Trinidad, Malaysia and South Australia.

London was a good place to carry out the research. While not much related research (regrettably) is currently being undertaken in Britain, a wealth of source material is available. Among the libraries that I used (and whose library staff were unfailingly helpful, especially Ted Maloney and the late John Barrick) were my own University of East London, the University of London (Senate House, London School of Economics, School of Oriental and African Studies), the Institute of Commonwealth Studies, professional institutes such as the Royal Institute of British Architects, Royal Town Planning Institute, Royal Institution of Chartered Surveyors, and Institute of Civil Engineers, and the Development Planning Unit. I also used the Public Record Office at Kew.

It is perhaps also appropriate to state my attitude to the material. Much British writing on the subject of the British Empire has been frankly celebratory and self-congratulatory, portraying it as, for example, 'Rosebery's great and secular force for good, which left memorials behind of which everyone could be proud, and for which everyone could be thankful' (Winchester, 1985, p. 126). An opposing view, with which I identify more, was that expressed by Samuel Johnson, who in 1744 censured:

. . . those Crimes which have been generally committed by the Discoverers of new Regions, and to expose the enormous Wickedness of making War upon barbarous Nations because they cannot resist, and of invading Countries because they are fruitful. (quoted in Holmes, 1993, p. 46)

My view is that British colonialism inflicted much suffering on millions of people. It was an important episode in world history, and especially in the processes of world urbanization. Its effects were both good and bad, or good for some and bad for others.

Many people have helped and encouraged, particularly those met through the International Planning History Society, with whom I have spent many happy hours of discussion. The faults and errors of the final product are mine. My especial thanks are due to the following (in alphabetical order): Linda and Tony Buckley, the late Gordon Cherry, Michael Hebbert, Alan Hutchings, Ben Hyman, Tony King, Goh Ban Lee, Jonathan Lim, Alan Mabin, Michael Mattingly, John Muller, Tony Sutcliffe, John Tregenza, Steve Ward and Brenda Yeoh. I wish to thank Hilda Matthews, who as my research assistant assembled much useful material, Ann Rudkin, my commissioning editor, and Simon Pattle, who helped with the illustrations. Finally I acknowledge the stimulus given by my students over the years.

Introduction: 'The Chief Exporter of Municipalities'

Among history's imperialists the British were certainly not the greatest builders, but they were the greatest creators of towns. Conquerors since Alexander the Great had seen the strategic and cultural advantages of establishing their own cities across the world, but as the first modern industrial power, Britain was the chief exporter of municipalities, and through the agency of her empire broadcast them everywhere. Half the cities of the American East owe their genesis to the British Empire, most of the cities of Canada, many of the cities of Africa, all the cities of Australasia and the tremendous city-states of Singapore and Hong Kong. Sporting pastimes apart, and the English language, urbanism was the most lasting of the British imperial legacies.

(Morris, 1983, p. 196)

World population has more than doubled in the past fifty years, and is increasingly concentrating in the towns and cities of what is still called the Third World. Many of these have been created in the process of British colonial expansion over the past four hundred years. While the history of planning and the built environment in 'Western' cities has been well researched, particularly in Europe and North America, comparable study of these Third World cities is still limited. This book aims to make a contribution to that study. The book's main focus is upon what is conveniently called the Third World, although that is an increasingly irrelevant term. It is not intended to offer a history of urbanization in the British Empire, but to explore some of the ideas and policies applied to the creation of colonial towns and cities, and the 'power-knowledge relationships' at work (to use a Foucaultian term).

Some Definitions

This book approaches the colonial city in the context of the world economy. One can hardly improve on Braudel's words in explaining the rise of world-economies (1984, p. 51):

At the centre of the world-economy, one always finds an exceptional state, strong, aggressive and privileged, dynamic, simultaneously feared and admired. In the fifteenth century it was Venice; in the seventeenth, Holland; in the eighteenth and still in the nineteenth, it was Britain; today it is the United States . . . it is to these governments, who never hesitated to employ violence, that we can readily apply, at a very early date and without fear of anachronism, the words colonialism and imperialism.

The formation of cities was a key part of this process. While the concept of the colonial city is still useful for the development of theory, all cities are in a way colonial. They are created through the exercise of dominance by some groups over others, to extract agricultural surplus, provide services, and exercise political control. Transport improvements then allow one society or state to incorporate other territory and peoples overseas. The city thus becomes an instrument of colonization and (in the case of the European overseas empires) racial dominance.

The words 'planting' and 'planning' in the title of this book need some explanation. For two centuries British overseas expansion was achieved through the 'planting' of colonies. The predecessor of the Colonial Office (created in the late eighteenth century) was called the Board of Plantations. The Oxford English Dictionary records the first use of the word 'plantation', with the meaning of settling people, from the year 1586. The word later acquired its more accepted modern meaning, referring to a mode of production – the plantation system. This evolved in the New World, particularly in the seventeenth and eighteenth centuries, to organize the various forms of imported labour, whether slaves, convicts or indentured labourers. It contained elements of both feudal and capitalist modes of production. To a leading historian of the American South, E.T. Thompson, the plantation existed:

(1) as a way of settling and concentrating a population of mixed origins on a frontier, a broad and moving area in transition from a lower to, presumably, a higher form of civilization; (2) as a way of producing an agricultural staple for a metropolitan market within geographical limits fixed by the means of transport; (3) as a way of disciplining a population for labor under the authority of a planter; and (4) as an institution which develops in time through collective activity a distinctive style of life or culture. (Thompson, 1975, p. 39)

Planters were intolerant of state intervention, and spent much of their energy feuding with colonial governors. From the ordering of a private estate evolved the concept of a regulatory role for the state. So in the late nineteenth century a Colonial Secretary, Joseph Chamberlain, could speak of a policy of 'developing the tropical estates'. Much of this book is concerned with the conscious planning of colonial built environments and urban forms by public authority.

Planning is now a familiar modern term. The author indeed has been professionally trained as a town planner, in its particular British formulation. Sutcliffe in his definition (1981) refers to 'the deliberate ordering by public authority of the physical arrangements of town or parts of towns in order to promote their efficient and equitable functioning as economic and social units, and to create an aesthetically pleasing environment.'[1]

For most of the period covered by this book, however, the term town planning was unknown. Until the early twentieth century, one might talk of laying out a town, but not of planning one. When the term arrived it was in a colonial context. Its first use in Britain has been attributed to the year 1906, and to the Birmingham politician and screw manufacturer, J.S. Nettlefold, supposedly in a direct translation from the German. Significantly for this book, however, an earlier use of the term has been traced to Australia.

In the year 1890 a British-born architect, John Sulman, gave a paper to the Australian Association for the Advancement of Science in Melbourne. Entitled 'The Laying Out of towns', this paper has been called 'the first lecture on town planning' by the *Australian Encyclopaedia*. In it Sulman criticized the grid system used in most Australian cities, and argued for a more rational, efficient and aesthetic approach, for which he used the term town-planning (with a hyphen). He was afterwards to become a father figure of Australian planning, and an influential figure in the early planning of Canberra.[2]

IDEOLOGIES

Over the first two centuries of British overseas expansion one can trace three co-existing (and sometimes competing) ideological positions which exercised a continuing influence over the colonial urban landscape.

The first, which one might call the ideology of state control, saw colonies as an initiative by the state, or more particularly the crown, through its agents. After the successive upheavals of the English Civil War, the American War of Independence and the French Revolutionary Wars, the crown sought tighter control over its colonies. The Restoration period after 1660, when Shaftesbury and Locke were operating, was such a time, with the crown determined to bring the plantations under a 'uniforme inspeccion and conduct' (quoted in Sosin, 1980, p. 13). After the disastrous experience of the American War of Independence, more than a century later, the pattern was repeated, with the creation of the Colonial Office and new policies of crown colony government which could be better controlled from London.

Colonial governors and ruling elites often sought to express their political authority through the physical form of ports and towns, using the civic design language of baroque avenues, esplanades and public buildings. The crowded mediaeval streets of Dublin in the eighteenth century, for instance, were extensively replanned by the aptly-named Wide Streets Commissioners, created under an Act of 1757, and comprising the Lord Mayor and Irish Members of Parliament, who undertook all manner of redevelopments and sent the hefty bill to a less than pleased Treasury in London (McParland, 1972). At the turn of the nineteenth century the Governor-General of India, Wellesley, asserted his authority by remaking the physical space of the capital, Calcutta, which was redefined as a seat of European Empire (Archer, 1994).

The second ideology was capitalist, and was adopted in the colonies to achieve the accumulation of wealth from trade, extraction and production. Planters and the businessmen of the chartered companies (of which the East India Company was the greatest) wanted public expenditure kept to a minimum, and that included municipal planning and administration being reduced to a minimum. When Wellesley was recalled from India in 1805, the main reason was that the costs of his viceregal pretensions were reducing the East India Company's profits, and other governors who came into conflict with local business interests could expect the same fate. Thus colonialism was a mixed venture, combining private enterprise with state or crown control. In the words of Braudel (1984, p. 54), central government was 'more or less dependent on a precocious form of capitalism already sharp in tooth and claw. Power was shared between the two.' Thus the plantation of Ulster was undertaken by private companies formed by the City of London in partnership with the King. Private capitalism involved itself little in the physical shaping of colonial ports and towns, other than through private displays of wealth (such as the grand houses which gave Calcutta its name as a 'city of palaces'), and indeed the colonists of Ulster complained bitterly at the neglect and parsimony of their backers in the City.

A third ideology, which one might call utopian, saw colonial settlement as an opportunity to experiment with forms of social organization (such as communal control of land) that were less achievable at home. A colonist was escaping to a new society. In the words of William Penn, the proprietor of Pennsylvania, in the 1670s,

A Plantation seems a fit place for those Ingenious Spirits that being low in the World, are much Clogg'd and oppress'd about a Livelihood, for the means of subsisting being easie there, they may have time and opportunity to gratify their inclinations. (quoted in Thompson, 1975, p. 229)

In the Restoration period political theorists were exploring new philosophies, and the ruling elite was exploring the new forms of physical planning based upon ordered, harmonious principles. The Fundamental Constitutions of Carolina, devised by Shaftesbury and John Locke in 1669, advocated a plan of land settlement which would balance the interests of the proprietors with those of freeholders and a colonial hereditary aristocracy.

Such alternative societies usually had a religious basis. The Pilgrim Fathers were fleeing religious persecution, and the Quakers had a continuing influence upon colonial settlement (as well as upon the town planning movement in Britain) from William Penn through Granville Sharp to the South Australian colony in the 1830s, which was a veritable 'paradise of dissent', to use the title of one of its histories (Pike, 1957). In the eighteenth century the new colonies in Georgia, British North America and Sierra Leone were to be a haven for either debtors or for those displaced by the American Revolution.

SCOPE AND APPROACH

The geographical space covered by this book is the British Empire. At its zenith, which for Christopher (1988) was in the year 1931, Britannia claimed dominion over a quarter of the land area of the globe (excluding Antarctica), and claimed to rule the waves as well. This dominion extended to a quarter of the world's population, some five hundred million people, of which India alone accounted for three-quarters.

During the nineteenth century twenty million emigrants left the British Isles (including Ireland), of whom about 40 per cent went to the colonies. This book, however, is not primarily concerned with white settlement in Canada, Australia and New Zealand, for the most part because they have already been relatively well served by planning historians. The focus is rather on the British colonies in the tropics and the Third World, particularly India, Africa and the Far East.

In time the book covers the whole period of British overseas expansion. It starts at the beginning of the sixteenth century with the plantation of Ulster under James I. (Earlier colonizations, by the Normans in Ireland and Wales and the Elizabethans in Ireland and the New World, are referred to only in passing.) The majority of the book relates to the nineteenth and early twentieth centuries, when the British Empire acquired its greatest extent.

It ends when the various colonies became independent nations. For the United States of America this was the late eighteenth century. For the white settler dominions it was the beginning of the twentieth century, apart from the special situation of South Africa. For most of the tropical colonies it was the mid-twentieth century, starting with the independence and partition of India in 1947.

Inevitably, with such an ambitious coverage of space and time, there are omissions and variations in emphasis. Being more concerned with the 'official mind', or the role of political authority in urban growth, I have included relatively little on unplanned or *laissez faire* urban growth and individualism.[3] The approach is interdisciplinary, and draws upon different academic disciplines and areas where necessary. What started as a historical investigation into how Third World cities were planned by the British 'colonial masters', led into other areas: sociological work on the professionalization of knowledge and bureaucratic structures; new insights from recent work in history and cultural geography on contested urban landscapes; the legal and political development of governmental institutions. I am less concerned with the designed capital cities such as New Delhi or the great public buildings that were symbolic representations of empire, than with the practical impact of ideas of colonialism upon urban form.

Some episodes in colonial town planning have already been well covered, and so this book deals with them only briefly. Among these are the planning of New Delhi, Patrick Geddes' work in India, and the founding of probably the two most famous planned cities of the British Empire, Adelaide and Singapore. The book does, however, draw upon the rich new material which has emerged during the past decade. Interest in planning history has widened from Europe and North America to embrace the extension of European planning concepts into their colonial empires. In the white dominions one can refer to the work of Freestone and Hamer. Oldenburg on Lucknow and Yeoh on Singapore are important studies of the clash of different cultures over the shaping and control of urban space. Sociological work, particularly of Anthony King, explores the social origins of building forms and urban landscapes. The emergence of South Africa from apartheid has prompted a small explosion of good planning history on the origins of that unfortunate application of land use planning. The Australian bicentennial in 1988 (together with the 150th anniversary of the creation of South Australia in 1986) has generated some important new research.

I have chosen to emphasize the contribution of individuals to the shaping of urban landscapes, but to place them within the context of the structures, particularly the structures of professional knowledge and political authority, within which they worked. If the emphasis is overwhelmingly upon white individuals, I hope that this is not from any white supremacist leanings on my part, but rather reflects the reality of the one-sided political structures which created colonial cities. Because many of the individuals are little known, I have given brief supporting biographical information in most cases, located mostly in the footnotes. Certain individuals (specifically Sir William Simpson, Charles Reade and Albert Thompson) I have considered more fully within the text, where I felt that this was appropriate.

Chapter Organization

The structure of the book is both thematic and chronologically sequential. Each chapter seeks to identify a major theme, which is traced successively through time, usually overlapping with the next.

Chapter 1 examines, for the period between 1600 and 1850, the formulation and application of a centrally directed model of town planning, which was intended mainly for settler colonies in the New World and in the Antipodes. Its final flowering was Light's Adelaide.

Chapter 2 explores the British context within which approaches to colonial settlement planning were developed. It concentrates upon the emergence of new professional groupings during the nineteenth and early twentieth centuries which successively claimed control over the ordering of urban landscapes.

Chapter 3 charts the rise of colonial port cities, particularly in the tropics, from the seventeenth century. It concentrates upon the response of colonial government, in the period 1850–1900, to growing urbanization pressures. Municipal improvement measures culminated in the last years of the nineteenth century in an assault upon other urban traditions, mostly in response to outbreaks of plague and justified on health grounds.

Chapter 4 deals with the influence of colonialism upon a particular built form, housing. It explores the neglected history of housing which was planned by the colonial authorities and business interests to accommodate migrant workers.

Chapter 5 explores what has been for many the central aspect of colonial urbanism, racial segregation. It tracks the growth of residential segregation, starting with Raffles in Singapore, and concentrates particularly on the period from about 1880 to 1930. Segregation was justified at the time on health grounds, the so-called 'sanitation syndrome' being closely associated with racial zoning.

Chapter 6 reconstructs the sudden arrival of the new idea of town planning, which occurred in a relatively short period after about 1910. The application of the new idea in many colonies was justified by the trusteeship or indirect rule principle of colonialism, and for a time appeared to offer a modern approach to colonial administration.

Chapter 7 describes the evolution of a legislative framework for the new planning function of government. This began with the 1915 Bombay Town Planning Act and other legislation in Palestine and Malaya. The improvement trust or board idea for urban renewal became a model for later development authorities, while suburban planning schemes for town extensions drew upon British legislation. The 1932 English Town and Country Planning Act provided an expedient legislative framework for new policies of colonial development and welfare, expanding town planning to embrace regional and national physical planning.

Chapter 8 explores the period of decolonization and post-war reconstruction. In its latter stages coercive colonial power created camps to control dissident populations. Pressures of large-scale population growth and redistribution led to the application of the British new towns programme, decentralization and other planning approaches to a whole range of new political situations.

SOURCES

Such a wide-ranging study relies more upon secondary sources than primary and field research. Fortunately, there is a wealth of suitable material available in London, and new work is emerging, particularly through journals such as *Planning History* and *Planning Perspectives*, and through academic groups for the study of planning history (the International Planning History Society, and similar groups in Australia and South Africa).

Opportunities for field visits were limited. Nigeria, the subject of my PhD over twenty years ago, is one local case. The largest of Britain's African colonies, some idea of its importance in the British Empire can be recognized from the fact that, among colonial governors, Nigeria's received the highest salary after the Viceroy and Governor-General of India. It was also the place where Governor Lugard's indirect rule doctrine for racial segregation was applied.

Another field visit was to the island of Trinidad. Although one of the smaller British colonies in area and population (less than half a million inhabitants during the colonial period), it was used more than once as a laboratory for testing new approaches to colonial administration. Foreign Secretary Canning called it 'an experimental colony', and Robert Peel wrote in 1812:

Trinidad is like a subject in an anatomy school or rather a poor patient in a country hospital and on whom all sorts of surgical experiments are tried, to be given up if they fail, and to be practiced on others if they succeed. (quoted in Wood, 1968, p. 31)

Material from Trinidad is included on the housing of indentured labour 'barracks', the 1938 Town and Regional Planning Ordinance, and the development of colonial town planning.

Briefer field visits, combined with other work, were made to Pakistan, Malaysia, Hong Kong, South Africa, Australia, Israel and the American South. Fortunately, the local researchers and library staff were so helpful that these visits generated much valuable material for me.

Finally, some readers may have cause to complain about omissions, particularly if their town or country is neglected. I plead the pressures of space and time, but also confess to the failing of Dr. Johnson, who, when asked why he had got something wrong in his massive dictionary of the English language, replied: 'Ignorance, Ma'am, pure ignorance'.

NOTES

1. The Oxford English Dictionary definition of *town-planning* is: 'The preparation and construction of plans in accordance with which the growth and extension of a town is to be regulated, so as to make the most of the natural advantages of the site, and to secure the most advantage conditions of housing and traffic, etc.' The word is related to 'plantation' through the Latin *planta* (sprout, slip or cutting).

Another similar word with a similar meaning is 'plat', the North American terminology for a cadastral plan, but this has a different origin, being linked to the Middle English for a flat surface.

2. John Sulman (1849–1932) was born at Greenwich. As an architectural student he was awarded a Pugin Travelling Scholarship, which he used to travel widely in Europe. He designed many large houses and churches in England, and was a friend of William Morris. Emigrating to Australia in 1885, he designed many buildings in and around Sydney, and from 1887 lectured in architecture at the University of Sydney. He wrote a series of articles in 1909 on the problems of designing a Federal capital for Australia, and from 1921–24 was chairman of the Federal Capital Advisory Committee, for which he was knighted in 1924. He was also Vice President of the International Garden Cities and Town Planning Association from 1923 until his death. In 1926 he gave £2500 to establish a Chair in Town Planning at the University of Sydney (See Freestone (1983) and DAustB).

3. For instance, the growth of Sydney, Australia, was sufficiently uncontrolled that a review of the history of planning there had the title 'The Accidental City' (Ashton, 1992).

1

THE 'GRAND MODELL' OF COLONIAL SETTLEMENT

Ashley declared no concern of more consequence for the security and thriving of our Settlement, than that of planting in Townes, in which if men be not overruled theire Rashnesse and Folly will expose the Plantation to Ruin.

(Lord Ashley [later 1st Earl of Shaftesbury] quoted in Brown, 1933, p. 163)

For over two centuries – from the early seventeenth century until the advent of *laissez faire* doctrines in the 1840s – England planted new settler colonies in Ireland, the New World and the Antipodes in accordance with a centrally devised scheme. Lord Shaftesbury deserves to be credited with formulating, or at least refining, what he called the 'Grand Modell' in the 1670s. The overseas expansion had begun in earnest after the accession of the Stuarts to the combined thrones of Scotland, England and Ireland in 1603. Its aims included commercial gain, strategic manoeuvring in the game of international geopolitics, and, later, the removal of unwanted social groups (political or religious dissenters, debtors, and the unemployed). In the nineteenth century emigration was also a means of reducing population pressure at home.

Over this period a standard model of colonial town planning gradually emerged. The systematic plantation of Scottish and English settlers in Ulster (which for half a century received more settlers than any other overseas colony) was followed by the Shaftesbury model, developed in the Restoration period.

Elaborated during the eighteenth century, it reached its most sophisticated expression in South Australia, with the celebrated Adelaide city plan of Colonel Light in 1836–37. Certain colonial settlements have a particular importance in the evolution of this model: Londonderry and Coleraine in Ireland, Charleston, Philadelphia and Savannah in North America, Freetown in West Africa, and Adelaide in South Australia. The application of the model varied from place to place, but there is an underlying consistency of approach, directed from London. Lord Shaftesbury referred to his 'Grand Modell', the Georgia Trustees to their 'design', Lord Dorchester and Granville Sharp devised 'regulations', and the South Australia Colony Commissioners drew upon Edward Gibbon Wakefield's 'systematic colonization' theories in their 'instructions'.

The plan form of these colonial plantations has been much studied. Origins have been traced to the *bastide* towns of mediaeval northern Europe, to Renaissance and Baroque revivals of ancient Roman planning, to the Spanish Laws of the Indies, and even to a seventeenth century plan of Peking. More recent studies have explored the wider political and social forces shaping the urban environment. This research has inevitably been geographically scattered, and this chapter tries to link together the evolution and elaboration of the model over time, and its influence upon later planning thinking.[1]

THE COMPONENTS OF THE MODEL

One can summarize the main components of this British model of colonial town planning as follows:

1. a policy of deliberate urbanization, or town planting, in preference to dispersed settlement;
2. land rights allocated in a combination of town, suburban and country lots;
3. the town planned and laid out in advance of settlement;
4. wide streets laid out in geometric, usually grid-iron form, usually on an area of one square mile;
5. public squares;
6. standard-sized, rectangular plots, spacious in comparison with those in British towns of the time;
7. some plots reserved for public purposes; and
8. a physical distinction between town and country, usually by common land or an encircling green belt.

Policy of Deliberate Urbanization

A policy of deliberate urbanization had its mediaeval origins in Britain with the granting of corporate charters by the crown, and earlier with the colonies of the Roman occupation (Bell and Bell, 1969). It was consistently applied by the British government to its overseas plantations and colonies. Towns were to be centres for trade and defence, and a civilizing influence.

Edmund Spenser expressed this view as a colonist. One of the great English poets, he settled in Ireland after 1580 and became the mayor of Cork. He wrote in 1596 that:

nothing doth sooner cause civility in any country than many market towns, by reason that people repairing often thither for their needs will daily see and learn civil manners . . . Besides there is nothing doth more stay and strengthen the country than such corporate towns, as proof in many rebellions hath been proved. (quoted in Gillespie, 1985, p. 167)

The Puritan colonists of New England, escaping from persecution, reflected the same approach, adopting as their settlement ideal the nucleated village. This acquired over time a romantic tradition associated with the covenanted community, cultural enlightenment and democratic self-government. (It was, however, a largely invented tradition, since Puritan communities in England had been usually dispersed in rural areas.[2])

After the Restoration in 1660, the crown sought to bring its New World under tighter central control. One of its first legislative measures for the colonies was the 'Act for Building a Towne' of 1662, which became a model for subsequent legislation in Virginia and Maryland. This required the governor to build a town by each river, to comprise 32 houses, regularly placed 'in a square or such other forme as (the governor) shall appoint most convenient' (quoted in Reps, 1965, p. 93).

The unsatisfactory alternative to such a policy, as perceived by Shaftesbury, was that settlers 'will expose themselves to the inconvenience and Barbarisme' of 'stragling and distant Habitations' in the countryside (quoted in Brown, 1933, p. 323). The policy was intended to avert the danger of a rejection of central authority, as occurred with Bacon's rebellion in Virginia in 1676. (Two centuries of urban growth later, the opposite policy was being applied. Decentralization, the main aim of the garden city and new town movement, saw authority and social order best preserved by moving away from the turbulent and politicized urban masses to places of safety, such as Port Sunlight and New Delhi.)

The policy laid down in the Restoration period was maintained through the eighteenth century. The trustees for the Georgia colony in 1733 saw themselves as city founders:

The first Honours of the ancient World were paid to the Founders of Citys and they were esteemed as the Parents from whose Wisdom whole Nations had their being and were preserved. (quoted in Reps)

The Board of Plantations, predecessor of the Colonial Office, adopted a standard wording in its instructions to colonial governors during the eighteenth century:

. . . it has been found by long experience that the settling planters in townships hath rebounded very much to their advantage, not only with respect to the assistance they have been able to afford each other in their civil concerns, but likewise with regard to the security they have thereby acquired against the insults and incursions of neighbouring Indians or other enemies. (Labaree, 1935)

Allocation of Town and Country Land Rights

The policy of deliberate urbanization was to be secured through the land settlement, by structuring a symbiotic relationship between town and country. Under the Shaftesbury 'Grand Modell' land was allocated to the settlers in both town and country lots (and sometimes suburban or garden plots as well). Thus a land-owner would have both types of property to occupy him, and would divide his time between them. One can interpret this, especially when the Restoration was seeking to restore royal authority after the civil war and Commonwealth, as an attempt to replicate the power relationships of town and country. Royal authority over the aristocracy was partly maintained by a seasonal pattern of attendance at court and London residence, alternating with periods living on the landed estates. It is not fanciful to see in this the origins of the distinctive wording still used for Britain's system of land use regulation – 'town and country planning'.

The settlement scheme for Carolina in the 1670s specified town or 'home' lots (300 feet square, about a quarter of an acre), and required 'that all the Inhabitants of every Colony should set thear houses together in one Place.' Ten-acre garden plots were to be laid out in a semi-circle around the town, and beyond them were country lots of 80 acres. Rents on land were set high at a penny an acre, to prevent the 'common people' from taking up large land grants and living on them.

The later Georgia colony at Savannah followed a tightly controlled and less generous land settlement scheme. Each settler would receive a fixed allocation of some 50 acres in three separate parcels: country lots of 45 acres, garden or suburban lots of 5 acres, and a town lot of less than an acre. Similar schemes were proposed for later settlements, but the holdings tended to be larger. Lord Dorchester's land policy for Upper Canada increased the standard size of farm lots to 200 acres.

Such attempts to control the land market, sometimes accompanied by a land tax or quitrent, proved unsustainable in practice. The colonists spread out over the land and amassed larger holdings, with or without the permission of the colonial administration. The Georgia settlers, allowed only 50 acres, complained at their unfavourable situation when compared with the larger holdings in South Carolina. All over the American South cheap slave and indentured labour allowed the establishment of larger plantations.[3]

Town Planning in Advance of Settlement

The town site was to be laid out in advance of occupation, according to a prepared plan. This assumed a sufficient number of colonists to begin the settlement, a figure which was set, for instance, at forty families in Ulster, and fifty in New Hampshire. Such advance planning was intended, in the words of an observer of the Carolina colony in 1680, to avoid the 'undecent and incommodious irregularities which other Inglish Collonies are fallen unto for want of ane early care in laying out the Townes' (quoted in Reps, 1965, p. 177).

Granville Sharp's instructions for the Sierra Leone colony (1788) stated that the settlers were to be 'restrained from purchasing land for private Property until the Bargains for the Publick land are concluded' and the town had been laid out by an 'Agent-conductor'. This position (more usually called the surveyor-general) was a key appointment in colonial settlement, requiring close co-operation with the committee of proprietors or trustees. Surveyors of ability won an honoured place in their colony's history, as well as a permanent influence upon its physical form. Among such men were Holme at Philadelphia, Oglethorpe and Bull at Savannah, and Light at Adelaide. Less able surveyors, however, failed to establish a lasting plan form. Thus Charleston and Freetown took a different form from the visions which Shaftesbury and Granville Sharp had for them respectively.

The slow process of laying out the town often caused discontent among the new settlers, who might be required to camp in temporary tents and huts for months. In 1793 the Sierra Leone colonists complained in a petition to their London directors that after ten months the surveying was still unfinished because of the slowness and incompetence of the surveyors. They claimed that they could have done the work themselves in only two months (Wilson, 1976).

By contrast, the Savannah colonists waited with relatively little complaint from February to July 1733 for the town to be laid out. They then met in the main square for the allocation of plots. This was followed by a general feasting, which resulted in the deaths of several colonists from the effects of bad liquor (Reps, 1965).

The most famous victim of settler rancour was Colonel Light at Adelaide. A conscientious and talented man, he completed the 1042-acre survey in two months, compared with the five months it took Hoddle to lay out the 240-acre town of Melbourne. His trigonometric survey method was subsequently found to be more accurate than the alternative of 'running surveys'. But criticism by the colonists, and lack of support from his superiors, led him to resign his position (together with most of his staff). He wrote in his journal preface a self-justification which is now inscribed on the base of his statue in Adelaide:

The reasons that led me to fix Adelaide where it is I do not expect to be generally understood or calmly judged of at the present. My enemies, however, by disputing their validity in every particular, have done me the good service of fixing the whole of the responsibility upon me. I am perfectly willing to bear it; and I leave it to posterity and not to them, to decide whether I am entitled to praise or to blame. (Elder, 1984)

The judgement has been one of praise.

Wide Streets in Geometric Form

The physical form of the colonial planned town was a rectilinear or grid-iron layout of wide streets, embodying classical ideals of symmetry, order and proportion. This has been called 'the ultimate symbol of the imposition of human order on the wilderness' (Hamer, 1990, p. 198).

The sixteenth and seventeenth centuries saw the revival in Europe of classical plan forms, used by monarchs to symbolize their authority to re-order society. Great Britain acquired such baroque fashions from the continent relatively late. From the mid-seventeenth century symmetrical grid-iron layouts (usually without diagonals) became a feature of the estates developed by aristocratic land-owners in London, starting with the Bedford estate at Covent Garden in the 1630s (Morris, 1979). These layouts were applied all over the colonies, often with scant regard for topography. Brisbane was a striking example of the failure of the rectangular plan in undulating or hilly country, sometimes generating road gradients as steep as 1 in 3 (Lanchester, 1925, pp. 196–199).

Although there was some common practice, there was no model book of physical planning standards, as the differing sizes of streets, squares and plots in the various colonies show. Charleston (1672) and Philadelphia (1682) were both planned with main streets of 100 feet, and secondary streets 60 feet wide at Charleston and 50 at Philadelphia. Savannah had main streets 75 feet wide. In Kingston (Jamaica) they were 50 or 66 feet, in Freetown 80 feet (twice that for the main street), in Adelaide 132 feet. Colonial town plans usually also divided the street blocks longitudinally by a conservancy or back lane for the removal of refuse and night soil, varying between about 12 and 22 feet (Home, 1990b).

Public Squares

The centrepiece of this regular grid of wide, straight streets was the square reserved for public use, often framed by four or more satellite squares. As early as 1638 New Haven was laid out in nine regular squares, the central one given to public use (Illick, 1976, p. 33). This was contemporary with London's first square, at Covent Garden.

In seventeenth-century town developments the square might be occupied by a market building, and was sometimes dominated by the house of the proprietor. This was the case in the Ulster plantation towns, the London aristocratic estates, and the unrealized plan for the Margravate of Azilia (precursor of Savannah).

The square's public function was sometimes

lost. Thus a description of Charleston in 1680 referred to a square of two acres into which four main streets centred, but it was not preserved as an open space: corners were soon built upon, for a market, a church, an arsenal and a courthouse (Reps, 1965, p. 177). By the later eighteenth century, however, the public role of the colonial square was predominant, and was defended against threats of development.

The use of the square in colonial town settlement reflects the influence of London, and indeed the square has been called 'London's principal contribution to town planning'. After the Restoration the square became the principal feature of the planned developments of the aristocratic estates in London. The adoption of the word 'square' in leases of 1663 for the development of Bloomsbury Square may be the first instance of its use in the topographical sense. The various plans submitted for rebuilding London after the Great Fire of 1666 showed a city of broad streets and piazzas of various shapes, recalling the great plan imposed on Rome by Pope Sixtus V. The justification for these open London squares was mainly sanitary, with good ventilation then being regarded as the key to good health.[4]

In London the squares were usually reserved for private use as promenades and gardens (at least until the nineteenth century), but in the more egalitarian colonies they fulfilled a multitude of public purposes. A commemorative plaque in Johnson Square, Savannah, for instance, gives some indication of these many uses. The first square in the new city, it was named after the Governor of South Carolina, upon whose protection the settlers depended. In 1735 Chief Chekilli stood there to recite to Oglethorpe's new settlers the origin myth of the Creek Indians. In 1776 the Declaration of Independence was read out to an enthusiastic audience. In 1819 President Monroe was entertained at a ball in a specially erected pavilion. Lafayette, Henry Clay and Daniel

Webster were among the eminent politicians to speak there. In 1737 the preacher John Wesley posted a public notice there, announcing his intention to return to England, after attempts to indict him for the conduct of his ministry in Savannah. The militia drilled there in times of trouble. On the trust lots around it were built the public store, guest house, church and public bake oven. Trees and gardens were planted on it. Memorial statues and tablets followed, including the statue of a Revolutionary War hero in the centre.

This list of activities and functions does not exhaust the possibilities of the public square. It could be used for parades to impress the local population with the coercive power of the colonial rulers. With the rise of organized sports in the nineteenth century, it could accommodate equestrian activities and games of cricket.

The town squares varied greatly in extent. Charleston's first square (the one later built over) was two acres. Penn in Philadelphia set aside five squares for public use, the central one ten acres and the rest eight acres each. The Savannah squares were much smaller, 315 by 270 feet (two acres), similar to London squares of the same period. Lord Dorchester for Upper Canada recommended squares of four acres. Light's Adelaide squares were so large that a critic said that: 'if there were any inhabitants in them, a cab would almost be required to get across them' (quoted in Hamer, 1990, p. 180).

Standard-Sized, Rectangular Plots

The street blocks of the colonial grid were subdivided into large, rectangular town plots. Plot dimensions could vary between different town foundations, apparently according to the personal preferences of the original planners. Shaftesbury recommended a plot size of 300 square feet for Charleston. In Savannah town lots were 60 by 90 feet, in Kingston (Jamaica) they were 50 by 150 feet. Granville Sharp engaged in highly elaborate calculations of plot

sizes for the Sierra Leone colony, and arrived at a dimension of 96 feet 3 inches frontage and 288 feet 9 inches depth (some two-thirds of an acre). His agents ignored these instructions, and the actual plots laid out at Freetown were much smaller, at 48 by 76 feet. Lord Dorchester's rules for Upper Canada specified one-acre plots (dimensions unstated). In the South Australia colony town plots were to be half an acre.

Such precision became irrelevant once plots began to be subdivided. Sometimes the splitting up became so excessive that legislative control was imposed. An example comes from the extreme free-market individualism of Queensland, Australia, where in 1885 an Undue Subdivision of Land Act was belatedly passed, prohibiting subdivision into plots of less than a certain size (16 perches) (Fitzgerald, 1982, pp. 315–317).

Plot frontages of 50 feet wide, or more, were two or even three times those found in British towns of the period. In them we can see the origins of the British and North American pattern of low-density urban and suburban development. The colonial plan actively discouraged continuous built-up frontages, partly reflecting the ready supply of land, but more as a response to the two great dangers of urban life at the time – fire and disease. Thus did London's Great Plague of 1665 and Great Fire of 1666 (which both Shaftesbury and Penn lived through) leave their mark on colonial planning.[5] In Philadelphia, according to Penn,

every house be placed, if the person pleases, in the middle of its plot, as to the breadth way of it, so that there may be ground on each side for gardens, or orchards, or fields, that it may be a green country town, which will never be burnt, and always be wholesome. (quoted in Morris, 1979, p. 266)

An account of the Savannah colony in 1745 said that:

The Houses are built some Distance from each other, to allow more Air and Garden Room, and prevent the Communication, in Case of any Accident by Fire. (quoted in Reps, 1965, p. 192)

Public Land Reservations

Land was to be reserved for public purposes or as a source of public revenue. In Penn's Philadelphia the central square was to be surrounded at each angle by 'houses for Public Affairs, as a Meeting House, Assembly or State House, Market-House, School-House, and several other buildings for Public Concerns.' Around the Savannah squares were four so-called Trustee lots, intended for churches, markets, stores, and other public purposes. In Upper Canada Lord Dorchester's township scheme sought to reserve on each side of the central square four acres for public buildings: worship, parsonage, schoolhouse, courthouse, prison and workhouse, and more land at the outer corners of the town plot was reserved for hospitals, burial places, and markets (Wood, 1982).

Granville Sharp proposed a particularly elaborate – and muddled – formula for public lands. In his scheme for Sierra Leone (which was not put into practice) the 'Agent-conductor' was to receive every tenth plot 'on account of his extra-ordinary care and trouble in the agreeing for the land, and for laying out the plots.' His land was held in guarantee for the payment of public debts. In addition, for every ten private plots, two were to be set aside for cultivation by public labour, the produce being used to fund health and education services. Finally, for every hundred private plots, ten additional public lots are to be reserved, one each for a male and a female asylum, poor families' asylum, hospital, prison, glebe land, land registry, parish clerk and assistant clerk, and the tenth for 'any other public use'. If implemented Sharp's formula would have reserved in total more than a third of the laid-out land for public purposes (Sharp, 1788, quoted in Home, 1991).

The public lands reservation was that feature of the colonial town planning model most often abandoned in the transition to *laissez faire* individualism after about 1840. The South Australian Colonization Commission was economical with its public land allocation. The utilitarian and *laissez faire* approach to colonial settlement meant that its rules and regulations merely stated that:

The streets, market place, wharf, public promenade and other places of general resort will be reserved as public property: the remaining portion will be divided into sections of ½ acre each . . . and will be offered for sale. (1838 Report of Colonization Commissioners, quoted in Bunker and Hutchings, 1986)

This was more typical of the hundreds of town creations which sprang up across the New World (Hamer, 1990).

Green Belts

In the colonial model we find a source for that most famous of British planning concepts, the Green Belt, or the physical separation of town and country by a building-free zone, usually encircling the town. The exact term 'Green Belt' apparently originates with Ebenezer Howard around 1900, but the concept was there in early colonial plantations, such as Ulster and Philadelphia, which reserved a common for sheep pasturing. Subsequently more general public uses were envisaged. The 1717 plan for Azilia advocated 'a large void space, which will be useful for a thousand purposes and among the rest, as being airy and affording a fine prospect of the town in drawing near it' (quoted in Reps, 1984, p. 114). The famous Adelaide plan proposed an encircling parkbelt, for which the case was put by Maslen (1830) in his book, *The Friend of Australia*:

All the entrances to every town should be through a park, that is to say a belt of park of about a mile or two in diameter should entirely surround every town . . . This would greatly contribute to the health and pleasure of the inhabitants; it would render the surrounding properties beautiful, and give a magnificent appearance to a town, from whatever quarter viewed.

Maslen suggested a parkbelt 'about a mile or two in diameter', but his later book (1843) reduced it to 'about half a mile in width'. Granville Sharp (1794) had been content with even less for his ideal colony: 'Common land round the Town 110 Yards broad or half a Furlong broad.'

Sometimes the green belt had a defensive role. Granville Sharp's 1794 plan required it to include 'small redoubts of Earth or Sod, for the outPosts of the nightly Guard', 'Parapets or Entrenchments to command the general Avenues', and an encircling dike and ditch 'which will enable the Inhabitants to defend themselves against very superior forces of Invading Chiefs or Robbers' (Sharp, 1794). This was certainly appropriate for his Freetown colony, which had to defend itself against outside attacks from both the French and local tribes. In Georgia and South Australia the settlers found the aborigines unthreatening,

and the defensive role was minimal. In Adelaide the aborigines continued to use the parklands for seasonal camping, like gypsies on the commons of twentieth-century Britain (Hamer, 1990, p. 216).

The concept of a common or parkbelt did not always survive *laissez faire* capitalism. Savannah developed southwards over its common land. In New Zealand the park belts for New Plymouth and Christchurch gradually disappeared, either because Maori hostility forced the settlers to move closer in, or because the colonization company needed to boost its shaky finances by selling the land for development. In South Australia such pressures were less, and protection of the parklands enjoyed strong public support. In 1990, of the 930 hectares set aside by Light for Adelaide's parklands, about 700 still remained in that use.[6]

THE EVOLUTION OF THE MODEL

The model for colonial settlement presented above emerged early in Britain's overseas expansion, and its essential features were modified and elaborated relatively little over the succeeding two hundred years. The process of plantation was cyclical, with new initiatives emanating from London at intervals of about fifty years. The intervening periods were times of war and disruption, and of slow digestion of territorial gains. We can trace the main episodes in the history through the successive founding of settlements that became exemplars of the art (or science) of town planning.

If one explores how, and by whom, the ideas or ideologies of colonial settlement were transmitted, the picture emerges of a small network of individuals within the political elite, men of education and influence, usually London-based, and personally connected through long periods of time. Key figures in the period before 1800 are Lord Shaftesbury, Benjamin

Martyn, and Granville Sharp. Shaftesbury, in touch with experienced colonizers and with Baroque planning ideas from the continent, not only launched the Carolina colony but also seems to have largely created the urbanization policies which the Board of Trade and Plantations followed for over a century. The less known Benjamin Martyn, in his day a renowned man of letters, seems to have been the prime mover in the sophisticated Georgia plan which Oglethorpe implemented so successfully in Savannah. Granville Sharp's publications associated with the Sierra Leone colony had a continuing influence.

Colonial planning also attracted some important political thinkers. John Locke was private secretary to Shaftesbury at the time of his colonial involvements and succeeded him for a time as chairman of the Board of Trade and Plantations. Bishop Berkeley, the founder of subjective idealism, was closely involved with the Georgia colony, corresponding with Oglethorpe and contributing funds from his failed college in Bermuda. The Benthamite utilitarians were closely associated with South Australia and the colonizers of New Zealand.

Although these individuals influencing colonial settlement were separated from each other by periods of fifty years or more, they had personal knowledge of each other's activities. Thus Martyn was commissioned to write the life of his predecessor in town planning, Shaftesbury, by the Fourth Earl. Granville Sharp personally knew Oglethorpe, the founder of Savannah, and was himself connected with the Nonconformist political reform movement which, two decades after his death, gave rise to the South Australia colony.

The chronological evolution of the model starts with the settlement, or plantation, of Ulster.

1610–40: The Plantation of Ulster

Ireland had been a testing ground for Anglo-Norman colonization techniques from the Middle Ages, and the pace of activity increased from the late Elizabethan period through the seventeenth century. The forfeiture of lands after the so-called 'Flight of the Earls' in 1607 created a particular opportunity for the recently united English and Scottish crowns to undertake a plantation of Ulster.[7] James I entered into a partnership with the livery companies of the City of London, under which some thirty thousand people settled in Ulster by 1659. Among those who went to Ulster to plan the new settlement were Thomas Raven and Sir Thomas Phillips.[8]

The Ulster scheme of plantation proposed market towns for each county, of which sixteen were incorporated during James I's reign. The more planned layouts at Coleraine (developed by the supervising Irish Society) and Derry incorporated a simple grid-iron layout. The focal point of the towns was the market-place (called then and since the diamond). This contained a market cross or (as at Londonderry) a public building which combined as the town hall and market. The local landlord's house was the centre of civic and commercial life.

The land settlement of each town distinguished between burgess, common and corporation land. Land was reserved for house and garden plots, a church and churchyard, school, streets and a market-place. About a third of the corporate land was set aside to be a common meadow for cattle and to grow food reserves for times of bad harvest. Corporation land next to the town was rented to finance urban development, and was not to be enclosed until the town was sufficiently peopled (forty houses built).

These plantation methods thus contained most elements of the planning model, and were applied elsewhere in Ireland during the subsequent settlements of Cromwell and William of Orange. Many of Britain's overseas colonists had Anglo-Irish connections, starting with Sir Walter Raleigh. William Penn was familiar with Ulster. Thomas Holme, who laid out Philadelphia, had been an officer in Cromwell's army in Ireland in the 1650s, and received a land grant there. Berkeley and Percival, who were involved with the planning of the Georgia colony, are known to have corresponded about the Londonderry foundation. Lord Dorchester, who laid down the land settlement policy for Upper Canada in the 1780s, was born in Strabane, a descendant of one of the first Protestant settlers in Ulster, and had an estate in Newry, County Down.[9]

At the same time as the Ulster plantation, colonies in the New World were also attracting settlers. Initially the numbers were small: some twenty-five thousand in New England in the period 1620–1650, and about eight thousand in Virginia and around the Chesapeake. Among the Caribbean islands St Kitts was the most populous, with a population of fourteen thousand in 1640 (Craven, 1949, p. 183, and Thompson, 1975, p. 317). These colonies,

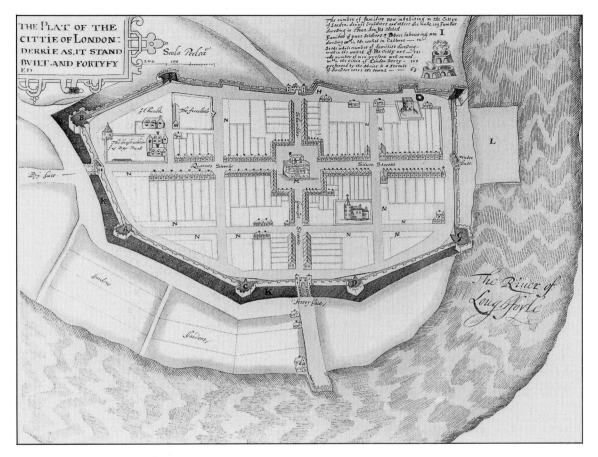

Plan (or 'plat') of Londonderry, Northern Ireland, in 1622. Planned as the chief town of the Ulster Plantation, it shows some of the early elements of the colonial town planning model, such as grid layout, regular plots, central square (or 'diamond'), and garden belt. This drawing by Sir Thomas Phillips and Ralph Hadsor was published in 1884 in Gilbert's Facsimiles of National Manuscripts *of Ireland. (Source: Reproduced from the facsimile by Historic Urban Plans, Inc., Ithaca, New York, of a map in Cornell University)*

however, were not planned according to any centrally devised model. It was only with closer central control in the Restoration period, and the emergence of a new form of settlement, the proprietary colonies of Carolina and Pennsylvania, that individual proprietor/entrepreneurs were able to direct the settlement process, laying out the streets ahead of the buildings according to a preconceived plan.

Restoration Planning 1660–1685: Charleston and Philadelphia

After the turbulence and uncertainties of the Civil War and Cromwellian interregnum, the Restoration in 1660 returned to power a crown determined to bring together the 'loose and scattered' plantations under a 'uniforme inspeccion and conduct' (Sosin, 1980, p. 13). A

Council of Foreign Plantations was created. Later reorganized into a Council or Board of Trade and Foreign Plantations, it was eventually replaced in the late eighteenth century by the Colonial Office. According to Wood (1982):

We might visualise the secretariat, with its ready access to progressive theory of all kinds and with relative stability in which to develop its thinking, as a shelter where innovative ideas could take root and metamorphose over lengthy periods.

This is perhaps a rather idealized view of how a bureaucracy operates, but certainly the Council brought a continuity of policy, from which crystallized the colonial planning model. From its inception the Council emphasized towns as the basis for colonial prosperity, as was reflected in the legislation of 1662 requiring the Governor of Virginia to build towns upon each river.

The key figure in colonial affairs during the Restoration period was unquestionably Lord Shaftesbury. The playwright John Dryden characterized him as:

For close designs and crooked counsels fit.
Sagacious, bold and turbulent of wit,
Restless, unfixed in principles and place,
In power unpleased, impatient of disgrace.[10]

He was active on the various councils and committees concerned with trade and plantations for some twenty years, under both the Commonwealth and the Restoration, until dismissed by Charles II in 1673. According to one of his biographers, he was 'the nearest to a minister for colonial affairs that England had yet seen,' and after his dismissal 'it was to be many years before a statesman of Shaftesbury's qualifications, influence and ability to get things done was able to appraise the problems of colonial government' (Haley, 1968, pp. 228 and 263). In Shaftesbury's writings, and those of his secretary, the political philosopher John Locke, one finds the essential elements of the colonial town plan. He called it his 'Grand Modell', and tried to put it into practice in the Carolina colony.

Shaftesbury disapproved of 'stragling and distant Habitations' in the countryside:

If men are not overruled in this wee find by the experience of both Virginia and Maryland that men will expose themselves to the inconvenience and Barbarisme of scattered Dwellings in unknown Countreyes. (Brown, 1933, p. 323)

He believed that New England had developed faster than Virginia because of the practice of 'planting in Townes', which he saw as the 'Chiefe thing that hath given New England soe much the advantage over Virginia and advanced that Plantation in so short a time to the height it is now at' (Brown, 1933, p. 163).

He got the opportunity to put his ideas into practice when a new colony south of the Chesapeake was created by royal charter in 1663. It was named Carolina after the King, and Shaftesbury was the most active of the eight proprietors. He called the project 'my darling', and after his fall from political power considered going into exile there, although he never did cross the Atlantic (Weir, 1983, p. 53). His instructions to the pioneer expedition of 1669 laid down his plan. The port was to be built on high ground, with the main street a hundred feet wide, other streets at least sixty feed wide, and alleys between the houses at least eight feet wide. Each householder was to be allotted a square of 300 feet for his house.

Be the buildings never so meane and thin at first yet as the Town increases in Riches and People the voyd spaces will be filled up and the buildings will grow more beautyfulle. (quoted in Brown, 1933, p. 164)

The first colonists did not execute the full detail of his instructions, but when Charles Town was relocated in 1680 it became the first American town to follow a grid-iron layout, albeit in a somewhat cramped style.

Shaftsbury added to the Ulster plantation approach new baroque planning concepts derived from the European mainland. Political theorists in England were exploring new philosophies, and the ruling elite was belatedly exploring the forms of Renaissance planning based upon ordered, harmonious geometric principles. The Earl of Bedford had been first to imitate Italian and French models with the Covent Garden piazza from the 1630s. After the Restoration the square became the principal unit of major layouts in the West End (Morris, 1979, chapter 8). Shaftesbury himself had little land, and no great London estate to develop, but he aspired in his plan for Charleston to a modest version of the Renaissance model. His Fundamental Constitutions of Carolina in 1669 prescribed a plan of land settlement which would balance the interests of the proprietors with those of freeholders and a colonial hereditary aristocracy. The land was to be laid out in squares of twelve thousand acres each, with large town or 'home' lots, ten-acre garden plots around the town, and country lots of 80 acres (Craven, 1949, pp. 338–40, and Brown, 1933, p. 168).

Shaftesbury's land settlement contributed to the development of Carolina as a slave-owning planter society, although his attempt to control the size of land holdings failed. South Carolina was the most prosperous of the American colonies in the years before the Revolutionary War. Shaftesbury's creation, Charles Town, from a population of less than two thousand in 1700, grew rapidly to 6800 by 1742, the fourth largest city in the North American colonies. Many of the richest American and Caribbean colonists lived or spent time there, and it supported a large service sector of artisans and traders. After a fire in 1740 it was rebuilt as a gracious city, with a riverside park and promenade, and, according to a gazetteer of 1794:

In no part of America are the social blessings enjoyed more rationally and liberally than in Charlestown. (Morse 1794, p. 539)

It was renamed Charleston in 1783, at the end of the American War of Independence, and became a cultural capital of the American South (together with New Orleans after the Louisiana Purchase). South Carolina led the South out of the Union in 1860, and the American Civil War broke out at Charleston, with the bombardment of Fort Sumter.

In the 1950s Edgar Thompson identified Charleston and New Orleans as the great capitals of plantation society:

The individual plantations fed their experiences, beliefs, problems and lore to the wise men and prophets of the capitals; these experiences and this lore came back in standardized form as ideology and conviction . . . If the capital cities of the Southern plantation system belonged to the planters, the heterogenetic cities of the present South belong to the merchants and adventurers. Atlanta and Dallas . . . have taken the place of Charleston and New Orleans, and chambers of commerce have taken the place of planters' associations. (Thompson, 1975, pp. 321–322)

Charleston was a quintessential orthogenetic city, in the Redfield and Singer typology. One can speculate to what extent its cultural predominance was a result of Shaftesbury's 'Grand Modell' of land settlement and town planning.[11]

Shaftesbury's settlement scheme for Charleston and Carolina, which contained the elements of the colonial planning model, was not fully implemented. A more complete realization of the Renaissance town plan was achieved in another proprietary colony of the period, that of Pennsylvania. When in 1681 the Quaker, William Penn, drew up a detailed brief for Philadelphia, the capital of his proprietary estate, he followed Shaftesbury's approach, and also the Newcourt plan for the rebuilding of London after the Great Fire. Philadelphia had by far the largest acreage of any seventeenth-century North American town. Its Surveyor-General, Holme, described it thus:

the city consists of a large Front-Street to each River, and a High-Street (near the middle) from Front (or River) to Front, of one hundred foot broad, and a Broad-Street in the middle of the city

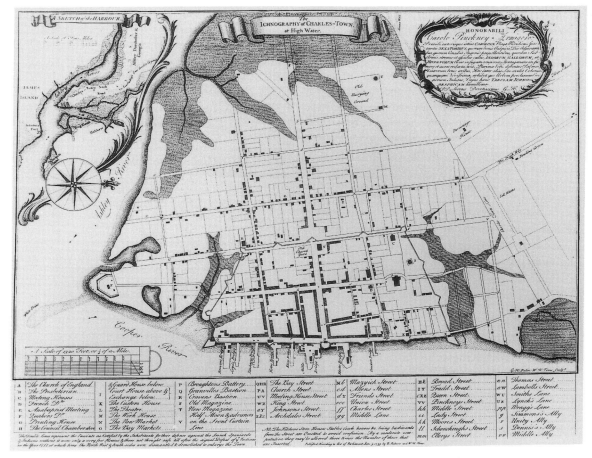

Charleston in 1739 (still known as Charles Towne in honour of King Charles II), relocated from the original site and undergoing expansion beyond the city walls. In 1717 the town had been enlarged by the creation of several new streets and a civic square. The square is beginning to be built over by a market, and divided by fortifications. (Source: Reproduced from the facsimile by Historic Urban Plans, Inc., Ithaca, New York, of a map in Cornell University)

from side to side of the like breadth. In the centre of the city is a square of ten acres; at each angle are to be houses for Public Affairs, as a Meeting House, Assembly or State House, Market-House, School-House, and several other buildings for Public Concerns. There are also in each quarter of the city squares of eight acres, to be for the like uses, as the Moore-fields in London; and eight Streets (besides the High-Street), that run from Front to Front, and twenty Streets (besides the Broad-Street) that run across the city, from side to side; all these streets are of Fifty-Foot breadth.[12]

Thus during the reign of Charles II all the main elements of the colonial town planning model were brought into existence. Only in Charles Town and Philadelphia, of the North American colonies, did the laying out of streets precede the erection of buildings. According to Bridenbaugh (1938), p. 13:

. . . elsewhere the evolution of a highway system was largely fortuitous. Paths appeared from house to house as they were needed, and an occasional road pushed to a nearby settlement. The first paths tended naturally to follow the configuration of the terrain with little thought of symmetry; ease of travel was the prime consideration.

Some of these planning approaches were at the time relatively new to Britain. The use of squares and the baroque style of street planning, for instance, derived from continental Europe. They were more fully implemented in later foundations, notably at Savannah, Georgia.

The 1730s: The Johnson Townships and the Foundation of Savannah, Georgia

After Charles II's reign new settlements in the New World were inhibited for fifty years by various happenings, the political upheavals of 1688, further wars, and the financial upheaval of the South Sea Bubble. In Jamaica the destruction by earthquake of Port Royal in 1692 was followed by the founding of a new planned town at Kingston, but it was not until the 1730s that a new colonizing initiative in the New World led to the most complete realization of the colonial town plan model in pre-Revolutionary North America, at Savannah.

Forerunner to the foundation of Savannah was an abortive scheme for a 'Margravate of Azilia'. Sir Robert Montgomery, a Scottish baronet, proposed this to the lords proprietors of Carolina in 1717 as a new buffer colony against the Spaniards in Florida to the south. It was to be settled with citizen-soldiers recruited from the poor of Britain. The promotional literature envisaged a colony twenty miles square (or 256,000 acres), with individual farm holdings one mile square, and four great parks. A grandiose town plan centred on the palatial residence for the 'Margrave', and there was provision for a green belt separating town and country. The scheme never left the planning stage, but was abandoned in 1720, when business confidence collapsed with the South Sea Bubble.[13]

Within a few years Shaftesbury's successors as proprietors of Carolina were bought out by the crown, and the first royal governor, Robert Johnson, introduced what was called 'Johnson's township scheme' to settle the colony's frontiers. Eleven townships were each to be allotted twenty thousand acres, within which each family would receive a town lot as well as fifty acres of country land. The crown would pay for the survey and grant, and assist emigrants with tools, food and transport. Although these townships attracted few immigrants, Johnson's scheme influenced the settlement shortly afterwards of Georgia, the colony immediately south of Carolina. This was the last to be established of the thirteen American colonies which declared independence in 1776, and the only one founded in the eighteenth century.[14]

The Georgia settlement at Savannah was the result of a royal charter granted in 1732 to a group of trustees. These were English philanthropists concerned to relieve the plight of insolvent and unemployed debtors who had been recently freed from prison under an Act of 1729. The debtors were to be given an opportunity to retrieve their fortunes as colonists 'after the Roman method' (quoted in Rand, 1914, p. 277). Samuel Johnson a few years later wrote a typically pungent critique of the society which could devise such a venture:

. . . Men driven into other Countries for Shelter, and obliged to retire to Forests and Deserts, and pass their Lives and fix their Posterity in the remotest Corners of the World, to avoid those Hardships which they suffer or fear in their native Place. (quoted in Holmes, 1993, p. 46)

The leader of the enterprise, and personal representative of the Trustees, was James Oglethorpe. He now has an honoured place among American colonial founders, and a statue of him stands in one of Savannah's main squares.[15] Although Oglethorpe is remembered as the founder of Savannah, Reps (1984) has identified Benjamin Martyn, the young and studious secretary to the Trustees, as the likely deviser of the Savannah plan, consciously seeking to apply Vitruvian town planning principles. Martyn had a personal connection with the Shaftesburies, having been commissioned by the 4th Earl to write the biography of the 1st Earl, the founder of Charleston.[16]

Also active in the Georgia colony was a Carolinian landowner, Colonel William Bull, who had been involved in laying out Johnson's townships and did the same for Savannah. He accompanied Oglethorpe's colonists and supplied labour (probably African and Indian slaves) to lay out the town, for which he was rewarded by having one of the main streets named for him.[17]

The plan which Oglethorpe implemented at Savannah includes all the elements of the Shaftesbury 'Grand Modell', but with tighter control than Shaftesbury and the Carolina

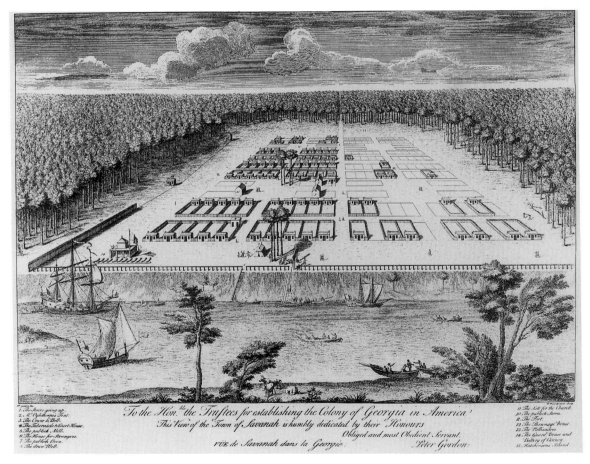

To the Hon.ble the Trustees for establishing the Colony of Georgia in America'
This View of the Town of Savanah is humbly dedicated by their Honours
Obliged and most Obedient Servant
vūe de Savannah dans la Georgie. Peter Gordon.

1. The Stairs going up.
2. M.r Oglethorpes Tent.
3. The Crane & Bell.
4. The Tabernacle & Court House.
5. The publick Mill.
6. The House for Strangers.
7. The publick Oven.
8. The draw Well.

9. The Tolt for the Church.
10. The publick Stores.
11. The Fort.
12. The Parsonage House.
13. The Pallisadoes.
14. The Guard House and Battery of Cannon.
15. Hutchinsons Island.

'A View of Savannah as it stood on the 29th of March 1734.' Baine and Vorsey (1989) analyse in detail this 'arresting high oblique perspective view', drawn at the end of Oglethorpe's time in Georgia. One of the rarest of American urban prints, it shows how Oglethorpe laid out the town in four wards, each consisting of forty house plots and four sites for public building arranged round an open space. (Source: Reproduced from the facsimile by Historic Urban Plans, Inc., Ithaca, New York, of a print in the U.S. Library of Congress Division of Prints and Photographs)

Statue of James Oglethorpe (1696–1785) in Johnson Square, Savannah, Georgia. He is represented in armour as not only the founder but the defender of the new colony. (Source: The author, photo taken in 1991)

proprietors had been able to achieve. The land was subdivided into town, garden and farm lots. There were squares, a grid-iron road layout, public lands and a common. A basis for local government was provided by the organization of wards (each consisting of forty house lots) and tythings. The colonists were expected to complete their house within eighteen months, and to clear and put into production their ten acres of farmland within ten years (Reps, 1965, p. 187).

Notwithstanding the carefully devised scheme of settlement, the practical difficulties of making a new life in the American wilderness soon soured relations between the Georgia colonists and the trustees. In 1752 the colony was transferred to the crown, as the proprietary colonies had been. Bad relations then continued with the British government, and culminated in the colony joining the independent States of America less than fifty years after its creation.

The planned approach to settlement was, however, kept. The Savannah plan was followed in all towns created in Georgia in the Trustee period, and the grid of 50-acre farm holdings around Savannah was still apparent on maps of 1875. While the belt of common land was mostly taken up for development, Savannah replicated the basic plan form of grids and squares as it expanded. Eighteen new squares were added to the six laid out in the colonial period. Only in the late twentieth century, when zoning practices and highway planning for the motor car changed the form of urban development, was the pattern of grids and squares abandoned in favour of road hierarchies and peripheral estates. Thus the Georgia colony forged a tradition of strong public involvement in planned urban development, drawing much of its inspiration from the experience of the London estates. Given this tradition, it is surely no coincidence that Savannah should now be a leader in the American movement for the preservation of historic buildings. In the words of Reps,

Like the seedlings for the Trustees' Garden, those original squares came as transplants from the London estates whose first English rootstock was put down in the soil of Covent Garden. Ignored for a time, allowed to wither and decay, the squares of Savannah's incomparable city now flourish under a new generation of urban caretakers.[18]

The 1780s: Settling Loyalists in Canada and Sierra Leone

The fifty years after the founding of Savannah were a period of wars and convulsions. Britain acquired new colonies, and, in the American Revolution, lost thirteen of her North American ones, with nearly four-fifths of her overseas population. New territories now had to be found, not only for her unwanted population, but also for those Americans and freed slaves who had remained loyal. A convict settlement at Botany Bay (later Sydney, New South Wales) was founded in 1788, the beginning of British Australia. The most detailed instructions hitherto formulated for colonial settlement were propounded for the

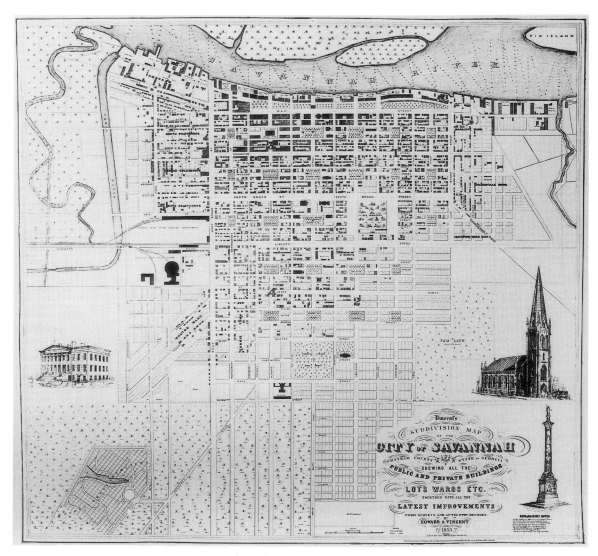

Savannah in 1853. Prepared a decade before the American Civil War, when Savannah narrowly escaped destruction by General Sherman's army, this subdivision map shows the location of every building, all plot lines, and names the numerous squares and wards. Savannah was expanding southwards into the surrounding countryside, the layout still closely following Oglethorpe's original concept. (Source: Reproduced from the facsimile by Historic Urban Plans, Inc., Ithaca, New York, of a subdivision plan by the Office of City Engineer, Savannah, Georgia)

new free settlements of Upper Canada and Sierra Leone, by Lord Dorchester and Granville Sharp rspectively. These drew upon proposals published in the *Gentleman's Magazine* after the Seven Years War for defensive settlements (Robison, 1992).

British North America (now Canada) had a population of only 110,000 in 1775, and about 40,000 loyalists and disbanded soldiers migrated there from the United States at the end of the Revolutionary War. Of these some 32,000 settled in Nova Scotia and 8,000 in the former French colony of Quebec. General Carleton, who had defended Canada against American attacks and was ennobled as Lord Dorchester, returned there in 1786 as Governor and Commander-in-Chief for Quebec, Nova Scotia and New Brunswick.[19]

He brought with him detailed rules and regulations for a new land settlement, elaborating upon earlier models. Townships, ten miles square, were planned around a town plot one mile square, which was to be divided into one acre lots. There was to be a central public square or parade, and four other public squares of similar size at equal and convenient distances from the centre. Public plots adjoined the central square, and further four-acre reservations at the corners of the 'Town Plot' were to accommodate markets, hospitals and cemeteries. The town was cordoned with a defensive belt half a mile wide. In practice only three such townships (Niagara, Johnstown and Cornwall) were realized in anything approaching the Dorchester concept.

Among the loyalists were thousands of former slaves, some of whom had fought on the British side in the Revolutionary War (the so-called 'loyal blacks'). These were now either displaced to the cold wastes of Nova Scotia (where they were racially discriminated against), or found themselves as impoverished refugees in London. In 1787, largely on the prompting of the abolitionist Granville Sharp, the Committee for the Relief of the Black Poor sponsored some four hundred of these refugees to found a free and self-governing settlement in West Africa. This first settlement (called Granville Town in Sharp's honour) was destroyed by the local tribespeople in 1790, but Sharp and others persevered to form the Sierra Leone Company. This founded a new settlement nearby at Freetown in 1792, from which grew the British colony of Sierra Leone. Over a thousand of the Nova Scotia refugees crossed the Atlantic to Freetown in what has been called 'the largest free migration of blacks in history.'[20]

Granville Sharp provided detailed regulations for the guidance of the new colony, which were published in 1787 and sold well, going into three editions. He had direct personal links with General Oglethorpe in his latter years (Oglethorpe died, aged nearly ninety, in 1785), and drew upon the experience of the Carolina and Georgia colonies.[21] Sharp prescribed a complete new system of government, as Shaftesbury had tried to do with his 'Fundamental Constitution' for Carolina, but he rejected Shaftesbury's quasi-feudal one for something more egalitarian. This was based upon his interpretation of Anglo-Saxon 'mutual frankpledge, or free suretyship, given by all the householders, for themselves and each other, in exact numerical divisions of tens and hundreds'. It proved to be a forerunner of the co-operatives of the nineteenth century, and for Ebenezer Howard's communal ownership model for the garden cities.

In 1794 Sharp published a shorter pamphlet than the Sierra Leone regulations, his 'General Plan for laying out towns and townships on the new-acquired lands in the East Indies, America or elsewhere'. This was also well received, and was revised in a second edition in 1804. It influenced later town planning both in Australia and North America (Robison, 1992). Sharp recommended a town or township:

laid out within the Compass of One Square Mile, or 640 Acres, Containing 40 Town Lots, for Planters or Farmers, having large Outlots beyond the Township, also Town Lots for 4 Public Officers, and for

132 Tradesmen, Clerks Artificers, Fishermen, Seamen or Labourers in all 176 Town Lots, with small Outlets, of a Quarter of a Square Furlong, of 2½ Acres each, for the said officers, labourers &c. within ¼ of a Mile from each side of the town. (Sharp, 1794)

Sharp's 'Regulations' for Sierra Leone had not included any guidance on defence or physical layout, but in the 1794 pamphlet Sharp included a diagrammatic plan, which showed an encircling belt of defensible common land.

Certainly the infant Freetown colony had need for defensive measures. Sharp never visited Sierra Leone, and the reality turned out rather differently from his detailed plan. His agents were incompetent and did not carry out his wishes. Defence was provided by a palisaded fort, rather than the encircling belt which Sharp had envisaged. The French raided and destroyed the town in 1794, the local tribes attacked it periodically, and the settlers themselves rebelled in 1800 against a proposed property tax.[22] In spite of these difficulties, Freetown after ten years had a population of some twelve hundred settlers, living in four hundred houses on an 80-acre site. Nine streets went inland at right angles to the coast, and were intersected by three avenues parallel to the shore. The streets were surfaced in Bermuda grass, which wandering sheep, cattle and goats kept cropped.

Granville Sharp's plan for new colonies was soon eclipsed by the turbulent years of the Napoleonic Wars. Britain emerged from these with a much enlarged empire after the political settlement at the Congress of Vienna in 1815. A new Colonial Office replaced the old Board of Trade and Plantations, and continued to apply the planned settlement policy. (Some of the new settlements, however, failed, such as that at Albany, in the Cape Colony of South Africa.) When the Colonial Office sent Governor Darling to bring greater order to the former convict settlement of New South Wales, he prepared regulations in 1829 for the planning of towns, developed with the

Surveyor-General, Major Mitchell. A simpler version of the colonial planning model was applied by Robert Hoddle, surveyor of the new settlement at Melbourne, then under the New South Wales jurisdiction. He laid it out in ten-acre blocks, with back roads 33 feet wide to give access to the back of each settler's allotment.[23] It is, however, the foundation and planning of Adelaide in 1836–37 which offers the most complete realization and final flowering of the colonial town planning model.

The 1830s: Systematic Colonization in Australia and New Zealand

Adelaide and the settlement of South Australia have all the essential elements of the model, preserved largely intact. The Adelaide city plan has been much praised for the choice of site – 'a brilliant statement of symmetrical urban forms related to river and land form' – at a time when town layouts were encouraged to ignore natural features. The quality of the plan as realized makes it hardly surprising that the city's foundation is much studied by historians and planners.[24] The immediate stimulus for the South Australia colony, and its so-called 'systematic' approach to colonization, came from the Benthamite Utilitarians and Edward Gibbon Wakefield. The new colony was promoted as a joint venture between the Colonization Commissioners and the Colonial Office.

The credit for the Adelaide plan is given to Colonel William Light, the first Surveyor-General of the new colony, who died there of consumption in 1839. His statue now looks across the parklands which he planned, towards the city centre of Adelaide. He is much honoured by the citizens, who have added several commemorative plaques around the base of the statue over the years. His second Adelaide memorial, in Light Square, is a model of the surveying instruments, which is also surrounded by commemorative plaques, the most rececent marking the 150th anniversary of his death.

Light is a romantic figure. He was of mixed race, born in 1786 at Penang. His father was Francis Light, founder of the British colony there; his mother, Martina Rozells, was probably part Portuguese and part Malay. He served with gallantry as a cavalry officer in the Peninsular War, gaining valuable experience of appraising territory through the perilous forward reconnaissance of enemy battle positions. At the end of the War, married to the illegitimate daughter of the Duke of Richmond, he toured the Mediterranean in a yacht, but the marriage failed. He then served as a mercenary with the Egyptian armed forces, commanding a gunboat. When he took up the South Australian appointment in 1836 he was fifty years old and his fortunes were at a low ebb. He had no settled home, no close family, and no secure income. As he later wrote, when he was dying of consumption in Adelaide,

I met with such misfortunes in the loss of my patrimony, and being besides hitherto naturally very careless of money, that in my old days I am obliged

William Light (1786–1839), the founder of Adelaide. This self-portrait from the 1830s shows his mixed race origins. (Source: Frontispiece to Elder, 1984)

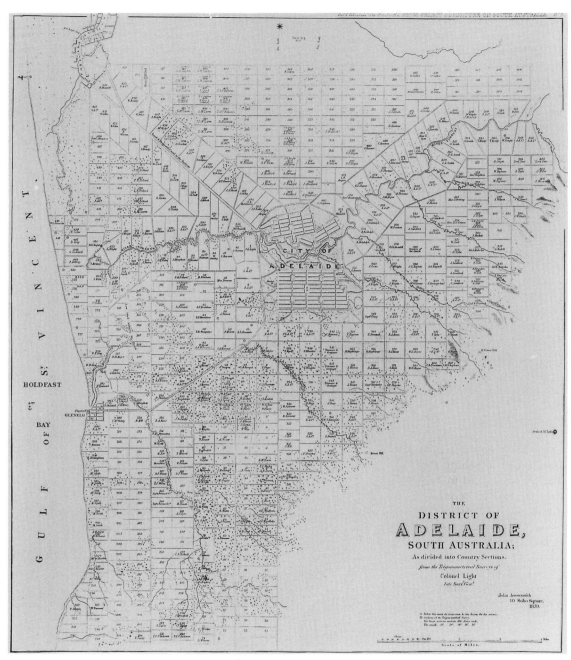

William Light's inspired plan of Adelaide and the suburb of North Adelaide, surrounded by parkbelt and divided by the Torrens River. Surveyed rural subdivisions are spreading over the countryside. (Source: Reproduced from the facsimile by Historic Urban Plans, Inc., Ithaca, New York, of appendix to the Parliamentary Select Committee Report of South Australia, 1839)

to do something; however I believe it to be for the best.[25]

Probably Light's most significant contribution to the history of the colonial town planning model was the Adelaide park belt intended for public recreation. Commons or defensive zones on several sides of, if not encircling, the town plantation had been included in most of the earlier plans, but were usually built upon as the settlements expanded. The recreational use of these green belts was a concept that Montgomery had suggested in his Azilia plan, and was urged in the book by F.J. Maslen, *Friend of Australia* (1830), upon which Light seems to have drawn.[26]

At the time when Light was being given his instructions by the South Australia Commissioners, the idea of public parks was being promoted by certain new Radical Members of Parliament, Roebuck, Hume and Buckingham, in the Parliament elected after the Great Reform Act of 1832. In 1833 a Select Committee of Parliament on Public Walks was considering 'the best means of securing Open Spaces in the Vicinity of populous Towns and Public Walks and Places of Exercise calculated to promote the Health and Comfort of the Inhabitants' (Chadwick, 1966, pp. 49–52). In 1835 Buckingham unsuccessfully proposed a Bill for establishing public gardens in towns and villages, and in 1838 Roebuck and Hume campaigned to require open space provisions in all enclosure bills.[27] Light was well informed about the Radicals' ideas, and was able to give Adelaide a public park to beat them all – the circular parkbelt. (Charles Reade, nearly a century later, mentioned in jest a contrary view of public parks, telling of an early Governor of Victoria (probably Bourke), who refused to consider squares and open spaces 'inasmuch as they merely afforded convenient places for idle persons to congregate and preach social sin and radical gospels' (quoted in *JTPI*, 1926, **11**, pp. 10–12).)

From the foundations laid by Light South Australia grew rapidly in the 1840s (from a population of 14,000 in 1840 to 64,000 by 1850), and established a tradition of government-promoted land use planning which has lasted to the present day. After Light the post of Surveyor-General remained of key importance in the opening up of the colony. A total of 370 government townships were surveyed and recorded on the cadastral plans of the State (compared with only 140 private townships). Two-thirds of them incorporated the colonial town planning model: for each 'hundred' (an area of about a hundred square miles), there was to be a government township of about a hundred acres, with a central square and four smaller squares, plots of half an acre, and a park land reservation about half a mile wide. South Australia also originated the Torrens system of land registration which influenced land law all over the world.[28]

A few years after South Australia, New Zealand was opened up to settlement by the system of colonization associated with Edward Gibbon Wakefield, his family and supporters sometimes known as Wakefieldians. Parkbelts were included in the new towns, although government control was less vigorous than in South Australia. Wellington was the first such town in 1840, with its road and section lines marked out on the ground only after the sale of plots. Canterbury was the fifth and last Wakefield foundation, in 1852.

THE INFLUENCE OF THE 'GRAND MODELL'

The parkbelt towns of South Australia and New Zealand proved to be the last ones under the old colonial model. Colonizing theory was moving from central direction to *laissez faire*

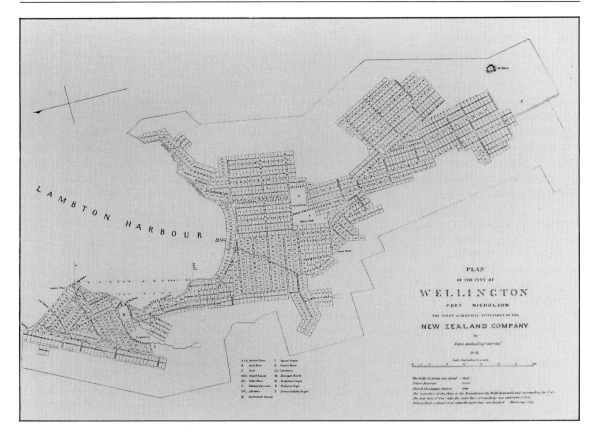

Wellington, New Zealand, in 1841. The Wakefields' New Zealand Company was more interested in cutting up real estate than in perpetuating the colonial town planning model, although there is an attempt at a parkbelt around the urban area. (Source: Reproduced from the facsimile by Historic Urban Plans, Inc., Ithaca, New York, of a plan in Colonial Office Command Paper on New Zealand, Command 569, in Olin Library, Cornell University)

doctrines. In the 1840s the influential followers of Wakefield were arguing against government-controlled urban development, and for private enterprise. Felix Wakefield in 1849 proposed 'leaving to individual judgment and enterprise the business of establishing towns and dividing waste land into Town Lots, and Suburban and Rural Sections' (quoted in Hamer, 1990, pp. 28–30).

In both the British Dominions and the United States government-regulated town planning was swept away in a tidal wave of migration. The population of Britain's New World colonies in 1775 had been less than three million, but in the hundred years after 1815 the New World and Antipodes were swelled by the emigration of 25 million people from the British Isles alone.[29] The colonial model could not cope with these pressures. In Upper Canada, for instance:

There was a retreat from the extreme elaboration of Ontario's ambitious earliest plans, perhaps because of the failure of those plans to cope with the demands of rough-and-tumble pioneer settlement. (Wood, 1982)

Some elements of the model survived. The policy of deliberate urbanization was privatized as boosterism, and the grid-iron of wide streets, sometimes with squares, was the usual urban form, albeit somewhat debased. A version of the model was recommended in 1877 by the Chief Engineer on the Canadian Pacific Railways, Sandford Fleming, in a report on the planning of railway towns. His diagonally-orientated grid-iron layout radiated outwards from the station on either side of a 2000-foot wide railway reservation. Town, park and village plots would increase in size with distance from the railway. Fleming's version of systematic colonization, however, was not favoured by the government, which prevented the railway company from controlling urban development (Gilpin, 1992).

The last new area to be opened to white settler colonization was East, South and Central Africa in the years between 1890 and the First World War. A little of the colonial town planning model was borrowed, as well as Dutch land surveying practices from the Cape of Good Hope. The British South Africa Company, when planning Salisbury and Bulawayo after 1890, used South African experience to lay out a grid, with wide streets, although sometimes the grid alignment had to be varied to bypass large anthills (Christopher, 1977). In the same decade the grid and square plan was deployed, admittedly in crude form, by Kitchener when planning the new city of Khartoum (Home, 1990b).

While the intellectual tradition of the colonial town planning model was submerged for fifty years during the hey-day of colonial immigration, it re-emerged as an influence upon the Garden City movement. Ebenezer Howard,

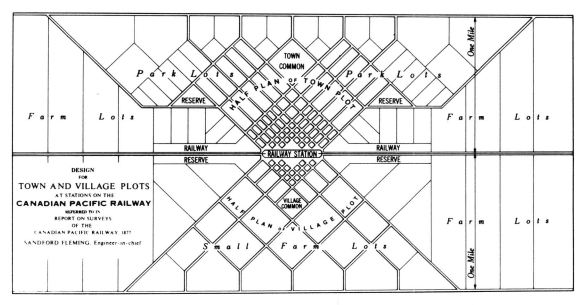

Model plan of a railway town in Canada (1877). The Canadian Pacific Railway's version of the colonial town planning model had town, park and farm plots, but was turned diagonally to focus on the railway station. It was the work of the Railway's Engineer-in-Chief, Sandford Fleming and appeared in the Report on Surveys and Preliminary Operations (1877). *(Source: Gilpin, 1992)*

who drew upon many sources, involved himself in attempts to create a 'Home Colony' on Wakefieldian lines in the 1890s, some years before publishing his garden city ideas (Beevers, 1988). He included Adelaide as the only plan of an existing city in the illustrations for his book, *Garden Cities of Tomorrow*, citing it to support his argument for a park belt in communal ownership:

Consider for a moment the case of a city in Australia which in some measure illustrates the principle for which I am contending. The city of Adelaide, as the accompanying sketch map shows, is surrounded by its 'Park Lands'. The city is built up. How does it grow? It grows by leaping over the 'park-lands' and establishing North Adelaide. And this is the principle which it is intended to follow, but improve upon, in Garden City.

The colonial planning model of the self-contained town is therefore one of the influences upon the garden cities and new towns movement. A key figure linking the two was Charles Compton Reade, who was the South Australian Government's Town Planner from 1915 to 1920 (see pp. 158–159). Drawing upon the Light tradition, he recommended the creation of an outer ring of parklands (not implemented), and also planned a garden suburb, at Mitcham, later renamed Colonel Light Gardens. Also in Australia, when John Sulman delivered the first lecture on town planning in 1890, he criticized the grid system of the old model, advocating a more aesthetic approach and more curvilinear roads. Sulman still followed the green belt tradition in recommending 'That no town or suburb contain a greater area than one square mile, with a belt of reserved land at least ⅛ of a mile in width between the same and the adjoining suburb.'

The evolution of the colonial town planning model thus shows a remarkable continuity of approach and concept from the Restoration period, with only slight modification and refinement. Much depended upon the personal authority and competence of those responsible

for executing the plan. Neither Charleston nor Freetown were laid out in accordance with their founder's wishes, but at Philadelphia, Savannah and Adelaide the determination and technical competence of the founders created urban forms which lasted.

The different implementation mechanisms combined private enterprise with state or crown control, and reflected the historical development of both government and capitalism. Thus the plantation of Ulster was undertaken by private companies formed by the City of London in partnership with the King. Carolina and Pennsylvania started as proprietary enterprises under royal charter, but were eventually purchased by the crown. Georgia and Sierra Leone were initiated by boards of trustees, and also came under government control after a few years. South Australia was from the first a partnership venture between the Colonization Commissioners and the Colonial Office.

While the colonial town planning model assumed a strong public authority, often a strong control over land use was not maintained in the years after foundation. The need to attract immigrants and investment could erode the initial concept, park belts and squares could be lost for building development at an early stage. Prescribed plot sizes and land allocations were soon ignored, as town plots were subdivided and country plots enlarged. Control over subdivision, minimum plot widths, use zoning and protection of public open space came much later in the history of these settlements.

They also had to contend with the harsh realities and uncertainties of pioneering life. It is hardly surprising that the elaborate plans laid down in far-away London were less than fully realized. Georgia, for instance, was eloquently described by a historian of its early years:

Located in the depths of a primeval forest, the tangled brakes and solemn shadows of which proclaimed loneliness and isolation; the vast Atlantic rolling its waters between it and the mother-country;

the Carolina settlements at best few in numbers and contending in a stern life-struggle for their own existence; Spaniards in Florida jealous of this disputed domain, and ready at any moment to frustrate by stealthy approaches and with force of arms all efforts of the English to extend their plantations along the southern coast; and, above all, Indian tribes in the occupancy of the country attached to their grand old woods and gently flowing streams, watchful of the graves of their ancestors, imposed upon by Spanish lies, disquieted by French emissaries, cheated by Carolina traders, and naturally inclined to resist all encroachments by the whites upon their hunting grounds, it did indeed appear that the preservation and development of this province were well nigh impossible. (C.C. Jones in 1888, quoted in Reese, 1963, p. 5)

Adelaide took years to realize Light's vision. In the year of his death, two years after he had laid it out, it was described as 'a seedy collection of shacks, tents and stores its streets muddy scratches through the grass, its squares a tangle of gum trees and wombat holes' (quoted in Hamer, 1990, p. 36).

NOTES

1. The classic study, of the North American experience, remains Reps (1965). See also Morris (1979) and Vance (1977). For the possibility that a printed plan of Peking influenced the design for Savannah, see Bell (1964).

2. For this interpretation of New England settlement, see Wood (1991). For the New England towns, see Garvan (1951), Lemon (1984), and Reps (1965), chapter 4.

3. For Carolina see Brown (1933), p. 163, and Craven (1949), pp. 338–40. For Georgia see Reese (1963) and Reps (1965). For Dorchester in Canada see Wood (1982).

4. See the entry on 'Planning' in Weinreb and Hibbert (1983). Of the substantial literature on the London Squares, see Olsen (1964), pp. 17–19, and Rasmussen (1937). For the similarities between the Savannah squares and the London squares, notably Hanover Square, see Reps (1984).

5. The effect of new building materials and low-density suburban development in reducing the incidence of large-scale urban fires is explored in Frost and Jones (1989).

6. The state of the Adelaide parklands in 1990 are reported in the *Adelaide Advertiser* of 25 May 1990. Parklands lost to other uses were usually for transport facilities (railways, bus depots). In 1912 the Mayor stopped the Commonwealth Government from building a barracks there (see Hutchings and Bunker (1986), p. 59, footnote 50). For parkland towns in Australia and New Zealand, see particularly Williams (1966).

7. The principal secondary sources on the Ulster plantation are Curl (1986), Gillespie (1985), especially Chapter Seven, Hunter (1971), Moody (1939), and Robinson (1984).

8. Thomas Raven (*c*. 1572–1640), the Surveyor of the Irish Society, laid out the fortifications at Londonderry between 1613 and 1618, and surveyed the lands for the various City Livery Companies. The town of Coleraine was planned by Sir Thomas Phillips (d. 1636), described by Moody (1939) as 'a pushing soldier of fortune and a protegé of Sir Robert Cecil.' He was active in the plantation from 1609, but became disillusioned by the inactivity of its backers in the City, and wrote a highly critical report on the condition of the plantation.

9. For the Irish connections of Penn and Holme see Illick (1976) and Soderlund (1983). For Berkeley see Rand (1914), p. 277. For Dorchester see Wood (1982).

10. *Absalom and Achitophel*, 11.152–5, quoted in Weir 1983, p. 52. Anthony Ashley Cooper (1621–83), created 1st Baron Ashley in 1661 and later the 1st Earl of Shaftesbury, held many high offices of state until his flight to Holland in 1682. Among his biographies see Brown (1933), especially chapter 10, and Haley (1968), especially chapter 12.

11. For Charleston see Weir (1983), chapter 9, Simons and Lapham (1970), and Fraser (1989). For orthogenetic and heterogenetic cities, see Thompson (1975) and Redfield and Singer (1954). They classified cities into orthogenetic ('carrying forward into systematic and reflective dimensions an old culture') or heterogenetic ('creating original modes of thought that have an authority beyond or in conflict with old cultures and civilizations').

12. Quoted in Morris (1979), p. 266.

Thomas Holme (1624–95), born in Yorkshire, served in Ireland with Cromwell, probably as a captain, and received a land grant there. He joined the Quakers, and in 1682 was appointed by Penn Surveyor-General of Pennsylvania, a position he held for life. He was later acting governor and a member of the assembly, and died in Philadelphia. See DAmB. For Philadelphia see also Roach (1968) and Soderlund (1983).

13. For Azilia see Montgomery (1717) and Williams (1974).

Robert Montgomery (1680–1731) was the 11th Baronet of Skelmorlie (DNB).

14. For Georgia see Weir (1983), pp. 111–112 and 208–209.

Robert Johnson (c. 1676–1735) was the first governor of royal Carolina from 1731 until his death in Charles Town in 1735. He was known as 'good governor Robert Johnson' (DAmB, DNB).

15. James Edward Oglethorpe (1696–1785) served in the army and was elected to Parliament as a High Tory in 1722. 'An ardent advocate of the spiritually oppressed', his exposé of penal conditions, *The Sailor's Advocate*, went through eight editions (DNB, DAmB). Biographies include Ettinger (1936) and Church (1932).

16. Benjamin Martyn (1699–1763) was a man of letters, secretary to the Georgia colony, and an original member of the Society for the Encouragement of Learning. He was instrumental in erecting Shakespeare's monument in Westminster Abbey. His epitaph described him as 'a man of inflexible integrity, and one of the best bred men in the land; which, with a happy genius for poetry, procured him the friendship of several noblemen'. His life of Shaftesbury was considered unsatisfactory and was suppressed. He travelled on the Continent, and his lodgings at Old Bond Street were a few yards from Hanover Square, identified by Reps as a source for the Savannah squares (DNB).

17. William Bull (1683–1755) was a member of the South Carolina Council and one of the three commissioners for the Indian trade, and went on to become lieutenant governor of South Carolina from 1738 until his death. His son, of the same name, was the last colonial governor of South Carolina (DAmB).

18. Other sources for Savannah include Baine and De Vorsey (1989), Chan Sieg (1984), Reps (1984), Coleman (1984), Stevenson and Feiss (1951), and Bannister (1961).

19. Guy Carleton, 1st Baron Dorchester (1724–1808), fought at the Battle of Quebec in 1759, and defended Canada in the American Revolutionary War. He was, in the words of Lord North, 'so much of a soldier and so little of a politician' (quoted in DCanB). See Wood (1982).

20. The main sources for the founding of Freetown are Fryer (1984) and Wilson (1976).

Granville Sharp (1735–1813) is described in the DNB as 'philanthropist, pamphleteer and scholar'. He was obsessed with the concept of individual liberty, which led him into many crusades. He established through the courts the principle that a slave became free when he stepped foot on English soil, campaigned against the press gang, and resigned from a government post because of his sympathy with the American cause in the American War of Independence.

21. Oglethorpe left Savannah after ten years, in 1743, married an heiress, and lived for over forty years in London and Essex. A congenial dinner host, he entertained Samuel Johnson, Boswell and Sharp. Sharp corresponded regularly with him, and was named trustee and executor under the will of Oglethorpe's widow. See Williams (1974).

22. The imposition of a form of property tax, or quitrent, was seen by the settlers to be turning them into wage labourers for the company instead of free yeomen farmers. Wilson (1976), pp. 361–363.

23. The Darling regulations advocated city blocks of 200 metres, and allotments of 20 × 100 metres fronting the main streets. The main roads were to be 100 ft wide, and lesser streets of 66 ft carriageway. See Lewis (1993).

24. For South Australia see particularly Bunker and Hutchings (1986), Cheesman (1986), Home (1991), Johnson and Langmead (1986), Pike (1951–52) and (1957), Price (1924), Statham (1989).

25. Quoted in Dutton (1960), p. 281. For the results of recent research into the life of Light, see Elder (1984) and Hutchings (1987).

26. Not much seems to be known about Maslen, which is surprising given his importance

in the history of the Green Belt concept. Williams (1974) identified him as a pseudonym of Captain Allen F. Gardiner (1794–1851), and I accepted this in an article (Home 1991b), adding further details of Gardiner's exotic career (he was an evangelist and missionary who died of starvation in Tierra del Fuego setting up a mission). Subsequently, however, David Elder has pointed out to me that we are in error because of a misinterpreted flysheet dedication, and Maslen was not Gardiner at all. (This is a pity, since Gardiner married into the Reade family of Oxfordshire in 1824. The connection with the later town planning missionary, Charles Compton Reade, would have made a nice link in the history of town planning ideas.)

Thomas John Maslen (1787–?1856), as it now appears, was not a pseudonym at all, but, as he states in his book, a former officer of the East India Company. India Office records provide some more information (L/MIL/9/116 f 524). Born on 18 July 1787, the son of Thomas and Mary Maslen, he was baptized on 20 February 1788 at St. Olave's Church, Silver Street, London. He entered the Madras Army as a cadet in 1806, and retired as a Lieutenant on 27 May 1821. He disappears from the list of Madras Presidency pensioners in 1857. As well as *The Friend of Australia*, he wrote a book on town improvement in Britain (Maslen, 1843).

27. For the Radicals see Hyde (1947) and Roebuck (1835). John Arthur Roebuck (1801–79) was a Utilitarian disciple of Jeremy Bentham. See his entry in Baylen and Grossman (1979 and 1984), and DNB.

28. The Torrens system was established by the South Australian Real Property Act of 1858, which created a public register where indefeasible title could be recorded. It was a solution to the disarray into which by the 1850s the system of land titles had fallen: of some forty thousand titles that should have existed, three-quarters were estimated to have been lost. It was named after Sir Robert Torrens (1814–84), who promoted the Act, and was himself called the 'king of the land jobbers' because he acquired many titles of doubtful validity. The origins of the system lie in Hamburg and the Hanseatic towns of North Germany, the agent of the innovation being Ulrich Hubbe (1805–76), who emigrated to Adelaide in 1842 and wrote pamphlets advocating the system (DAustB). Its success was such that by 1875 of the guarantee fund of £30,000, created to compensate for errors under the scheme, only £308 had been paid out. For the Torrens system, see Hinde (1971).

29. Wells (1975), Table VII-5, p. 284; and Christopher (1988).

2

'PLANTING IS MY TRADE' THE SHAPERS OF COLONIAL URBAN LANDSCAPES

Planting is my trade and I think I may without vanity say I understand it as well as most men.

(Sir Peter Colleton to John Locke, 28 May 1673, in De Beer, 1976)

THE NEW PROFESSIONALS OF COLONIAL SETTLEMENT

Shaftesbury and Locke, in forging a policy towards colonial settlement, drew upon the practical advice of Sir Peter Colleton, an experienced old salt who was active in the Caribbean region during the turbulent years of the Protectorate and the Restoration. He regularly corresponded with Shaftesbury and Locke, sharing his hard-won knowledge of the business of planting new colonies with those London-based servants of the crown. Between them they helped to formulate the policy or 'Grand Modell' associated with Shaftesbury. To Colleton managing colonial settlement was a job of work, a trade or profession, requiring special knowledge and skills. Such a man learned 'on the job', and it was not until the nineteenth century that new professions emerged with organized structures of knowledge.

After two centuries of British overseas expansion, the nineteenth century confirmed Britain as a world industrial and maritime power, with a vast empire to manage. To begin with, the task of planning the new colonial ports and towns fell to governors, usually with a military background from the Napoleonic Wars. Among these military governors were Brisbane and Darling, Bourke and D'Urban, some of whom gave their names to new cities.[1] The most individual and influential of these colonial governor-planners in the two decades after Waterloo was undoubtedly Stamford Raffles at Singapore. Not himself a soldier, he was exceptionally studious and diligent, and laid out a new and carefully planned city with minimal support, and indeed hostility, from his employers, the East India Company.

The demands of colonial management, as well as the new technologies of the Industrial Revolution, soon created new occupational roles. New professions rapidly diversified from the traditional three of law, divinity and medicine. It was also the time, after the Reform Act of 1832, when a new breed of professional government inspectors arose, committed to improvement, demanding state intervention, and deepening government's hold on civic society. The new professions, with their qualifying associations, sought to identify a reserved body of knowledge, and to control entry through training and testing. Their specialist knowledge was 'collegiate controlled', with distinct cognitive structures, claiming universality and a theoretical orientation. The extent to which professionals could 'solve' social problems conferred on them prestige, power and social position. They saw themselves as fulfilling a civilizing mission and a public service of trust. If (as has been claimed) the British empire operated as a vast system of outdoor relief for the English middle classes, then the new professions were an effective job creation scheme.[2] Headrick (1981) has summed up the rapid diffusion of new technologies and ideas around the colonial empires in a telling sentence: 'It is the Europeans who had the "talking drums" ' (p. 208). Certain professions, notably the land surveyors, engineers, doctors, and architect-planners, left their distinctive marks, both positive and negative, upon colonial urban landscapes, the empire offering them wider scope and opportunity than they might have had at home.

Some of the new professionals had public school educations and were already socially well-placed: Sturt, the explorer and Surveyor-General of South Australia, was educated at Harrow School. Others rose from humble origins. Sir William MacGregor, for instance, the son of an Aberdeenshire crofter, trained as a doctor and ended his career as a highly-honoured colonial governor. Robert Hoddle, the land surveyor who laid out the city of Melbourne, was described by a fellow land surveyor from the officer class, Major Mitchell, in supercilious terms, that he 'can scarcely spell . . . this man can only be employed, as he has always been, at the chain'.[3]

One can see the different professions associated with British colonial expansion as enjoying their respective 'Kondratieff waves' of influence.[4] Successive professions each enjoyed a period of some fifty years of power to shape colonial urban landscapes, as will be seen. The land surveyors surveyed the new empire in the years after Waterloo (1820–1870). The engineers, civil and military, installed the basic physical infrastructure of transport and utilities in the period 1850–1900. The doctors, especially the sanitary specialists, tried to control public health through a drastic re-ordering of the urban fabric in the period 1880–1930. The architects and planners enjoyed their primacy in the period 1910–1960, evangelizing for the garden city and creating new physical forms to symbolize empire. In the post-colonial era this professional sequence appears to continue with the rise of the valuers, specialists in making and selling space in the market.

The Land Surveyors

As new lands were acquired, a first priority was to survey them. The mapped cadastral survey was one of the most powerful instruments available in the colonies for allocating the prime resource – land. In the long-settled lands of Europe, the land surveyor's work was largely confined to demarcating and mapping, but in the colonies he was doing much more. He was the instrument for imposing a whole new economic and spatial order on the territory. In the process he usually extinguished precolonial land rights (or at least restricted them to defined areas), so that he was a figure regarded by the native peoples with little enthusiasm. The land surveyor was an explorer, resource appraiser, town planner, delineator of routeways, and the shaper of landscapes both urban and rural. Until he had traversed the land with chain and compass, and recorded the results on a map, it could not be fully converted into private property. In the New World township land subdivisions were published by subscription and hung in public places:

To landowners in the new states, the presence of their property clearly identified on a map in a published county atlas confirmed their stake in the new nation . . . etching the cadastre into the public mind.[5]

The Munster plantation of 1585–86 was one of the earliest examples of this power of the map, followed by the plantation of Ulster. The results of a survey could be the key to successful confiscation of land from the previous owners. Thomas Raven, who mapped the plantation of Ulster for the livery companies of the City of London (see pp. 16), can claim to be one of the first colonial land surveyors.

Over a century later, the settlement of the vast tracts of Canada, acquired from the French in the Seven Years' War and later a refuge for loyalists after the American War of Independence, created great opportunities for the land surveyor. The man most associated with this was the Dutch-born surveyor Samuel Holland. As a young man he surveyed the St. Lawrence River for the British assault on Quebec in 1759, and in the process trained James Cook, the future explorer of Oceania, in survey methods. When General Wolfe died in battle at the Heights of Abraham, Holland was close to his side. After the end of the American War of Independence in 1783, when the government of British North America decided to give large land grants to the loyalists, Holland and his assistant, John Collins, surveyed the sites of many new settlements in Upper and Lower Canada, laying out the so-called Haldimand six-mile-square townships.[6] Governors such as Dorchester and Simcoe tried to standardize the size and design of townships, but a variety of approaches remained until the 1867 British North America Act established the Dominion of Canada. Nine-square-mile townships and 600-acre sections then became the norm. In the year 1883 alone, as a response to demand generated by the Canadian Pacific Railway, 1221 townships and more than 170,000 farms, totalling some twenty-seven million acres, were surveyed in advance of incoming homesteaders. This has

been called 'an achievement probably unequalled in the survey history of any country' (Kain and Baigent, 1992, p. 303).

After the Congress of Vienna land surveyors were needed to map Britain's new acquisitions. The experience gained in the Peninsular War, and the training provided by the survey section of the Quartermaster-General's Department, equipped many leading surveyors at this time, notably Mitchell and Hoddle in New South Wales, and Light in South Australia. In these early years of Australian colonization the land surveyors were important and honoured public servants, the Surveyor-General ranking second to the Governor. When Colonel Light was too late to get the governorship of the new colony of South Australia, he was willing to settle for the position of Surveyor-General, which eventually won for him a higher fame (Dutton, 1960). Often, it has to be said, the governors and land surveyors quarrelled, for both seem to have been stiff-necked and intolerant. Examples of such conflicts were Light and Hindmarsh in South Australia, Mitchell and Darling in New South Wales, and Hoddle and Bourke in Victoria.

The Australian Surveyors-General also had a particular responsibility to prevent uncontrolled land grabbing, especially after the experience of the Swan River Colony in Western Australia. There land was granted in huge tracts of a hundred thousand acres or more, in 'the extreme case of profligate, effectively unregulated land alienation in the first half of the nineteenth century' (Kain and Baigent, 1992, pp. 307–313). Thereafter, governors and surveyors sought to impose a more ordered land settlement. In New South Wales, Governor Brisbane in 1821 experimented with six-mile townships on the North American model. His successor, Governor Darling in 1825 brought from London new instructions which abandoned townships in favour of an English hierarchy of counties, hundreds and parishes, trying to ensure contiguous and close settlement.

While Mitchell in New South Wales and Roe in Western Australia were important figures, it was in South Australia that the land surveyors achieved their greatest success in town planning. Light's inspired layout of Adelaide became a model for other settlements in that colony and in New Zealand. South Australia established a tradition of responsible government land survey which has lasted to the present day. Light was succeeded as Surveyor-General by a line of able and long-serving individuals, notably Sturt, Frome and Goyder, who were key figures in the opening up of the colony to white settlement.[7]

In India, surveyors gradually mapped the whole sub-continent, in the so-called Great Trigonometric Survey, and the Indian Revenue Survey replaced Mughal land tenure with British absolute proprietary rights of landownership (Edney, 1990). In South Africa the strong Dutch tradition of land surveying was followed, and the British South Africa Company in Southern Rhodesia used tight cadastral controls and a grid based upon South African experience, as being 'the quickest and simplest method of laying out the town' (Christopher, 1977).

Elsewhere in Africa land survey expertise was less available, and some crude methods were used. The Imperial British East Africa Company, for instance, allowed the town of Nairobi to grow with no proper survey or control (Trzebinski, 1985, chapter 3). Winston Churchill as Colonial Secretary in 1908 criticized that failure: 'it is now too late to change, and thus lack of foresight and a comprehensive view leaves its permanent imprint upon the countenance of a new country' (quoted in Christopher, 1988, p. 132). There were, nevertheless, some able land surveyors at work in Africa, notably Colonel Rowe in West Africa.[8] In 1911 a Governor of Northern Nigeria, Sir Hesketh Bell, offered some simple advice for the laying out of 'native towns:

The site of the new town having been cleared the officer, taking my plan in hand, would at once proceed to lay out on the land the lines of the central market square, the broad avenues and the main street. This would be done by running shallow furrows through the ground. He would then secure from the surrounding 'bush' a large quantity of poles about 8 feet in length and as thick as one's wrist. These poles would be set into the ground, 7 or 8 feet apart, all along the lines and furrows to indicate the boundaries of the avenues and roads. Then between these poles would be stretched rough grass mats, known locally as 'zanna mats', which measure about six feet by eight feet and cost only a few pence each. These poles and mats at once formed long lines of straight walls and, as if by enchantment, a town laid out in straight and regular lines, would suddenly rise out of the ground. The spaces enclosed within the mat walls would be subdivided into plots measuring 80 feet by 100 feet, and the town was practically ready for the tenants. (quoted in Urquhart, 1977, p. 28)

Three methods of surveying evolved for the colonial situation. In the New World the so-called 'Virginia system', survey from existing physical features (by 'metes and bounds'), was used to prove title after occupation. It was suited to the creation of large, capitalist plantations founded on slave labour. Later the running survey, imposing a grid of land sections by rectangulation, was used in Australia and by the Wakefield colonizers in New Zealand. The third, and most scientific, method was triangulation by trigonometric methods, setting out sections only after a regulatory framework of fixed points was in place. This came to replace the running survey method. It was a dispute over these methods of survey which led to the resignation of Light as Surveyor-General of South Australia, in what has become a famous episode in the history of that province and of land surveying. He had been using the latest triangulation method, equipped with the new transverse theodolite, but was over-ruled by his superiors in London and required to follow the running survey method, which was claimed to be quicker but was less accurate. Light had already surveyed

150,000 acres around Adelaide when this decision was imposed upon him by the London directors, advised by their own surveyor. He resigned with most of his survey team, and after his death his survey method was vindicated. J.T. Thomson, the chief surveyor of New Zealand, with experience gained on the Great Trigonometric Survey of India, finally established the importance of proper triangulation to fix cadastral detail accurately.[9]

The land surveyor was, therefore, the professional most responsible for the land settlement of the new colonies. It was he who subdivided the towns into their ample plots and thus decisively established the character of the low-density suburban landscapes of North America, Australia and New Zealand, and thereby also influenced the garden suburb style in Britain. The rectangular grid layout survived into the twentieth century until replaced by a design approach more sensitive to topography and aesthetics. When a town planning propagandist, Davidge, visited Australia in 1914 to promote the new approach, he commented upon the restraints which land survey methods imposed on suburban layouts: land registration procedure required the compass bearing of each length of road to be stated, so that, as he observed, curved roads were practically impossible to achieve, the nearest being a series of straight lines from point to point (Lanchester, 1925, p. 199).

The Engineers[10]

While the land surveyors were plotting out townships in Australia, New Zealand, and elsewhere, another new profession, civil and military engineering, was developing a technical expertise in urban infrastructure.

The civil engineers created their own institute in Britain in 1818. Its royal charter in 1828 included as its objectives, to improve the means of production and of traffic, and to protect property. King's College London introduced courses in civil engineering from 1838, and the first chair of civil engineering in Britain was established in 1840 at the University of Glasgow. In 1856 the first professional examinations were held in the subject. A separate cadre was the military engineers, who, following in the French absolutist tradition, enjoyed an elitist schooling, and the security and authority of state support, with royal recognition of the corps of engineers. In 1826 the school of military engineering at Chatham started a course in practical architecture, including the planning of cantonments, building and architectural principles. The vast demand for engineers in India, especially after Governor-General Dalhousie created the Indian Public Works Department in the 1850s, prompted the provision of local training at Thomason Engineering College (Roorkee) and the Madras Engineering College.

Surveyors and civil engineers, attached to town boards across the empire, worked on the layout and servicing of towns. These were only some of the many tasks that they might be called upon to undertake, which included railways, roads, bridges, fortifications, canals, drains, dams, and public buildings. Rudyard Kipling's father (the artist Lockwood Kipling) in 1884 wrote of the standardized plans produced by these engineer-designers: long facades which 'would answer equally well, or indeed much better for a dry goods store, a barrack, or a factory . . . cut up into longer or shorter lengths, they serve for law courts, schools, municipal halls, dak bungalows, barracks, post offices and other needs of our high civilization' (quoted in Metcalf, 1989, pp. 165–166).

Some of the more important colonial ports and towns were laid out by military engineers. When Rangoon was acquired by the British in 1852, Lieutenant Fraser of the Bengal Engineers, 'an engineer with a capacity for the then little studied art of Town Planning', was placed in charge of the port's development, and achieved 'the first Indian city to be planned on modern lines':

Whether by accident or by the exercise of exceptional foresight, Lieutenant Fraser adopted exactly the correct type of design needed for the planning of the central area of Rangoon. (Webb, 1923–24)

Fraser's obituaries (he died, a general, in 1898) give an indication of the relative unimportance attached to town planning in an engineer's career: they gave little or no attention to his work on the planning of Rangoon, emphasizing instead his achievements in railways and lighthouse building in India.

Engineers could also be involved in demolishing towns. Another Bengal Engineer, whose influence on urban form was less benign than Fraser's, was Robert Napier, better known as Lord Napier of Magdala. His experience of road building and environmental hygiene in military settlements involved him after the Indian Mutiny in replanning the old cities of Delhi and Lucknow, and in the creation of new cantonments. His memorandum on the City of Lucknow in 1858 offered a blueprint for reshaping the city, opening broad streets, and creating a 600-yard wide esplanade in its most heavily populated and built-up parts. The plans led to some two-fifths of the city being demolished, and Delhi suffered a similar fate.

Another town planning exercise by military engineers was the remaking of Khartoum in 1898 by Kitchener, who was later to use it to claim a link with the emerging town planning movement (see pp. 141–142). A Royal Engineer, he defeated the Mahdists at the battle of Omdurman, thus avenging the death of General Gordon (a fellow Royal Engineer), and declared an Anglo-Egyptian 'condominium' over the Sudan. His occupying army found that Gordon's Khartoum had been plundered to build the new Mahdist capital of Omdurman, and so, within a month of his victory, Kitchener ordered the building of a new Khartoum. According to a generally accepted tradition, Khartoum was laid out on a pattern of Union Jacks, in a symbolic statement of British dominance. Another explanation is that the convergence of roads allowed

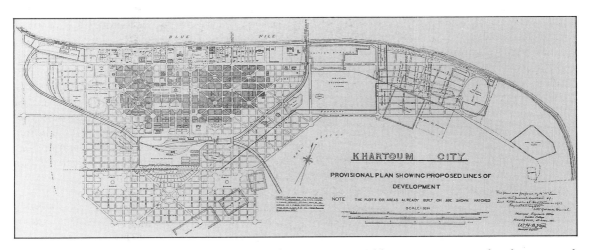

Khartoum City in 1910. It is endorsed 'This plan was prepared by Mr McLean under the personal direction of Lord Kitchener of Khartoum in 1912'. The plan shows the 'Union Jack' layout of streets, the spacious riverside plots for senior officials' housing, and the planned extension of the grid superimposed upon various existing 'native villages'. (Source: McLean, 1930)

machine-guns to command in all directions. There is, however, no contemporary evidence to support either version (although that does not mean that they are untrue). In the words of a historian of the British Sudan:

the hallowed association of the ruins gave it a legitimacy that Omdurman could not match . . . Kitchener's triumphal ideas for the rebuilding of Khartoum may well have been inspired partly by the need to impress the Sudanese with the permanence of the regime . . . The great conqueror . . . would raise up a new capital, found a seat of learning, lay down a charter by which the people should be ruled, and depart for new conquests.[11]

During the 1890s Joseph Chamberlain's policy of developing the tropical estates in West Africa created opportunities for engineers. Several Royal Engineer officers (McCallum, Girouard, Nathan and Guggisberg) transferred to become successful colonial governors in West Africa, supervising the development of railways and other infra-structure.[12] Civil engineering firms, such as Coode, Son & Matthews, and Howard Humphreys, were also active in colonial urban development, particularly the construction of docks, harbours, tramways, water supply and drainage. The commander of Australian forces in the First World War, General Monash, was in his early career an engineer for the Melbourne Harbour Board in 1892 (a time he apparently found frustrating).

Civil engineers were closely involved with the new town planning movement in the early twentieth century. Sir William McLean, perhaps best known for his Jerusalem plan of 1918, served for twenty years in the Sudan and Egypt (see pp. 152–154). In India Sir Frederick Temple (the brother of a later Archbishop of Canterbury) was the Town Engineer of the steel town of Jamshedpur (see pp. 152). John A. Brodie, the City Engineer of Liverpool, was a member of the committee which planned New Delhi, the chairman of which said of him:

Mr Brodie, of course, was a great man on roads, and when he went to Delhi his intention probably was to try to make the longest and widest avenue in the world. Mr. Brodie had got two roads three miles long, so that he had done very well.[13]

The 'Sanitation Syndrome': Doctors and Public Health Specialists[14]

The medical profession (and its handmaiden, public health) acquired a dominance over colonial urban landscapes in the latter years of the nineteenth century.

A common culture of medicine – sustained by the image of science as the universal agent of progress, and scientific medicine as its servants – became the hallmark of European empires throughout the world. (MacLeod & Lewis 1988, p. 3)

Western medicine had formerly been less domineering in its relationship with indigenous societies, but between 1880 and 1930 it obtained a wider importance in imperial ideology and practice, at a time when European empires were at their most expansive and assertive. There was a spate of laws, proclama-tions and decrees giving state sanction to draconian health measures, especially in response to the plague epidemics. Recourse to state power gave the medical profession un-precedented authority in public life and affairs of state. Doctors became all-purpose experts, authorities on matters as diverse as 'native affairs' and town planning, and were recruited as military advisers, impromptu diplomats, geologists and pioneer anthropologists. If sanitary experts were the new 'specialists of space' (in Foucault's words), then the colonial urban landscape offered almost untrammelled scope for their endeavours, far more than Europe at the time.

Public health measures were exported to India, as part of what Florence Nightingale called the 'noble task' of introducing a 'higher civilization'. Sanitary commissions, created in 1864 for the three Presidencies of Bombay, Madras and Calcutta, had no executive powers, but a duty to tour the province and prepare statistics for disease control, while at a district level the Civil Surgeon (an Indian Medical Service officer) advised on sanitation. Scientific investigation of the causes of cholera led to restrictions on movement and sanitary cordons around cantonments. New elected municipalities, created on the English model through various Municipal Acts in 1871–74, were given wide-ranging sanitary powers and employed untrained sanitary inspectors. After 1888 a sanitary board for each province provided technical advice, backed by funds from the provincial government (Arnold, 1988).

Tropical medicine, as a separate subject from medicine, was introduced in Britain with the creation of Schools of Tropical Medicine in London and Liverpool in 1898–99, and courses soon followed at the universities and colleges of Edinburgh, Durham, Aberdeen and Queen's Belfast. The Liverpool School was a business investment in increased colonial trade. It enjoyed the backing of companies like John Holt and Unilever, concerned to combat malaria in their trading region of West Africa, and was expected to extend to the empire the progressive public health philosophy of the city port. The new academic discipline of tropical medicine was raised to a pinnacle of importance in an already prestigious profession. In 1909 the Secretary of State for the Colonies created an Advisory Medical and Sanitary Committee for Tropical Africa (later extended to all dependencies in 1922), and in 1926 the first Chief Medical Adviser to the Colonial Office was appointed.

New perspectives on medical history now regard medicine and the treatment of disease as structurally embedded in contemporary political and social thought. Epidemics become events through which the workings of society are revealed. In combating them, medical men become agents of colonialism, rather than the socially neutral voice of disinterested science. In 1883, for instance, Dr. Jameson, the close associate of Cecil Rhodes, chose to misdiagnose an outbreak of smallpox among black migrants from Mozambique passing through the Transvaal. He knew that, if he confirmed smallpox, the mines at Kimberley would be quarantined, with a disastrous effect on their profitable operation. He chose to label it instead 'Felstead's disease' (after the farm where the sufferers died) or 'Kaffir pox', calling it 'a bulbous disease of the skin'. As a result no preventive action was taken until at least seven hundred miners had died between 1883 and 1885. The Cape Prime Minister later openly admitted that doctors 'had declared the disease not smallpox lest the result should be injurious to the mining interest'.[15]

Much of imperial medical history has concentrated on the great discoveries of the causes of disease: Pasteur and the 'germ theory', Manson and Ross establishing the link between mosquitoes and malaria. But it is in the public health area that the influence of the doctors on the urban landscape was most marked. Medical attention in the colonial ports shifted to public health measures that might combat the threat of disease to trade and commerce, and especially protect the health of Europeans. A new breed of sanitary experts emerged in the Eastern empire, attributing high death rates from disease to 'the insanitary and immoral lives of the Asiatic races'. Public health experts like Sir William Simpson advocated remedies derived from British practice: better ventilated houses, pure water and good drains, better waste and sewage disposal, open spaces, and (of particular importance to town planning) the ventilating effects of new roads.

The importance of Sir William John Ritchie Simpson (1855–1931) at this time, admittedly much of it discredited by his racist notions, deserves to be recognized, and his work will be referred to later (see pp. 75, 78 and 126–127). He is not to be confused with his namesake, the distinguished surgeon, Sir James Simpson. He trained in medicine at the University of Aberdeen, where he lectured in hygiene before serving as Health Officer for the Calcutta Municipal Corporation between 1886 and

1897. He achieved some notoriety when he diagnosed an early case of plague in Calcutta, only to be overruled by the colonial authorities because of the panic and disruption to trade that would be caused. When plague arrived in earnest shortly afterward, his position was vindicated. He returned to Britain to take up the important post of Professor of Hygiene and Public Health at the University of London, which he held continuously from 1899 until into his seventies, not retiring until 1927. He was a founder of the London School of Hygiene and Tropical Medicine, and a member of the advisory committee to the Secretary of State for the Colonies on medical and sanitary matters. He served on various public health commissions which influenced urban planning in the colonies: into dysentery and enteric in South Africa (1900–1), plague in Cape Town and Cape Colony (1901), plague in Hong Kong (1902), Singapore (1906), West Africa (1908), East Africa (1913–14), and the Gold Coast (1924), and Northern Rhodesia (1929). He wrote treatises and books on cholera, plague and hygiene in the tropics, some of which became standard texts. Knighted in 1923, he was described in an obituary as 'a man of great industry and an inflexible purpose that sometimes led to clashes with his associates' (Munk's Roll, quoted in Van Heyningen, 1989).

Simpson contributed to the medical profession's new status as the advocate of racial segregation, which became 'a general rubric of sanitary administration set by the Imperial government for all tropical colonies' (Dummett, 1968, p. 71). While there was scant scientific evidence to sustain a policy of urban racial segregation, the fear of catching 'native' diseases provided a sufficient pretext, especially in South Africa, as will be seen in chapter 5. Another public health specialist who was closely associated with early town planning and racial segregation was Dr. Charles Porter, the Medical Officer of Health of Johannesburg (Parnell, 1992).

Architects and Town Planners

Another profession to claim a role in shaping colonial urban landscapes was architecture, later linked to town planning. The Institute of British Architects came into existence in 1834, and received its royal charter in 1837. While architects mainly designed individual buildings, they also concerned themselves with public works and the laying out of towns. Architect-planners working in the colonies during the nineteenth century included George Coleman in Singapore, and Francis Greenway and John Sulman in Sydney.[16]

Town planning subsequently emerged as a new area of knowledge in the decade before the First World War, and the Town Planning Institute was formed in 1914. The urban problems which gave rise to the new profession were summarized by an Indian town planner in a sentence of splendidly mixed metaphors:

The galloping growth of towns under the stress of rapid progress of science and the consequent mechanisation of industries and transport has created many problems which are knocking at the doors of the best brains among the leaders of sociological thought. (Mehta, 1937–38, p. 386)

The architects were the first professional body to promote the town planning idea. Sulman in 1890 was apparently the first person to use the term town planning, and claimed the architect as 'the one man who by training and experience combines in himself a knowledge of all the conditions of town-planning, and to him should be entrusted the task of initiation' (Freestone, 1983). A later architect-planner, Albert Thompson, who had worked with Raymond Unwin, claimed in South Africa in 1924 that 'it is impossible to thoroughly understand town planning without a basis of architectural training' (quoted in Muller, 1993, p. 7). Many architects were active as town planners in the colonies – Lutyens at New Delhi, Lanchester in India and elsewhere, Holliday in Palestine, Longstreth Thompson in South Africa, Maxwell Fry in West Africa and

John Sulman (1849–1932), leading Australian architect and town planner. He is credited in Freestone (1990) with inventing the term 'town-planning' at a conference in Melbourne in 1890, and was later involved in the early planning of the Australian federal capital at Canberra. (Source: Freestone, 1989)

India, and Gardner-Medwin in the West Indies. Other town planners active in the colonies in the early twentieth century, however, came from varied backgrounds: Geddes a biologist, Reade and Adams campaigning journalists, Mawson and Dann landscape gardeners, Ashbee and Adshead arts and crafts designers.

The University of Liverpool can claim to have started the world's first town planning course. The Department of Town Planning and Civic Design was created there in 1909, and other courses followed at the University of Birmingham in 1912 and University College London in 1914. The first Professor of Town Planning at Liverpool, Stanley Adshead (who later advised on the planning of Lusaka) stated in the prospectus for his new course that:

Town Planning, although intimately connected with Architecture and Engineering, is a distinct and separate study in itself, and the primary object of the school is to equip Architects, Engineers and others with a knowledge of the supplementary subjects that Town planning connotes. (Batey, 1992, p. 54)

He argued that the town planner would 'occupy with credit those advisory and permanent positions which must necessarily be created as legislation affecting civic development and extension becomes increasingly efficient.' The new professional, 'empowered to control the aesthetics of cities', was to work alongside the Municipal Architect and the Medical Officer of Health. Although the Liverpool Department started as a night school for local engineers and architects, it was also closely associated with the colonies. Its very existence was made possible by a grant from W.H. Lever (the founder of Port Sunlight), the same grant which endowed the Liverpool School of Tropical Medicine. The first lecturers included several who were later active in the colonies: Abercrombie, Brodie, and Mawson. Among its early students were Clifford Holliday, the later Lord Holford (himself a South African by birth), and Linton Bogle (the town planner of Lucknow). Through its supply of graduates, it had a continuing influence on Australian planning.[17]

From the start the town planning idea was vigorously exported to the colonies. Representatives of the garden city movement, Reade and Davidge, toured Australia in 1914–15 (Hardy, 1991, p. 94). The eminent architect Herbert Baker promoted it in a speech at Pretoria in 1911:

I must add a few words on the art of town planning. It is an art which has but lately come to the front, and been raised to the rank of the older arts . . . There is no art which, in the long run, is more profitable to a city, nor any field in which good seed, well sown, will ultimately reap a richer harvest . . . Every large town, with any civic pride, in the old and new world, is now regretting past neglect, and considering schemes for improvements; so it is full time we in South Africa bestirred ourselves. (quoted in Muller, 1993, p. 5)

When Swinton left the London City Council to serve on the planning committee for New Delhi, he said that he was to apply Howard's garden city ideas:

The fact is that no new city or town should be permissible in these days to which the word 'Garden' cannot be rightly applied. The old congestion has, I hope, been doomed for ever. (quoted in *Garden Cities and Town Planning*, 1912, Vol. 2, April, p. 78)

Soon new colonial capitals (Canberra, New Delhi, Lusaka), as well as hill stations and suburbs (the Cameron Highlands in Malaya, Pinelands in South Africa) were all claiming garden city credentials. In 1916 the president of the Town Planning Institute, J.W. Cockrill, in his inaugural address could claim that:

Australia, Canada, India and New Zealand are all busy. Consider the splendid opportunities the men employed are getting, with plenty of space to work out problems of providing sites worthy of the civic centres and public buildings which will be a necessity as the townships develop. (Cockrill, 1916, pp.2–3)

The spread of the town planning idea, and its subsequent institutionalization as a function of government, are the subject of separate chapters.

THE SUPPORTING IDEOLOGIES

The new professions of the nineteenth century reflected both a strengthened role for the state and a scientific approach to the management of society in nations that were growing in population as well as industrializing fast. After the upheavals of the French Revolutionary Wars, restored conservative governments applied new methods to controlling their populations. Foucault has traced the development from the eighteenth-century Enlightment of systems of thought which redefined the 'power-knowledge relationship' between the state and social man. These provided much of the intellectual framework for new codes of social discipline and the ordering of physical space.[18] British colonial expansion was thus informed by new political thinking associated with positivism, utilitarianism and trusteeship. One paradox of colonialism in the nineteenth century was that a system ostensibly built on free trade and minimal government interference in Britain depended upon a high degree of regulation and control in the colonies.

Positivism provided a union of eighteenth-century rationalism with the nineteenth-century empiricist thought promoted by Comte and Mill. Human order and progress would be based upon the work of men of foresight, as well as the positive spirit of modern industrialism. This was an ideology well suited to colonialism and the formation of new nations, building a new state upon natural laws rather than the divine right of kings or the church, and planning a state-directed process of accelerated structural change in economic, social and political systems. It relied upon central authority, favoured grand cities and despised the natural environment and indigenous peoples. James Mill's history of India in 1818, for instance, maintained that India was bound to despotism and Hinduism, and superstition had to be rooted out and replaced by a new system of laws to ensure the happiness of India's people (Metcalf, 1989, p. 22). Colonialism was to be justified by material improvements through large public works, which would also secure greater political hegemony and continued colonial rule. This investment in infrastructure was to be secured by taxation of the colonial peoples and with as little cost to the home Treasury as possible. The Wakefieldian settlements in Australia and New Zealand sought to reproduce the English capitalist society based upon landlord and wage labourer. As for the indigenous peoples, a Wakefieldite put the view in 1856 that: 'All we can do is to smoothe the pillow of the dying Maori race' (quoted in Fryer, 1988, p. 43).

Positivism was linked, in the period after Waterloo, to Benthamite Utilitarianism, seeking to bring the benefits of the industrial revolution to society through 'the greatest good of the greatest number'. Utilitarian ideas, which have been called 'the largest contribution made by the English to moral and political theory', were absorbed into government in this period, and contributed to an increased regulatory role for the state over many aspects of society – classifying, segregating and controlling. They were associated with an increasing specialization of building form, especially for the control of groups of people. Bentham's *panopticon* (cited by Foucault as a paradigm of disciplinary technology), which subjected prisoners to solitary confinement under an all-seeing central supervision, was applied as the 'fan' design principle to colonial labour camps. As will be seen in chapter 4, the colonial situation created a need for all kinds of specialized buildings for the management of goods and people, such as the barrack for the efficient housing of workers, and the clock tower, a symbol of the industrial revolution's new time disciplines.[19]

Another element in the political thinking that informed nineteenth-century colonialism was the idea of trusteeship for the subject peoples. Earlier colonial expansion had paid little attention to the living conditions of slave labour or the indigenous peoples. Then the Quakers and Evangelicals, having achieved the abolition of slavery, continued to press government to ameliorate the conditions of the colonial peoples, through bodies such as the British and Foreign Aborigines' Protection Society (Rainger, 1980). This was associated with reformist pressure for municipal improvement in Britain, as expressed by one of the

South Australia promoters, Maslen, in 1843:

An opinion has for some time been gaining ground with the reflecting portion of the public, that something must be done to better the condition of the labouring classes, who are becoming so exceedingly numerous by the increase of the population, that their numbers alone are embarrassing, at the same time that their reverence for superiors, and respect for the classes above them is evidently much weakened, and likely to be succeeded by vindictive feelings and hatred, springing from their miserable condition, and what little education they may have, not being based upon a religious foundation. (Maslen, 1843)

The concept of trusteeship derived from the politician Burke, for whom colonialism implied a trust from humanity to protect native societies from the disruptive influence of Westernization. In 1834 the British Parliament passed a petition demanding the protection of the rights of native peoples, and the Colonial Office began to put in place an administrative machinery for regulating the legal and territorial relations between settlers and natives. In South Australia Colonel William Light, better known for his planning of Adelaide, also held the position of Protector of the Aborigines, and 'Protectors' in other colonies were created for the indentured labourers brought in to replace the freed slaves.

By the late nineteenth century, when British colonial control was being enlarged in Asia and tropical Africa, the trusteeship principle was restated as the doctrine of indirect rule, or the dual mandate. The terms were particularly associated with Lord Lugard, the governor first of Northern and then of all Nigeria between 1900 and 1919. As expressed by Lugard:

The British role here is to bring to the country all the gains of civilisation by applied science (whether in the development of material resources, or the eradication of disease, etc.), with as little interference as possible with Native customs and modes of thought. (Lugard, 1965)

After the First World War the extension of British rule over Palestine and former German colonies in Africa was justified as a mandate, or 'a sacred trust of civilization', conferred through the League of Nations.

Indirect rule created opportunities for experimentation with progressive ideas such as municipal improvement and town planning. It promoted the concept of the 'dual city', in which the 'modern' was kept separate from the 'traditional'. A movement to preserve the historic buildings and monuments of the colonized societies was promoted, particularly by Lord Curzon, who wanted to preserve India's architectural heritage. The era of indirect rule and the new imperialism was also associated with white supremacist ideas, applied to colonial urban landscapes through racial segregation policies. Europeans, once respectful of some non-Western peoples, began to confuse levels of technology with levels of culture in general, and finally with biological capacity.

London was the place where such ideas and ideologies were mostly forged. In the early days of British colonial expansion, the businessmen of the City of London, in partnership with King James, had planned and promoted the plantation of Ulster. In London, inspired in part by the designs for its rebuilding after the Great Fire, William Penn and Shaftesbury planned their colonies. The trustees of the Georgia, Sierra Leone, South Australia and New Zealand colonies met in London. There the professional societies and institutions held their meetings, assembled their libraries (still important sources for researchers), and built their grand headquarter buildings. London's local government also had a colonial impact, especially the London County Council, which was created in 1888: a former LCC member (Lord Pentland, the Governor of Madras) invited Patrick Geddes to introduce his new town planning ideas to India, while a chairman of the LCC (Captain Swinton) resigned his position in order to lead the planning of the new colonial capital for India at New Delhi.

Outside London there were important provincial centres of influence in the port cities of the western coast of Britain from which the slave trade, shipping, emigration and professional training were also organized. Of the city of Liverpool, home of the slave trade, it was said that every brick had been cemented with the blood of a slave (Fryer, 1984, p. 33). It also became the home of the first university schools of tropical medicine and civic design, largely funded by Lord Leverhulme, whose soap fortune was based upon colonial raw materials.

Also important were the colonies of the English, absorbed through Acts of Union into the United Kingdom – Scotland, Wales and Ireland. They produced a disproportionate number of colonial servants compared with England. Scotland, for instance, trained most of the colonial doctors and many of the colonial engineers in the nineteenth and early twentieth centuries. In the words of Linda Colley, the Scots had an active interest in British imperial expansion, since the Empire allowed 'Scots to feel themselves peers of the English in a way still denied them in an island kingdom'.[20] Among the Scots who influenced the form of colonial urbanism were the sanitarians, Simpson and MacGregor, and the engineers, Napier and McLean.

As long as the ideas were transmitted within a small elite, the medium of communication was personal meeting and correspondence, like Colleton's exchanges with Shaftesbury and Locke, referred to at the beginning of this chapter. Books and magazines became increasingly important from the eighteenth century. Proposals after the Seven Years War for new colonial defensive settlements were canvassed in the *Gentleman's Magazine* (Robison, 1992). Influential books in the eighteenth century were Martyn's *Reasons for Establishing the Colony of Georgia*, and Granville Sharp's *General Plan for laying out Towns and Townships on the new-acquired Lands in the East Indies, America or Elsewhere*, which ran to several editions. In the nineteenth century Maslen's *Friend of Australia* and John Stuart Mill's *Principles of Political Economy* offered guiding principles, and the report of the Royal Commission on the Sanitary State of the Army of India (1863) had an influence beyond the quartering of the military. In the early twentieth century Lugard's *Dual Mandate in Tropical Africa*, which was published in 1922 and reached a fourth edition by 1929, became the semi-official approach to British colonial administration in the years between the two World Wars, and offered a planning framework for racial segregation. Textbooks on public health and sanitation, notably Simpson (1908) and Kirk (1931), had a powerful influence.

The ideas and ideologies of colonial expansion largely disregarded the cultural traditions of the colonized peoples. Colonial settlement planning drew upon European Renaissance and baroque models, but largely ignored the much older urban traditions of India and China. In India, for instance, the positivist and progressive ideology interpreted the indigenous populace as having no significant political principles or forms of government, only religious customs and domestic concerns, so that Indian culture was effectively depoliticized. At a practical level this meant that the sophisticated pre-colonial irrigation systems of India were ignored by British civil engineers, and the municipal organization of Indian cities was allowed to fall into neglect (Oldenburg, 1984). Often, for instance in the Caribbean and Australia, pre-colonial populations were all but extinguished, their settlement patterns of mere passing archaeological or antiquarian interest to the conquerors.

Only in the twentieth century did the British begin to pay much attention to the rich urban traditions of India, China or the Middle East, and show a growing awareness of the need to repair the damage inflicted by their cultural domination. In the 1930s the Town Planning

Institute began to take an interest in early Indian planning, and the Chief Executive of the Nagpur Improvement Trust wrote for it a spirited paper extolling the virtues of the ancient planning methodology as recorded in Sanskrit texts (of which Geddes had spoken highly):

. . . the Zoning system of old India, in its courage of approach, in its extent of application, in its richness of details and in its fitness of purpose, is miles ahead of its modern prototype . . . the vandalistic tendency of civic life destroyed all (of the city gardens) and created a jungle of brick and mortar and worse still of tin sheds out of tune with its surroundings and depressing the mental, moral as well as physical well-being of the community.[21]

At the same time the Town Planning Institute was urging the Egyptians to adapt modern architecture and town planning to an Arabic style: 'to create a more supple formula, which while neglecting neither the picturesque nor the aesthetic, will accord with modern needs and harmonise with contemporary customs' (*Garden Cities and Town Planning*, 1935–36, Vol. 22, pp. 218–219).

Patrick Geddes was particularly aware of the contradictions in colonial rule and the trusteeship concept, which tried to preserve cultural heritage and at the same time pioneer a path into the 'modern' world, but he found himself out of step with the new Indian political leaders:

While Geddes was eulogising about ancient Indian urban forms, and the domestic arrangements, for example, of courtyard houses (usually the first target for demolition by British sanitary engineers), leaders of the Indian National Congress were taking their own families from traditional homes to the new-style bungalows. (Meller, 1990, p. 221)

The designs and ideologies of British colonialism not only had little regard for indigenous cultures, but also seem to have drawn little upon the experience of other European countries as colonizers, partly because they were rivals and competitors. While there are clear similarities between the British and the Spanish colonial town planning model (as set out in the *Laws of the Indies*, the Spanish crown's instructions on colonization practice), there is little direct evidence of conscious borrowing. Early colonists in the Caribbean region transferred experience to the American mainland, notably from Barbados to the Carolinas (Alleyne and Fraser, 1988). Renaissance and baroque concepts of political order filtered into Britain from the European mainland at the time of the Restoration, and from there were applied in colonial situations. In the nineteenth century the reshaping of Paris by Haussmann has its echoes in the demolition of large parts of Indian cities.

The closest direct borrowing seems to have come from the Dutch rather than from French, Spanish or Portuguese colonizers. This may be partly because of the historic links with their fellow Protestants, and also because the British acquired long-established Dutch colonies at the Cape of Good Hope, Ceylon, and Malacca. It was the expressed desire of Stamford Raffles (who was governor of the conquered Dutch colony of Java before he went on to found Singapore) to build upon and improve Dutch practices. The arcaded shophouse and the captain system of indirect rule (see pp. 103–107 and 120) are perhaps the best examples of this borrowing.

By the late nineteenth century a new era of competitive colonialism, and an assumption of British superiority after a century of imperial dominance, meant that planning ideas were not willingly shared between the European powers. Although two leading colonial town planners, Reade in Malaya and Karsten in Indonesia, were operating in the 1920s in colonies only a few miles apart, there is no record of them meeting.[22] (Reade did, however, visit the Philippines to learn from American colonial practices.) The importance of German town planning and infrastructure provision was recognized in the early twentieth century, but at the International Garden City Congress in London in 1904 the British

Dutch colonial architecture in Malaya: the Stadhuis in Malacca. The Dutch took Malacca from the Portuguese, and lost it in 1796 to the British, who demolished the fortifications and transferred power to Singapore. The governor's house, however, survived. (Source: The author, photo taken in 1985)

organizers viewed the enthusiastic response from Germany with some suspicion, partly because of imperial rivalries.[23]

The shapers of British colonial urban landscapes were not only narrowly British, they were also male. Colonial towns and cities, especially in the tropics, were made mostly by men, for use by other men. Women and families were intended to have a very limited place in them, both for the white colonizers and the non-white colonized peoples. To a greater extent than in contemporary Europe, colonial urban landscapes and building forms – the counting-house and cantonment, the maidan and the padang, the barrack and the jute mill – were intended for men rather than women to occupy. Family, social and community life was correspondingly under-valued and impoverished. Patrick Geddes was, almost uniquely, perceptive enough to recognize this situation, and sought to involve women in his teaching and projects. As he wrote to his daughter:

I cannot discover that it has yet at all adequately been grasped by women what an awful mess our masculine division of labour – into mechanical stupidities and so on – makes of the world.[24]

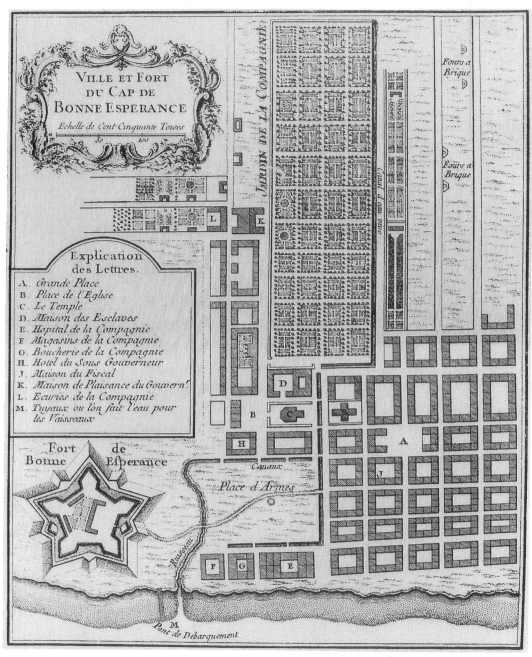

Explication des Lettres.

A. *Grande Place*
B. *Place de l'Eglise*
C. *Le Temple*
D. *Maison des Esclaves*
E. *Hopital de la Compagnie*
F. *Magasins de la Compagnie*
G. *Boucherie de la Compagnie*
H. *Hotel du Sous Gouverneur*
J. *Maison du Fiscal*
K. *Maison de Plaisance du Gouvern.*
L. *Ecuries de la Compagnie*
M. *Tuyaux ou l'on fait l'eau pour les Vaisseaux*

Cape Town in 1764. The oldest colonial settlement by Europeans in southern Africa was founded by the Dutch East India Company. The plan shows the regular street layout of the Dutch surveyors before the British conquest in 1796. (Source: Reproduced from the facsimile by Historic Urban Plans, Ithaca, New York, of Bellin's Petit Atlas Maritime)

The Colonial City as 'A Terrain of Conflict and Negotiation'[25]

The professionals concerned with creating the colonial city found themselves far from Europe. They had to grapple with very different climates, terrains and social practices, and were involved in local political processes and accommodations. What might seem appropriate in Britain or Europe could be disastrous on the other side of the world. A documented example is the introduction by the Dutch in Batavia of a system of canals similar to those of the Netherlands, which had the unsought effect of increasing the incidence of disease, and making Batavia into one of the unhealthiest places in the tropics (Blusse, 1985).

The political institutions and corporate structures of European colonialism helped to forge the colonial urban landscapes. The tension between the mercantile capitalism of the chartered company, and the colonial government representing the crown, has already been mentioned. From the late nineteenth century concentrations of capital in mining, railways and iron and steel production created new urban landscapes through a mixture of public and private sector enterprise. Examples include De Beers' closed compounds and white suburbs at Kimberley, the iron and steel towns of Jamshedpur and Vanderbijl Park, and the railway 'colonies' of India and Africa.

Structures of colonial administration expanded to incorporate the new professions. Departments of lands and survey, public works, medical and sanitary services were created in many colonies from the nineteenth century, although only rarely was a separate department created for that late arrival, town planning. Within these structures of colonial government the professional found his role circumscribed by the administrators: he was to be 'on tap but not on top', in a favourite bureaucrat's phrase. British colonial officials in Northern Nigeria, for instance, were particularly hostile to the new professional and technical services:

They did not want a wholesale influx of subordinate departmental officials from the South to come upsetting everyone by enforcing health regulations or forestry regulations . . . They felt sure that the native authorities, with the help of a few sympathetic white men who understood their ways and spoke their language, could make a better, more economical job of meeting the basic needs – simple roads, bridges and water-works, simple schools and dispensaries – than any centrally organized bureaucracy of professional specialists whose schemes were always too expensive. (Nicholson, 1969, p. 240)

Also from the late nineteenth century onwards, new municipal authorities were brought into existence in the colonies, and princely states subordinated to the indirect rule system. These local political structures found themselves circumscribed in what they could achieve, and British colonialism designed or modified them in order to limit local involvement. In Lucknow in the 1860s the municipal committees habitually used an English language medium, which most indigenous members at the time could not understand, thus effectively excluding them from decision-making (Oldenburg, 1984). The members of municipal corporations were elected on a limited franchise, and were drawn from a narrow group of Western-educated professionals and businessmen. The various boards and trusts which reshaped the docks and cleared the slums were controlled by appointed members and British officials. Their chairmen and executives, men such as Crawford, the Municipal Commissioner of Bombay in the 1860s, or Bompas, the head of the Calcutta Improvement Trust after 1911, only attended to local political opinion when forced to.

When local and municipal authorities wanted to draw upon professional expertise they were often frustrated. Even large authorities had difficulty persuading the British colonial administrators to allow them to employ white professional or technical staff. C.L Temple, a leading advocate of indirect rule, defended this situation as follows:

It is of no use to make any bones about it – the prestige of the white man, to use that hackneyed phrase, must be maintained.[26]

Nor was there much attempt to train local staff for senior positions, at least until the 1930s in India and Egypt.[27]

The colonial political structure was, therefore, a rigid one. It concentrated power in the hands of the colonizers, who sought to organize the urban built environment to express their aspirations and ideals. It was to be well-ordered, sanitized and amenable to regulation. The various strategies to achieve this included, as will be seen, surveillance and inspection, the modification of built form, the provision of municipal facilities, and the demarcation of space.

The urban landscape constructed by the colonizers was not, however, accepted without challenge by the subject peoples who had to live there. Urban space can be seen as 'a resource drawn upon by different groups and the contended object of everyday discourse in conflicts and negotiations involving both colonialists and colonised groups' (Yeoh, 1991, pp. 13–14). The indigenous communities through their group organizations resisted attempts at hegemonic control by the dominant colonizing culture. They tried to thwart the purposes of the colonial power through non-co-operation and even open rebellion. The people of Trinidad, denied normal political expression, expressed in the carnival tradition their protest against class and colonialism through popular culture on the streets

The town hall on Mapo Hill, Ibadan, Nigeria. This building in classical style was the work of 'Taffy' Jones, engineer to the Ibadan Native authority and an exception to the rule that white technical staff were not employed by 'native authorities'. (Source: The author, photo taken in 1965)

(Jackson, 1988 and 1989). Yeoh (1990) gives examples from the Singapore case, such as the disputes over street naming, over the definition and use of public space (in the verandah riots of 1887), and over the control of 'sacred' space (the Chinese burial grounds).

The allocation of street and place names might seem to be an uncontentious matter. To the colonial authority in Singapore accurate addresses and clearly sign-posted streets were important and necessary for the levying of house tax assessments and public utility rates. Portions of streets were renamed or re-numbered to accommodate the requirements of the municipal assessor. The municipal names accorded with the British vision of a vital, progressive outpost of empire. Chinese names, however, almost never indicate cultural influences from other parts of the world, while Asian communities pressed for the recognition of Asian names, in order to make their own claim upon the landscape. The contrast between municipal and Asian place names represented different ways of signifying the landscape. As Yeoh (1991, p. 269) comments:

The establishment of a network of official place- and street-names not only introduces order and differentiation into an originally amorphous landscape but also reflects the mental images of the dominant culture.

Another example of conflict over the control of urban space in Singapore is the British attempt to move cemeteries out of town, on religious as well as sanitary grounds. This was interpreted by the Chinese as an attack on their customary rituals, eroding their control over their own sacred places. In Chinese culture *feng shui* geomancy had to be taken into account in siting a grave, if harmony between society and the physical landscape was to be maintained. Any form of interference with the 'sepulchral boundaries' could destroy the transmission of power from the ancestors and lead to a reversal of family fortunes. Thus *feng shui* became 'a strategic discourse in the

encounter between the colonial authorities and the Chinese community', with the Chinese seeking to preserve 'the immunity of certain elements of the environment from colonial or municipal control' (Yeoh 1991, chapter 8).

Domestic building form was another way in which an alien urban environment could be adapted to immediate social needs, as will be seen in Chapter 4. African slaves in the Caribbean and the American South incorporated in their house styles their memories of the African compound – Genell Anderson's 'call of the ancestors' exemplified by the Charleston single house and the shot-gun house (Anderson, 1991). The 'shophouse Rafflesia' of Singapore and South-East Asia was essentially a Chinese vernacular style, adapted to a colonial context (Lim, 1993). Chinese *feng shui* has apparently exercised a strong influence upon the built forms of Hong Kong and Singapore.[28]

Thus in day-to-day living the physical forms of the colonial city could be adapted to the social practices of the indigenous populations, while control over urban space was contested through rituals of resistance. Notwithstanding the control exercised through colonial authority and its professions of the built environment, a plurality of cultures and ways of seeing could still be reflected in a plurality of landscapes.

Controlling Public Space:
The Wide Street

Perhaps the dominant physical form of the colonial urban landscape is the wide street. It was often imposed at considerable social cost through the demolition of crowded areas, as occurred in Indian cities after 1857, and in port cities during the plague epidemics of the early twentieth century. It proved to be environmentally unsuited to hot climates, although often justified on public health grounds. The assumptions behind this urge to create wide streets varied over the centuries of British overseas expansion, in a shifting discourse on the social significance of urban forms. One constant, however, was the attempt to impose a controllable public space upon societies which had different traditions and often mingled public with private space.

Indigenous urban cultures in the tropics tended to favour narrow rather than wide streets, for practical reasons as climatic regulators. The Spanish Laws of the Indies stated unequivocally that 'in cold climates the streets shall be wide; in hot climates narrow'. Yet the British laid down wide streets even – indeed especially – in the tropics. Street widths (typically 100–150 feet for main roads) were specified in regulations, and much attention was paid to maintaining the full width of road reservation against 'encroachments'. In one of the hottest climates in the world, the new Khartoum was planned by General Kitchener in 1898 with streets of 120 and 150 feet wide. The consequences were, as McLean, the City

Engineer, complained, that 'the great width of the streets and the very open development has so spread out the town that the cost of a drainage scheme was found to be prohibitive' (quoted in Home, 1991b).

Wide straight streets could fulfil a number of social and symbolic functions. They removed congestion, allowed the free movement of air, imposed a sense of order, facilitated police control, and broke up densely populated areas into manageable units. One of the earliest colonial agencies for urban renewal, in Dublin in the eighteenth century, was aptly named the Wide Streets Commissioners. Its original brief (under an Act of 1757) was simple enough, 'for making a wide and convenient Way, Street, or Passage, from Essex-bridge to the Castle of Dublin', but this it enlarged to undertake a large-scale replanning of the city (McParland, 1972).

In the free-enterprise Wakefield settlement of New Zealand, the land surveyors had no

A colonial wide street in Lahore, Pakistan. Such streets were typically 150 feet wide, designed for ease of surveillance and public health as much as for traffic movement. An open drain can be seen to the right. Building 'encroachments' were vigorously resisted. (Source: *The author, photo taken in 1991*)

The result of the Wide Streets Commissioners' work in Dublin in the eighteenth century, providing a setting for grand public buildings. (Source: McParland, 1972)

A similar perspective view from the other side of the world – Calcutta in the 1770s. (Source: Losty, 1990)

specific instructions on street widths (other than that they should be 'ample'). This resulted in exceptionally narrow streets of only 16 feet, until the Municipal Corporations Act of 1867 set a standard width of 40 feet, later increased to 66 feet. The argument in favour of wide streets was made on grounds of morality, rather than efficiency. As a member of the New Zealand House of Representatives said in a speech in 1878:

If they looked for crime, vice, destitution, and everything that was bad, they would go to the narrow slums and lanes, where these evils were actually engendered. If they made good wide streets, depend upon it they would greatly promote the virtue, morality, and health of the people, so that, in the interests of every community, the Government should insist upon the laying out of wide streets. (quoted in Hargreaves, 1992)

Later the argument in favour of wide streets was made on public health, rather than moral or efficiency grounds. It was believed that they would ventilate the towns and blow away smells and disease. Dr. William Simpson's textbook on tropical hygiene (1908, p. 305) advocated wide straight streets with shade-giving trees, preferably aligned to the prevailing wind 'in order that they may act as ventilating conduits to the town or village'. These streets were to be not less in width than the height of the proposed buildings on either side, and he advocated no street in a new district less than 50 feet, while principal ones should be 60, 80 or 100 feet. He also advocated back lanes of 15 feet, for the following reasons:

(1) They facilitate (a) drainage, (b) scavenging;
(2) Add to the air space between the rear of buildings and thus reduce overcrowding on area;
(3) Prevent encroachments and extensions backwards, which are detrimental to ventilation and a free circulation of air . . .;
(4) Form an alignment . . . essential to prevent the lanes being irregular and winding;
(5) Define the limits of the boundary of each plot . . . (Simpson, 1908, p. 307)

Apart from its public health role, the wide, straight street was represented as the imposition of colonial order upon indigenous culture. Maintenance of the road space, even when not needed for the movement of traffic, became a point of honour with colonial municipal administrators. There was much talk in the early twentieth century of the need to protect the public street against 'encroachments', and indeed the straight road was even justified on the grounds that it allowed encroachments to be more easily detected.

Patrick Geddes saw the damaging consequences of the colonial obsession with wide streets. He was concerned that roads broader than needed were being driven through poor districts, regardless of the hardship caused to the displaced inhabitants. The harsh approach of the colonial municipal administrator was expressed by C.H. Bompas of the Calcutta Improvement Trust, in a discussion of street width in 1928, when he voiced his resolute opposition to narrow roads:

Plotting based on 20-feet roads was not successful as the people took every advantage they could of the flat area and the place rapidly degenerated into a slum. (Temple, 1928, p. 27)

An analysis of what the British were about with their wide streets is given by Archer (1994), writing of the plans for reconstructing the Indian parts of Calcutta in 1803:

Instead of building neighbourhoods in which traditional relations were embedded in the material fabric of building and street, the new paradigm . . . was a matter of corridors, avenues, straight lines, and grids. This paradigm was not just a matter of enhanced fire protection or drainage, or even augmentation of the city's imperial splendor. Rather, it was also the imposition of new means of control (through sectorization), visibility and identification (plotting holdings as positions within a matrix) and, more insidiously, socialization (replacing tight-knit, well-surveilled neighbourhoods with open corridors as places of primary contact, communication, and leisure for the indigenous population.

NOTES

1. Sir Thomas Brisbane (1773–1860) was Governor of New South Wales 1821–5, and the capital of Queensland was named for him. His successor from 1825 to 1831 was Sir Ralph Darling (1775–1858). Sir Richard Bourke (1777–1855) was Governor of the Eastern Cape 1825–28, and of New South Wales 1831–37, where he was involved with the planning of Melbourne. Sir Benjamin D'Urban (1777–1849) was Governor of the Cape 1834–38 and founded the city that bears his name. All were Peninsular War veterans (DNB).

2. For the growth of modern professions see Larson (1977), and Torstendahl and Burridge (1990). Their links with colonialism, however, have hitherto been little studied.

3. Sir William MacGregor (1847–1919) was educated at Aberdeen and Glasgow, and served in the Seychelles, Mauritius, and Fiji. In 1888 he declared British sovereignty over New Guinea as the first Administrator. He was Governor of Lagos 1899–1904, where he worked with Ross on anti-malaria measures, and he represented the West African colonies and protectorates at the coronation of Edward VII in 1902. Subsequently he was governor of Newfoundland and Queensland (WWW, DNB).

Robert Hoddle (1794–1881) trained in the Ordnance Department and came to New South Wales (after a year in the Cape Colony) in 1823. Governor Darling had a different opinion than Mitchell, regarding Hoddle as one of the most competent men in the department. See DAustB, Lewis (1993) and Selby (1928).

4. Kondratieff waves are long economic cycles, averaging fifty years, often associated with major technological changes such as the Industrial Revolution. See Lloyd-Jones (1990) for an introduction, and Braudel (1984), pp. 80–85.

5. Kain and Baigent (1992), p. 307. This section draws heavily upon their book. Information on individuals is drawn mainly from DAustB, DCanB, and DNZB.

6. Samuel Johannes Holland (1728–1801) emigrated to England from the Netherlands in 1754, and went to North America in 1756. According to the DCanB, 'It is the many maps and the layout of townships in Upper and Lower Canada under his competent administration that constitute the chief legacy of the Canadian career of this great surveyor and cartographer.'

His deputy was John Collins (d. 1795), who surveyed townships for loyalists at Kingston, Ernestown, Fredericksburgh and Adolphustown (DCanB). See also Kain and Baigent (1992), pp. 298–303.

7. John Septimus Roe (1797–1878) laid out Perth and Fremantle, as Surveyor-General of Western Australia 1829–70.

Thomas Mitchell (1792–1855) was Surveyor-General of New South Wales 1827–55 and died in the field.

Of the South Australian Surveyors-General, Charles Sturt (1795–1869) went to Sydney in 1825, succeeded Light, and was a famous explorer of the Australian interior before he retired to England in 1853. E.C. Frome (1802–90), an instructor from the Chatham Royal Engineer's college, held the post 1839–49, and was an innovator whose book on trigonometrical survey went through four editions. G.W. Goyder (1826–98), who held the post 1861–94, as 'the king of the lands department' quadrupled the colony's revenue from land sales, and also chose the site of Darwin for the capital of the Northern Territory.

See Foster (1985) on Mitchell, Lines (1992) on Australian mapping, Hall-Jones (1992) on Thomson, and Jones (1989) on the mapping of Tasmania; see also DAustB and DNZB.

8. Colonel R.H. Rowe (1883–1933) became Surveyor-General of the Gold Coast in 1920, and in Nigeria was the first chairman of the Lagos Executive Development Board before his premature death. WWW.

9. See Davies (1989) for Light's survey methods, and Kain and Baigent (1992), pp. 307–313. I am grateful to John Porter (former Surveyor-General of South Australia) for helping me understand the dispute over Light's survey methods. Johnson and Langmead (1986) claimed that Light's deputy, Kingston, was the true source of the Adelaide plan, but this view has few adherents. In the words of John Porter to me, 'Kingston was a dork'.

10. For the Royal Engineers see Smithers (1991) and Watson (1914). For the military engineer in India see Sandes (1933).

11. Daly (1986), pp. 25–28. See also Home (1990b). Kitchener left the detailed work to two other Royal Engineer officers on his staff, who were later Lt. General Sir George F. Gorringe (1868–1945) and Colonel Hon. Milo Talbot (1854–1931) (WWW).

12. Frederick Guggisberg (1869–1930), a Canadian, was Director of Survey in the Gold Coast 1905–8, and returned as Governor from 1919 to 1927. He developed the first deep-water harbour in Gold Coast at Takoradi, and made the first colonial ten-year development plan.

Colonel Sir Henry MacCallum (1852–1919) worked on naval installations at Hong Kong and Singapore in 1877–79, and after a spell at Penang was Colonel Engineer and Surveyor-General of the Straits Settlements 1884–97 (for which he received the C.M.G. in 1887). He then became Governor of Lagos 1897–99, at the time of the construction of the railway into the interior, and was Governor of Natal 1901–7.

Sir Matthew Nathan (1862–1939) was successively Governor of Sierra Leone, the Gold Coast 1900–3, Hong Kong 1903–7, and Natal 1907–9.

Colonial Sir Percy Girouard (1867–1932), a French Canadian, was director of railways in the Sudan and South Africa 1896–1902, High Commissioner and Governor of Northern Nigeria 1907–9, and Governor of East Africa 1909–12.

13. Captain Swinton in *JTPI*, 1921–22, Vol. 8, p. 73. John A. Brodie (1858–1932) was City Engineer of Liverpool 1898–1926, and Engineer to the Mersey Tunnel Committee after 1926. Lutyens described him as 'a great apple-shaped man full of drains' (Hussey, 1953, p. 246) (WWW).

14. The term comes from Swanson (1977). There is a growing literature on medicine and the British Empire, to which the edited collections in Arnold (1988) and McLeod and Lewis (1988) provide an introduction. See also Curtin (1985) and (1989), Dumett (1968), Headrick (1981), Hume (1986), Klein (1986), Lyons (1985), Mayne (1982), Phimister (1987), Spitzer (1986), and Swanson (1977).

15. Quoted in Marks and Andersson (1988), pp. 262–263. For this shameful incident, see also Wasserfall (1990), p. 86.

16. George D. Coleman (d. 1844) first visited Singapore in 1822 and settled there permanently in 1826. He became the government surveyor and supervisor of public works, and prepared the first comprehensive map of the town. He retired in 1841. He widened and standardized many of the roads, and designed many public buildings, including the market, courthouse, gaol, and cathedral. See Hancock (1986), and Turnbull (1972), pp. 37–43.

Francis Greenway (1777–1837) was a Bristol architect transported for forgery to Australia in 1814, who, after obtaining his ticket of leave, was civil architect and assistant engineer from 1816 and 1822, designing many Sydney buildings, including a barracks and compound for male convicts. DAustB. For Sulman, see Freestone, 1983.

17. See Batey (1993) and Wright (1982). Colman (1993) deals with the Liverpool connection of Australian planners.

W.H. Lever, Viscount Leverhulme (1851–1925) developed Port Sunlight and was a Liberal M.P. 1906–9. He used the damages from a libel case to endow tropical medicine and civic design at the University of Liverpool in 1909, and subsequently was made a baronet in 1911 and a peer in 1917 (WWW, DNB).

18. Rabinow (1986) introduces Foucault's ideas, and the influence of social theory upon town planning is explored in Benevolo (1967).

19. Plamenatz (1966) deals with the political thought of the Utilitarians, Finer (1972) with their influence upon government, Hyde (1947) with their place in town planning, and Markus (1993) with their influence on building design. Brine (1993) discusses the panopticon and Adelaide.

20. Colley (1992), pp. 123–130, deals with the Scots role in Empire. As she points out, in the century after 1750 Oxford and Cambridge produced five hundred medical doctors, but Scotland produced ten thousand, and a quarter of the East India Company's army officers were Scots.

21. Mehta (1937–38). See also Dutt (1925) on early town planning in India, and a short note on the early Indian village in *GCTP*, 1924, Vol. 14, pp. 3–4.

22. Thomas Karsten (1884–1945) worked for many years in Dutch Indonesia, and died in a Japanese internment camp. Probably influenced more by German than British planning, he

advocated planning and housing strategies to shape cities as an organic whole, including decentralization. For his work see Van der Heiden (1990) and Cobban (1992). For Dutch colonial buildings, see Greig (1987).

23. See Hardy (1991), p. 94. Hietala (1987) compares in detail the practice and diffusion of infrastructure provision in different European countries around 1900.

24. Letter in 1918, quoted in Kitchen (1957), p. 279. See also Meller (1990), pp. 7 and 226.

25. The phrase is from Yeoh (1991), pp. 12–13. This dissertation (to be published) is a striking analysis of disputed urban landscape in Singapore. Other important studies of the colonial shaping of cities are Oldenburg (1984) on Lucknow and Gupta (1981) on Delhi. Jackson (1989) provides an overview of the new cultural geography which these studies represent.

26. Temple (1918), pp. 38 and 77. A notable exception to this general policy was the Ibadan Native Authority's road engineer, Robert A. (Taffy) Jones (1882–1949). He worked in Southern Nigeria 1910–44, starting as a road foreman, and was seconded to the Ibadan Native Authority in 1923, where he remained until his retirement to his native Wales. He built a wide road through the heart of Ibadan (known as Taffy Highway), obtaining the agreement of the local community for the necessary demolitions (he spoke Yoruba). He also designed the Ibadan Town Hall at Mapo. See Home (1974), p. 181.

27. One exception was Sabry Mahboub Bey in Egypt, who had studied civil engineering in England, was a member of the Town Planning Institute and became first Director General of the Tanzim Department in Cairo and then Director General of the Egyptian Roads and Bridges Department (Sabry Mahboub-Bey, 1934–35). Another Egyptian, Meligy Masoud, was trained in Britain by Barry Parker and became the Municipal Engineer of Cairo.

28. For *feng shui* see Lim (1993) and Shelton (1914). For a fascinating case study of the conflict between *feng shui* and Western planning concepts of the cul-de-sac, see Nishiyama (1988).

3

PORT CITIES OF THE BRITISH EMPIRE: A GLOBAL THALASSOCRACY

Among empires, the most unusual is that of the sea. The Minoans, the Greeks, the Phoenicians, and the Vikings all dominated for a time the seas around them. But only once has there been a truly global thalassocracy, a nation whose fleet and merchant marine were dominant on almost all the seas of the world. This was Great Britain in the nineteenth century.

(Headrick, 1981, pp. 174–175)

Many of the largest cities in the world today are creatures of British colonialism – Bombay, Calcutta, Hong Kong, Singapore and Lagos, to mention some of those in developing countries. They are links in a world economy and global network of cities, through which trade and production is organized. Braudel (1984, chapter 1), in his great study of world history from the fifteenth to eighteenth centuries, has shown how, by the late eighteenth century, the 'octopus grip of European trade had extended to cover the whole world'. He has linked this to the existence of a dominant capitalist city: London by 1775, he says unequivocally, was 'the centre of the world'. The parts of the world economy each developed their own core, middle zone and periphery, each with its dominant city. Friedmann (1986) has formulated a present-day version of world-economy theory with his world-city hypothesis. Recent academic work now combines world-city theory with colonial urban development theory (King, 1990), to recognize the import-ance of ports in the development of colonial and post-colonial economic systems.

While the plantation colonies of North America and the Antipodes, as has been seen, occupied territory and imported their own labour, the ports of the tropics were not intended for permanent white settlement, but to open up the vast markets and populations of India and the Far East to European trade. No 'Grand Modell' was applied to these tropical colonies, other than the demands of trade and profit. Their port towns were not planned as Savannah or Adelaide were planned. There were no social theorists, like John Locke or Granville Sharp, devising the physical form of an alternative society. Most importantly, the colonists under the 'Grand Modell' did not expect to return to Britain, but to make new lives for themselves under foreign skies. British merchants in the tropics, on the other hand, generally expected to make their fortunes as quickly as possible and return home before their health, and indeed their lives, gave out.

THE RISE OF PORT CITIES IN THE COLONIAL ECONOMY

The history of port creation in the British empire can be briefly summarized. Its first great port cities were the three 'Presidencies' of the British East India Company, which became the cornerstones of British power in the Far East. Madras was acquired in 1639. Bombay was part of the marriage dowry of the Portuguese Princess Catherine of Braganza when she married Charles II in 1665. Calcutta was founded by Job Charnock in 1690.

Bombay and Calcutta were particular commercial rivals from the start, and grew to become two of the largest ports in the world. In the late eighteenth century Calcutta was recognized as 'inferior only to the first capitals of Europe . . . in its extent and in the number of its inhabitants', and estimates of its population suggest that it was then larger than any British city apart from London. A century later Bombay overtook it to become the most populous port city in the East after Tokyo.

From the Presidency towns the British tightened their grip on the Indian sub-continent. In the Seven Years' War (1756–63) they displaced the rival French, and conquered Bengal, which created a whole new class of English nabobs within a few decades of Clive's victory at Plassey in 1757. The British in Bengal administered an economy that systematically exported wealth to England, a flow of tribute aptly titled 'the great drain', amounting to tens of millions of pounds by the late eighteenth century. As Edmund Burke described the behaviour of the East India Company's servants to the House of Commons:

animated with all the avarice of age and all the impetuosity of youth, they roll in one after another, wave after wave; and there is nothing before the eye of the native but an endless hopeless prospect of new birds of prey and passage, with appetites continually renewing for a food that is continually wasting. (quoted in Moorhouse, 1984, p. 45)

To safeguard their sea routes and open new markets the British went on to found or seize other ports. In the Mediterranean, Gibraltar was captured from the Spanish in 1704, and the island of Malta from the French in 1800. One of the East India Company's 'country traders', William Light, saw the strategic opportunity of the Straits of Malacca, the most direct sea passage from India to China and the Eastern Archipelago, and founded a colony on Penang Island in 1786 which proved to be the foundation of British power in the region. During the French Revolutionary Wars British force of arms relieved the Dutch of ports at Cape Town, Colombo and Malacca. Cape Town, called by its first British Governor in 1797 'the master link of connection between the western and eastern world' (quoted in Ross and Telkamp, 1985, p. 107), was also known as 'the Tavern and Brothel of the two Oceans', albeit with a modest population of less than twenty-five thousand by 1850. Colombo in Ceylon was of similar importance strategically: 'the Clapham Junction of the Far East'. While Cape Town and Colombo went from strength to strength, Malacca was less fortunate: the fortifications were razed, and it was rapidly overtaken by Singapore as the trading emporium of the region.

These gains were confirmed by the Treaty of Vienna in 1815. In the century of British maritime supremacy which followed, more ports consolidated a world-wide trade network. When the 1815 peace settlement returned Indonesia to the Dutch, and left the British with Penang Island and the much reduced port of Malacca, Stamford Raffles obtained the cession of Singapore island in 1819 from the Malays, against the initial disapproval of his masters in the East India Company and the opposition of the Dutch. He saw it as a 'commanding and promising Station for the protection and improvement of all our interests in this Quarter', 'a great commercial emporium and fulcrum, whence we may extend our influence politically, as circumstances may require' (quoted in Cangi, 1993). So it proved. Singapore soon came to supplant Penang and Malacca as the most important of Britain's 'Straits Settlements', commanding the trade routes between India and China.

A generation after the founding of Singapore, the British acquired Hong Kong Island in 1841 as their beach-head into China. It was soon followed by the international 'Treaty Ports' through which European traders gained access to the huge markets of China: Guangzhou, Amoy (now Xiamen), Foochow (Fuzhou), Ningpo and Shanghai. By the end of the century Lord Curzon could write that:

No Englishman can land in Hong Kong without feeling a thrill of pride for his nationality. Here is the furthermost link in that chain of fortresses which from Spain to China girdles half the globe. (quoted in Morris, 1988, p. 138)

The creation of the port of Rangoon in 1852 consolidated British influence over Burma. In Africa smaller ports came under their control, such as Lagos in 1851. The Caribbean, although collectively important, was a scatter of small islands, and had only relatively small ports. When the Presidency of Bombay initiated steam communication between Britain and India in the 1820s by the Red Sea route, the port of Aden was raised to prominence. The opening of the Suez Canal in 1869 further cut the travelling time and distance between Europe and the East. A global achievement, it benefited mainly British interests, and brought Egypt, Cairo and Aden more firmly into the British sphere of influence.

Other additions to the British imperial port network came with the First World War. Port Harcourt was created in 1915 to open up the Eastern Nigerian coal deposits. The British mandates from the League of Nations at the end of the War brought control of Haifa in Palestine, and Dar-es-Salaam in Tanganyika.

This world-wide network of ports was linked to improvements in land transport. Railways, canals and roads fanned out from them, opening up the hinterlands to economic development (or exploitation). Plantation agriculture embraced the tea estates of India and Ceylon, the rubber estates of Malaya and the sugar estates of the Caribbean. Mineral extraction included tin in Malaya, copper in Northern Rhodesia, gold and diamonds in South Africa. Some ports developed their own processing industries, notably the jute mills of Calcutta and Bengal and the cotton textile mills of Bombay. In 1908 184,000 Indians worked in the Calcutta jute mills, and in 1931 a quarter of Bombay's working population, 136,000 hands, were employed daily in the cotton mills.[1]

The ports processed not only goods but people, and had an insatiable demand for labour, especially unskilled dock labour. All across the empire there was a shortage of labour, which after the abolition of slavery in 1834 was solved by the importation of migrant and indentured workers. The vast populations of the Indian and Chinese subcontinents provided an ample supply of usually docile workers. India, China and Africa fed workers to their new colonial cities, such as Bombay, Calcutta, Madras, Lagos, and Johannesburg, through internal migration. Smaller, less populated colonies, such as the geographically remote islands of Mauritius, Fiji and the West Indies, had to organize the mass importation of labour.

This colonial network of ports can be seen in the rankings of population and tonnage in 1911 in tables 3.1 and 3.2. The greatest cities after London were Calcutta and Bombay. These were the 'half-caste offspring of London', in the words of an astute Indian commentator, Nirad Chaudhuri (quoted in Tindall, 1982, p. 26). In 1894 Calcutta had combined imports and exports to the value of £60 million, and Bombay £50 million, compared with Hong Kong's £45 million, Singapore's £40 million, and Madras' £10 million.

Table 3.1. Main ports in Britain and the British Empire in 1911 (ranked by population in thousands).

London	4,522
Calcutta	1,222
Bombay	947
Glasgow	784
Liverpool	746
Manchester	714
Madras	518
Belfast	387
Singapore	303
Rangoon	293
Colombo	211
Cape Town	162
Penang Island	142
Durban	90
Lagos	73

Table 3.2. Annual average tonnage of vessels entered and cleared at ports in Britain and the British Empire (1907–11, millions of tons).

Hong Kong	22.5
London	20.1
Liverpool	14.7
Cardiff	14.5
Singapore	14.2
Colombo	13.3
Gibraltar	10.3
Valletta	8.0
Aden	6.7
Glasgow	4.8
Durban	4.7
Calcutta	3.5
Bombay	3.5
Cape Town	3.4
Montreal	3.0
Victoria, BC	3.0

Source: Oxford (1914).

THE MUNICIPAL GOVERNMENT OF *LAISSEZ-FAIRE*

The Industrial Revolution in Britain created new forms of municipal government to cope with the needs of large cities, but the rapidly growing colonial port cities lagged behind. In the early days their municipal administration was limited to justices of the peace (appointed by the governor-general), with powers to levy a property rate and hire scavengers and watchmen, thus following a similar structure to smaller English towns of the time. This minimalist approach was espoused by a governor of St. Lucia, who in 1807 wrote that: 'Few things can be of less interest, than the interior details of a Colony' (quoted in Wood, 1968, p. 33). If such an attitude was to be found in one of the planter colonies, the transient populations of the tropical port cities were even less considered. The British and American rejection of a planned approach has been contrasted with the port city planning of French absolutism:

Private property and social order became so closely linked in England that government interference with the former was thought to disrupt the latter. How different this was from the situation on the Continent! (Konvitz 1978)

The ports of the Indian presidency towns were divided between the 'White Town', where the white traders lived, and 'Black Town', where the wealthier Indians were allowed to lay out their own grid of streets, surrounding which was an unplanned and largely unmanaged periphery of villages for the common people.

In the early days of a colony the founding governors had the opportunity to lay out a street pattern, which some (like Governor Aungier in Bombay or Raffles at Singapore) did with more enthusiasm and foresightedness than others. Until the threat from colonial rivals and native opposition was over, the ports were periodically replanned or consolidated for defensive reasons. After 1763, for instance, having driven the rival French from India, the British reshaped the presidency towns, perhaps borrowing from the absolutist traditions of their defeated opponents. Fortifications were consolidated, and the white population was brought closer together and segregated within or close to the defensive walls. Around the consolidated white town, the ground was levelled and cleared of buildings and trees, to create a free field of fire, usually 800 yards wide (later extended to 1000 yards). This became the maidan, a place for horse-riding and other recreation. In Bombay it was to be for two centuries the divide between 'white' Bombay ('prestigious giant buildings, new and old, the Bombay of western road systems') and Indian Bombay ('the bazaar, the small workshops, the stalls, the rag-trade, the temples, the mosques: the Bombay of the people') (Tindall, 1982, p. 35). At Madras the former Black Town was demolished for a defensive zone, and rebuilt further out, but with less spatial or social cohesion (Neild, 1979).

If one seeks to contrast the planned or planted towns of the 'Grand Modell' colonial settlements with the largely unplanned trade ports of the tropics, then Penang and Adelaide offer good case studies, being creations of father and son unique in the history of planning. We are fortunate in having a detailed comparative study by Goh Ban Lee (1988a) of Adelaide, planned for permanent white settlement, and George Town, intended to be a place of trade. In the attention and care he gave to the planning of Adelaide (see pp. 26–29), Colonel William Light sought to emulate and improve upon the work of his father, half a century earlier, in founding George Town, Penang Island. Goh describes the capitalist ideology at work in Penang:

As far as the Directors of the EIC and the British Governor-General in India were concerned, the founding of George Town was only to make money. The spatial structure and the urban form of the town were the least of their concern. (Goh, 1988a, p. 60)

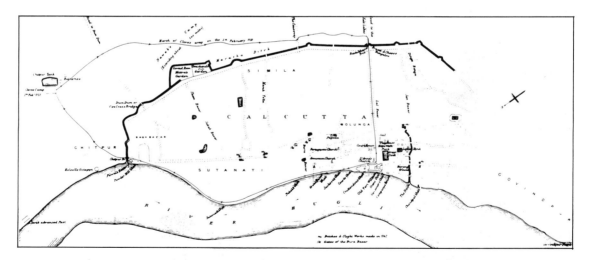

Calcutta in 1757, at the time of the 'Black Hole' incident, showing the dispersed low-density character of early colonial ports. After driving the French from India, the British reshaped the Presidency towns of Bombay, Calcutta and Madras, consolidating white settlement. 'Black Town' is off this map, which should be contrasted with that on page 69 (Source: Ross and Telkamp, 1985)

Francis Light was a trader, not a surveyor nor a social engineer. Penang was his own creation, and it was, unfortunately, a poorly chosen site, difficult to defend, prone to flooding, and short of drinking water. He laid out a small grid of streets, but with no proper land survey or system for recording land ownership. Instead he issued 'cutting papers' which granted permission to clear the jungle, and 'measurement papers' indicating general boundaries, but these were quite amateur, and within a few years land disputes were rife, each settler building as fast as he could. Clearing the land for development was allegedly achieved by 'the ingenious expedient of loading a cannon with a bag of silver dollars and firing it into the virgin forest' (quoted in Goh, 1988*a*, p. 54). The early settlers, of many races,

Malays, Sepoys, and Lascars were to find 'the Axe their only title'. Little thought was given to public ownership, so that, when it was decided to build a Government House in 1804, no land was available. It is not surprising to find that Penang has been called that 'botched rehearsal for Singapore', and William Light at Adelaide set out consciously to do the job better than his father had.[2]

The largest of the cities of *laissez faire* was Calcutta, with its extremes of wealth and poverty. To the British it was made a 'city of palaces' by the private wealth of their traders. In the eighteenth century they erected many such 'spacious and showy houses', attempting 'some order of architecture' with 'porticos, columnades, galleries etc. etc.' (1773 comment, cited in Marshall, 1985, p. 90), but these were

Central Calcutta as an imperial capital of wide avenues and public buildings. The crowded Indian city was kept separate. (Source: Christopher, 1988)

abandoned when East India Company rule ended. An Englishman coming to Calcutta at that time (1858–59) as an official of the new Crown administration, remarked on 'one of those huge palaces, half in ruins, situated in the remains of spacious grounds half overgrown with jungle that one often sees in the neighbourhood of Calcutta' (Beames, 1961, p. 87). The other side of the coin was the squalor of the streets, and neglect of municipal administration. A visitor to Calcutta in 1790 was appalled that carcasses were left to rot in the streets, and jackals had for two nights preyed on a human corpse thrown down at his gate (quoted in Dodwell, 1914, p. 523). To the Victorian humorist, Edward Lear, who visited the city, it was not so much a city of palaces, but 'a humbug of palaces' (quoted in Morris, 1983).

For all its squalor, Calcutta acquired the status of an imperial capital. The new view was that India ought to be ruled 'from a palace, not a counting-house; with the ideas of a Prince, not with those of a retail dealer in muslins and indigo' (Lord Valentia in 1803, quoted in Metcalf, 1989, p. 13). When Lord Wellesley arrived as Governor-General in 1798, he accordingly carved out an imperial island of 26 acres at the centre of the city. He demolished the old Government House, Council House and sixteen private mansions, some of them only erected in the previous five years. In their place he erected a vast and imposing new Government House, which still stands as a symbol of state authority.

The new Government House now framed and dominated the south side of the administrative and cultural centre of the city, adding the voices of imperial supervision and bureaucratic control in a rhetorical discourse of increasingly ominous proportions. (Archer, 1994, p. 5)

Wellesley also reluctantly acknowledged that Calcutta's urban growth could not continue uncontrolled. He appointed in 1803 an Improvement committee, one of whose duties was:

to ensure that the irregularity of buildings should be forbidden and that streets and lanes, which have hitherto been formed without attention to the health, convenience or safety of the inhabitants, should henceforth be constructed with order and system.

Buildings were demolished, and a new grid of streets was laid out, based upon huge half-mile street blocks. Each of these eventually became 'filled in with a tangle of wretched lanes, alleys, passages and footpaths, tortuously separating sanitary and insanitary property of all kinds' (Richards, quoted in Lanchester, 1914). A Lottery Committee was formed in 1817, and its proceeds were deployed to excavate new public water tanks, fill in ditches, open new streets and build bridges, under the executive authority of the Chief Magistrate (Ghosh *et al.*, 1972).

The new government-directed approach did not achieve much. In 1841 the Superintendant of Conservancy for Calcutta, Lieutenant Abercrombie, proposed a new street layout, drainage system, and water tanks for the native town, but this was only partly implemented many years later.[3] Some ambitious plans were made for Calcutta, but the reality of its municipal government was what has been described as:

. . . the civic planning of laissez-faire: one of the Victorian Empire's nearest approximations to an ideology: if the starving millions of Ireland, during the 1847 famine, were to be left to the mercies of the market economy, the Indians who flocked in search of livelihood to the great emporium of Calcutta must arrange their own social affairs. (Morris, 1983, pp. 209–210)

A more directed approach to municipal government of the colonial cities did, however, emerge during the nineteenth century, similar to that being applied to British towns and cities experiencing the problems of industrialization and rapid population growth. Raffles at Singapore, for instance, devoted much care and attention to the planning of his creation, in conscious contrast to Francis Light at Penang.

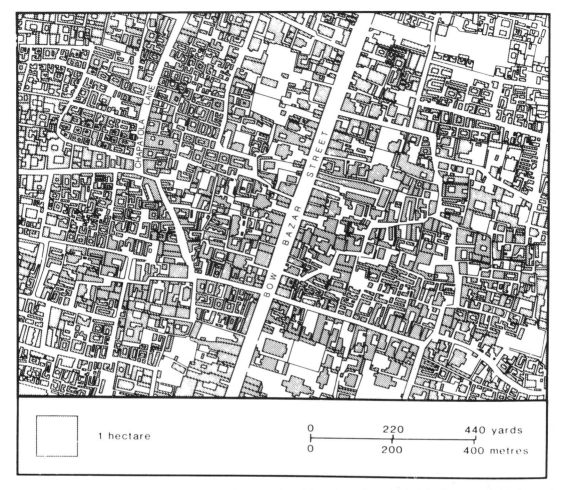

Indian suburb of Calcutta. This shows the 'tangle of lanes' within the grid of streets laid down in the early nineteenth century. (Source: Christopher, 1988)

He echoed (probably unawares) the words of Shaftesbury over the Carolina project in the 1670s, saying of Singapore that:

It is a child of my own and I have made it what it is. You may easily conceive with what zeal I apply myself to the clearing of forests, cutting of roads, building of towns, framing of laws, etc., etc.[4]

On his second visit to the new colony, in 1822–23, he replanned much of it, having appointed a 'Land Allotment Committee' of three prominent men, which selected a site for the warehousing and main commercial area, which was then drained and banked. A 'Town Committee' made detailed regulations, and Lieutenant Jackson prepared the first official plan of the town in December 1822 or January 1823. Hundreds of people were relocated in this replanning of the town, nonconforming buildings torn down, and standard street widths demarcated according to the street's importance in the town. Raffles's instructions included details of the 'ground reserved for the Government, European Town and principal mercantile establishments, native divisions or campongs', and he established by edict the principle of freedom of trade and equal rights for all, with protection of property and person.

Thirty years later, when Rangoon in Burma was acquired by the British in 1852, Dr. Montgomerie from Singapore advised on the planning of the new port, applying some of Raffles' principles. The urban area was declared to be government property, and the profit from the sales of land parcels was used to pay for roads, drainage and infrastructure. Lieutenant Fraser laid out a simple grid-iron of streets 100 feet wide, enclosing blocks of land 800 × 850 feet. According to a later writer:

Despite the well known defects of the rectangular design for town planning, it is doubtful whether any other system would have suited the needs of Rangoon equally well. Communications parallel with, and perpendicular to, the river bank, have proved themselves after seventy years' experience, to be excellently suited to the requirements of the city. Whether by accident or by the exercise of exceptional foresight, Lieutenant Fraser adopted exactly the correct type of design needed for the planning of the central area of Rangoon.[5]

REFORMING THE PORT INFRASTRUCTURE

When in 1858 the Indian Mutiny forced the crown formally to take away the government of India from the hated East India Company, the period of the 'city of palaces' came to an end, and a period of new activity in municipal administration began, accompanied by a heavy investment in transport infrastructure. It was done by 'a mixed economy of state and private capitalism, a system designed to temper the efficiency and greed of the private sector with the inefficiency and social conscience of government' (Headrick, 1981, p. 187). Outside the cities nearly a hundred million pounds of private capital (guaranteed a good profit by the Indian Treasury) was invested in Indian rail-roads between 1845 and 1875, resulting in the construction of 26,000 miles of track by 1902 (Headrick, 1981, chapter 13). A vast network of irrigation canals was also built.

During the nineteenth century successive innovations in shipping technology profoundly affected the colonial ports. The replacement of sail by steam propulsion and screw propellers allowed ships to travel faster, without refer-ence to the wind system. Reliable timetables of arrivals and departures could be drawn up. More efficient steamships incorporated high-pressure compound engines that did not use seawater. Steel hulls instead of timber vastly increased the carrying capacity of ships and reduced shipping costs. In 1828 the largest steamer afloat was 500 tons, but by 1840 the P.&O. Company's largest ships were over 1,000 tons, and the *Great Britain* in 1845 was nearly 3,000 tons. By 1890 the average vessel was 4,000 tons. The economics of shipping led to ever larger and more specialized vessels, improvements in harbours and other naviga-tional infrastructures, and larger and more efficient shipping companies. Freight rates fell rapidly, and Britain's trade with India grew threefold by value between 1860 and 1910. Whole fleets of ships could now be controlled from headquarters half a world away. As described by Jan Morris:

if there was one thing the imperial British knew how to do, it was to organize a port . . . You sailed your ship from Port Said to Aden, from Aden to Bombay, from Bombay to Penang or Singapore, from Singapore on to Hong Kong, and everywhere there were British charts to guide you, British pilots to see you into port, British harbour-masters to accommodate you, British agents to reprovision your ship, British shipwrights to make your repairs, and ships of the Royal Navy, swinging at their anchors in the roadsteads, to protect you on your way. (Morris, 1983, pp. 148–149)

These developments in transport led to trade being concentrated in fewer, larger ports. By 1903 the experts considered that all first-class ports in the future would need to provide for ships up to a thousand feet in length, with a hundred feet breadth of entrance, and up to 35 feet depth of water (*PICE*, Vol. 171, 1908, p. 15). Such facilities required vast capital expenditures in dredging, harbour and dock construction, warehousing, graving docks for the repair of ships, and also investment in the supporting city infrastructure. Port building and improvement continued throughout the colonial period, into the twentieth century. Major projects included the reconstruction of Haifa to handle the export of Iraqi oil, the building of new ports in West Africa at Port Harcourt and Tema, and the construction of naval defences at Singapore in the 1920s.

Sometimes the ports were unsuitably located for expansion, and heavy costs were incurred. The port of Calcutta had four screw-pile jetties before 1869, increased to eight by 1881. An ambitious new dock to accommodate the larger vessels was projected at Kidderpur, and opened in 1902, eventually providing 27 berths. But the new docks created costly engineering problems because of poor ground conditions which led to movement of the dock walls, and a great debate among civil engineers on the possible remedies, all of them expensive (Bruce, 1895). Bombay also had poor ground conditions, so that new land had to be formed from 'the great epic of reclamation which has been in process for two-and-a-half centuries and of which the end is not yet in sight', as a commentator in *The Times* put it in the 1930s (quoted by Tindall, 1982, p. 41). The most ambitious project, to reclaim the entire Back Bay, ended in financial disaster in the 1920s. Colombo port had to accommodate the rapid

expansion of tea production for export (which grew from 115,000 pounds (about 51,400 kg) exported in 1880, to over 32 million pounds (about 14.25 million kg) by 1888. Huge breakwaters were built, enclosing the largest artificial harbour of its day, 660 acres in extent. Madras was another difficult port to enlarge, and two vast converging piers had to be built to create a new harbour.[6]

Many of these large projects were supervised by the civil engineering firm of Coode, Son & Matthews. Its senior partner, Sir John Coode, chose as the theme of his presidential address in 1890 to the Institute of Civil Engineers in London: 'Colonies as fields for the employment of the Civil Engineers, – past – present – and future.' He declared harbours and docks to be:

. . . the terminal links of those great chains of communication which, stretching across the 'great and wide seas where go the ships' serve to bind together the Mother country and her Colonies; or – to suggest another simile – they may be regarded as abutments to those floating bridges, which, spanning the great ocean highways, do really, in the words of the poet just cited, 'bring man nearer unto man'. (Coode, 1890)[7]

The remodelling of the colonial ports also involved investment in roads, trams, and water supply and drainage systems. Industrialization proceeded apace, particularly with the cotton mills of Bombay and the jute mills of Bengal. When it was reluctantly acknowledged that urban growth could not continue unmanaged, municipal administration was also overhauled, with more elaborate arrangements of commissioners and committees, but these created new political tensions. Granting greater local autonomy in the administration of urban affairs was viewed with suspicion by the colonial power as leading to the domination of local, non-British interests in city government.

Bombay in the 1860s was a particular battleground in this struggle. It had a thrusting business community, and an active programme of public works, opening the first railway east

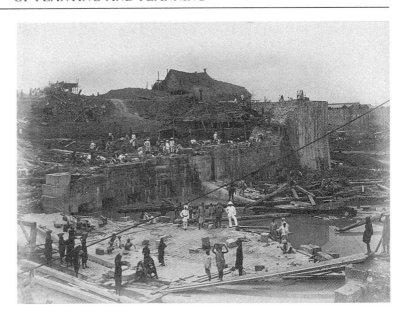

Prince's Dock. Extension work to the port of Bombay in 1887. These pictures, taken by the Port Trust, show the labour-intensive methods for large-scale excavation, and the drainage difficulties encountered. (Source: India Office Library)

of Suez in 1853. During the American Civil War (1861–65) cotton prices boomed when supplies to Britain from the American South were cut off by blockade, and new mills were established. The population of the city grew from 236,000 in 1838 (larger than Birmingham or Leeds at the time), to 644,000 in 1872 (overtaking Calcutta), reaching 822,000 in 1891. Governor Frere embarked upon a programme of improvements, hoping to make the 'new Bombay' *Urbs Prima in Indis* (Tindall, 1982, p. 31). One of his first actions, in 1864, was to demolish the old castle walls, and turn the fort area into a modern business district.

At this exuberant time Bombay sought constantly to compare itself favourably with the industrial cities of Britain, and turned itself into 'one of the most characteristically Victorian cities in the world, displaying all the grand effrontery of Victorian eclecticism' (Morris, 1983, p. 212). Frere boasted in his valedictory speech as Governor in 1867 that Bombay was twice the population of Glasgow. A self-conscious catch-phrase of the time was that 'Bombay has long been the Liverpool of the East – she is now becoming the Manchester also' (Tindall, 1982, p. 219). When new water-works and piped water were opened, the city for a time boasted of being healthier than London or Manchester, and Florence Nightingale wrote to its governor that 'If we do not take care, Bombay will outstrip us in the sanitary race. People will be ordered for the benefit of their health to Bombay' (quoted in Moorhouse, 1970, p. 256).

This was also, however, a time of conflict between the colonial authorities and the un-represented inhabitants who were expected to pay for the new public works. A young and dynamic Indian Civil Service official, Arthur Crawford, was appointed the first Municipal Commissioner when the unelected Bombay municipality came into existence in 1865. He used his wide powers to reform the drainage works, construct new roads and markets (among which was Crawford Market, completed in 1869 and decorated by Kipling's father Lockwood), and take drastic measures against cholera and smallpox. But these projects had to be paid for. A detailed property survey, followed by demands for back-dated municipal taxes, resulted in a rate-payers' demonstration in 1870, Crawford's resignation in 1871 and the creation of an elected Bombay Municipal Corporation in 1872. While the franchise was limited by rate-paying qualifications, leaving control in the hands of landlords, mill-owners and large merchants, these political battles contributed to the emergence of Indian nationalism.[8]

The other Indian presidency towns of Calcutta and Madras evolved similar arrangements for municipal government. A large corporation was kept under the control of the colonial administration through a strong executive centred on a British government official with considerable freedom of action. It was a hybrid form of local government with which to address the basic needs of water supply, drainage and conservancy. In Madras the new municipality created in 1884 had thirty-two commissioners, of whom twenty-four were elected by rate-payers and the rest appointed. Calcutta Municipal Corporation, in 1876, had seventy-four commissioners, a third appointed by the government and the rest elected by rate-payers.

Municipal authorities followed in other port cities, and were gradually extended to most towns under direct British control. These city councils were 'among the earliest institutions upon which Britons and Indians sat ostensibly as equals' (Morris, 1983, p. 107), but the emphasis should be on the word 'ostensibly'. In practice power remained firmly in the grip of the municipal commissioner, 'a British official with a concern for efficiency, but none for innovation' (Gupta, 1981, p. 207). Constrained by such a system, the young Nehru resigned his position as a Delhi councillor when he realized the limits of his capacity to effect change, writing in his autobiography in 1936 that:

The whole steel frame of municipal adminstration as erected by government, prevented radical growth or innovation. (quoted in Gupta, 1981, p. 207)

When it came to reshaping the colonial ports, this was considered too important a task to be left to the new municipal authorities. A form of democratic urban government might have been conceded, but the colonial authorities made sure that they kept control over dock development, vital as it was for British capital and colonial interests. The mechanism deployed was that of a trust, with mainly appointed members, and supported by direct grants from central government. The Bombay Port Trust came into existence at the same time as the new Municipal Corporation, after attempts at dock reconstruction by private enterprise had failed through corruption and mismanagement. Similar port trusts or dock boards were created in Calcutta (1870), the other ports of the Bombay presidency (Karachi in 1880, Aden in 1889), Singapore (1908), and elsewhere. In creating these bodies the colonies were ahead of practice in British ports. The London docks continued to be managed by various companies and authorities for many years, until its port authority was created in 1909 (following a Royal Commission report).

The Effect of the Plague: Sanitary Surveillance and the Improvement Trusts

Within a few years of the creation of the port trusts, the same administrative device was being used for a much greater assault upon the physical fabric of the port cities. Improvement boards and trusts, created in response to the spread of plague, resulted in unprecedented demolition, slum clearance and urban renewal. While the role of disease and medical practice in imperial history is now a growing area of research, the full destructive impact of harsh sanitary measures upon the colonial cities have received only passing mention. Kostof has called it, with some cause, the *éventrement* (Kostof, 1991, p. 86), or disembowelling, of colonial cities.[9]

By the end of the nineteenth century the cities of Bombay and Calcutta were among the largest cities in the world, with probably the worst slums in the world. The railways changed life for millions:

Liberated from nature's timeless constraints on human mobility, Indians flooded the cities and places of pilgrimage. (Headrick, 1981, p. 189)

Mortality rates were three or four times the equivalent rates in Britain at the time. In Bombay bad drainage and waterlogged land, combined with an influx of starving migrants from famine in the interior, created a particularly receptive environment for disease. Into this situation came bubonic plague. It had moved from the interior of China in 18794 to Hong Kong, where in the space of five months some 2,500 people died, and eighty thousand fled the colony. It remained endemic in Hong Kong, causing over a thousand deaths a year through the 1890s, and spread to Bombay in 1896.

By 1899 over 2,800 people a week were dying of plague in Bombay, and half the population had fled back to the countryside, putting the city's economic position at risk. Spreading from Bombay and Calcutta through the railway network, the plague went on to kill an estimated seven million people in India in the period 1896–1914, reaching a peak of 1.5 million deaths in 1904. It spread to other port cities around the empire, arriving in Cape Town in 1900, during the Boer War, and in Nairobi in 1902. It reached West Africa in 1908. Extreme and drastic reactions followed wherever it occurred. When it was diagnosed among the Indian population of Nairobi, the administrator responded by immediately burning down the Indian market, which temporarily halted the disease (Trzebinski, 1985, p. 44).

Epidemics are social as well as medical events, through which disease takes on a wider social, political and cultural significance. For the British colonial community, fear of the 'Black Death', deep-rooted in the European collective consciousness since the depopulation of the fourteenth century, combined with fear and uncertainty about whether Britain's imperial dominance could be maintained: the 'illusion of permanence' was being exposed. So the outbreak of bubonic plague in the 1890s evoked a profound hysteria. When Dr. William Simpson, then the Medical Officer of Health for Calcutta, reported cases of plague in 1895 and 1896, the colonial administration of Bengal chose to reject his diagnosis, claiming instead that they were a form of venereal disease. The Calcutta business community, particularly that concerned with tea and jute exporting, breathed a sigh of relief that trade was not to be disrupted, while nevertheless working themselves into a state of frenzy over the insanitary state of the city. Simpson stuck to his diagnosis, and was pilloried for it. 'His obstinacy and conceit are beyond control,' exclaimed the Secretary of the Municipal Department of the Government of Bengal. Simpson was not a member of the Indian Medical Service, but was employed by the Calcutta Municipal Corporation, which conferred a lower position in the complex colonial hierarchy of status, but also freed him from formal responsibility to the government authorities. When plague incontrovertibly broke out in 1898, the Government of Bengal had its revenge upon Simpson. Anti-plague measures were seen as too important to be left in the hands of doctors, and were taken out of the hands of the corporation into the Municipal Department, the Corporation's powers being curtailed in the Calcutta Municipal Act of 1899. 'Plague provided an appropriate occasion for an assault on what had been, for some years, to a considerable extent the preserve of talkative but supposedly dilatory Bengali babus' (Catanach, 1988, pp. 155–156).

In 1897 combating the plague was the subject of an international sanitary conference, held in Venice. In an era of increasingly competitive imperialism, persistently high levels of epidemic mortality were seen as a mark of poor colonial management, and

British India was already being censured internationally as the 'factory of cholera'. The Venice conference, egged on by Britain's new colonial rivals, the French, proposed closing ports to passengers and cargo from India. This would have had a disastrous effect upon British imperial trade, but the threat was successfully fended off by arguing that there was no evidence of the disease being transmitted in that way. Had the disease vector been known at the time, the British would not have succeeded, the embargo would have been imposed, and countless lives might have been saved. It was to be a decade before the Indian Plague Commission, appointed in 1907, eventually established the cause as being transmission by rat fleas.

With so little being then known about the causes or treatment of plague, colonial medical authorities chose to allocate the blame to the living practices of the indigenous population. High death rates in the port cities, which the colonial authorities had hitherto been reluctant to spend money in combating, were blamed upon 'the insanitary and immoral lives of the Asiatic races', in the words of a Presbyterian missionary in Singapore in 1907 (quoted in Yeoh, 1991, p. 110). Following the Indian Epidemic Diseases Act of 1897 sanitary intervention against plague involved the vigorous digging up of earthen floors (where it was thought the plague bacillus lived), drastic disinfection measures, house-to-house searches for plague victims by British soldiers, the isolation of victims, and control over population movement. Such aggressive measures soon provoked a violent response, which included the assassination in 1897 of the British official placed in charge of plague control in Pune (Poona). For a time the British feared another Indian Mutiny, suspecting that recently improved Hindu-Muslim community relations might lead to a coalition against 'constituted authority' (Gupta, 1981, pp. 138–139 and 193–194). The British colonial authorities chose to blame the situation at

Pune upon poor medical adice from visiting sanitary specialists (the 'Hong Kong doctors') rather than admitting to any excess of zeal by the official concerned. Such bullying intervention in public health was given up after 1899, once the discovery of an anti-plague vaccine reduced the immediate risk to the European population. The Sanitary Department of India could then abandon wide-ranging preventive measures, preferring to regard the living conditions of the general population as beyond the influence of enlightened sanitary effort.

Medical attention in the colonial ports now shifted to public health measures which could combat the threat to trade and commerce, and protect the health in particular of the Europeans. In the words of Sir William MacGregor, the Governor of Lagos, such measures were to aim at 'curtailing the toll of

Chinese dock workers' housing in Singapore, from Sir William Simpson's 1907 report on anti-plague measures. The picture shows the ground floor of a 'tenement house', with the family shrine in the middle ground, and the partitions of workers' living cubicles either side of a narrow corridor. (Source: Simpson, 1907)

our fellow citizens in those insalubrious, over-sea territories of the empire' (quoted in Yeoh, 1991, pp. 99–100). The new breed of sanitary experts still chose to attribute the high death rates from disease in the colonial port cities to insanitary living practices and racial characteristics, rather than to the inequalities and contradictions of the colonial situation, poverty and economic privation. The remedies proposed, which derived from British practice,

were better ventilated houses, pure water and good drains, better waste and sewage disposal, open spaces, and (of particular importance to town planning) the residential segregation of the races. A range of new sanitary measures thus emerged which attacked not just the health practices, but the whole way of life, of the subject populations in the colonial port cities.

Even if the more extreme steps were

This picture, also from Simpson's 1907 report, shows the interior of a cubicle (described as a 'windowless room and pitch dark'), with the dock worker's few possessions (chest in the foreground). (Source: Simpson, 1907)

politically unimplementable, indigenous customary practices were subjected to inspection, regulation and disciplinary action by an army of sanitary inspectors. Their by-law powers conferred wide authority to control 'any act, omission or thing . . . occasioning or likely to occasion injury, annoyance, offense, harm, danger or damage to the sense of sight, smell or hearing,' in the words of the Singapore Municipal Ordinance of 1896 (quoted in Yeoh, 1991, pp. 136–37). As colonial control over Asian medical practices and living habits increased, the populace responded with non-compliance and the withholding of information. In 1907 the Singapore Municipal Inquiry Commission of Dr. Simpson reluctantly acknowledged the existence of 'so much hostility to sanitation, and so little belief in its utility on the part of the bulk of the population' (quoted in Yeoh, 1991, p. 164).

Dr. Simpson, who went from Calcutta to become an influential professor of public hygiene at the University of London, was an enthusiastic advocate of the new style of sanitary surveillance. He claimed, for instance, that pure water was hard to come by in the tropics, 'mainly due to the pollution to which the water is subjected by the customs of the people' (quoted in Curtin, 1989, p. 109). In his manuals on hygiene and tropical medicine, he made the following remarks about Eastern cities:

The narrow streets, the winding alleys, the crowding together of houses, form an insanitary labyrinth, which cannot be efficiently cleansed nor purified by a free circulation of air. The mischief has been done in old towns and frequently to such an extent as to be irremediable without the largest measures of demolition and reconstruction. In olden times the fashion in many parts of the East was for each king to build a new city, which no doubt originated from the fact that after a certain number of years each city became so unhealthy that it was advisable to leave it. (Simpson, 1908, p. 294)

Despite his long experience in Calcutta, he seemed quite unaware, or unconcerned, that the insanitary and overcrowded conditions were more due to British neglect of local services other than within the white man's city. He made no mention of the often sophisticated drainage and water-tank systems of traditional Indian cities, which had become choked by neglect and the lack of resources from the colonial authorities. In Lucknow, for instance, borrow pits, ordure piles, and demolition lands combined to create an unhealthy urban jungle. European conservancy contractors only cleaned the main streets, leaving the by-lanes for the inhabitants' own efforts, so that two-thirds of the city was not cleaned at all (Oldenburg, 1984, pp. 99–116).

Simpson also recommended tough building and planning controls, and had little understanding of the causes of overcrowding and housing shortage, which he apparently attributed to the dirty habits of the people. In his view:

If streets are not laid out on a definite plan and on sanitary principles or when so laid out the houses are not subject to regulations as regards their height, depth, site, the area they cover, their relation to one another and the amount of air space to secure a free circulation of each, a congested area is soon formed in which there is too much crowding together of houses and too many houses on too small a place. These congested areas are always filthy and always unhealthy. (Simpson, 1908, p. 297)

New roads were believed to help prevent disease. According to a report on the administration of Oudh in 1863–64, 'affording as they do, a free passage for a current of air through the heart of the city, (they) are not less important in a sanitary than in a military point of view' (quoted in Oldenburg, 1984, p. 103). Large-scale demolitions were carried out to achieve this ventilating effect. One such project, in the town of Tanjore, was later described by Patrick Geddes:

. . . as usual, it is proposed to drive a new gridiron of forty feet streets through a congested and insanitary area. Again as usual, this dreary and conventional plan is quite unsparing to the old homes and to the neighbourhood life of the area. It leaves fewer housing sites and these mostly narrower than before and the large population thus expelled would, again as usual, be driven into creating worse congestion in other quarters, to the advantage only of the rack-renting interests . . . The policy of sweeping clearances should be recognised for what I believe it is; one of the most disastrous and pernicious blunders in the chequered history of sanitation. (Tyrwhitt, 1947, pp. 40 and 45)

As well as roads, water supply was a major public health concern for the British, especially with increased demand from the new docks and wharves, and suburban housing. Expensive reservoirs and piped water systems were built. Traditional water tanks and wells were filled in or closed as anti-malaria measures, and replaced by standpipes and water metering. The standpipes, however, while supplying abundant piped water, without any safeguards against wastage were found to increase the risk of malaria, as the waste water gathered in stagnant pools. In practical terms, these measures for water supply according to Western technology meant the neglect of the traditional Indian systems. While British engineers were largely unconcerned, Lanchester and Geddes noticed the situation, expressing regret that the traditional system of surface water drainage through tanks was being neglected, so that they flooded in heavy rain (Lanchester, 1916–17, p. 102). Geddes believed, probably correctly, that a properly maintained system of water tanks would not contribute to malaria, as long as the water was not allowed to become stagnant, and if ducks were kept to eat up the mosquito larvae.

While piped clean water was considered essential, the cost of mains sewerage was prohibitive in the teeming port cities. Dr. Simpson recommended instead the construction of backlanes for conservancy, and claimed that the more expensive option of main sewers was dangerous and inappropriate for an Asiatic population (perhaps because people might start living in them, and fugitives from justice might escape down them). Traditional methods of night-soil removal with scavengers and cesspits were also replaced by less flexible municipal services. From the 1880s a system of public latrines was introduced in many cities, and summonses were issued against market gardeners for keeping nightsoil for more than 24 hours. The system of pail vans was replaced with pumping by Shone ejectors to barges which carried the sewage out to sea. The protracted attempt at municipalizing Singapore's water supply and sewage disposal, examined by Yeoh (1991), demonstrates that these were not 'neutral, scientifically-sanctified engineering works which could be arbitrarily imposed, but were subject to negotiation between those who impose them and those who had to live with them.' Geddes had his idiosyncratic ideas here also, advocating the use of human wastes for garden manure, which would eliminate the need for an infrastructure of drainage pipes.

It was direct, simple, cheap, depended on arousing new social and civic consciousness, and it resulted in the enhancement of gardens. It was the socio-biological answer.[10]

From the surveillance of daily health practices it was but a short step to direct intervention in the built form of housing. Colonial building regulations discriminated against traditional designs, whether the Indian courtyard house or the airwells of the traditional Chinese shophouse, in spite of their suitability for hot climates and for privacy, evolved over thousands of years. Instead the British favoured through ventilation, bungalow designs with plot ratios that prevented 'over-development', and back-lanes. Dr. Simpson accused the Chinese shophouse of offering insufficient daylight, and disregarded the contribution of the airwell. As a result, British-driven urban renewal demolished and re-planned large areas of housing (Oldenburg, 1984, pp. 96–144, and Yeoh, 1991, pp. 99–167).

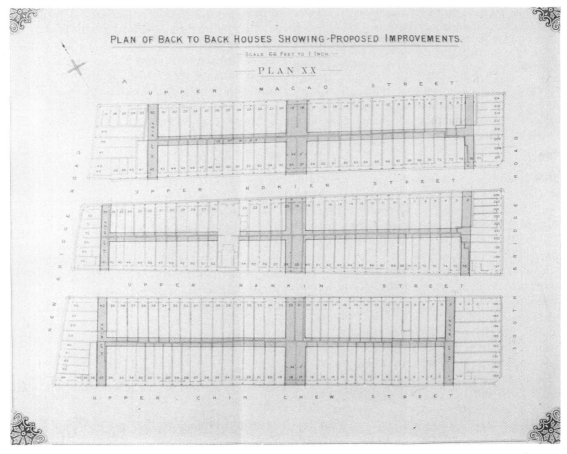

Slum improvements in Singapore. Following standard practice at the time, the rear of the houses are to be demolished to create back-lanes for conservancy and daylight. (Source: Simpson, 1907)

To carry out the drastic remodelling of the cities that they envisaged, the authorities turned to the mechanism of the trust, which had already been used for port development, in preference to operation through democratic municipal institutions. Plague led directly to the creation of the first of them, the Bombay Improvement Trust, in 1898 (Tindall, 1982, pp. 253–254). It busied itself with the control of development, making new streets, opening out crowded localities, reclaiming land from the sea to provide room for the expansion of the city, and constructing dwellings. Other port cities followed suit, notably the Calcutta Improvement Trust in 1912, the Rangoon Development Trust in 1920, the Singapore Improvement Trust in 1927, and the Lagos Executive Development Board in 1928. These trusts were perhaps best known for their ambitious slum clearance and road schemes, which were justified less on grounds of transport efficiency, or even housing need, than as public health measures to bring light and air to areas of high population density.

Those British planners who had the temerity to criticize the approach soon fell foul of the colonial authorities, notably Captain Richards in Calcutta. Geoffrey Moorhouse's book on Calcutta includes a dedication 'to E.P. Richards, sometime Chief Engineer of the Calcutta Improvement Trust, who restored some of my national pride' (Moorhouse, 1984). Calcutta was the largest and most influential of the improvement trusts. Richards, the newly appointed planning engineer, wrote a massive survey report, four hundred pages long, on the condition of Calcutta, which included scathing criticisms of the authorities' neglect of urban poverty:

... we have all heard of Calcutta described glowingly – and quite sincerely – as the fairest city in the east. That opinion arises from a civic patriotism that can be of great value, but the speakers are plainly unaware of the real conditions . . . It should be made thoroughly known that the city is in a most serious condition, and that only prompt, big and concerted action will maintain our commercial supremacy and save Calcutta and Howrah from becoming the largest slum in the world. Calcutta has lagged and muddled for 50 years, and is now far behind other cities of the same size and importance.

Richards was totally pessimistic that the Calcutta trust's powers would be sufficient for the task, saying that 'only a completely authoritarian regime with huge resources and a vigorous policy of demolition would make any impact whatsoever.' Although his report on Calcutta, summarized in the *Town Planning Review* in 1914–15, was acclaimed by British planners of the time as a model of planning survey method, Richards' views were unpopular with his superiors, presumably the autocratic chairman, C.H. Bompas, in particular, and had to be published privately in Britain after he had been 'invalided' to Britain with a 'breakdown' in 1914.[11]

It is hardly surprising to find that the activities of the improvement trusts soon encountered local opposition. Demolition could result in communal riots, as tensions between castes or between Muslims and Hindus was brought to the surface by the destruction of a religious building, or the location of an abattoir. A minor improvement scheme in Kanpur, involving the part demolition of a temple, led to serious rioting in 1914 (Meller, 1990, p. 212). In 1907 the Viceroy of India's private secretary wrote that:

Hitherto with our accustomed energy and self-confidence we have been trying to do everything for the people, and we have only succeeded in rousing their prejudices and irritating their religious and social susceptibilities. (quoted in Catanach, 1988, p. 162)

The improvement trusts achieved little to combat the underlying problems of urban overcrowding and poor housing, for various reasons including the scale of those problems, their limited powers and resources, and the opposition of both property-owners and the general population. In Singapore, for instance, only 22 backlane schemes had been completed by 1918, affecting a mere 426 houses. In Calcutta by 1921 the new housing provided for those displaced by slum clearance was heavily under-occupied (GCTP, **11**, 1921, pp. 113). Patrick Geddes was one of the few who dared to criticize the whole approach, which he called 'death-dealing Haussmannising' by 'the well-intentioned fanatic of sanitation'. The aim of creating a healthy city failed to recognize the need for more housing, or to take account of valid traditions of building and organizing space, and so led to the conflicts which made the trusts intensely unpopular.

The plague placed India at the mercy of vast impersonal demographic forces, and there was very little that the practitioners of Western medicine, or the officials, could do about it. Even knowledge of the causes of plague did not lead to a rapid reduction in cases. Among the factors in the reduction of the occurrence of plague from the 1920s were increased knowledge of the ways that it could travel in merchandise, the development of immunity in rats and other vectors, and perhaps also changes in the virulence of the plague bacillus.

Public health measures apparently had little effect. The improvement trusts may have been drastic, but they did little to curb the plague and other diseases, and indeed probably assisted their spread by the scale of disruption to human and animal populations in the cities. Plague-carrying rats, in spite of the bounties paid for rat-killing, were almost certainly displaced from slum clearance areas to spread the disease more widely.

CONCLUSIONS

'Think of what our nation stands for . . . democracy and proper drains.' So wrote the English poet John Betjeman (as usual with tongue slightly in cheek) at the beginning of the Second World War ('In Westminster Abbey', originally published in 1940, Betjeman, 1988, p. 73). As far as the British colonies were concerned, however, such self-ascribed national attributes were more usually found in conflict with each other: the advocates of sanitation were little concerned with, and indeed hostile towards, democracy. Urban renewal measures were often carried out in colonial cities with less regard for their social impact than would have been possible in Britain at the time.

Colonial ports were clearing houses for both commodities and labour. The British wanted them to be constructed and regulated in a manner which facilitated trade, communication, movement and a high turnover of people. In the Victorian era, they were also to manifest the advancement of science and civilization through modern techniques of town planning and sanitary engineering, and they aspired to the same range of urban services as European cities of the time, albeit with fewer resources. Usually it was Bombay and Calcutta, the two greatest ports of the British Empire, which took the lead, establishing a tradition of large-scale construction projects (which could create profitable opportunities for British contractors and consulting engineers).

The port cities evolved similar hybrid forms of local government to address basic needs of water supply, drainage and conservancy, but the colonial authorities had no intention of subjecting the development and control of docks and harbours, which were vital for imperial commerce and capital, to the vagaries of local democratic control. So port administration was kept separate by deploying the mechanism of a port trust, with appointed members and direct grants from central government.

The colonial port cities shared most of the characteristics and problems of other nineteenth-century cities in other parts of the world, such as overcrowding, poverty, disease, industrialization and physical restructuring. The professional expertise available, particularly the public health experts and civil/military engineers, and the solutions on offer, were similar in both colonial and metropolitan cities. But in the tropical port cities there was the added dimension of racial diversity, with political dominance by one racial minority group, which affected the mechanisms and solutions adopted. If local government was allowed to become democratically representative, then the British racial minority would lose political control of municipal affairs. Programmes for major infrastructure upgrading and urban renewal were consequently transferred to trusts or boards, which the colonial authorities, could control. The port trusts from the 1870s were the first such mechanisms, and the policy continued with the improvement trusts and boards after 1898.

The arrival of plague from the 1890s put colonial city management to a severe test, and provoked massive demolition and renewal in the name of public health. It was easier to blame urban problems upon the cultural deficiencies of the subject populations rather than face up to the deficiencies and contradictions in the colonial situation. Overcrowding in the cities was a more or less inevitable consequence of maintaining a market for unskilled labour (one which hugely favoured the employer). Colonial government was not prepared to spend money building working-class housing on the scale needed. Overcrowding was attributed by the British less to the underlying pressures of population density and housing shortage than to 'Asiatic ignorance and apathy' in the arrangement of living space. Richards, working in Calcutta at the time of some of the grander imperial building projects, found with the British attitude to the port city, that it was 'easier to embellish its face than sound its depths' (Warren, 1986, p. 213).

NOTES

1. For the growth of Bombay and Calcutta see Kooiman (1985), Marshall (1985), Tindall (1982), and Moorhouse (1980).

2. Penang as a 'botched rehearsal' for Singapore is in Barley (1993), p. 11.

Francis Light (1740–94) was the illegitimate child of a Suffolk country squire. He served in the navy during the Seven Years War, and then traded in India, China and Malaya. He persuaded the East India Company to sanction a colony at Penang Island in 1786, and stayed on as the superintendant until his death there of malaria in 1794. His son William, the founder of Adelaide, was born there in 1786. See Dutton (1960) and Elder (1984).

3. See Archer (1994). It is tempting to speculate that this Abercrombie, with his Haussmann-style urban renewal plan for Calcutta, was related to the famous planner, Patrick Abercrombie (who spelled his name the same way), but I have been unable so far to trace a connection. Patrick was born in 1879, the son of a Fife stockbroker who moved to Cheshire, and was brought up in the Wirral.

4. Quoted in Cangi, 1993, p. 173.

Sir Thomas Stamford Raffles (1780–1826) was born in London (the 'Prince of Puddle Dock'), went to Penang as secretary to the governor in 1805, and accompanied the expedition which captured Java from the Dutch. He was lieutenant governor there from 1811 until it was returned to the Dutch in 1816, as part of the post-Napoleonic peace settlement. He then became lieutenant governor of the small port of Bengkulu (or Bencoolen) in 1818, from which he founded Singapore. He left Singapore for Bengkulu in June 1823, returned to England in April 1824 and died there in 1826. See biography in Barley (1993) and Cangi (1993).

Unfortunately little is recorded on the sources of his ideas regarding town building and government because his personal effects were destroyed in a shipboard fire as he was preparing to return home to England. William Light's personal effects were also destroyed in a fire at the Adelaide encampment in 1837, so that valuable source material on the two greatest city founders of the colonial period was lost because of the hazards of early settlement.

5. Webb (1923–24). Alexander Fraser (1824–98) entered the Bengal Engineers as a lieutenant in 1843, and rose to become the colonel commandant in 1884, and a general in 1886, and a member of the Governor-General's Council. He saw active service in the Sikh Wars, and was known as the Star of India for the lighthouses he built on the Burmese and Indian coasts 1856–65 (based upon Alan Stevenson's plans for Scottish lighthouses). He was also active in railway construction as chief engineer of the Public Works Department of the North-West Province 1873–9. According to his obituary, he was 'universally loved for his sterling qualities of mind and heart, his unassuming manners, and retiring disposition' (*The Times*, 13 June 1898).

6. These capital works were described in the Proceedings of the Institute of Civil Engineers in London, for instance articles on: Hooghly River improvements, Vol. 21 (1861–62), pp. 2–24; Rangoon River improvements, Vol. 202 (1916), pp. 143–242; Karachi Waterworks, Vol. 83 (1886), pp. 333–350; Tansa Waterworks (Bombay), Vol. 115 (1894), pp. 12–42; Madras Harbour, Vol. 194 (1914), pp. 240–246. For Kidderpur see Bruce (1895).

7. Sir John Coode (1816–92), a Cornishman,

received a knighthood for his work on the harbour of Portland, England, 1847–72, and worked on Colombo, Melbourne, Cape Town and other colonial ports. See DNB and obituary in *P.I.C.E.*, **113** (1893), pp. 335–343.

8. See Dobbin (1975), Dossal (1989) and Kooiman (1985).

A former East India Company official, Sir Bartle Frere (1815–82) was Governor of Bombay 1862–7, and Governor of the Cape 1877–80, at the time of the Zulu War.

Arthur T. Crawford (1835–1911) served in the Bombay Civil Service 1854–89, receiving a C.M.G. in 1887. He later published his reminiscences (WWW).

9. For the impact of medicine on cities, see Arnold (1988), MacLeod and Lewis (1988), and Furedy (1982). For the plague see Catanach (1988) and Condon (1900).

10. Meller (1990), p. 220. Geddes was influenced in his composting ideas by J.A. Turner (1858–1922), the Executive Health Officer of Bombay from 1901 to 1916, who published a book on sanitation in India (WWW). Similar practices existed traditionally in the close settled zone of Kano, Northern Nigeria, and were studied by the British. For Singapore see Yeoh (1991), pp. 237–262.

11. Lanchester (1914), pp. 126, and 219–20. Geddes called the Richards report 'a stately volume' (Meller 1990, fn 37, p. 231, in *Cities in Evolution* 1915 edition).

In spite of his importance in the history of colonial town planning, I have been able to find out little about Captain E.P. Richards. He was a founder member of the Town Planning Insitute. A subsequent period as planning adviser in Singapore (1920–24), where he worked for a time with C.C. Reade, ended in similar frustration. 'Like all planning pioneers, he was regarded as an unrealistic dreamer and in 1924 he gave up the unequal struggle' (Fraser, 1957).

4

THE 'WAREHOUSING' OF THE LABOURING CLASSES

. . . all have for their object the housing – one is almost tempted to use the expression 'warehousing' – of large numbers of the labouring classes in as cheap a manner as possible.
(Burnett Hurst, 1925, p. 20, writing of the chawls of Bombay)

Much has been written on the architectural history of the British Empire, especially India. This literature has often adopted a celebratory or elegiac tone, and has generally concentrated on the buildings made and occupied by the British themselves – the great public buildings that symbolized empire.[1] Now that the pioneering work of Tony King, Amos Rapoport and Tom Markus has placed building form in a new sociological context, the building forms of Empire can also be viewed in their relation to the power structures of colonialism. Tony King has urged the case for 'a carefully documented comparative account of the actual buildings' to assist in understanding the function and organization of the colonial city.[2] Olsen has identified the emergence of a 'professional building' during an important period of the British Empire:

After Waterloo there appeared one after another new types of building designed from the outset for a specialized function . . . Prior to that period, most urban buildings were amateur, adaptable for a variety of purposes. (Olsen, 1974)

There were many types of public building which expressed political, and specifically colonial, symbolisms, and the civilizing role of western urban civilization. They included

A colonial clock-tower, symbolizing western time disciplines. This one, in Oshogbo, Nigeria, is the assembly point for Independence celebrations. (Source: The author, photo taken in 1960)

government offices, town halls, and educational institutions. The Post Office symbolized the world-wide network of communications which Empire helped to create. The clock tower symbolized new time disciplines:

With its hourly gongs chiming far above their heads, the clock helped to remind students and passersby not only of the supremacy of the Raj but of the virtues of punctuality. The modern world in India, as it had been for the peasant-become-factory worker in Britain a century before, was to be marked by discipline and orderliness. (Metcalf, 1989, pp. 78–80)

The theatre, which Raffles saw as a source of authority, was to impart the values inherent to civilized society, especially the villain being punished for his crimes.

Public buildings were often (at least before the rise of the corporate office building) the grandest and most visible structures in the urban landscape, as indeed they were intended

to be. The major land use, and the commonest building, however, in any city is housing in one form or another. This chapter is concerned with the adapted and new forms of housing that British colonialism created, especially for the millions of migrant workers who came to live in the cities. Of the various types of housing, attention has hitherto focused particularly on the bungalow, which has been called 'the basic residential unit of the colonial community'. Bungalows, however, only ever accommodated a tiny proportion (less than 1 per cent) of the populations of the colonial cities, predominantly the white colonists. The history of mass housing in Europe and North America is becoming well researched, including its links with town planning, and we now need a history of how the common people lived in the colonial city, from the chawls of Bombay to the mine workers' hostels of South Africa.

The Search for New Housing Forms

Colonialism relocated peoples in their millions to distant places, and often to unaccustomed climates. They were both white and non-white, both temporary migrant workers and permanent settlers. They took with them the building traditions of their homelands, and deployed many building materials and constructional techniques to build (or have built for them) their new homes in strange lands. They had to make new living and working relations. In the process building forms were created and modified, and the evolution of colonial housing forms shows a fascinating interaction of cultures upon built form and urban landscapes.

The Bungalow

Early white colonizers adapted their building techniques and styles to their new environment. If resources permitted, they might try to

imitate the Georgian-style country house as a symbol of success, even in the tropics where their design might be inappropriate to the climate. By the middle of the nineteenth century the colonials could benefit from technological advantages in smelting, and the increased carrying capacity of merchant shipping, to import prefabricated and portable iron buildings in kit form. The first Superintendant of the Port Phillip Region, which later became the State of Victoria, erected such a house, LaTrobe's Cottage, which is still preserved in a prominent position in Melbourne.[3]

These buildings were often not well adapted to the available building materials or climate. Iron walls and roofs absorbed the sun's heat and radiated it to the inside, while two-storey structures were expensive to build and maintain, especially in the climatic extremes of the tropics. Accordingly during the nineteenth

'Of the hut I builded'

Figure 6.8(a) Stylistic sequence of Australian houses. *Left*: Georgian Primitive. *Right*: Colonial Georgian. (After Boyd 1952.)

EXTRACTING HISTORY FROM HOUSES

Figure 6.8(c) Stylistic sequence of Australian houses. *Left*: Boom Style. *Right*: Queen Anne or Federation Style. (After Boyd 1952.)

Figure 6.8(d) Stylistic sequence of Australian houses. *Above*: Californian Bungalow. *Below*: Spanish Mission. (After Boyd 1952.)

Figure 6.8(b) Stylistic sequence of Australian houses. *Above*: Gothic Revival. *Below*: Italianate. (After Boyd 1952.)

Stylistic sequence of Australian bungalow designs. This shows the evolution from one or two room structures with hipped roofs to the ornate borrowings from Italian and other architectural traditions as a market in housing developed. (Source: Connah, 1988)

century the more environmentally suitable bungalow (a name derived from the word Bengali) became the basic residential unit of the white colonial community. Described in 1803 as 'stationary tents which have run aground on low brick platforms', it derived as much from the Indian service tent, in permanent materials, as from the Bengali native hut, although borrowing from the latter the high pyramidal roof. The bungalow was a solution to the sudden demand for mass housing from the increased population of new colonial officials, planters and the military. From its origins in the tropics it was adopted in the settler colonies, and soon absorbed into the British housing tradition.[4]

The bungalow was usually framed by a veranda, a feature of colonial and settler housing found all over the Empire and America. It functioned as a climatic regulator, keeping the main house walls cool and dry, and providing a relatively cool transitional space between interior and exterior. It was a place of hospitality and refreshment. When located on the outside of the dwelling rather than in a courtyard, it allowed surveillance of the surrounding landscape, and was, therefore, an important feature for planters and colonial officials. Psychologically, in the words of one of its historians, the veranda was

a nagging reminder of the frailty of white European occupation, its thinness on the ground, an almost

Governor LaTrobe's Cottage, Melbourne, Australia. This prefabricated house was erected in 1840 for the first Superintendent of the Port Phillip Region (later Melbourne). (Source: Hudson and McEwan, 1986)

defiant acknowledgment, signalling an unwillingness to be more deeply rooted in the country. In that quality of uprootedness, of uneasy detachment, it is tempting to read a covert nomadism.[5]

Housing the 'Invisible Man'

The bungalow and veranda have been the subject of a growing literature, as have other house types of the white settlers and colonizers. There is also a substantial academic literature on the working-class housing of the industrialized countries of Europe and North America.[6] It is, however, a different story when we look for the housing of the black workers – the slaves and migrant labourers who found themselves often far from their homelands. These

were the 'invisible men', in the words of a leading historian of slavery, Michael Craton. He called his meticulous study of the records of the Worthy Park sugar plantation in Jamaica 'In Search of the Invisible Man', because he was seeking to recover the lost history of the slaves – 'the lives of the ordinary toilers who made the plantation system possible' (Craton, 1978, p. vii). Central to those lives was the housing which accommodated millions of slaves, indentured labourers and other workers in the colonial economic system. This has also remained largely invisible, until recent research, geographically scattered, has allowed the main outline to be pieced together. The housing environments created for the non-white workers of the British Empire show a great mixture of influences, including African compounds, the great urban cultures of India and China, and British army barrack design and utilitarian theories of spatial organization and public health.

The colonial economic system, from the early days of plantation slavery in the Caribbean and the American South, treated black people primarily as units of labour. Housing made little or no provision for family or communal life. Indeed it often sought deliberately to extinguish their cultural traditions and social practices, for slavery was a form of 'social death'.[7] Slave quarters, where they were allowed the opportunity, often followed the African compound tradition of grouping rooms around a central courtyard, with rooms in rows. One variant of this building form was the Charleston 'single house' in the American South, which appeared in the eighteenth century: a one-room wide structure, two rooms deep, with a central stairway, and a porch or veranda. Another building type was the so-called 'shotgun house'. This was a row of rooms opening onto a corridor, where the front and rear door were in line with each other; the name is said to refer to the opportunity to command the corridor with a shotgun so that slaves could not escape. Building regulations in Jamaica sought to facilitate searches for runaway slaves by controlling the number of entrances to huts and compounds. They required huts to have no more than one door, and where more than four huts were built together the inhabitants were required to build a surrounding fence, seven feet high, with only one entrance to the compound. As long as supplies of fresh slaves were obtainable from Africa, the system had no incentive to encourage slave reproduction, and this was reflected in the form of slave housing. When fresh slaves became harder to obtain, especially after the abolition of the slave trade in 1807 (which preceded by a generation the abolition of slavery itself), family housing became more common, albeit often based upon unstable family relationships. Free black villages

emerged as 'distinct social entities where black society flourished'.[8]

The slaves of the Caribbean had very little chance of returning to their homelands, but after the abolition of slavery the assumption in most colonial towns and cities was that black workers were temporary sojourners, and would return to their homes at the end of their period of service. So non-white worker housing in the colonial economic system was expected to be:

(a) *Intended for temporary workers*. Burnett-Hurst (1925), for instance, described dwellings for the Bombay 'wage-earning classes' (the so-called 'zavli sheds') that were crude shelters, made of palm leaf or flattened kerosene tins, often shared with domestic animals. Even when the structures were more permanent than that, their inhabitants were not expected to stay long.

(b) *Not intended for family occupation*. The worker's labour was wanted, but not his relatives and dependants, and all across the empire family life was discouraged. The Indian Factory Labour Commission in 1908, for instance, maintained, conveniently and cheaply for British interests, that the migrant who came to dislike factory labour had the option of returning to his village, where the joint family system would secure him against want. The port cities and indentured labour systems created a huge gender imbalance: in Singapore the ratio of males to females was 3:1 in 1871, and in Calcutta in 1911 2.4:1.[9]

(c) *Not recognizing social bonds other than the work relationship*. The labour demands of the colonial economic system dissolved, or at least submerged, ties of family, tribe, caste or region in the greater cause of industrial capitalism. It was only in the twentieth century that indirect rule doctrines led to the segregation of workers by race and tribe.

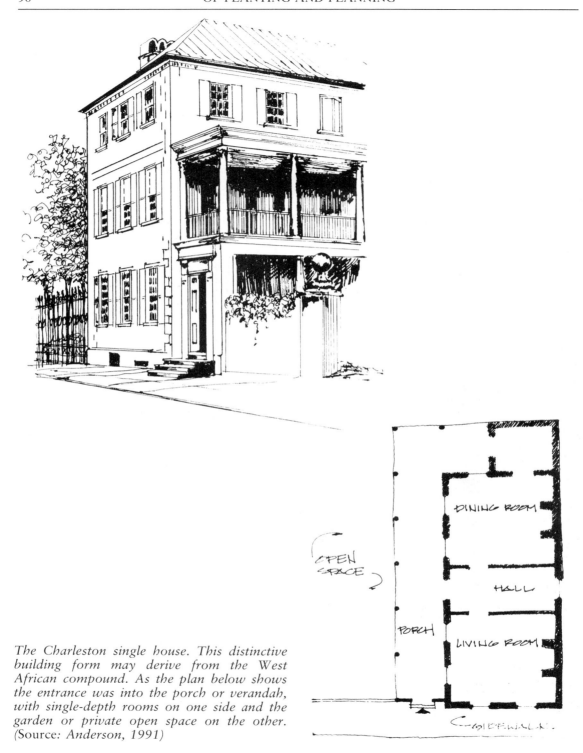

The Charleston single house. This distinctive building form may derive from the West African compound. As the plan below shows the entrance was into the porch or verandah, with single-depth rooms on one side and the garden or private open space on the other. (Source: Anderson, 1991)

The Charleston town house of Governor Rhett, in the single house form. The slave owner Rhett took South Carolina out of the Union in 1860, an act of secession which led to the American Civil War. (Source: The author, photo taken in 1991)

Row-house for the middle-income black families in Savannah, Georgia. The 'shotgun house' style evolved into the deep-plan houses in the background, with porch added. (Source: The author, photo taken in 1991)

Temporary houses for workers in Bombay. In the foreground are sheds made from flattened kerosene tins, in the background chawls built by the colonial authorities. (Source: Burnett-Hurst, 1925)

A few quotations from the long sad story of the Calcutta slums will illustrate the point. Captain Richards, in his massive planning report on Calcutta, wrote that:

The first thing that usually strikes an Indian newly arrived in Calcutta is the enforced mixture of castes, creeds, and races found in every street, and in nearly every dwelling-house or place. Only an intense housing pressure could produce conditions so un-natural and repulsive to Indian requirements. (Lanchester, 1914, p. 126).

The consequences of this approach in the early twentieth century has been described by an Indian historian:

Family-life was powerfully discouraged in Calcutta. The lack of women brought in an excess of vice. The unique preponderance of males over females in the city was to be explained in terms of the floating and migrant character of male labour. For men would certainly have brought their families, if the possibility of a decent life had existed. Under existing conditions, the workers preferred to maintain connections with their native village by going back every summer to look after their families and lands. There was, therefore, no question of their undergoing a thorough process of urbanization and losing their traditional, rural identities. The European business-men had a perennial complaint about the poor quality of labour, its temporary character, and the seasonal shortage of labour during the summer. Had they invested in creating suitable living conditions in the working-class quarters in Calcutta, a better and more stable labour force could easily have been obtained. In fact, the extremely crowded slums, by squeezing large numbers of people in small areas, kept down the cost of maintenance of labour, while the overpopulated rural areas in Bihar and UP provided for the reproduction of labour at no cost to capital. (Ray, 1979, p. 51)

From the early days of colonialism such dis-regard for the needs of the non-white labour force resulted often in the cheapest and most primitive forms of shelter. A British woman wrote disdainfully of Calcutta in the late eighteenth century:

the appearance of the best houses is spoiled by the little straw huts, and such sort of encumbrances, which are built by the servants themselves to sleep in; so that all the English part of the town, which is the largest, is a confusion of very superb and very shabby houses, dead walls, straw huts, warehouses and I know not what. (Mrs. Kindersley in 1777, quoted in Losty, 1990, p. 37)

The migrant labourers of the Empire might live in grass or mud shelters, or, as Burnett-Hurst (1925) described in Bombay, structures of bamboo matting, with roofs of kerosene tin sheets, rags, gunny sacks, reeds and hay. Housing for temporary workers, however, need not itself be temporary. By the second half of the nineteenth century unprecedented numbers of workers were needed for the cotton and jute mills of Bombay and Calcutta, the estate plantations of the Caribbean and Ceylon, and the mines of southern Africa. New housing forms were devised and enforced through building regulations which were replicated in many colonies. It was also increasingly impressed upon employers that they had the responsibility to house their workers, at least on the estates, if not necessarily in the port cities. Stamford Raffles, the Utilitarians and the mining capitalists of South Africa addressed the question of accommodating the workers in housing that was (for the employer rather than the occupier) cheap, convenient and controllable. From this process emerged various building forms: the barrack, the chawl, the shophouse, the closed compound.

Barrack Housing: 'Comfort, Privacy and Decency are Impossible'

The commonest type of worker housing in the empire was variously known as the barrack, the barrack range, the barrack yard, the hostel, or the coolie lines. Its essential features were the same and the resulting accommodation is aptly summarized in the phrase above (Williams, 1962, p. 106). Early ones might house forty or more workers in a room, but later practice was for each room to accommodate up to six workers, at space standards of 250–350 cubic feet per person. The building was typically a long, narrow, single-storey structure, about a hundred feet long and constructed of sawn timber with a cast iron frame. The internal arrangement would be a single or double row of standard-sized rooms (each about 10 × 12 feet square). A single communicating veranda or corridor ran the length of the building, and was sometimes open-sided for ventilation. Cooking, washing and toilet facilities, where these existed at all, were communal and usually grouped at one end of the building.

The term 'barrack' is defined in the Oxford English Dictionary as a 'temporary hut or cabin, e.g. for the use of soldiers in a siege'. It is etymologically linked to the 'barracoon', which was a building for quartering slaves in transit. The origin of the word is uncertain, but it appears early in Spanish and Catalan as 'barraque'. Soldiers through the centuries have been housed, either by billeting them upon civilian households, or by accommodating them in purpose-built barracks, the latter having the advantage to military authority of segregation and greater control.

The building form of the barrack was adapted by plantation owners in the Caribbean region, who, like the military, had to house and discipline large groups of young male workers in relative social isolation. Slave captives in West Africa were kept in barracoons before being shipped across the Atlantic, and on arrival in the New World were often herded into communal barracks, while seasoned local slaves lived in their own family homes. Some planters built planned 'lines' for their slaves' houses, especially from the late eighteenth century, and most regarded the provision of housing as one of their obligations. Some plantation owners tried to provide communal barracks of stone, but the slaves often refused to occupy them, 'stating that they were so much exposed to their neighbours they did not like to let them know what they were doing on all occasions'.[10]

With the growth of new mass armies in the period of the French Revolutionary Wars, the scale and design of barracks developed rapidly. After 1815 Britain's greatly expanded imperial role required the maintenance of standing armies, both home and colonial. The quartering, training and control of such large groups of men was best undertaken in isolation from the general population. In 1818 responsibility for construction and maintenance of the British Army's barracks was transferred from a civilian department to the Corps of Royal Engineers, whose training school at Chatham included it from 1826 in a course in practical architecture. New industrialized building technologies and materials were available, such as machine-sawn timber, mass-produced wirecut nails, and cast-iron framing.

A major development in barrack history occurred in the mid-nineteenth century. The British Army during the Crimean War experienced more deaths from disease than from enemy action, and the high death rate in the army at the time became part of a wider public discourse on public health in crowded conditions. In British India, where throughout the nineteenth century a large British standing army was maintained, barrack design was severely criticized by the Commander-in-Chief, Sir Charles Napier. He resigned his position because of policy differences with the civilian administration, and in a book written upon his

return to England he attacked the Military Board for the squalid housing conditions of the troops:

Murdering Board should be its name, for directly or indirectly it causes more loss of life, more extravagance than can be described.

Napier, whose family was of a Radical style of politics, and closely connected with the Utilitarian movement, recommended space standards of at least a thousand cubic feet per person, claiming that:

with less, insufferable heat and a putrid atmosphere prevails, death is the result![11]

The new form of barrack which emerged from these debates followed a pavilion style of design. Minimum space standards were prescribed of 300–400 cubic feet per soldier, later increased to 600 cubic feet, which had the effect of reducing by a third the numbers that could be accommodated in the existing barracks. For India, where the climate necessitated somewhat different designs and standards, the Commission recommended the higher standard of a thousand cubic feet, with a minimum floorspace of 80 ft^2 and rooms 16 ft high (Curtin, 1989, p. 161). Barrack ranges were recommended of 250 × 24 ft, with a 10-foot verandah, along with bungalows for married soldiers, privies, cookrooms and guardhouses. As a result of these reforms,

the verandah'd barrack-block, so inescapable a part of the Indian scene, was thought as suitable for Aldershot as for Rawalpindi, while high in the Blue Mountains of Jamaica Newcastle Barracks faithfully followed the guidelines for health and happiness laid down on behalf of his soldiers by C.J. Napier far away.[12]

Within a few years the new barrack designs were being used all over the British Empire, and not only for the military. They were found particularly suitable for housing the large numbers of indentured and migrant labourers. The abolition of slavery in 1834 had created a serious labour shortage in the Caribbean, as

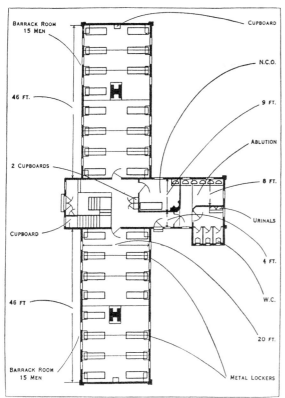

Ground floor plan of a two-storey barrack design for the British Army, from the period between the two World Wars. Early barrack designs were simpler. (Source: Encyclopaedia Britannica, 1937 edition)

Mauritius	453.1	Trinidad	143.9
Malaya	250	Fiji	61.0
	(estimated)	Jamaica	36.4
Guyana	238.9	Surinam	34.3
Natal	152.2		

Singapore received 100,000–250,000 Chinese labourers every year between 1900 and 1930, and Hong Kong processed similar numbers (Christopher, 1988, p. 81). Many labourers returned home on completing their indentures, and many died in service. After the system had been abolished it was estimated, in 1928, that some 2.3 million Indians were living outside India as a result of this diaspora, as well as large numbers of Chinese.[13]

The colonial government sought to regulate this new kind of labour more closely than ever it had the slave plantations. Protectors of immigrants were appointed, and model ordinances circulated to the colonies, which sought to regulate virtually all aspects of the labourers' living and working conditions. Housing standards were established, and pass laws governed the movement of the labourers away from their place of work. From their origins in the indentured labour system, the regulations were transferred to other places with large migrant labour requirements, such as the mines of Malaya, Southern Africa and Nigeria. Although they were justified as ensuring adequate living and working conditions for the labourers, in practice they operated more to the employers' advantage, for actual labour conditions were so poor as to ensure a high death rate for much of the colonial period, in spite of all the regulations.

Barrack housing was not only linked to the indentured labour system, but appeared all over the colonies. Similar bachelor accommodation of the 'range' type was described in West Africa in the 1930s: rows of twelve rooms (10 × 12 × 8 feet), built of concrete, with a corrugated-iron roof, provided with pit or bucket latrines and a communal kitchen. In South Africa rental barracks or single-sex hostels were built for migrant workers of

FIG. 1.—GROUND FLOOR PLAN OF A MODERN TWO-STOREY BARRACK BUILDING. THE PLAN OF THE FLOOR ABOVE IS SIMILAR

freed slaves left the plantations in droves to set up smallholdings, ignoring the disapproval of their former owners. The solution adopted for the Caribbean, and extended to other island plantation economies, was to import indentured labourers from the overpopulated sub-continents of India and China. Between 1845 and 1917 (when moral outrage brought an end to this 'new kind of slavery') India supplied the following numbers of labourers (in thousands):

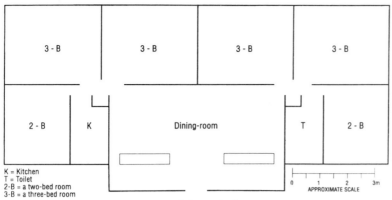

| 3 - B | 3 - B | 3 - B | 3 - B |

| 2 - B | K | Dining-room | T | 2 - B |

K = Kitchen
T = Toilet
2-B = a two-bed room
3-B = a three-bed room

0   1   2   3m
APPROXIMATE SCALE

Fig. 1 A hostel 'door'

Crowded hostel accommodation, intended as single-sex, in Cape Town, South Africa. The floor plan of a hostel 'door', with 13 bed-spaces sharing a communal room, toilet and bathroom. (Source: Ramphele, 1993)

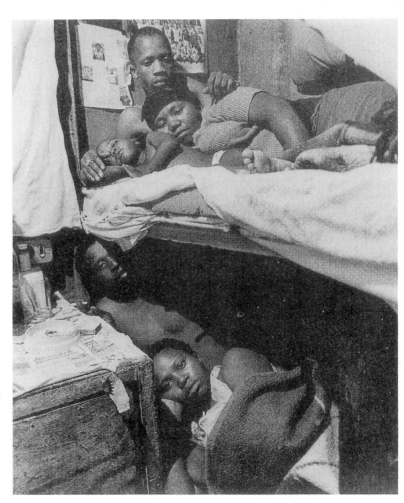

This picture of couples with children sharing a single bed-space in a hostel shows the extent of overcrowding. (Source: Ramphele, 1993)

Exterior of African hostels in Gugeletu (Cape Town). Designed on the barrack principle for single-workers, they now accommodate families in grossly overcrowded and insanitary conditions. (Source: The author, photo taken in 1995)

Row houses in Bo-Kaap (Cape Town). This is one of the few older housing areas for coloureds to survive the demolition and forced removals of the apartheid era in South Africa. These well-kept homes preserve some of the diverse cultural influences upon Cape Coloureds. (Source: The author, photo taken in 1995)

Post-apartheid African housing in Cape Town. Lack of money makes it difficult for the new government to improve the standard of housing. These model dwellings are smaller and built to lower specification even than 'cottage' housing of the colonial period. (Source: The author, photo taken in 1995)

different races and became one of the symbols of urban apartheid. In Durban, an important port for indentured labour, the first barrack was built in the dockside work zone in 1878.[14]

The contrast could hardly be greater between this type of accommodation and that which British colonial administrators thought suitable for themselves. Standard accommodation for white officials was the bungalow, set in a one or two-acre compound. As expressed by Lugard, the colonial official's 'dwelling-house should be as superior to those of the native as he is himself superior to them' (1893, quoted in Fryer, 1988, p. 70).

Sharing was disapproved of. When C.L. Temple wrote in his book on Indirect Rule about 'The housing problem', he was thinking, not about the appalling living conditions of many black workers, but that the bachelor white colonial officials should not have to share their accommodation. He called this the principle of separate housing ('one man, one roof'), and estimated that it cost only about eighty pounds per head more to build one-man rather than two-man bungalows. To him this was money well spent:

. . . owing to the extra space covered by a number of small bungalows compared that covered by one large building, the cost of upkeep of roads and sanitation is slightly increased. But in my opinion, it were far better to reduce some other head of expenditure (if such a course is considered absolutely necessary) than to secure so diminutive a saving at the cost of the comfort, i.e. the health, of even one Government officer, though he be of the most junior grade conceivable. (Temple, 1918, pp. 248–50)

Presumably his unspoken fear was of homosexuality among these scions of the English public schools.

Barrack Housing in Trinidad

The island of Trinidad is offered as a short case study of barrack housing. It received some 144,000 indentured labourers between 1845 and 1917, mostly from India. In 1901 its population was some 255,000, and today 40 per cent of its population is descended from these Indian indentured labourers.

Detailed regulations covered virtually all aspects of the immigrants' lives. They were not allowed to leave their estates without a ticket of leave or similar document, on penalty of fine or imprisonment: until at least the 1870s, freed slaves might taunt them with the gibe, 'Slave, where your free paper?' (Wood, 1968, p. 131). Estates were required to provide hospital facilities at a rate of about one bed for every ten immigrants (a ratio which suggests a high level of sickness). Educational facilities remained minimal until the early twentieth century (Tikasingh, 1973, pp. 310–317).

Regulations were devised for housing from about 1872, when barracks became the norm for estate labourers' housing, replacing the earlier slave cottages. Such barrack housing was built of machine-sawn timber planking, and was required to be white-washed every two years. The roof was of galvanized iron, and the floor either earth (mixed with dung) or raised planking. A wooden verandah 4–6 feet wide at the front provided a cooking space, and a Dutch barn door gave entry.

These barracks were cheap to build: the meanest overseer's house was valued at ten times the annual value of a barrack room. A critic called them 'a legacy of slavery, being little more than a modified form of the old slave barracoon.' His evidence to the Royal Franchise Commission in 1888 was that:

All noise and cooking smells pass through the open space from one end of the barrack to the other. There are no places for cooking, no latrines. The men and women, boys and girls, go together into the canes or bush when nature requires. Comfort, privacy and decency are impossible under such conditions . . . With all this, can anyone wonder at the frequent wife-murders and general demoralisation among the Indian immigrants? In fact the barrack life is approaching to promiscuous intercourse . . .' (Memorandum by L. Guppy, in Williams, 1962, pp. 106–107)

The Trinidadian newspaper, *The Observer* (which called itself 'a monthly organ of Indian opinion') in 1942 attacked the continuing legacy of indentured labour thus:

The system, it was acknowledged, caused a vast and terrible amount of suffering; bitterness was engendered in the minds of thousands; and their interest in life was destroyed . . . The ever-burning question is the plight of the hundred thousand on the estates whose lives are of oppression and sorrow. (Mahabir, 1942)

It is hardly surprising that the barracks were much hated by those forced to live in them. Perhaps their worst fault was the profound lack of privacy, especially for families. They offered no separate room for the women members of a family, and partitions between rooms were flimsy. In such conditions the labourers' past traditions of caste, privacy and family loyalty were broken down, and crime rates (especially wife-murder) were high. When estate labourers completed their term of indenture, there was often not the money to repatriate them, and many had in any case lost contact with their home communities. Offered land in commutation of their contractual right to a paid passage home, they settled, either officially or unofficially, as squatters on unclaimed land. On these small-holdings they hoped to re-establish an independent existence based upon the social practices of their lost homelands. A typical family house on a small-holding was small, measuring some 15 × 15 × 8 feet, but that was still 800 cubic feet larger than the average barrack room, as well as giving far greater family privacy.

From their origins on the estates the barracks became the principal form of mass housing for the urban poor in the Caribbean, mainly because of their profitability to landlords. A typical urban barrack range was a long wooden shed, built against the back wall of a shop and hidden from the street, with up to ten rooms sharing a single tap and cesspit. A building ordinance in Port of Spain in 1868 prohibited the use of wood construction in new buildings (for fire prevention reasons), but the ordinance, far from improving conditions, had the effect of stopping new barrack construction, because the alternative of brick cost more, and thus added to the overcrowding (Brereton, 1979, p. 118).

After the abolition of indentured labour in 1917 the sugar and oil companies used a modern version of barrack design for accommodating their workers, believing that they were improving living conditions. This new-style estate housing was a major factor in the riots of 1937, so deep-rooted was the popular revulsion against barracks. In the words of the Trinidadian architectural historian, John Newel Lewis:

This second wave of compounds was particularly anathema to Trinidadians . . . The alienation is complete. No expense has been spared, it is even extravagant! Yet it is soul-less and because of . . . the Trinidadian addition to individual freedom it comes as a shock to find such an alien establishment in the countryside . . . The foreign company prides itself upon the utility and generosity of its compounds but it is this, the alien life as expressed in this piece of foreign regimentation, which may be the worst aspect of the imposed presence. (Lewis, 1983)

The Forster Commission of Inquiry into the Trinidad labour riots of 1937 judged the barracks to be 'indescribable in their lack of elementary needs of decency'. It recommended that the term 'barrack' should be discontinued, associated as it was with regimentation and harsh discipline. Instead family life was to be encouraged by the building of more semi-detached cottages. The characteristics of the much-hated barrack were not absorbed into Trinidad's subsequent building styles. Very few, if any, examples of barracks survive, nor is the present-day government concerned to preserve them. Yet their negative influence remains, for the rejection of estate living had a profound effect upon the island's settlement pattern. The former indentured labourers rejected the crowded life of the estates, and adopted a pattern of low-density housing in small-holdings scattered over the rural areas, with little or no attempt at settlement planning.

The Closed Compound in South Africa[15]

The barrack style of worker housing was applied in South Africa from the 1880s, particularly in the diamond mines of Kimberley in the form of the closed compound. It was a product of the consolidation of diamond mining production in the hands of the De Beers Consolidated Mines Ltd, and the introduction of deep-shaft mines instead of open digging. New mining technologies required a smaller, but better disciplined, work force, and the new type of compound allowed the companies not only to control their 'boys', but also to prevent pilferage of the diamonds: the mining companies claimed to lose a quarter of production in this way. The DeBeers Company experimented with convict labour in a closed compound in 1884, and found the arrangement so suitable that by 1889 all ten thousand of its African mineworkers were accommodated in closed compounds. The experience of Brazilian mine labour practices was apparently drawn upon, introduced by a Cornish mining engineer, Thomas Kitto.

The closed compound arranged barracks around a large open square. It was enclosed by a corrugated iron fence 10 feet high, and a 15-foot open space between it and the outer wall of the barracks, patrolled by guards with Alsatian dogs and cross-bred bull mastiffs. The camp was lit by arc lights, with a watch tower, and a single gate. Cabins of 700 square feet floorspace for 20–25 workers violated even a modest space standard of 300 cubic feet per worker. The compounds were complete settlements, with their own chapel, hospital/dispensary, and baths, but they were planned more for labour control than social welfare. As described by one writer in 1896, 'The compound is one vast prison'. Later development of the closed compound incorporated

three types of accommodation, the short-term workers being accommodated in the inner square of barracks, surrounded by longer-term miners, and a separate area for the huts of married workers.

Mortality rates in the compounds were high, as much as 5–10 per cent each year. The usual cause of death was lung disease, the result of overcrowding, poor diet and inadequate protection against major changes in temperature. The doctors followed the conventional wisdom of the time about the health advantages of fresh air, and designed the compound buildings to incorporate large ventilators blowing cold drafts of air. Under the extremes of temperature experienced on the high veldt, combined with the high temperatures in the underground mines, it is hardly surprising that the workers became susceptible to pneumonia and tuberculosis. By blaming the incidence of tuberculosis upon the 'biological character' of the African, the doctors deflected attention from the need for costly improvements in compound accommodation and underground working conditions. One of the more enlightened doctors reported in 1900 that, until the compounds were 'extended and re-modelled with an increased air-space, proper lighting and impermeable floors, this terrible disease (pneumonia) among the natives will continue its ravages' (quoted in Turrell, 1987, p. 161).

After the South African War the new British administration of Lord Milner, under pressure from the Colonial Office, appointed a commission to investigate the mortality rates in the compounds. This recommended a minimum standard of 200 cubic feet of living space per worker. It was the risk of an acute labour shortage, and the possibility of having to import Asiatic labour, that finally forced improvements. The compounds were extensively redesigned in 1903–4, with increased space standards and dormitories for 30 workers in three-tier bunks. Mortality rates fell from 65 per thousand in 1897 to 20 per thousand in

1903–12, and allowed De Beers to claim its compounds as models of enlightened company housing. Even so, the American engineer Gorgas, who had achieved excellent health conditions constructing the Panama Canal, visited the Witwatersrand in 1913, and was appalled at the poor hospital facilities, untrained medical staff, crowding and poor sanitation. He recommended replacing the barrack system with family housing, but this was rejected. More expensive housing for mine workers was not introduced until their managers were convinced that cheaper, laboratory-based measures would fail.

The closed compound appears to have become a model for forced labour camps in Russia and Nazi Germany, the Birkenau camp at Auschwitz being designed on space standards of 60 cubic feet per worker. Its legacy in South Africa can be summarized in the words of Wasserfall:

Rather than improving the lives of black workers, they were notable chiefly for what they achieved in terms of creating a disciplined, experienced and cheap African workforce for the underground mines . . . the manner in which housing has been utilised is the social pivot for black labour control throughout the country's history of industrial development. This manipulative use of worker housing has found spatial expression in the compounds and the segregated township . . . Compounds, and latterly hostels, have formed the central thrust of the housing arrangements for 'single' black workers at South African mines and in its industries, while the segregated townships, with their endless rows of almost identical technically-functional houses, have been the typical form assumed by black family accommodation in the urban areas' (Wasserfall, 1990, pp. 297–302)

OTHER TYPES OF WORKER HOUSING: 'PESTILENTIAL PLAGUE SPOTS'

The barrack and its variants were probably the most widespread form of worker housing in the British colonies. It proliferated in the estates, mining camps and towns, and was encouraged by a range of government regulations and public health specialists. Other distinctive regional housing forms also emerged, with the aim of housing and controlling a large migrant unskilled labour force. Two examples are the chawls of India and the shophouse of South-East Asia.

The Chawl[16]

While single-storey barrack accommodation was built in Bombay and Calcutta (usually made of corrugated iron), the usual form of mass housing in those cities, dictated by pressure of population on land, was a tenement building of up to five storeys, called a chawl.

Bombay became an exporter of cotton during the American Civil War, and a textile industry was created by Parsi capitalists. The first cotton mill was built in 1854, in 1914 there were 264, and by 1935 365. In 1931 a quarter of Bombay's working population, 136,000 hands, were employed daily in the cotton mills. On the other side of India the jute mills of Bengal created a similar demand for high-density worker housing near the workplace: in 1908 there were 38 jute mill companies employing 184,000 Indian labourers in Calcutta. The accompanying housing pressures were enormous. According to one study, Calcutta housing stock grew by 20 per cent in the nineteenth century, but the population by 373 per cent. The number of persons per house, measured by the sanitary statisticians, deteriorated from 2.6 in 1831 to 6.7 in 1850, improved slightly to 6.5 in 1901, and deteriorated to over 20 per house after 1921, because of in-migration to escape famine and disease in the countryside.

The chawl emerged as one solution to the

problem of housing this tidal wave of migrant workers. Mostly they remained out of sight and out of mind for the British, but Burnett-Hurst (1925) did describe for Bombay some of the conditions in these 'pestilential plague spots'. In one ward he found that 97 per cent of the working-class households lived in single rooms (sometimes six families to a room), and he estimated that over 60 per cent were overcrowded by English official standards. Some chawls had begun as single-family houses, later extended and subdivided. As new floors were added, up to four or five storeys high, tall narrow frontages and excessive depths were created, often structurally unsound and liable to collapse. Others were speculatively built, the ground-floor rooms facing the streets being let out as shops. A central or side staircase would lead to the upper-floor verandas or central corridors. Washrooms and toilets were communal, and a piped water supply was rare. Burnett-Hurst wrote a horrified description of a typical chawl:

. . . ground-floor rooms are invariably dark, dismal and unhealthy, and often permeated with obnoxious effluvia . . . A personal recollection may be pardoned. On the occasion of a visit to a slum area in the company of the late chairman of the Improve-

Chawl housing in Bombay. Above: *'typical street scene in working-class quarters'.* Right: *'Sweepers' gully' between two chawls.* (Source: Burnett-Hurst, 1925)

ment Trust, entrance was gained to a private dwelling-house which had been converted into a set of one-room tenements. Here was a room with a floor space of 6 ft by 9 ft, part of the space being occupied by the chula (fireplace). The sole window of the room overlooked a gully reeking with filth into which we had previously witnessed a basket of human excreta being emptied by a sweeper woman. The room was occupied by two adults, a boy of three years and an infant. The tenants had been paying Rs. 2 per month for the room, but in 1918 the landlord demanded double the amount, finally agreeing to Rs. 3.8 – an increase of 75 per cent. (Burnett-Hurst, 1925, p. 22)

The Improvement Trusts of Bombay and Calcutta tried to build better chawls, offering rooms 10 feet square, and one bathing space and a latrine for every six to eight tenements, but cost constraints resulted in low-quality materials and minimal maintenance, and even then the economic rents of 12 rupees per month per room proved too expensive for the workers, who would not take them up at 5 rupees. Geddes called the Improvement Trust chawls 'Bolshevik barracks', and likened them to prisons, with no access to any kind of natural light and stifling in crowded conditions, although they were better than the alternatives available at the time.

The 'Shophouse Rafflesia'[17]

Another regional variation in colonial workers' housing emerged in the port cities of the Far East – the Chinese shophouse. Although the term 'shophouse' seems only to have come into general use from Malaya as late as 1949, it is a

Shophouses in Ipoh, Malaysia. This shows the influence of Chinese building form and Raffles' five-foot way in a tin-mining town in Northern Malaysia. (Source: The author, photo taken in 1986)

literal translation of the Chinese, and the association of ground-floor shop with housing accommodation over is as old as urban life itself. The traditional house of mainland south China was designed as a hierarchical arrangement of spaces, which extended from the more public at the front, to the more private at the back, and was similar to the European, and especially British, tradition of terraced housing.

As its name implies, the shophouse combined housing with economic activity. It was usually two or three storeys high, with a narrow street frontage (16–18 ft). Its depth might be two or three times its width, sometimes extending back as much as two hundred feet because of the deep plots allowed by the colonial grid-iron layout. The narrow frontage was dictated by property values, and apparently also by the size of transverse timber beams available as lintels. Each floor could be subdivided into semi-private compartments or cubicles, with an average space per occupant of 25–68 ft^2. The front room would usually contain a table with ancestral tablets, images of gods and ceremonial paraphernalia – the ritual heart of the house. Airwells provided some ventilation and helped keep the interior relatively cool. Yeoh (1991, p. 180) has summarized the role of the shophouse in Singapore:

The essence of the shophouse-tenement tradition was the internal division of the house using partitions, which were not part of the permanent structure of the building, to create distinct compart-

*Stamford Raffles' 'five-foot way'. It was a requirement of his regulations for the new colony of Singapore, and was subsequently applied all over South-East Asia. This example is in Georgetown, Penang Island. (*Source: *The author, photo taken in 1990)*

ments which could be let to individuals, families or business users who would have the use of the common stair, kitchen and bathroom . . . It was a system well-adapted to the needs of immigrants in search of cheap lodgings, and to the labouring classes who spent little time at home but were dependent on hawkers for cheap and quick meals and on the social life in the streets.

Thus a city of shophouses, such as Singapore and Hong Kong, could absorb high population densities and intense economic activity, offering low travel costs and easy access to employment.

A distinctive feature of the colonial shophouse in South-East Asia was the inclusion of a veranda or open arcade, forming a continuous walkway along the terrace front. The British version originated in Singapore, and derived directly from Stamford Raffles' vision of social engineering. It has been called by Lim the 'Shophouse Rafflesia', in allusion to the Rafflesia orchid, the largest flower in the world, and named after Raffles. The veranda was also known as the 'five-foot way' because of the width required in Raffles' original decree of 1822, which said that 'each house should have a verandah of a certain depth open at all times as a continued and covered passage on each side of the street' (quoted in Yeoh, 1991, p. 299). It stipulated that buildings be

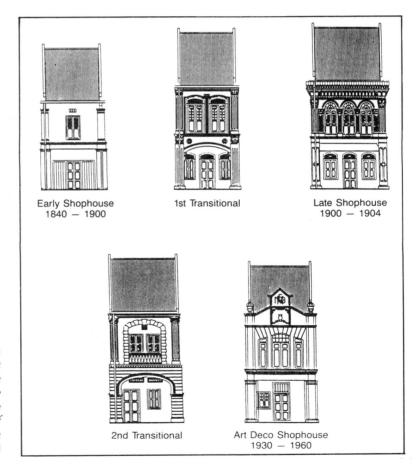

Early Shophouse
1840 — 1900

1st Transitional

Late Shophouse
1900 — 1904

2nd Transitional

Art Deco Shophouse
1930 — 1960

Shophouse styles in Singapore. These front elevations show the extremely narrow frontages, and the successive elaboration of style. (Source: Koh-Lim Wen Gin, 1989)

aligned with each other, and should provide a free passage in front of the building line for purposes of ventilation and scavenging.

The design feature of an arcade maintained as a public way had not existed in the Presidency towns of India or in Penang before the coming of Raffles. It seems to have been his personal contribution, and was probably based upon the buildings he had seen in Dutch Batavia while Governor of Java. They were in turn based upon the arcaded streets and squares of southern Europe, which afforded pedestrians shelter from sun and rain, and safety from passing vehicular and horse traffic. From Singapore the building type spread, through the application of standard by-laws, across much of South-East Asia, to Burma, Hong Kong and the Treaty ports of China. The King of Thailand personally ordered its adoption after a visit to Singapore in 1871. Chinese traders introduced it from Penang to the border towns of south Thailand at Haadyai and Patani. It appeared in Kuala Lumpur when the town was rebuilt in brick after the great fire of 1884. The Rangoon Development Trust in the 1920s built four and five-storey shophouses, some with five-foot ways.

The five-foot way became drawn into the conflicts and negotiations that characterized the shaping of colonial urban landscapes. Raffles had intended it to be an open, un-obstructed public space for the convenience of pedestrians, but there were many competing claims upon it, such as the disposal of rubbish (even corpses), the sorting and selling of merchandise, and informal meetings and negotiations. As Yeoh puts it:

As social, economic and highly mutable space, it was crucial to the social reproduction of a casual labour force dependent on unreliable sources of income and inadequate housing . . . The verandah and adjacent streets were hence latticed with many timetables and competing claims, not just the explicit ones of the municipal scavenging crew or the routine police patrol, but also those of the itinerant hawker on his daily rounds, celebrations dictated by the cycle of Asian festivities as well as the covert activities of secret society gangs staking territorial claims on the urban environment (Yeoh, 1991, p. 313)

With the strengthening of the colonial municipality's determination to impose standards of acceptable behaviour, and permissible activities in public streets and spaces, the threshold between public and private domains became less ambiguous and more defined. Conflict was ensured over the

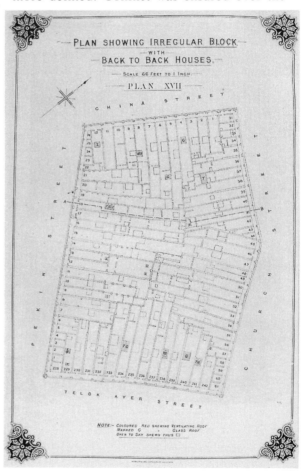

Shophouse plots and air-wells in Singapore. This street block plan, part of Simpson's report on plague, shows the irregular plots and back-to-back houses, punctuated by the air-wells that he campaigned against. (Source: Simpson, 1907)

use of that valuable commodity, space. An attempt by the Singapore authorities in 1888 to clear obstructions from the five-foot ways led to the so-called 'verandah riots'. In the same year the Hong Kong authorities passed an ordinance to prohibit the enclosure of shop-house verandas. Later the advantages of a segregated pedestrian way became apparent with the growth of motor traffic, and there were attempts to restructure and widen the verandahs to six or seven feet.

The interior airwell was another aspect of shophouse form to be disputed between the occupiers and the colonial authorities. It maintained a flow of fresh and relatively cool air, but was unacceptable to the sanitarian, Dr. Simpson. His report on Singapore sanitation (1907), following the plague, attributed disease in the shophouses to Chinese living practices and racial characteristics, rather than to over-crowding and poverty. He refused to acknowledge the positive contribution of the airwells to house ventilation, and did not allow them to contribute toward the total amount of open space which regulations stipulated. His expensive remedy was partial demolition of the shophouses to create backlanes, a policy later applied by the Singapore Improvement Trust to many thousands of shophouses. It had the effect of reducing the amount of space enclosed as private territory within the house plot.

HOUSING IN THE TWENTIETH CENTURY: NEW DIRECTIONS

Squatters and Informal Settlements[18]

Most black migrants to the colonial town had to find, or often make, their own housing, rather than getting it from their employer. Under traditional attitudes to land, it was assumed that vacant land had no owner and no value, so that anyone could clear it and lay claim to it, without acknowledging the position of a chief or headman, and new immigrants might not recognize any local authority at all. As the landless urban community grew, and the legal and bureaucratic maze also grew, the immigrants simply put up their own houses. The exotic (to them) law of private property, giving a landowner exclusive rights, often presented migrants with no choice but to squat in unauthorized structures in informal settlements (Mutale, 1993, pp. 15–16).

An example of the plight of the landless can be given from the Caribbean after the abolition of slavery. The former slaves' bodies might have been freed, but they had few other rights, and the planters continued to control the land. Slave owners were compensated for the loss of their property, but not the slaves for the original deprivation of their freedom, and their forcible uprooting. In Barbados, where land was totally dominated by the large plantation, the landless proletariat created by slave emancipation was allowed to occupy self-built houses on 'spots' assigned by the plantation owner, usually in an infertile or inaccessible corner of the plantation. Because the in-security of tenure meant that the property might have to be moved at short notice, a prefabricated house form developed known as the 'chattel house'. The house was on a loose rock-pile foundation, with pit latrine rather than water-borne sewage disposal, so that there would be little to mark its passing, and as recently as 1980, over half of the homes still had pit latrines (Watson and Potter, 1993).

To call the inhabitants of such informal settlements squatters illustrates, not so much their lawlessness, as the injustice of the colonial land settlement and legal-political structures, which numerous examples can show. The informal settlements of South Africa predated apartheid by decades and reflect colonialism's refusal to accept Africans (and to a lesser extent Asians) as legitimate

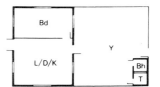

A. Basic timber chattel

B. Bipartite timber chattel

Evolution of the chattel house design in Barbados. A two-bed structure on a loose rock-pile foundation added extra rooms over time, but tenure remained insecure and at the whim of the plantation owner. (Source: *Watson and Potter, 1993)*

C. Tripartite timber chattel (gable roof)

L Living room	Y Backyard
D Dining room	Bh Bathroom
K Kitchen	T Toilet
Bd Bedroom	

urban dwellers and participants in land and property markets. The refugees created by the 1948 partition of India and Pakistan were deprived of their land as victims of a political situation not of their making. Such inequalities of land and housing have roots deep in colonial history.

The colonial authorities' attitude to squatters and informal settlements varied widely. Typically there seems to have been no systematic policy towards squatters, sometimes evicting them, sometimes tolerating them, sometimes negotiating with them. Squatters sometimes organized to petition government for better services and some security of tenure, as occurred in Madras in 1920 (Lewandowski, 1984). Not until the 1970s, and then only sometimes, was there much recognition that government might have some responsibility for the situation of landless people and informal settlements.

Employer Housing

Sometimes employers provided housing for their workers, and some even attempted to build housing according to their workers' preferences. The Tata iron and steel town of Jamshedpur in the 1920s designed for its Hindu workers 'group housing', comprising typically twelve families grouped around a central space, instead of an open suburban style of layout, but still aiming at the garden city ideal of twelve houses to the acre. Muslim workers instead were allocated plots 40 × 20 feet, in lines with a 40 ft space front and back. In a discussion of the Jamshedpur approach, at the Town Planning Institute in 1928, the Lucknow town planner, Bogle, commented:

Where the Englishman wanted his house surrounded by a garden, the Indian wanted his garden surrounded by a house. The latter liked to have a garden in the form of a courtyard where Purdah could be observed and if there was to be an open garden, quite a small one was usually preferred between the house frontage and the road. (Temple, 1928, p. 27)

In Ceylon a tea estate company planned a town at Medamulla for its two thousand workers in the 1920s, adopting the latest community planning principles. Designed by a Colombo-based architect planner it included a civic centre (with town office, post office, chapel, hospital, school, club), septic tank drainage, bakery, laundry, baths, incinerator, clock tower combined water storage tank, museum (*JTPI*, 1927–28, Vol 14, p. 235).

The more usual picture was one of neglect, with the workers clustered in unplanned 'locations' around their place of work. The housing, health and social conditions of black workers should be placed in the context of company profits repatriated to Britain. Dividends from the South African Rand Mines averaged over 100 per cent per annum over a forty-year period. Tate and Lyle, which controlled over half of British sugar consumption, paid similar handsome dividends. Commenting during the Second World War on the Moyne Commission report (see p. 18), Russell wrote:

Is it too much to hope that people will perceive some relation between the exploitation which these profits reveal and the background of extreme poverty, bad social conditions, scandalous housing, starved health services, feeble education and rampant illegitimacy which is the direful picture revealed – or at least partly exposed – by those extracts from the report of the Royal Commission which the Government has allowed to be published? Perhaps the full story would be too painful – or too damaging – for even our hardened consciences. (Russell, 1944, pp. 40–42)

Government agencies, particularly the large employers like the mines and the railways, sometimes took responsibility for housing their workers, although standards could be low. In Nigeria a colonial administrator in 1927 described the railway town of Kafanchan as the 'insanitary grass hovels of the old railway camp . . . a cesspool of vice' (quoted in Home, 1974, pp. 99 and 102). Railway colonies or housing estates stood near the railway station on the outskirts of most Indian cities, inhabited mostly by Eurasians (Morris, 1983, pp. 134–6). Oldenburg described the style of housing for Indian government employees in Lucknow:

These endless straight rows of small brick cells with a small front verandah and kitchen were as ill-adapted to the environmental and climatic conditions as they were ugly, although some of the barren architecture was compensated by the zealous garden and tree planting that was undertaken during the period. (Oldenburg, 1984, p. xviii)

In Kitchener's new Khartoum land was zoned into three 'classes', based on social and racial rather than land-use differences, and arranged in bands parallel to the river. Second Class land was reserved for Egyptian officials, businessmen and others of lesser social status. As one British administrator later recalled:

The British went home to their charming houses on the river with their well irrigated gardens and trees while their subordinates were relegated to dismal

*Aerial photograph of Khartoum in the 1920s. This shows the transition from the British officials'
'charming houses on the river with their well-irrigated gardens' to the 'dismal rows of houses in the
dusty back parts'. (Source: McLean, 1930)*

rows of houses in the dusty back parts. (quoted in
Daly, 1986, p. 357)

Regulations for indentured labour were
gradually extended to other colonies as Labour
Ordinances, seeking to create 'Labour Health
Areas' under government sanitary inspection,
especially in the period of colonial development and welfare after the 1920s. Sometimes
expatriate firms could be compelled to provide
better housing, although in general the
controls were weakly applied and inadequate.
The Colonial Office's Labour Adviser, Colonel
Orde-Brown, fulfilled a similar role to Dr.

Simpson, writing reports as a consultant on
labour conditions in many colonies.[19]

Beginnings of Public Housing

Action by the colonial authorities to remedy
bad housing conditions came only because of
the fear of plague. Earlier, when in 1872 the
Health Officer of Calcutta pressed the
Municipal Commissioner on the desirability of
building artisans' and labourers' dwellings ('the
filthy dens in which the labouring classes of the
city live are among the chief causes of the very

New-style chawls built by the Bombay Improvement Trust (about 1920). The plan was for one family to a room, with wide central corridors and through ventilation. (Source: Burnett-Hurst, 1925)

high death-rate'), nothing was done (Burnett-Hurst, 1925, p. 30). The outbreak of plague in the 1890s shifted medical attention in the colonial ports to public health measures which could combat the threat to trade and commerce. Dr Simpson's activities as a sanitary consultant in many port cities after 1900 were part of a new wave of municipal improvement activity which resulted in an increased state role in the direct provision of housing, following closely upon similar initiatives in Britain.

The 'new style' chawls built by the Improvement Trusts of Bombay and Calcutta sought to raise standards of worker housing. They were three, four and five storey buildings, the early ones being built of brick or stone, later of reinforced concrete (justified as being less affected by the weather and less harbour for vermin). The usual sunshades of matting or iron were replaced by asbestos, which was claimed to be 'neater and lighter and keep the veranda and rooms cooler'. There was a wide (8 feet) central corridor, room sizes of 10 × 12 feet together with a front balcony or verandah. The areas between the blocks were tarmac-surfaced and intended as play areas. The Bombay City Improvement Trust claimed for its new style chawls a death rate a third or a quarter that of the whole city, but even a sympathetic writer like Burnett-Hurst was appalled by the face of poverty and irked by the apparent dirty habits of tenants:

Two-storied chawl with shops on the ground floor. (Source: Burnett-Hurst, 1925)

All sense of cleanliness appears to be absent. Spitting of pan and betelnut juices and other nuisances are committed everywhere, especially on the staircases, in the passages and corridors. These places also serve as the chief repositories for the sweepings of the rooms. Goats, fowls and other animals belonging to the tenants are often to be found in the corridors. It is in these surroundings that one sees babies crawling, children playing and mothers nursing their infants. The interiors of the rooms are little better than the rest of the building. Windows and sometimes verandas are enclosed with rags, gunny cloth, clothing hung out to dry, etc. Where woodwork and glass ventilators are provided . . . they are frequently blocked with firewood, etc. The verandas are fitted with cooking places, but tenants prefer to cook in their living-room, especially on a windy day. It is not surprising, then, that the walls and ceiling are blackened, as there is little escape for the smoke . . . The floors are daily 'cleaned' with cow-dung – a practice common throughout India; the occupants of the room eat their meals on the floor and sleep on it where space does not provide for charpoys. Cooking and eating vessels are cleaned with earth, road scrapings and any kind of water which is procurable. . . . It is no exaggeration to say that the masses are utterly unacquainted with even elementary ideas of hygiene and sanitation, and little improvement can take place until they have been educated to a different standard of living. (Burnett-Hurst, 1925, p. 27)

The Improvement Trust chawl remained a standard form of government housing for some sixty years. Probably the largest such housing programme was initiated in Hong Kong after the Second World War, when disastrous fires in the squatter camps north of Kowloon (at Shek Kip Mei) led to the establishment of a Resettlement Department in 1954. The design of its so-called Mark I accommodation was recognizably derived from the chawl. In seven-storey H-shaped blocks, single rooms of 120 ft^2 were allocated for families of five adults, using space standards of 24 ft^2 per individual (children under 10 being counted as half an adult). Off each side of a central corridor were 14–18 flats, in a row, and communal bath and toilet facilities were located in the link between the long blocks. Some 240 blocks of that type were built before the design was superseded in 1964, each block accommodating some 450 families (Dwyer, 1971).

These mass housing schemes in Asian cities reflected the new colonial development and welfare approach, and a shift towards government taking responsibility for low-income housing, as illustrated by the new housing legislation in Trinidad in the 1930s. As put by a member of the Trinidad Legislative Council:

this Government is becoming slightly communistic in the sense of its awakening to its responsibilities to its citizens. (quoted in Home, 1993b)

Following a survey in 1931–32 which found a third of the population of Port of Spain (some 25,000 people) living in 'barrack-yard conditions', a start was made on redevelopment with the Slum Clearance and Housing Ordinance of 1935, based upon the British Housing Acts of 1919, 1925 and 1930. Britain was at the time developing a programme of slum clearance and redevelopment by the public sector, alongside a growing interest in industrialized housing. Trinidad's housing ordinance followed pressure for better housing conditions from the Legislative Council, which had been created in 1924 to provide a limited form of representative government. A Council member who earned an honoured place in Trinidad's political history, Captain Cipriani, called this legislation 'the most far-reaching scheme for the benefit of the working classes ever undertaken by any administration in this Colony'. He was forthright as usual:

Whether we are red or blue or any other colour, there is one thing that honest-minded men are agreed upon and that is that the housing of the working classes has grown to be such a menace that it is nothing short of a blot on our civilization. My friends argue that the bill is drastic and they even go so far as to say that their land is being filched from them. That may well be; but I would remind them of the time when they filched that land from that section of the community which could not help

itself, and if today we are filching the land back from them, it is only giving them a dose of their own medicine. (quoted in Home, 1993b)

Towards 'Cottage' Housing

The growing colonial government interest in worker housing was accomplished by a shift in policy from the provision of 'block dwellings' (tenements) to 'cottage' housing. A repeated theme from about 1910, probably prompted by the British experience of building low-density garden cities and suburbs, was for cottage-style family accommodation for the workers. Massive tenement blocks and barrack styles were no longer seen as the only solution. Captain Richards in Calcutta was an early critic:

Block-dwellings are not productive of good citizens . . . The present new chawls of Calcutta are a disgrace to any city . . . the author is no advocate for this type of housing, and much prefers single-family dwellings or cottage flats built on such suburban areas as are suitable. (Lanchester, 1914, pp. 219–220).

With reluctance the authorities were forced to concede that workers had families, and wanted to live with them.

In South Africa in 1920 the Housing Commision enthused about the potential of new-style town planning for housing the poor, and the advantages of family houses, which were neater and more easily controlled than the congested slums. Detailed research was undertaken into the design and construction of houses for urban blacks, with tribal precincts under a headman, and grouped around separate educational institutions (Robinson, 1990).

The progressive thinking on colonial worker housing was forcefully expressed by the Forster Commission of Inquiry into the Trinidad riots of 1937. The commissioners were particularly shocked at the housing conditions which they found:

In no aspect of our inquiry have we been more impressed by the evidence placed before us and by our own investigations than as regards the conditions in which large numbers of the working population, both urban and rural, are housed. (Forster Commission, 1938, p. 35)

Earlier commissions in Trinidad (in 1897 and 1930) had criticized the bad housing provided for estate labourers, blaming it for what was seen as 'the absence, among a large section of the population, of a due sense of the value of home and family life.' The Forster Commission, appalled at barracks that were 'indescribable in their lack of elementary needs of decency', recommended that family life be encouraged by the building of more semi-detached cottages with gardens. It repeated the arguments of British housing writers nearly a century before (Gaskell, 1987) about the advantages of the family house and garden for creating 'a sense of self-respect among the people and the feeling that their house is their own, and in the encouragement of family life'. The Forster Commission made eighteen recommendations on housing (more than on any other issue), including sites-and-services schemes, village housing developments, and a review of estate housing.

Following the Commission, a new Slum Clearance and Housing Ordinance was passed for Trinidad in 1938, based upon the English 1936 Housing Act and the experience of other colonies (such as the Straits Settlements, Northern Rhodesia, Tanganyika, and Jamaica). It conferred powers for slum clearance, 'the improving of congested areas by radical re-planning and redevelopment', new working-class housing (including hostels for single men and women), and a betterment levy (Home, 1993b).

CONCLUSIONS

The history of the mass housing of black workers in the British Empire offers nothing much to be proud of. Colonial economic systems from the early days of plantation slavery treated people essentially as units of labour. The housing arrangements made little or no provision for family or communal life, and deliberately sought to override the cultural traditions of the subordinate peoples. Housing, such an integral part of everyday life, was the building form in the urban landscape which, perhaps more than any other, revealed the conflicts and interactions between the colonial authority's views of social order and the cultural values and traditions of the mass of the population living in colonial cities. The housing created for the non-white workers of the British Empire shows a bewildering mixture of influences, army barracks and Utilitarian theories of spatial organization and public health coming from the colonizer's side, and African compounds and Chinese shophouses coming from the cultures of the colonized and enslaved.

To the extent that it cared about the living conditions of its black workers, the colonial system tried to make mass housing in the colonial cities on a standardized and industrialized model, intended to dissolve, or at least submerge, ties of family, tribe, caste and region in the greater cause of industrial capitalism. The designs discouraged workers from bringing their families to live with them, and where provided by the employers the housing was located near the workplace (whether this was an estate, a factory, dock or railway depot), under maximum employer control. The physical division of space was intended to assist the authorities in a process of fixing, dividing, recording, and opening up homes and public places to 'the gaze of power'. Colonial authority, through agents like the sanitarian Dr. Simpson, sought to control its subject populations by rendering their living areas

Fig. 27 Compound diagram, Sabon Gari, Zaria

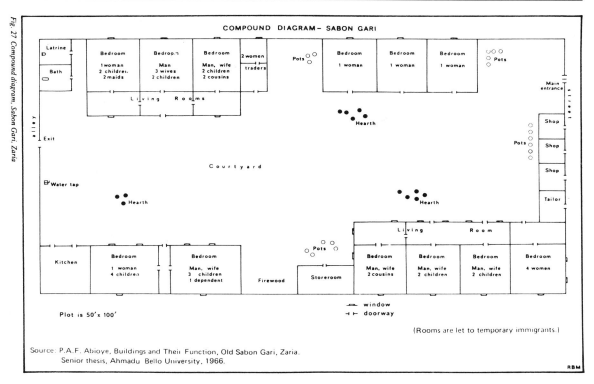

The influential African compound style of communal housing. This diagram shows a modified form of compound adapted to the rectangular plot of the Sabon Gari ('strangers' quarter') of Zaria, Northern Nigeria. Traditionally for an extended family, this example was mainly let to temporary immigrants. (Source: Urquhart, 1977)

open to this gaze, especially after the panic induced by the plague epidemic of the 1890s.

On the ground the reality could be very different, with the new migrants to the city building where and how they could, and drawing upon their various cultural traditions. The African compound, the Indian village house, the Chinese shophouse were all domestic building types which pervaded the colonial urban landscape, and survived by a process of conflict, negotiation, and adaptation to the demands of colonial social order. In the twentieth century colonial government eventually conceded to the pressures for normal family and community life to be expressed in housing form, with the shift from 'block dwelling' to 'cottage housing'. The recognition that squatters and informal settlements were a consequence of colonial land policies, and, therefore, a matter for which government should accept some responsibility, was to come more slowly.

NOTES

1. For examples of this approach see Davies (1985), Losty (1990) and Morris (1983). For a critical view of the contemporary debates on architectural style in Victorian India, see Metcalf (1989).

2. For new approaches to the social relations of building form, see King (1980), Markus (1993) and Rapoport (1982).

3. See Hudson and McEwan (1986), pp. 8–9, and Connah (1988), chapter 6. The National Trust of Australia preserves several prefabricated buildings, which include LaTrobe's Cottage, The Domain (which was his home from 1839 to 1854), and three portable houses in South Melbourne. For Australian building design see Connah (1988), Drew (1992), Hudson and McEwan (1986), and Irving (1985).

4. For the bungalow see Edwards (1990) on Singapore, King (1984), and Morris (1983), pp. 39–46.

5. Drew (1992), p. 41. He provides a detailed and perceptive history and account of the veranda. The word itself is probably of Portuguese origin.

6. For an introduction to the extensive literature on worker housing in Europe (which is outside the scope of this book), see Daunton (1983) and (1990), Gaskell (1987), and Pooley (1992).

7. *Slavery and Social Death* is the title of Patterson (1982), in which see p. 113; see also Davis (1984).

8. Walvin (1992), pp. 79–83. See Anderson (1991), pp. 17–26, for the Charleston single house; Beckles and Shepherd (1991), and Higman (1973), on household structure; Vlach (1976) on the shotgun house; Clarke (1985), p. 161, on Kingston; and Smith (1985) and McDaniel (1982) on plantation life in the American South.

9. Labour Commission quoted in Kooiman (1985), p. 217. Singapore figures in Yeoh (1991), p. 44, Calcutta in Lanchester (1914), p. 126.

10. Walvin (1992), pp. 79–83. Alleyne and Sheppard (1990) describe the barracks provided for the garrison at Barbados, which was originally of stone construction (two floors measuring 265 × 44 ft and accommodating 450 men). Later the building used iron girders and joists (after 1842) to provide added strength against hurricanes.

11. Napier (1853), p. 205.
Sir Charles James Napier (1782–1855) served in the Peninsular War, conquered the province of Sind, and was Commander-in-Chief of the British Army in India. He was described by Thackeray as 'a beak like an eagle, a beard like a Cashmere goat', and has his statue in Trafalgar Square at the foot of Nelson's Column.

12. Morris (1983), p. 225. There is an excellent short account of 'Barracks' in *Encyclopaedia Britannica* (see particularly 1911 and 1937 editions). See also Abdul Sattar (1965), Home (1993a), and King (1976), chapter 5.

13. There is a growing literature on identured labour, although the housing aspects have been relatively neglected. See Saunders (1984), Tinker (1974) and Campbell (1923).

14. For West African ranges see Russell (1944), pp. 33–34. For South African hostels see Lemon (1991), pp. 76 and 186, and tables of the numbers of hostels in different South African cities in Wilson (1972).

15. See Butchart (1994), Mabin (1986), and Turrell (1984) and (1987), chapter 8. Wasserfall (1990) examines the physical form of the compounds in detail. For a general account of colonial mining development see Christopher (1988), pp. 101–4, and Blainey (1993) on Australian mining.

16. For the chawl, see Burnett-Hurst (1925), and Chitale (1928), which has a plan of one. For labour relations in the Indian jute mills, see Chakrabarty (1981) and (1983).

17. There is a small but growing literature on the Asiatic shophouse. This section draws heavily upon Lim (1993) and Yeoh (1991), especially chapters 3, 4 and 7. My thanks also to Detlef Kammeier for the opportunity to clarify some aspects.

18. There is a substantial literature on present-day problems of informal settlements in Third World cities, but relatively less on the historical background in the colonial period. See, however, articles by Blouet (1977), Doebele (1987), Furedy (1982), Lewandowski (1975) and (1984), Maharaj (1992), Mutale (1993), Neild (1979), Rakodi (1986), and Tikasingh (1973).

19. Sir Granville St. John Orde Brown (1883–1947) served in the Royal Artillery 1902–20, and was Labour Commissioner in Tanganyika 1926–31. He undertook special investigations of labour conditions in Northern Rhodesia 1937, West Indies 1938, West Africa 1939, and the Far East 1941. He was adviser on colonial labour to the Secretary of State for Colonies from 1938, and was knighted in 1947. For his work in Nigeria, see Home (1974), pp. 149–153, and Orde Brown (1941). For Southern Rhodesia, see Phimister (1987).

5

'THE INCONVENIENCE FELT BY EUROPEANS': RACIAL SEGREGATION, ITS RISE AND FALL

The first object of the non-residential area is to segregate Europeans, so that they shall not be exposed to the attacks of mosquitoes which have become infected with the germs of malaria or yellow fever, by preying on Natives, and especially Native Children, whose blood so often contains these germs. It is also valuable as a safeguard against bush fires and those which are so common in Native quarters, especially in the dry season in the Northern Provinces. Finally, it removes the inconvenience felt by Europeans, whose rest is disturbed by drumming and other noises dear to the Native.

(Lugard, 1919, p. 420)

Race has always been a part of colonialism and of colonial urban landscapes. In the words of Anthony King 'The distinctive social characteristic of the colonial city . . . is the fact of race' (King, 1990, p. 34). The spatial separation of races maintained both cultural differences and power relationships, and was not unique to the colonial cities of European expansion. Ancient Indian cities, for instance, were segregated according to occupation and caste. European colonialism, however, increasingly separated the races as an object of urban policy.

Christopher (1992) has attempted to establish the historical extent of segregation within the British colonies. He analysed census returns according to the recognized statistical measure of segregation (the index of dissimilarity). While handicapped by gaps in the statistical and archival record, and by the different racial categories used in different colonies, his broad finding was that Dominion territories in the mid latitudes rarely had to deal with sizeable minorities. Even in the tropics European populations were largely transitory, and structural segregation was only loosely enforced. He found the most severe examples of structural segregation in Africa, especially in South Africa.

Early studies of colonial residential segregation were morphological. More attention is now being given to the dynamic processes over time, to the conflicts and contradictions associated with capital accumulation in a colonial context, and also to the wider implications of ethnic policy for post-colonial nation states' integration into the world economy. The evolution of segregation in the British colonial city was complex, and rarely was there rigid enforcement of legalized segregation. Significantly, the term 'segregation' (in the context of some formal residential separation of races) seems to have arisen at the same time as 'town planning'. Dubow (1989) has traced it to around the year 1908, and it was subsequently associated with the new planning concept of land-use zoning. Formalized racial segregation reached its peak for a brief period between 1900 and 1930. It then declined in importance (other than in South Africa), when extreme applications in Nazi Germany discredited the concept, and the need to maintain loyalty in the colonies made it politically unacceptable.

This chapter is not concerned with exploring the development of racist and social Darwinist thinking, or the elaborate social distinctions which racial classification could create, but to trace their application in practice through land-use policies. Segregation served different purposes in the British Empire over its history.

Here I examine certain defining situations in that evolution: the creation of a new multi-ethnic trading city at Singapore, the impact of defensive and public health requirements in post-Mutiny India, the application of Indirect Rule philosophy in tropical Africa (particularly by Lugard in Northern Nigeria after 1900), and the management of a multi-ethnic society for the interests of mining capitalism (South Africa after 1900).

Throughout this history the inherent difficulty of laying down racial categories was recognized by the architects of racial segregation, and dressed up as something else. Raffles used the word 'respectable', for anyone of whatever race who had adopted western ways and achieved commercial sucess. Lugard said that 'what is aimed at is a segregation of social standards, and not a segregation of races' (1965, p. 150). In South Africa the move towards apartheid was justified as segregation by class.

SEGREGATION AS TAXONOMY: STAMFORD RAFFLES AT SINGAPORE

Racial segregation in the British Empire was developed during the nineteenth century. In the earlier centuries of colonial expansion the whites certainly assumed their racial superiority. Some indication of the resentment it caused is illustrated by the example of a Parsi shipbuilder of Bombay, who during the Napoleonic Wars carved on one of his warships for the British, 'Made by a damned black fellow' (Tindall, 1982). But the whites were few in number, and often lived alongside other races or ethnic groups. On the plantations of the West Indies and the American South slaves and planters lived close together, although on the larger plantations the field slaves had their separate quarters and villages.[1] In India the white traders lived in scattered dwellings, while the non-white population lived in peripheral

areas appropriately labelled 'Black Town'. In Madras, for instance, the Indian merchants laid out their own 'Black Town' near the fort, with its own market and temples, and separate streets for the different castes and trades. While taxed by the British Collector, Black Town operated largely outside the municipal administration, and the British had little interest in its affairs.

The 'Black Hole' of Calcutta incident during the Seven Years War seems to have been instrumental in bringing about a sharp change in European racial attitudes, as a result of which the white population of the Presidency towns became concentrated inside a walled settlement (similar to the Anglo-Norman bastide towns of Wales, Scotland, Ireland, France and elsewhere). The indigenous population was largely banished outside the walls (except for servants), and a maidan or open field of fire was created, which in Madras required the demolition and relocation of Black Town. This racial separation has its legacy in the urban form of Bombay down to the present day.

Stamford Raffles, in his foundation of Singapore in 1819, introduced a more elaborate scheme of racial segregation. It can be best characterized as a taxonomist's approach, based as it was upon Raffles' own hierarchical classification of societies. He reserved separate geographical areas for the different ethnic groups, going beyond a crude division into 'whites' and 'blacks' to distinguish six main groups: European, Chinese, Malay, Indian (called Chulia at the time), Arab, and Bugis (from Celebes). Raffles also sought to distinguish 'the classes engaged in mercantile speculation and those gaining their livelihood by handicrafts and personal labour.' Since Singapore was his planned creation, his role justifies examining in some detail.[2]

Raffles was a conspicuously visionary and capable imperialist, and his ideas anticipated the Indirect Rule or paternalist style of colonialism. One of the few British colonial governors to study in depth the culture, language and customs of the peoples under them, he also acquired a knowledge of Dutch colonial practices as governor of Java during the Napoleonic War. If his vision of the future Singapore as a great trading emporium was to

Statue of Sir Stamford Raffles (1780–1826) on the waterfront in Singapore. His ideas on town planning applied there were widely copied, including the 'five-foot ways' and racial segregation. (Source: The author, photo taken in 1985)

become a reality, he had to attract traders from far and wide, and this was best done by pragmatically guaranteeing them freedom of trade and security in their own areas. He was also establishing a new colony on a largely unsettled island (although Singapore, like other islands acquired by Britain, was not the uninhabited place or *terra nullius* that the British alleged). Raffles seems genuinely to have enjoyed cultural diversity, and sought not only to order the physical landscape, but to the influence the moral and social habits of the people as well. Based upon his study of local history and culture, and his classification of races and classes, he aimed to teach the natives the values of their past, and at the same time introduce them to British laws and customs.

His detailed instructions to the Town Committee in 1822 allocated the 'ground reserved for the Government, European Town and principal mercantile establishments, native divisions or campongs'. The best land went for the government buildings and a padang. The next best land was for 'European Town', where twelve lots of equal size were set aside to be sold at a nominal rate to the first European traders. The street layout was a rectangular grid-iron, with a 'circular carriage road' connecting the different parts of the town. First preference in land allocation went to merchants, second to artisans, and third to farmers.

The Chinese were vital to the success of the new colony. In June 1819, within a few months of taking possession, most of the reported population of five thousand were Chinese. They were allocated land second only to European Town in position, in spite of Raffles' personal dislike of the 'lower classes' of Chinese (whom he called 'supple, venal and crafty'). The Chinese quarter was further subdivided geographically by province, because, as he said, 'the people of one province are more quarrelsome than another, and continued disputes and disturbances take place between peoples of different provinces'.

Three other groups, Arabs, 'Chuliahs' and Malays, were each allocated their own quarter. The Arabs, estimated at between one and two thousand in the early years, were kept as far as possible from the Europeans, and the followers of Islam were grouped together. The least civilized group (in Raffles' view), the Bugis from Celebes, were allocated the farthest edge of the settlement, but even they were incorporated in the plan, with regular roads. The huts they had built on first arrival were pulled down on Raffles' orders, and rebuilding was only allowed in accordance with his plan and regulations.

To manage this multicultural society Raffles appointd headmen or captains for each ethnic group, apparently drawing upon his knowledge of Dutch and Portuguese practice in Java and Malacca. The Dutch in Malacca had taken over from the Portuguese the Kapitan or Captain system, itself probably derived from Malay and Muslim practice, whereby a headman was personally responsible to the authorities for law and order within his own community. A captain was normally appointed for life, and it was not unusual for a post to become hereditary, creating a kind of local aristocracy. The captain was often responsible for revenue raising through tax farms, and might have a monopoly of certain goods and services (such as the rice market, the slaughter-house, and the town tavern). This administrative device relieved the government of the problem and expense of raising a revenue through personal taxation from among a heterogeneous population. Malacca's governor decided in 1828, however, that the captain system was 'of a nature which cannot be accommodated to the new system of judicial administration'. He discontinued the system and pensioned off the office holders, although an informal version survived through the president of the Chinese temple,

For the socially and culturally tenacious Chinese at least, the captaincy had responded to a felt need for intelligible leadership within the framework of a

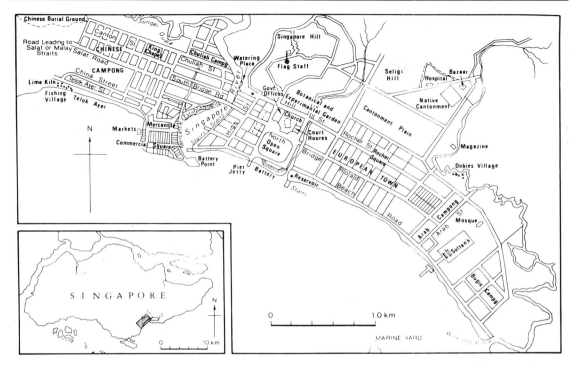

Raffles' plan for the segregation of the races in Singapore, derived from Lt Jackson's plan of 1822. The European town and Chinese kampong are either side of the central business and government area, while the other ethnic groups (Arabs), Bugis, Chuliahs, and 'natives', i.e. Malays) are in smaller campongs around the periphery. (Source: Eng, 1992)

society governed by the unfamiliar methods of the West. (Harrison, 1985, pp. 11–12 and 105–106)

From his time in Java Raffles had noted that Malay society was based upon detached village societies with elected chiefs, and at Singapore he allotted each group a kampong or village, to act 'as a stabilizing influence on the natives as they became acclimatized to urban society'. He appointed 'one native Captain or Headman with one or more lieutenants or Assistants' to be responsible for the different groups, and instructed his Town committee to 'call upon the heads of the principal classes of natives to be present at your deliberations, explaining to them the object of your appointment and the desire of the Government in associating them with you, that the interest of all should be only

considered in the arrangements adopted. This was a precursor of later Indirect Rule practice.

Raffles' Town Committee allocated street and place names associated with the different ethnic and regional groups, and these names continued an unofficial dichotomy between European and Asian residential areas. The naming of places proved to be an important negotiated area in the control of urban space. A proposal to name a street Bombay Road in 1925, for instance, was opposed by the Indian community, because it preserved an unwanted association with Indian convicts who had been transported to Singapore. Asian names for streets and places developed informally within certain conventions and parameters set by each community. By contrast with municipal street names, Chinese place names seldom performed commemorative functions, but used daily landmarks and material symbols (e.g. 'foot of the big well' 'eight small buildings' or 'mouth of the gambling houses'), or reference to headquarters of secret societies (Yeoh 1991, chapter 2).

Although there was no legalized racial segregation, Raffles' scheme of ethnic segregation in Singapore worked for a while, since territorial concentration by race and dialect group accommodated new migrants' need for mutual support mechanisms. His methods were remembered and copied by later colonial administrators, especially Lugard in Nigeria.

Segregation for Defence: Indian Cantonments and the 1857 Revolt

In India, as the British extended their control from the Presidency towns into the interior, they found that, instead of the Indians living outside cities of European creation, it was the turn of the Europeans to live outside the Indian cities. From this situation grew the cantonment or garrison camp, an important mechanism for racial segregation.

The first cantonment created by the occupying British seems to have been at Pune (Poona) in 1817. The idea of a separate, self-sufficient camp for the military was not, however, new to India: ancient Vedic texts classify as many as seven types of such camps (Begde, 1982, chapter 2). The British cantonments, most of which were built between 1845 and 1855, were usually located a few miles from the native city. They were complete, self-contained communities, comprising infantry, cavalry and artillery quarters (subdivided between European and Indian), parade grounds, cemeteries, religious buildings, and bazaars. There were separate barracks for married and unmarried soldiers, and spacious residential plots for the European officers. Army manuals recommended the proportional land areas: for instance, cavalry 23 per cent, officer compounds 21 per cent, infantry 18 per cent, bazaar 18 per cent, artillery 15 per cent, community buildings 5 per cent (Abdul Sattar, 1965). The cantonment has been described as 'a petrified camp . . . in strictest lines of symmetry . . . entirely devoid of grace. All was

logic and functionalism' (Morris, 1983, pp. 89–93). As Tony King, in his study of the sociology of the cantonment, has written:

segregation . . . helped the group to maintain its own self-identity, essential in the performance of its role within the colonial social and political system. They provided a culturally familiar and easily recognisable environment which – like dressing for dinner – was a formal, visible symbol providing psychological and emotional security in a world of uncertain events. (King, 1976, p. 39)

The violent events of 1857–58 (called the Indian Mutiny by the British, the Great Revolt by the Indians) painfully exposed the defects and excesses of East India Company rule, which was soon replaced by direct Crown Rule. The numbers of white troops were substantially increased to about a third of the Indian Army's total strength, reaching over seventy thousand in the 1880s. The British had learned that 'traditional' societies would only tolerate less direct and obvious control, and the cantonments became racially and physically more separated, as the British civilian population moved in with the military. Defence and public health arguments, combined with theories of white racial superiority, were used to justify this segregation of the white colonial community. We are fortunate in having meticulous studies of these changes for two of the cities of northern India closely involved in the Mutiny. Gupta (1981) has traced the history of Delhi over a century, while Oldenburg (1984) has analysed in depth the British reconstruction of Lucknow in the two decades following the Mutiny. Delhi was the great Mogul capital, while Lucknow, capital of the nawabs of Oudh, could claim to be the largest and most prosperous precolonial city in the subcontinent.

The trauma of the Mutiny broke many links between British and Indian political and cultural institutions. Behind the 'illusion of permanence' a lasting fear of revolt was implanted in the minds of the British, a sense of insecurity best summed up in the phrase 'mutiny-watching'. Before the Mutiny British officials and Indian citizens had often lived and worked side by side, and British officials involved themselves in urban improvement projects in the cities. After it British officials moved away from the city into the so-called 'Civil Lines'. Even the missionaries rather shamefacedly opted to live there instead of in the city, where their work would have been more effective. In Delhi after the Mutiny, following a prolonged debate, the civilian and military dispositions were reversed: European troops were stationed within the walled city, with a 500-yard open fire zone around the Fort, while the Civil Lines were located to the north, away from the native city, in which Englishmen had formerly worked and lived. The land within the walls of the fort became 'a kind of howling desert of barracks, hideous, British and pretentious' (Val C. Prinsep in 1879, quoted in Gupta, 1982, p. 57). From the 1890s the club and those British offices which had remained inside the city of Delhi also moved out, partly because of the fear of plague.

A consequence of the Revolt was also that large parts of those Indian cities associated with the violence, especially Delhi, Lucknow and Kanpur, were systematically destroyed by the British, for reasons of revenge and military security. Some two-fifths of the city of Lucknow were demolished, removing the twisting lanes which had made it an ideal city for riot and insurrection. Places of public assembly, such as mosques and temples, were singled out for destruction, and houses were demolished without even notice to the inhabitants to vacate. The mosque was used as a military barracks where 'British troops ate pork, swilled alcohol, trampled the sacred hall in regimental boots, and manifested every other kind of contempt for the religion of the old rulers of the province' (Oldenburg, 1984, p. 36). Gupta has described the psychological effect of the demolitions in Delhi:

At one sweep the face of the city, so lovingly built by Shahjahan, was transformed. What the Government decided was necessary for its security led to some of the loveliest buildings of the city being destroyed . . . When the dust of the demolitions had settled down, the people of Delhi rubbed their tired eyes and looked in vain for their familiar landmarks, and did not find them. 'Where is Delhi?,' moaned Ghalib. 'By God, it is not a city now. It is a camp. It is a cantonment . . .' (Gupta 1981, p. 30)

These destructions of Delhi and Lucknow were largely planned by one man, Colonel Robert Napier of the Bengal Engineers, later Lord Napier of Magdala.[3] He had observed the public works improvements in English towns, worked on the building of Darjeeling after 1838, and already designed a new cantonment at Ambala. His 'Memorandum on the Military Occupation of the City of Lucknow' (March 1858) contained the blueprint for remodelling the city by opening broad streets with a 600-yard wide esplanade in the most heavily populated and built-up area of the city, as well as the plan for the new cantonment.

This crude assertion of power carved straight new roads, typically 150 feet wide, through the crowded city. In Lucknow the British ignored the river-oriented logic of the city and destroyed the integrity of the *mohallas* (aristocratic quarters). Patrick Geddes was later, in 1916, to criticize these wide streets as 'monotonous' and 'unbeautiful as they are destructive and costly' (Oldenburg 1984, chapter 2). In Delhi the railway was built through the city, instead of outside, adding to the destruction but making for greater security in the event of a local uprising.

The new Lucknow cantonment, one of the largest in India, came into being after a reconnaissance by three key local colonial officials – the civil surgeon, political commissioner and the military engineer. A plateau of high land was chosen, well drained and well raised with no trees, and several villages demolished to make way for the cantonment. More than three thousand acres of valuable land, more than a third of the city's total area, with an annual revenue demand of nearly twelve thousand rupees, was confiscated. There was no prior negotiation with the lawful owners, and compensation was eventually paid at a fraction of its value.

These cantonments imposed a new order on India's cities. As described by Oldenburg (1984, pp. 59 and 263):

In their own unflamboyant, understated, and bureaucratic style the military and civilian officers who undertook the reconstruction of Lucknow and other war-ravaged cities of the north Indian plain unleashed a revolution in social control and with a quiet efficiency succeeded in institutionalizing it . . . The old city of Lucknow was blighted and is today a striking example of urban decay that is ubitiquitous in the old sections of the once splendid regional centers of northern India. What thrived was the 'new city', which was a spacious complex of the cantonment, the civil, police and railway 'lines'. The British created, as the nawabs had once done, an alien and exclusive cosmos that was based on the culture and value system of the metropolitan society.

When the British architect-planner, H. V. Lanchester, Patrick Geddes' associate, visited India during the First World War, he wrote of the physical environment of the cantonment that:

It is generally loosely and somewhat carelessly laid out, sites having been taken up from time to time according to the taste of the official requiring a house, and subsequently linked up as far as practicable under the Public Works Department. Every European likes to isolate himself in a large compound so as to secure privacy from his neighbour, or rather from his neighbour's servants; everyone drives, so distance is of little consequence (the Cantonment often covers a larger area than the town), but such large compounds are far too extensive for cultivation as gardens; at their best they simulate a park, at their worst a desert . . . The European pins his faith to the Cantonment because its open layout and scattered houses secure it against epidemics and against noise and other drawbacks. It has few other merits, though there is no reason why it should not have been properly laid out at the start, and even now some are not past redemption. (Lanchester, 1916–17, pp. 92–93)

Ultimately the biggest example of defensive segregation in British India arose from the decision to move its capital to New Delhi. The British portrayed this as an example of their unfaltering determination to maintain British rule in India. In practice it was largely undertaken to escape the violent political atmosphere of Calcutta since Curzon's 1905 partition of Bengal, the revocation of which was Britain's first defeat in dealing with Indian nationalists (Metcalf, 1989, chapter 7). After a lengthy discussion of how the new capital should be administered, it was eventually decided that the Cantonment Code was the appropriate model, because it conferred many powers not given by the various Municipal Acts. A segregated administration was maintained, and within the new city residential areas were highly classified according to status. The urban design of New Delhi was used to highlight the locus of imperial power, and at the same time to remove it from general public access.

The cantonment in India was not only physically distinct and racially segregated, but was a separate administrative unit managed by a committee. Although it received a municipal subsidy from the city, it was considered outside the municipal limits and without any reciprocal obligations to it. A separate regulatory code was consolidated in a Cantonments Act in 1889, and later revised in 1910 and 1924. The seventeen chapters of the Cantonments Act of

1924 amounted to a complete code of local government. They dealt with the definition and delimitation of cantonments, constitution of cantonment boards, liquor licensing, property tax and finance, contract administration, nuisance control and public safety, sanitation and disease prevention and control, street and building control, market and trading controls, water-supply and drainage, and 'suppression of sexual immorality' (Butt, 1990). These privileged enclaves, of which over a hundred were created in British India, often survived and were even enlarged in the post-Independence period, with their colonial management regulations still intact.

Segregation for Health: The 'Sanitation Syndrome'

Entwined with the defensive considerations in the creation of cantonments were concerns of public health and sanitation. As the Cantonments Manual put it in 1909:

it should be carefully borne in mind that the cardinal principle underlying the administration of cantonments in India is that the cantonments exist primarily for the health of British troops and to considerations affecting the well-being and efficiency of the garrison, all other matters must give place' (King, 1976, p. 118).

The fear of death or invaliding from epidemic diseases haunted the British in India. Within a few years of the Crimean War and the Indian Mutiny the high death rates among British troops at home and abroad brought about a radical review of health provisions (see pp. 94–95). A Royal Commission on the sanitary state of the army in Britain in 1857–61 was soon followed by similar commissions on India and the Mediterranean stations. The Royal Commission in India (1863) found annual death rates of 69 per thousand enlisted men over the period 1800–56, compared with 38 for officers and 20 for European civil servants. Apart from the scale of human tragedy implied by these figures, the Commission calculated that a force of 70,000 Europeans would cost £200,000 annually in Europe, but an additional £388,000 in tropical service because of sickness alone.

In the absence of scientific knowledge about the causes of epidemics before the advent of microscopy and the 'germ theory', the Chadwick model for improving public health assumed disease to be caused by bad air, atmospheric impurities linked to decaying animal and vegetable matter. The conditions which could temper the intensity and frequency of disease were known: proper drainage, better housing and ventilation, better sewage disposal and watersupply. In the tropics an additional measure was the creation of distinct areas for European residence. The Royal Commission in India set a target of reducing the death rate to 20 per thousand, and that was met within a decade, not because of specific medical remedies, but a range of empirical measures, which included relocation. The Military Cantonments Act XXII of 1864 was the first comprehensive public health legislation for the British in India, instituting sanitary police under the overall charge of medical officers. Physical separating walls were to be built between the European and Indian populations to prevent the spread of 'miasmas'. The principles of cantonment planning were also extended to the native areas through the Sanitary Commissions created in 1864 for the three presidencies (Curtin, 1989, pp. 159–160).

After this success in reducing European mortality in the tropics, doctors grew in status and became all-purpose experts, and Western medicine obtained its greatest importance in imperial ideology and practice between 1880 and 1930. This was the period when European empires were at their most expansive and assertive, and new trade, transport and imperial ties were assisting the spread of disease vectors, particularly mosquitoes, flies and lice. A spate of laws, proclamations and decrees gave state sanction to various health measures, especially in response to the plague epidemics. In an era of competitive imperialism persistently high levels of epidemic mortality were a mark of poor colonial management, and the association of diseases like smallpox, plague, cholera and malaria with the indigenous population deepened European suspicions of that population. Fear of catching native diseases thus provided a pretext for segregation, which became 'a general rubric of sanitary administration set by the Imperial government for all tropical colonies' (Dumett, 1968, p. 71). The campaign for better sanitation was concerned with order, openness, ventilation and the spatial demarcation of different activities.

The leading expert on tropical sanitation in the early twentieth century was Dr. Simpson, who was happy to blame dirty 'native', and especially Asiatic, health practices for causing disease. He claimed, for instance, that the lack of pure water in the crowded tropical cities was 'mainly due to the pollution to which the water is subjected by the customs of the people' (quoted in Curtin, 1989, p. 109). Lecturing in South Africa on plague prevention in 1900, he declared that Cape Town was, after Bombay, the city most suited to plague, because of its heterogeneous population and their dirty habits, thus displaying prejudices 'which were a good deal more rampant than any expressed by local doctors' (Van Heyningen, 1979, p. 470).

Simpson also advocated putting as much distance as possible between the races, particularly between the Europeans and Asians:

The [European] house should not be surrounded by nor close to native huts. Native children are seldom not infected with malaria, and hence living in a dwellinghouse in this position increases the risk

of infection from that disease. (Simpson, 1916, chapter 3).

Lugard was soon echoing these words in his writing on Indirect Rule:

malarial germs – and at times those of yellow-fever also – are present in the blood of most natives, especially of native children, and their dark huts and insanitary surroundings foster mosquitoes, by which these diseases are conveyed. Doctors, therefore, urge that that Europeans should not sleep in proximity to natives, in order to avoid infection.' (Lugard, 1965, pp. 148–150)

Simpson and Lugard thus echoed the views of Dr. Ross, the discoverer of the cause of malaria, who thought children were a prime source of infection. Lugard's first annual report on Northern Nigeria in 1900 described moving the native town some six miles from the army camp, which he claimed would have the benefit of removing 'the proximity of a haven for thieves and prostitutes, the infection of mosquitoes with malarial germs, and the insanitary condition inevitable around a large native town' (quoted in Urquhart, 1977, p. 26).

From these medical ideas came the segregation of European Reservations by a non-residential area (sometimes called a building-free zone). Lugard advocated a width of 440 yards, while Simpson in East Africa in 1914 was content with 300 yards (Curtin, 1985). Although the flying range of a mosquito was probably not known, Lugard wrote of the need for the zone to be wide enough not to offer 'resting-places for mosquitoes' (Lugard, 1965, p. 150). The arbitrary nature of the recommended widths is shown by the view in the 1930s of a planner working on the Haifa Bay project that the flying range of an anopheles mosquito was quite different, about three kilometres (Hyman, 1994, p. 613), a distance which, if it could have been proven, would have made both Simpson and Lugard wrong.

The enforcement of strict racial segregation by a non-building zone was, however, soon abandoned. The Colonial Office decided in

1923 that segregation in East Africa by legislation was unjustified, while recognizing that 'in practice the different races will, by natural affinity, keep together in separate quarters' (quoted in Curtin, 1985). The colonial administrators recognized 'that rigid insistence on racial segregation, as laid down by Professor Simpson, would involve fatal dislocation of trade and unwarranted expense to the Government' (Mirams, 1931–32).

SEGREGATION AS 'TRUSTEESHIP': LUGARDIAN INDIRECT RULE

Apart from defence and health arguments, the British also justified racial segregation in the context of a trusteeship for the 'subject' peoples. As expressed by Lugard for Nigeria:

The British role here is to bring to the country all the gains of civilisation by applied science (whether in the development of material resources, or the eradication of disease, etc.), with as little interference as possible with Native customs and modes of thought. (Lugard, 1919, p. 9)

Renamed the 'Dual Mandate' or 'Indirect Rule' it became the semi-official approach to British colonial administration in the years between the two World Wars, and strongly influenced the apartheid ideology in South Africa. Indirect Rule can be traced to British colonial practice in the princely states of India after 1857, those two-fifths of Indian territory which remained under traditional rulers. The British strengthened princely authority, but supervised it with British 'resident commissioners'. The princes were expected to become both traditional and modern, 'rooted in the past yet participants in the creation of a new India'.[4] The Indian approach was then transferred to the Malay States and Africa in the expansion of British colonialism in the late nineteenth century.

An ardent advocate was C.L. Temple, Lieutenant Governor of Northern Nigeria between 1914 and 1917, a 'speculative and rather individual kind of Socialist' who 'believed almost fanatically that (native society) should be kept inviolate from the disintegration of western influence'. After his retirement to South Africa he wrote a book, *Native Races and Their Rulers* (1918), setting out his philosophy and showing 'some reflection of local views of social segregation' (introduction to Temple, 1918). An autocrat and indeed proto-fascist, he believed in strong leadership:

I submit that the phrase 'Government by the masses' is meaningless, however admirable may be the ideal which it is intended to convey. It is an obvious truth that the actions of weaker individuals are controlled by the stronger individual.[5]

Much of Temple's thinking seemed to have been absorbed by the more famous Lord Lugard, his boss in Northern Nigeria whom he heartily disliked. Lugard's book, *The Dual Mandate in British Tropical Africa*, which he wrote 'to get on paper all his long accumulated ideas about colonial government', was published in 1922, went into four editions by 1929, and was reprinted in 1965 during the 'winds of change' period of African independence. In it he wrote:

Europe is in Africa for the mutual benefit of her own industrial classes, and of the native races in their progress to a higher plane . . . it is the aim and desire of civilised administration to fulfil this dual mandate . . . As Roman imperialism laid the foundations of modern civilisation, and led the wild barbarians of these islands along the path of progress, so in Africa to-day we are repaying the debt, and bringing to the dark places of the earth, the abode of barbarism and cruelty, the torch of culture of progress, while ministering to the material needs of our own civilisation.[6]

He combined this with a white supremacist view of the subject peoples, describing the 'typical' Bantu African as:

a happy, thriftless, excitable person, lacking in self-control, discipline, and foresight, naturally

Traditional African compound in Kano, Nigeria. Lugardian Indirect Rule or the 'Dual Mandate' sought to keep 'native' society separate from western influence. The old walled city of Kano was one place kept free of urban renewal schemes. (Source: The author, photo taken in 1985)

courageous, and naturally courteous and polite, full of personal vanity, with little sense of veracity, fond of music, and loving weapons as an oriental loves jewelry . . . it is extremely difficult at present to find educated African youths who are by character and temperament suited to posts in which they may rise to positions of high administrative responsibility. (Lugard, 1965, pp. 69 and 488)

To achieve the so-called 'dual mandate' Lugard in Nigeria created a dual structure of local government: Native Authorities for the 'native' population, and, in an evolution from the Indian cantonment, the Townships. The Townships Ordinance of 1917 abandoned the terms 'Government Station' and 'Cantonment' (which had been used in the earlier Cantonment Proclamation of 1904), and instead the township was defined as 'an enclave outside the jurisdiction of the native authority and native courts, which are thus relieved of the

difficult task (which is foreign to their functions) of controlling alien natives and employees of the government and Europeans' (Lugard, 1919, p. 419). The 1917 Ordinance dressed up the cantonment concept as a progressive approach to municipal government, providing for 'the creation, constitution and administration of all towns and municipalities in Nigeria with the exception of those native towns where the population is sufficiently homogeneous for it to be administered by a Native Authority' (which in practice were the vast majority of towns). Townships mostly had the same physical relationship to existing towns as the cantonments had to Indian towns and cities. A total of 74 Townships were gazetted under the Ordinance (all but two of them before 1920), and were graded into three classes 'according to the degree of municipal responsibility'. First class Townships (of which Lagos was the only one in Nigeria) had an appointed town council, and the other classes were administered by a British colonial official, assisted in the case of second-class townships by an advisory board. Many of the third-class townships were never actually brought into operation.[7]

The workaholic Lugard prescribed highly detailed regulations for the physical planning of Nigerian Townships in his political Memorandum No. 11, which was more detailed than the cantonments regulations in India. The Europeans were to be segregated from the Africans in a cantonment-style

REVISION OF

INSTRUCTIONS

TO

POLITICAL OFFICERS

ON SUBJECTS CHIEFLY

POLITICAL & ADMINISTRATIVE.

1913-1918.

PRINTED BY
WATERLOW AND SONS LIMITED, LONDON WALL, LONDON.
1919.

Title page of Lugard's Political Memoranda. Written when he was Governor-General of Nigeria, it was later revised and incorporated into his best-selling Dual Mandate. Memorandum No. 11 deals with regulations for townships and segregation. (Source: Lugard, 1919)

European Reservation (later called a European Residential Area or ERA). Plots or 'compounds' were large: Lugard recommended 100 yards deep, with 70–100 yard frontages (i.e. a total area of up to a hectare), the house to be set back usually 20 yards from the frontage. Servants' quarters and stables were to be located near the backline of the plot, where there was to be a conservancy lane. No natives except *bona fide* domestic servants' were allowed to live in the European Reservation. There were also detailed rules for roads and land subdivision in the Native Reservations: main streets to be 100 feet wide, no specification of plot sizes, but site coverage with buildings not to exceed a third, eaves of all buildings to be at least 6 feet from the boundary, the number of occupants not to exceed ten. The Native Hospital should be near the prison, 'so that the Medical Officer can visit both at the same time, and sick prisoners can be easily transferred, a single guard sufficing for both' (Lugard, 1910, pp. 405–422). The Lugardian doctrine of Indirect Rule required not only that Europeans lived in ERAs but also that they should not live anywhere else. In 1915 Lugard forced two British ex-administrators, who had created a trading company, to stop living in the old city of Kano, and the government paid the not inconsiderable sum (for those days) of a thousand pounds in compensation for them to relocate (Home, 1983).

This space-consuming planning approach needed a large acquisition of land by the government, to the practicalities of which Lugard adopted a lofty attitude:

It is still a matter of indifference to the people whether Government takes up a few square miles, here for a township, or there for a railway, or elsewhere as leases to commercial, mining, agricultural or ranching companies. Even if occupiers are expropriated in the neighbourhood of a large town, there is as a rule abundant land elsewhere in the great unoccupied spaces of this vast country. (Lugard, 1919, p. 29)

In practice, however, conflict often arose over the colonial government's demands for land, especially to maintain the building-free zone (BFZ, sometimes called the 'neutral zone' or 'green belt'). When the Ibadan BFZ was to be extended in 1941, seventy houses in the Sabo quarter would have needed demolition, and the chiefs felt that no money payment could compensate the people for the loss of their homes and land.

Within a few years of Lugard's departure from Nigeria in 1918, colonial doctors were no longer convinced of the medical justification for segregation. They pressed at the West African Medical Conference in Accra in 1925 for the abolition of B class townships, because of the large area required for their layout and the sacrifice of valuable building sites for the BFZ (Home, 1974). In 1928 the Residents' Conference resolved that Europeans should not be permitted to live in native towns, but in practice it became increasingly difficult to stop, for instance, merchants, hospital staff and missionaries from doing so. They were, however, subjected to minor inconveniences, such as not being able to claim special police protection, and having their postal services in the European area. It also became increasingly difficult to justify the racial exclusiveness of ERAs. Non-Europeans were gradually allowed to live in the ERA, with revised building leases to preserve the standards and amenities, and

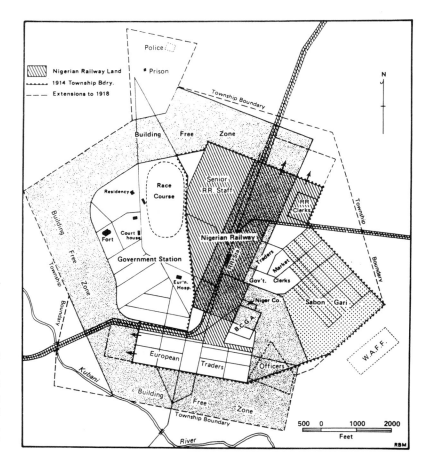

Applying segregation in Zaria Township, Northern Nigeria. This 1914 plan shows the application of Lugard's Indirect Rule principles. (Source: Urquhart, 1977)

the ERA was renamed the Government Residential Area (GRA) in 1938 to reflect changing reality and remove the racial connotations. By 1945 official colonial policy in Nigeria was to allow residence according to 'standard of living and not colour of skin', although the rent would be reduced for Europeans compelled to live next to an African! By 1948 the official view was that it was 'objectionable' for government to acquire and lay out special residential areas for occupation by its own servants and by other Europeans, which should be a function for the newly-created Town Planning Authorities.

The colonial administration in Northern Nigeria thus found racially-segregated zoning

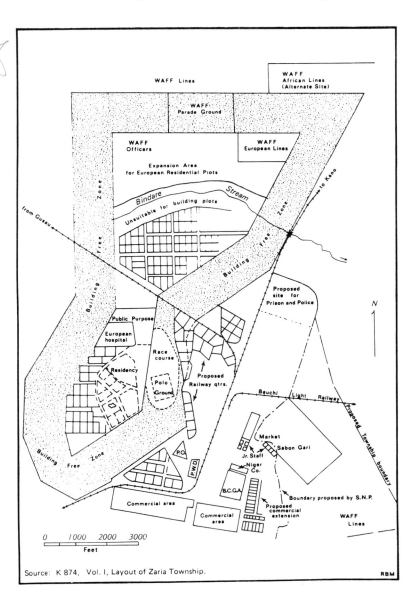

This 1926 plan for the expansion of Zaria Township further separated the white colonial administrators from the commercial areas and the 'Native' population. (Source: Urquhart, 1977)

Source: K 874, Vol. I, Layout of Zaria Township.

increasingly impracticable and embarrassing. It could also no more preserve the 'native' society from outside influences (including the other ethnic groups migrating into and within Nigeria) than King Canute could keep back the waves. Specific tribal or racial classifications would have been politically unacceptable, not to mention unenforceable, so Lugard resorted to other clumsy and overlapping categories: aliens, strangers, native foreigners, non-native foreigners. He distinguished an 'alien' (someone not subject to the native courts and not allowed to acquire rights in land) from a 'stranger', whom he defined as 'a Native of Nigeria who does not belong to the tribe or community having control of the land'. He further subdivided 'strangers' into:

(a) Strangers who enter a community with the intention of identifying themselves in all respects with it, and who are content to hold land on such terms as Native customary law allows.
(b) Strangers who wish to acquire land for permanent cultivation, or to erect permanent houses for trade, and who desire to substitute an individual interest and title for the communal tenure under which the members of the community hold their land, and to obtain safeguards for undisturbed occupation.
(c) Strangers who acquire land for speculation, etc. (this group being defined by Lugard, one is not surprised to learn, as 'undesirable'). (Lugard, 1919, p. 417)

'Native foreigners' were Africans from outside Nigeria, usually from the Gold Coast or Sierra Leone, and 'non-native foreigners' embraced such small groups as Syrian or Lebanese traders. Such categories as a basis of residence became impossible to sustain in practice, and created absurdities. Thus Yoruba whose parents were born in Kano and who submitted to Native Authority law were allowed to continue living in the walled city, but not if they wore European clothes.

Between the 'native' population on the one hand, and the 'Europeans' on the other, were a proliferation of other groups, defined in relation to the Dual Mandate principle, which

Lugard intended should usually stay in the Townships in a 'Non-European' or 'Native' Reservation. In his words,

Only Aliens not ordinarily subject to the jurisdiction of a Native court, who reside for purposes of trade and access to a railway siding, or Natives who are employees of Europeans, or artisans, and those who minister to the requirements of the community, should as a general rule be allowed to live in the actual precincts of a Township. Carriers and temporary labourers will not usually do. (Lugard, 1919, p. 417)

Later, when tin mining developed in the Plateau region of Northern Nigeria, the local tribes were discouraged from working in the mines, and 'Hausa village areas' were created under a separate administration. The numbers of labourers in the tin mines grew from 12,000 in 1912, to 38,000 in 1931, and to 71,000 in 1942 (Home 1974, chapter 5). No 'stranger' was allowed to spend more than one night in any Hausa settlement without satisfying the village head of his character.

In other colonies alternative segregatory strategies were devised. In the Sudan, under the joint Anglo-Egyptian 'condominium', Khartoum was zoned into three 'classes', arranged in bands parallel to the river. First Class land, reserved for British administrators, was on the banks of the Nile, where 'owing to the proximity of the water supply, gardens, which are so necessary for the comfort of Europeans, can be much more easily and economically made' (McLean in 1912, quoted in Home, 1990b, p. 5). Second Class land was reserved for Egyptian officials, businessmen and others of lesser social status. The native Sudanese were relegated to Third Class land, furthest from the river. In practice relatively few of them chose to live in Khartoum, but preferred Khartoum North or Omdurman, which, being both 'native' towns, were allocated no First or Second Class land. These distinctions were reflected in the building regulations. Mud structures were only allowed on Third Class land, while on First and Second

Class land the outer walls of all buildings were required to be of 'stone, burnt brick or concrete, or of mud brick faced with burnt brick'. Plot ratios were specified of 0.5 for First and Second Class housing ('in order to permit the free circulation of air'), 0.67 for Third Class housing, and 0.75 for non-residential buildings.

If, in Nigeria, segregation of the Europeans in Reservations proved ultimately impracticable, Non-European Reservations based upon some muddled 'dual mandate' principle of keeping 'natives' apart from 'strangers' and 'native foreigners' stood even less chance of implementation. In some Northern towns, notably Kano and Zaria, Sabon Garis (or Strangers Quarters) were established. In Kano, the arrival of the railway was followed by the laying out of a 'Traders' Township' or Sabon Gari, initially with 300 compounds of 100 × 50 feet and a market square. But this created problems for Township administration. Its residents became too vocal, pressing for improved services which the township budget could not (or would not) provide, and for more representation on the Township Advisory Board. There were constant disputes over land and tenancies. Perhaps most important of all, to the British, it was an anomaly in the Indirect Rule system. So in 1926 the Residents' Conference decided to transfer the Kano and Zaria Sabon Garis to Native Authority control, and it was finally done in 1940. The Resident of Kano Province in 1926 showed the acute distaste felt by Indirect Rule administration for these 'native foreigners':

The hordes of Gold Coast middlemen and so on hang about the skirts of the market in the busy season, infest the roads, and tout for produce when they can, and in the slack season appear to live mainly on the earnings of immoral women, or by acquiring plots and subletting rooms and huts to prostitutes . . . The existence in proximity to the City of an enclave of disrepute is an obvious danger to the Emirate, from a general point of view and in particular in view of the fact that intoxication is more prevalent in Sabon Gari than elsewhere.

(Resident Alexander in 1926, quoted in Home, 1976)

The main, if spurious, justification for transfer at the time was given as financial. The British claimed that the major programme of road and drain construction, which the Sabon Gari needed, was beyond the Township's financial capacity, but could be afforded by the Native Authority (although that body afterwards made no attempt to undertake it). In 1951 the political and physical separation of the indigenous and immigrant communities in Kano was confirmed by the creation of separate councils: the Kano City Council for the old city and the Waje Town Council for the Sabon Gari. The latter soon established a sound revenue base from market and lorry park dues, and became a successful local authority. Such separation of communities, which British Indirect Rule had actively fostered, contributed to the intercommunal violence of 1966–67 which preceded the Nigerian civil war (Home, 1976).

The Cantonment/Township model, being based on segregation of people rather than activities, proved incompatible with the new-style land-use zoning which began to make its appearance in the 1920s. The British officials debated the possibility of dividing Lugard's 'European Reservation' into an ERA and a Residential-cum-Business Area, where Europeans could both trade and reside, and non-Europeans could trade but not reside. The mining town of Enugu, for instance, was divided into an ERA, a Residential-cum-Business Area, a Building-free zone, and native 'locations' forming a crescent around the periphery. In 1928 a stricter approach to separating residential from other activities was being advocated: Townships were to be divided into ERAs and Business Areas 'which may be further subdivided into Administrative and Business, Commercial, Industrial and African Residential Zones'. In practice such clumsy land-use zonings proved unpractical, and those Cantonment/Townships that have

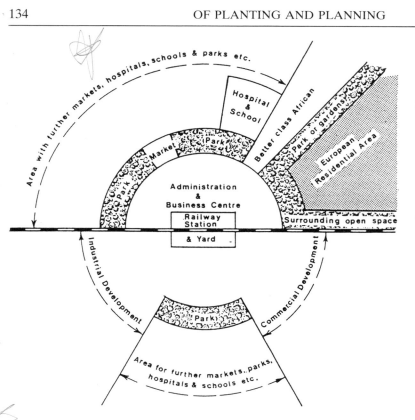

'Suggested principles for the planning of new towns'. This application of Lugard's approach was produced by the Directors of Public Works and Medical Services in Nigeria after his departure. First prepared in 1929, it was revised in 1939. The European Residential Area, segregated by a park, soon became politically unacceptable in the Second World War and was renamed the Government Residential Area. (Source: Evans and Pirie, 1939)

Below: Trading plots by the railway line in Northern Nigeria. This shows the separation of European from non-uropean plots. (Source: Urquhart, 1977)

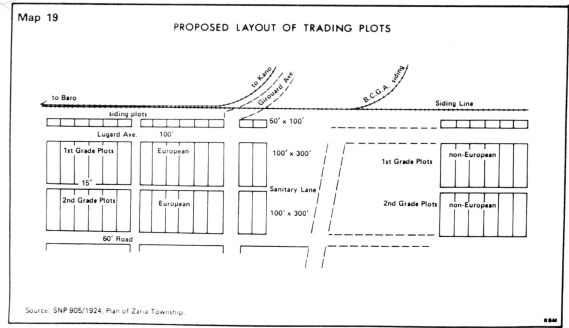

Map 19

PROPOSED LAYOUT OF TRADING PLOTS

Source: SNP 905/1924, Plan of Zaria Township.

survived in India and Africa remain mixed use areas, subject to a gradual process of densification as large plots are subdivided.

In other colonial empires similar approaches were followed. In French North Africa, for instance, Marshal Lyautey's concept of the dual city replaced the French colonial concept of assimilation with one of association, and preserved the traditional alongside the modern town, with a separating zone (Wright, 1987).

The underlying planning approach, however, remained, and contributed to fragmenting the urban form of many Nigerian towns, especially in Northern Nigeria (Mabogunje, 1968). Winston Churchill, a confirmed racist, as Colonial Secretary in 1921 had been proposing elaborate rules for the 'segregation of races and town planning' in Nigeria, proposing five categories of Township (more even than Lugard) according to the degree of physical segregation, and these were modified in memoranda in 1926 and 1927. In 1929 the Directors of Public Works and Medical Services prepared a document, *Memorandum on the General Principles to be followed in the Selection of Sites for, and the Laying Out of, Towns and European Residential Areas in Nigeria* (Evans and Pirie, 1929), which contained some principles of segregation, and was still nominally official policy into the 1950s (Urquhart, 1977). So Lugard's model of Indirect Rule and Townships, based upon the unachievable aim of protecting 'native' society against corrupting outside influences, contained such contradictions that it was soon seen to be largely unworkable. By 1934 (only sixteen years after Lugard's departure) the official policy in Nigeria was progressively to abolish Townships.

Segregation by Zoning: The South African Case

Both Simpson and Lugard (who were close contemporaries) had passed their sell-by date when land-use zoning appeared as a new concept in the 1920s, deriving from German and American experience. Had it been available, they would probably have seized upon it as an instrument for segregation. Zoning in the United States was intended to protect good-quality residential areas from incompatible uses such as apartment-blocks and other forms of low-income housing, and was applied by southern progressives to enforce racial segregation, Baltimore passing the first racial zoning ordinance in 1910. Although racial zoning was soon declared unconstitutional by the Supreme Court in 1917, it survived in the American South as 'expulsive' zoning, which allowed the intrusion into black neighbourhoods of disruptive uses. Racial discrimination was also evident in the use of public health powers to displace small independent Chinese laundry operators with steam-powered machines in California in the years before the First World War (Logan, 1976; Silver, 1991).

Within the British Empire the white settler societies had attempted segregation by regulation in the second half of the nineteenth century, particularly with the arrival of Asian immigrant labour (both Indian and Chinese). In the 1870s, for instance, the town of Lawrence, New Zealand, had regulations forbidding Chinese miners from living in the town, so that a separate Chinese shanty settlement grew up outside. In Singapore in 1904 the public health officials were concerned by the risk of 'the increasing invasion of the European residential quarters by native houses, especially those of the Chinese shophouse class' (Dr. Kirk, quoted in Yeoh, 1991, p. 102).

It was South Africa that experienced the most complex reaction to the multi-racial character of the new colonial societies, and proved the most fertile soil for segregation through land-use planning (Mabin, 1991).

There the combination of cultural and structural segregation in the early colonial period was transformed into the rigidly segregated *apartheid* city. At the meeting place of two great oceans, South Africa had a potent mix of populations: the Dutch-Afrikaner community dispossessed of its colonial parent and determined to keep its identity, a conquered African population dispossessed of much of its land, the migrant labourers for the diamond and gold mines (African, Indian and, to a lesser extent, Chinese), the racially-mixed coloured population (including strains of Malay and other ethnic groups), and the British settlers and mining interests. An intimate relationship existed between the segregation of South African cities and the early development of town planning in the country, which was highly segregated before the implementation of the Group Areas Act.

In seeking the origins of the *apartheid* city, one finds that slave emancipation in 1834 gave rise to separate quarters in the towns of the Cape for freed slaves. The term 'location' appears, in the sense of a land allocation on the edges of towns, in the context of resettling African refugees on the colonial side of the Kei river after the 1835–36 'Kaffir' war, and these locations became human buffer zones in the ongoing wars over land rights. The Eastern Cape was a frontier where various policies and approaches for regulating inter-ethnic relations were tested throughout the history of South Africa: 'locations' for black Africans on the urban edge separated by buffer strips, personal pass cards, and the blockhouse during the Boer War. The location emerged early as 'a means of governing non-disciplined, non-consenting populations who proved difficult to observe and record', and around it evolved 'a complex set of governmental, urban, racial and economic ambitions associated with ordering the residential and political domains of African people in cities' (Robinson, 1990).

The discoveries of gold and diamond deposits in the Eastern Cape and Transvaal in the 1870s led to new concentrations of population, the development of a migrant black labour force, and new threats of disease. These diseases included epidemics of smallpox and plague, but also diseases of overcrowded industrial societies – malnutrition, tuberculosis, typhus, cholera, typhoid, VD. The migrant labour system undermined divisions between urban and rural, white and black workers, and brought disease to a formerly relatively healthy population. Labour recruitment had serious health consequences both for the workers and the communities from which they were drawn. Crowded and insanitary conditions in mine compounds and plantations created environments favourable to the spread of disease, which was then carried back by returning migrant workers to their own families and villages. Rather than spend money on better housing and health facilities for the black workforce, the authorities preferred to listen to the public health advocates of segregation, such as Dr Simpson. Confronted by exotic and epidemic diseases, the holders of state power opted for short-term, politically popular solutions. It was left to the managers of capital to find their own solutions. In the circumstances it is hardly surprising that they did not solve the problem but shifted it from the work place to the rural areas, paying careful attention to the labour force at the work site and turning a blind eye to the origins of industrial disease and bad living conditions.

In the early twentieth century, public health officials were in the forefront of the demand for urban residential segregation. The move toward segregation quickened after 1900, with war and plague arriving at the same time. Minority Asiatic groups (Malays and Indians) were segregated in 'Asiatic Bazaars'. When these were burned down as an anti-plague measure, the inhabitants were moved out to new segregated locations. The Cape Medical Officer of Health wrote in a confidential memo in 1906 that:

THE SEGREGATION CITY

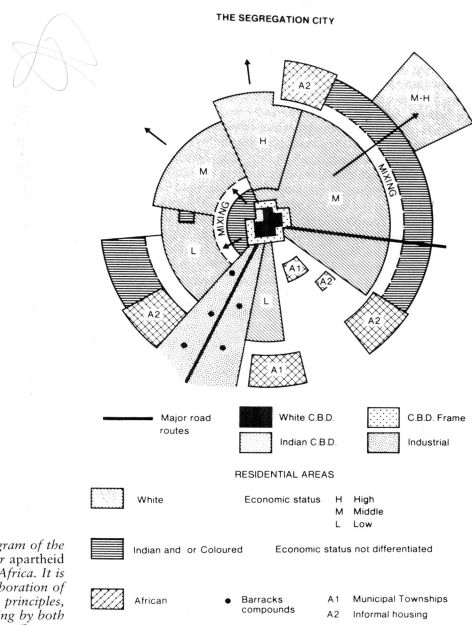

Major road routes

White C.B.D.

C.B.D. Frame

Indian C.B.D.

Industrial

RESIDENTIAL AREAS

White   Economic status   H   High
                                            M   Middle
                                            L   Low

Indian and or Coloured   Economic status not differentiated

African   ● Barracks   A1   Municipal Townships
                 compounds   A2   Informal housing

MIXING   Zones of racial mixing   Domestic servant quarters not shown

Schematic diagram of the segregation or apartheid *city in South Africa. It is an elaboration of Lugardian principles, segregating by both income and race. (Source: Lemon, 1990)*

the duty of excluding British subjects with a certain number of favoured exceptions, from a British country, is the most odious which a British Government could legitimately undertake . . . The real object we have in front of us is not to exclude dirty Asiatics and to admit clean ones . . . but it is to shut the gate against the influx of an Asiatic population altogether. (quoted in Denoon, 1988, p. 130).

High Commissioner Milner supported state regulation (Marks and Trapido, 1979), and sought to develop a new and efficient municipal administration, to build support among the white electorate. This included a stronger central direction of native affairs. The belief that the mixing of races led to incidence of disease provided a rationale for removing African segregated housing to the edges of the towns, while including them within the municipal boundaries to retain control. Disease was common in the poorly laid out and crowded locations, and the outbreak of plague prompted a new system of permanent locations outside the town, planned about 3–5 miles away from the European areas. Johannesburg on the outbreak of plague moved as many Africans as it could manage to its first native location at Klipspruit, and in this period Pimville (the precursor of modern Soweto) came into existence. The so-called 'sanitation syndrome', which equated black urban settlement, labour and living conditions with threats to public health and security, became fixed in the official mind.

Although reconstruction in Transvaal after the Anglo-Boer War included a Townships Board to guide land subdivision, public powers of racial zoning remained weak. The influenza epidemic of 1918 led to a Public Health Act in 1919 which conferred added public powers. The Lange Commission in 1921 recommended that municipalities have powers to create separate areas for Indian residence, and a Class Area Bill was introduced to Parliament in 1924, but not passed.

The African right to purchase land in urban areas was removed at the time of the Union of

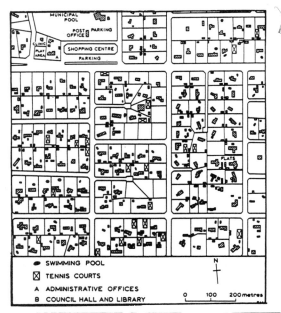

SWIMMING POOL
TENNIS COURTS
A   ADMINISTRATIVE OFFICES
B   COUNCIL HALL AND LIBRARY

0   100   200 metres

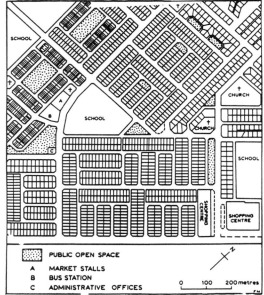

PUBLIC OPEN SPACE
A   MARKET STALLS
B   BUS STATION
C   ADMINISTRATIVE OFFICES

0   100   200 metres

Different standards for housing layout in Salisbury, Southern Rhodesia, Top: Low-density house plots for the whites, with swimming pools and tennis courts. Bottom: High-density plots in an African location. The plans are to the same scale! (Source: Kay and Smout, 1977)

South Africa in 1910. In 1922 Colonel C.F. Stallard, chairman of the Transvaal Local Government Commission, proclaimed the doctrine that the towns were essentially the creation of the white man. The African's presence there could only be justified insofar as he served the white man's needs, so he should have no political rights nor hold land in freehold tenure. Towns were thus perceived as primarily white places, leaving the indigenous population, whose lack of money excluded them from the property market, to fend for themselves on the periphery.

The Indirect Rule theorist, C.L. Temple, who had retired to South Africa, provided a justification for such policies by arguing against introducing freehold or individual land title for Africans. This was because of 'the mental condition of the African, his proneness to live in the present, his lack of thrift and foresight, rendering him willing to sacrifice the future to the present.' He also justified the erosion of individual land tenure in rural as well as urban areas:

In order to secure a good supply of cheap labour, which can be transported easily to whatever point in which it is required at the moment, you do not want a self-respecting class of yeoman farmers at all; what you want is a large thriftless population of more or less physically strong individuals who have no particular tie to attach them to one or other locality, to one or other class or section of natives. (Temple, 1918, pp. 139–146)

In 1923 the Natives (Urban Areas) Act gave local authorities powers to restrict Africans to townships and compounds. When the Transvaal Town Planning Commission in 1929 recom-mended the creation of Townships Boards, these were to have the power to reserve land 'for occupation by persons other than Europeans'. In the Cape Colony a Slums Act in 1934 empowered local authorities to clear buildings or whole neighbourhoods, and to move the occupants to new housing estates, on a racial basis. In Johannesburg the residents of racially mixed inner city slumyards in Doornfontein were moved to new areas, the whites closest in, then the well-off coloureds, poorer coloureds, and black Africans.

By the 1930s there was an increasingly noisy lobby among whites for racial zoning in South Africa, confronted by the uncomfortable fact that towns were losing their white majorities and becoming predominantly black. While there was still little formal regulation of racial segregation, the growing practice of town planning clearly had racial zoning in view. A draft Cape ordinance in the late 1930s would have allowed municipalities to segregate both residentially and in amenities, and defined whites married to blacks as blacks. A Depart-ment of Health Committee in 1939 (the Thornton report), considering 'irregular' settlement on the fringes of municipal areas, found a need to prevent the further establish-ment of 'peri-urban settlements': 'occupation of land and buildings irrespective of race with the result that Europeans are found to be occupying premises and living cheek-by-jowl with non-Europeans'. Local authorities con-tinued to press central government to act, and it was only a short step to the Group Areas Act, which followed the election of a Nationalist government committed to apartheid in 1948.

The Legacy of Segregation

The nineteenth century saw a more inter-ventionist approach by colonial authority (exercising what Foucault called the pastoral power) towards the urban environment, attempting to impose its image of order on society, including social and racial categories. This disciplinary power was much concerned with the organization of space, and medical campaigns (Swanston's sanitation syndrome) were key weapons in the subjugation of indigenous culture and the physical separation of ethnic groups.

Colonialism helped to create ethnically heterogeneous societies, which now categorize most of the world's independent states. Yiftachel (1992, chapter 2) has estimated that 90 per cent of the world's nation states are ethnically heterogeneous, and in 30 per cent the largest ethnic community is less than half of the population. Attempts by the colonial authority to create and maintain racial segregation, particularly in residential land use, has contributed to ethnic political polarization, which sometimes after independence resulted in forced population transfers, while other states managed a political accommodation through various multi-cultural policies. The most severe examples of structural segregation have occurred in South Africa, where the so-called *apartheid* city has imposed a lasting and inflexible land-use scheme.

NOTES

1. See especially Anthony (1976), but also McDaniel (1982), Smith (1985), and Walvin (1992). For racial attitudes see Davis (1984) and Patterson (1982). For later attitudes to evolution and race, see Brereton (1979) on Trinidad, Burrow (1966), Fryer (1988), Lorimer (1978), and Russell (1944).

2. Raffles has been the subject of several biographies, given his status as one of the creators of the British Empire, most recently Barley (1993). Recent work (Cangi, 1993; Eng, 1992; and Yeoh, 1991) has explored his role as a planner.

3. Colonel Robert Napier, later Lord Napier of Magdala (1810–90), born in Ceylon, was related to a sugar planting family, the Codringtons of Barbados. He was not related to C.J. Napier. He entered the Bengal Engineers in 1828, led the expedition to Abyssinia in 1868, and was Commander-in-Chief of India 1870–76. For his

work at Lucknow see Oldenburg (1984, chapter 2), and at Delhi see Gupta (1971).

4. Metcalf (1989), p. 106 and chapter 4. See also Jeffrey (1978).

5. Temple (1918), p. 485. Charles Lindsay Temple (1871–1929) served in Northern Nigeria from 1901 until his retirement in 1917. Some of his thinking seems to have derived from his father, Sir Richard Temple (1826–1902), who as Lieutenant Governor of Bengal and Governor of Bombay had sought to lessen the impact of British colonialism upon peasant societies. Temple throughout his career in Northern Nigeria quarrelled with his superior Lugard, who seems to have stolen his ideas on Indirect Rule. According to Nicholson (1969), who does much to attack the Lugard myth, Temple's book included disguised attacks on Lugard as being 'prolix with his pen, not from affluence, but from paucity of ideas' (see Nicholson, 1969, pp. 183–186).

6. Lugard (1965), pp. 570–574 and 617. Lord Lugard (1858–1945) served with the army in India 1879–88, in Uganda 1888–94, and Northern Nigeria 1897–1906 (High Commissioner 1900–6). Governor of Hong Kong 1907–12, he returned to Nigeria 1912–18, and became the Governor-General of a unified Northern and Southern Nigeria in 1914. He remained active in colonial affairs until the end of his long life, and received a peerage. See his biography by Perham (1956) and (1960), and the critical re-appraisal in Nicholson (1969), especially chapters 6 and 7. His *Political Memoranda* (1918) provide more detail on his policies, some of the more extreme of which he toned down or left out in the later book.

7. This section draws heavily upon the author's own research. The evolution of Township and segregation policy in Nigeria is in CSO 26/23061, CSO 26/06914, CSO 26/03272 (NNA). See also Home (1974), chapter 5, (1976) and (1983), and Urquhart (1977).

In Nigeria the township was basically a whites-only area outside the native city, while in South Africa it was a blacks-only area outside the white city, a term highly charged with negative associations. The history of this cross-over in meaning, and its early usage in South Africa, seems to have been hitherto unresearched.

6

'MIRACLE-WORKER TO THE PEOPLE': THE IDEA OF TOWN PLANNING (1910–1935)

The town planner fails unless he can become something of a miracle-worker to the people. He must be able to show them signs and wonders, to abate malaria, plague, enteric, child-mortality, and to create wonders of beauty and veritable transformation schemes. Sometimes he can do this in a few weeks, or even in a few days, by changing a squalid slum into a pleasant courtyard, bright with colour-wash and gay with old wall-pictures, adorned with flowers and blessed again by its repaired and replanted shrine. Within a few weeks he can change an expanse of rubbish mounds, befouled in every hollow and defiling every home with their germ-laden dust, into a restful and shady open space, where the elders can sit in the evening watching the children at play and watering the new trees they have helped to plant.

(Patrick Geddes, Report on Indore, 1918, quoted in Tyrwhitt, 1947, p. 38)

This rose-tinted view of the potential offered by the new 'art of town planning' was typical of Patrick Geddes, who was not burdened by excessive modesty. Already the most original and influential thinker in the field, he found himself a particular beneficiary of the sudden general enthusiasm for town planning. In the decade after 1910 it was rapidly elevated to a high social purpose and its practitioners sought after in many parts of the Empire. That decade also saw the First World War further enlarge the role of the State and add a sense of social urgency (Hardy, 1989). It was also a decade in which the British Empire's 'illusion of permanence' was challenged by the growth of political violence, notably the attempted assassination of the Viceroy of India, Lord Hardinge, by a Hindu nationalist on his state entry into Delhi.

A key event in the rise of the new idea was the First International Conference of 'Town-Planning', held in London in October 1910. After the passing of the 1909 Act the Royal Institute of British Architects wanted to put British ideas at the forefront of the international town planning movement. Thirteen hundred delegates attended the conference, plans, drawings and models were displayed at the Royal Academy, and the subsequent transactions were published in a handsome volume of eight hundred pages (RIBA, 1911). The colonies sent delegates, and among the sixty-four 'Honorary Vice-Presidents' were the

*Patrick Geddes
(1854–1932) conferring
with the ruler of Indore in
1919. When he became
unwelcome to the British
officials in India, Geddes
developed a lucrative
planning consultancy in
the princely states.*
(Source: *Tyrwhitt, 1947*)

Maharajah of Baroda (a sponsor of town planning, as will be seen) and Lord Kitchener of Khartoum.

At the conference Kitchener, newly returned from India (where he had been Commander-in-Chief), chaired a session at which McLean gave a paper on the planning of Khartoum. Kitchener allowed the ensuing discussion to go on so long that it stole from the time allotted to the following paper (by John Sulman on the new Australian capital city). Kitchener was made a Fellow of the RIBA for his planning of Khartoum, but his professed sympathy with the town planning movement was probably motivated by another objective. He was manoeuvring for a senior appointment, such as Viceroy of India, and sponsoring a Liberal cause such as town planning would help ingratiate him with the government of the

day. Although the Viceroyship went elsewhere, he obtained a consolation prize, the position of 'British Agent, Consul-General and Minister Plenipotentiary' in Cairo in 1911 (Magnus, 1958, pp. 238–251).

Geddes' star also rose. He belonged to a generation of writers, thinkers and philanthropists piecing together a critique of the Industrial Revolution and its social consequences. His ideas influenced other town planners who worked in the colonies, notably Abercrombie, Lanchester, Pepler and Ashbee, and supplied them with a new sociological rationale for their work. His collection at the Outlook Tower in Edinburgh became the nucleus of the Cities and Town Planning Exhibition, shown in London, Dublin, Belfast, Jerusalem, and other cities. It was visited in Edinburgh by Lady Aberdeen, wife of the

H.V. Lanchester (1863–1953). He was an active British architect-planning consultant in the colonies during the inter-war period, and was Geddes' collaborator on many projects. (Source: Burchell, 1987)

Lord Lieutenant of Ireland, who invited Geddes to Ireland and thus began his career of promoting the planning idea in the British Empire. Geddes also took the exhibition to Ghent, where it contributed to the founding of the International Garden Cities and Town Planning Association in 1914.

Geddes formulated an idiosyncratic but persuasive definition of the new art of town planning for his exhibition, which was later adapted for Indian use, as follows:

WHAT TOWN PLANNING MEANS UNDER THE BOMBAY TOWN PLANNING ACT OF 1915

CARE and PRESERVATION of human life and energy, particularly child life. NOT merely superficial beautification.

CONFORMITY TO A DEFINITE PLAN of orderly development, into which each improvement will fit as it is wanted. NOT the immediate execution of the whole plan.

THE BRINGING INTO THE MARKET OF LAND suitable for building, which without a Town Planning Scheme would in all probability never be anything but agricultural land. NOT the levying of heavy improvement charges without commensurate benefits.

PROVISION OF GOOD BUILDING SITES were no possibility of building with any success now exists. NOT the having of awkward and narrow-shaped plots

ENCOURAGEMENT of TRADE and increased facilities for business. NOT the interruption of trade.

PRESERVATION of HISTORIC BUILDINGS and buildings of religious veneration with all their traditions. NOT the destruction of old land-marks and temples.

The DEVELOPMENT of an INDIAN CITY worthy of civic pride. NOT an imitation of European cities, but the utilisation of what is best in them.

HAPPINESS, COMFORT and HEALTH for all residents, NOT merely expensive roads and parks available only for the rich.

MUTUAL INTERCHANGE of the cities' activities. NOT wholesale alterations at great expense, with no assured financial returns.

CONTROL over the FUTURE GROWTH of your town with adequate provision for future requirements. NOT HAPHAZARD laying out of buildings and roads with resultant COSTLY improvement schemes. ECONOMY. Not extravagant fads.[1]

Geddes had the ambitious notion that his style of town planning could have a key role in holding the British Empire together. Of his work with Unwin in Ireland between 1911 and 1914, which established his position in the British town planning movement, he was 'adamant that, if only the money had not suddenly stopped in 1914, and some of their ideas had been carried out, there would not have been an Easter Rising' (Meller, 1990, p. 189). In a similar vein he wrote during the 1919 Irish troubles that: 'I have had peculiar opportunities of investigating such connexion as might be between Irish urban unrest (so much more serious than the older rural form)

with the deplorable conditions of Dublin and other cities' (quoted in Meller, 1990, p. 282). He carried this conviction into his work in India, writing in 1915 to his son:

I increasingly feel the value of our own exhibitions in India and that of my conservative yet constructive attitude and influence in cities and towns to be of direct political as well as social value . . . an unexpectedly direct bearing on order and stability – even of the Empire – not only by economy etc. but by tending to check the revolutionary spirit by the Eutopian one – and cast out devils by ideals, so rendering a very direct form of service even in and for these times of war.[2]

Towards the end of his life Geddes was repeating the same theme, believing that his plan for the Wailing Wall in Jerusalem would have prevented the riots of 1929 (Hyman, 1994).

The main journals of the new town planning movement, particularly the *Journal of the Town Planning Institute* and *Garden Cities and Town Planning*, reported what work was being done in the Empire. Through their pages we can gain some appreciation of the relative levels and importance of planning activity in different colonies. India, Palestine, Malaya (through the active reporting of C.C. Reade) and South Africa received the most coverage. The regular contributors on colonial matters were Lanchester, Reade, Mirams and Holliday, of whom more later.[3]

DESIGNING THE IMPERIAL CAPITALS

The enthusiasm for town planning in the decade after 1910 coincided with Imperial federation. Grandiose plans for new capitals at New Delhi, Pretoria, Canberra and Ottawa were being formulated, and, as an editorial in 1913 in the *Town Planning Review* put it, 'what better reply to those who hold that there is no use for Town Planning, all our cities being built?' (Vol. 4, No. 3, p. 185). These new capitals in the Grand Manner 'transported

dominion and showcased it' (Kostof, 1991, pp. 217 and 271), highlighting the difference between the civilization of the colonizers and the old order of the indigenous population. As symbols of new nationhoods they remained an important feature of new towns throughout the twentieth century (Vale, 1992).

There were ambitious plans to reshape London to play its role as the capital of a great Empire. The construction of the Mall in 1913 was part of the plan, intended to enhance the position of the king-emperor as the focal point of the imperial system by providing a formal processional route. The rest of the plan was abandoned during the First World War, when national survival took the higher priority (Metcalf, 1989, pp. 177–179).

The building of New Delhi was the greatest expression of this celebration of Empire. Its story has been often told, and is not repeated at length here.[4] The decision to move the capital of India from Calcutta to Delhi was proclaimed at the Durbar which marked the accession of George V to the throne. The following year a committee was brought out from Britain to plan the new capital, chaired by Swinton, and including Lutyens, Brodie, and Lanchester (Swinton subsequently added Herbert Baker because of his work at Pretoria).[5] It had originally been intended to build the new capital north of the city, but the Town Planning Committee was given complete freedom of choice, and opted for a vast southern site. The so-called Delhi Enclave embraced an area of 1290 square miles, far larger than the 70 square miles of the plan for Washington, DC.

New Delhi was an attempt by the British to lay claim to India's past, and show their unfaltering determination to maintain British rule in India. It represented a British view of India as a timeless traditional society of different castes and faiths, which 'Britain alone could reconcile and so of necessity must rule' (Metcalf, 1989, p. 241). Its architecture was seen in explicitly political terms, with oriental-ized classicism representing the happy marriage between the ideals of East and West. New Delhi 'must not be Indian, nor English, nor Roman, but it must be Imperial' (Baker to Lutyens, quoted in Metcalf, 1989, p. 222). The Viceroy's House was probably the largest of all modern palaces, measuring some 600 feet from end to end, and 180 feet to the top of the central dome. It was described in 1931 as 'the shout of the imperial suggestion – a slap in the face of the modest average-man, with his second-hand ideals' (Robert Byron, quoted in Morris, 1983, p. 80). Although New Delhi is usually seen as the work of Lutyens (partly because he consistently sought to undermine the other planners involved), he saw himself as a grand designer in the Beaux-Arts classical tradition, rather than a town planner in the new style.[6]

But the architect-planners of New Delhi could not resolve in built form the fundamental problems confronting the British Empire in the twentieth century, the slow and inevitable loss of British control over India. The Indians were not consulted, there was no provision for a legislative building, and the new Indian modernizing elite were not interested in the architectural facadism represented by Indo-Saracenic design. New Delhi was 'a device to mask a growing insecurity by shouting forth an assertive magnificence' (Metcalf, 1989, p. 236). Its ultimate failure was symbolized by the disagreement between Lutyens and Baker in the famous 'gradient controversy' over the King's Way. The idea was that the Secretariat building should be seen throughout the ascent towards it, but it transpired that the volume of earth-moving was so great as to be prohibitive.

Town planning commentators in Britain at the time remarked upon New Delhi's concentration on architectural display to express the dignity of the Empire (Salkield, 1924). Later they were to criticize the hier-archical arrangement of housing, which accom-modated the poorer officials far from the centre. According to an anonymous commentator in *Garden Cities and Town Planning* (Vol. 14 (1924), pp. 11–12):

New Delhi will be the paradise of the garage owner. To live there without petrol is impossible . . . a town planned to surround the office desk of the chief bureaucrat, where converge the railway lines, the telegraph and the roads of our Empire, but where its soul will never rest.

Contemporary with New Delhi was the creation of a new capital of South Africa at

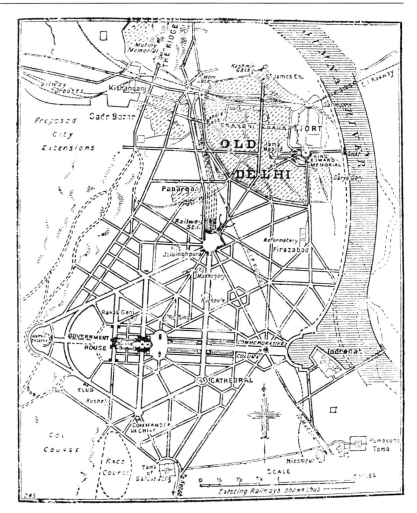

Plan of New Delhi. The scale of the enterprise is shown by the relative size of New and Old Delhi, and the network of avenues in the Beaux Arts tradition. (Source: Lanchester, 1925)

Pretoria. The Boer republics of the Orange Free State and the Transvaal were federated in 1910 with the Cape Colony and Natal to create a self-governing Union of South Africa. This final achievement of Milner and Cecil Rhodes secured Britain's interests in South Africa. When Pretoria, formerly a small sleepy town, became the new seat of the Union government, its official buildings were to represent in stone the dignity of the new South Africa.

Pretoria's buildings fit to celebrate Empire were created by the British architect Herbert Baker almost single-handedly. He had settled in South Africa in 1892 and was soon closely associated with Cecil Rhodes, who had a vision of a federated South Africa, with himself following in the footsteps of Pericles and Hadrian. Rhodes paid for Baker to tour the classical sites of the Mediterranean, so that in his designs he could crystallize in stone the soul and spirit of Empire. Baker reconstructed Rhodes' house at Groote Schuur, under the influence of the Dutch and Huguenot homesteads in South Africa, whose simplicity of design and handcrafted finish appealed to the ideals of the British arts and crafts movement. After Rhodes' death Baker was invited to Johannesburg by Milner in 1902, with the aim of (in Milner's words) 'introducing a better and more permanent form of architecture.' His design of the new Union Buildings subsequently embodied the classical ideals of Empire he had brought back from his Mediterranean tour.[7]

The new Pretoria, however, like New Delhi, reflected the uncertainties and insensitivities of British colonialism. Baker built two identical office blocks to symbolize the two partners in the new South Africa, the Dutch Afrikaners and the British, omitting the black Africans and other peoples. Baker himself became disillusioned that even the Afrikaners refused to accept the new order (in 1914 they rebelled unsuccessfully), and he left South Africa to join Lutyens in New Delhi.

In the more white dominions of Canada and Australia these uncertainties and insensitivities were less apparent. Thus Canberra, although designed by an American, was a project manifesting 'a widely shared vision of Australian nationality that complemented an emerging sense of equality, through participation in the British Commonwealth, with the former imperial master' (Metcalf, 1989, p. 241). The Australia Constitution Act authorized a new federal capital, to be located at least a hundred miles from Sydney, but within the state of New South Wales. A site at Canberra was selected in 1909, and in 1911 an international competition resulted in the selection of Griffin's plan for a garden city centred on a lake. In 1927 the administration officially moved from Melbourne, although Canberra's inhabitants still numbered less than nine thousand in 1931. It later evolved into 'arguably the epitome of the garden city tradition in Australia . . . one of the world's most massive urban design initiatives and an open air museum of 20th-century planning ideas.'[8]

Town Planning in India

As well as New Delhi, India created many opportunities for the emerging profession of town planning. A prime beneficiary was Geddes, whose work in India after 1914 consolidated his reputation as arguably the most innovative town planning practitioner of the century. The library of the Calcutta Improvement Trust was by the 1930s (rather paradoxically, in view of the trust's crude style of urban renewal) a Mecca for aspiring young British planners because it contained a complete set of Geddes' reports on Indian cities. After the Second World War Geddes' work in India was celebrated in an edited book of his writings (Tyrwhitt, 1947). The introduction to that, by Lewis Mumford, proclaimed Geddes as 'a global thinker in practice', and his conservative surgery method as 'particularly apt and timely for the days ahead'.[9]

Geddes' opportunity in India came through the sponsorship of a fellow Scot, Lord Pentland, the Governor of Madras. Pentland was a Liberal politician and former close associate of Campbell-Bannerman. Dropped from the Cabinet by Asquith when he became Prime Minister, he was sent out to govern Madras, to his own surprise and initial reluctance. Pentland had known Geddes' work in Edinburgh since about 1890. Indeed he had wanted to propose Geddes for a knighthood in the 1911 honours list, but Geddes declined, partly because he felt his income could not sustain such a position. Within a week of taking up his post in Madras Pentland invited Geddes to send literature on town planning. In February 1914 he followed up with an invitation for Geddes to bring his exhibition on town planning to Madras, and also to advise on 'not only the evils to be remedied but the limitations within which we have to work'. There was a political dimension, in that the National Indian Congress was meeting in Madras, and Pentland hoped that the exhibition would help reconcile the Congress members to the benefits of British rule.[10]

Geddes reached Madras in October 1914, after the outbreak of war. Unfortunately, his exhibition, the product of 35 years' work, which was following him by ship was sunk near its destination by the German raider *Emden*, along with 'Christmas consignments to the Madras shops, motor-cars for a member of council and lesser individuals, the season's supply of wine for Government House, all . . . scattered on the stream' (Pentland, 1928, p. 214). Fortunately a fresh exhibition was assembled in London and sent out through the good offices of Lanchester and others. It opened at the Senate Hall of Madras University in 1915, and Geddes gave a series of lectures, which were published with a preface by Pentland. He also trained Indian surveyors from the Madras Presidency towns in such matters as diagnostic survey, conservative surgery, the socio-biological approach and the importance of trees and open space. From Madras he took his exhibition to the other Presidencies of Bombay and Bengal, where Pentland's political friends, Lords Willingdon and Carmichael, were governors. He also held a chair of Sociology and Civics at Bombay University from 1919 to 1925 (although this was not a success with the students, and Geddes was often absent).

After his initial popularity, under the sponsorship of governors of Liberal political leanings, Geddes met with growing hostility from the British administrators of the Indian Civil Service, who did not care for his goading criticisms of their work in the municipalities. Geddes saw the damage that was being done to Indian towns by the demolition activities of the sanitarians. The town reports he prepared are rich with scathing comments, which deserve quoting at some length:

the usual wasteful super-blunder-bungle of a great 'Drainage Scheme'. (Kitchen, 1975, p. 278)

The policy of sweeping clearances should be recognised for what I believe it is; one of the most disastrous and pernicious blunders in the chequered history of sanitation. (Tyrwhitt, 1947, p.45)

It is clear that we must face the impossibility for years to come of completing those new and prosperous thoroughfares which were dreamed of at the outset of these clearances. The question is, therefore, how can these gaping slashes across the town be to some extent healed, so that their gradual revival and re-occupancy may take place. (Tyrwhitt, 1947, p. 47)

(Conservancy lanes and the new latrine) the sacred shrines of the sanitation engineers who originate these clearances. (Tyrwhitt, 1947, p. 53)

(On the sanitary authority of the Madras Government) its death-dealing Haussmannising and its squalid (Belfast 1858) industrial bye-laws . . . From the callous, contemptuous city bureaucrat at Delhi, I have now to tackle the well-intentioned fanatic of sanitation. (Kitchen, 1975, p. 257)

(On sanitary lanes) I am constantly compelled to wonder how this system, at once so costly and inefficient, can have become so general both in India and in Europe. True, to the professed utilitarian, the preservation of the old world picturesqueness of these courts and lanes is obviously anathema. It rouses all those deep-seated prejudices and readily excited sentiments towards a coldly fanatical iconoclasm of old-world beauty, which had such disastrous effects during the past century that they are hardly equalled by the savagery of war. (Tyrwhitt, 1947, p. 44)

Such criticism of what was, after all, standard colonial practice at the time, did not endear him to British colonial officialdom. Geddes thought in terms of primary human needs, rather than in terms of the business, health and engineering orthodoxies of the day. His 'Conservative Surgery' approach offered an alternative to destructive demolition and road-building, creating instead local open spaces, planted with trees. His aim was:

To give people in fact the same care that we give when transplanting flowers, instead of harsh evictions and arbitrary instructions to 'move on',

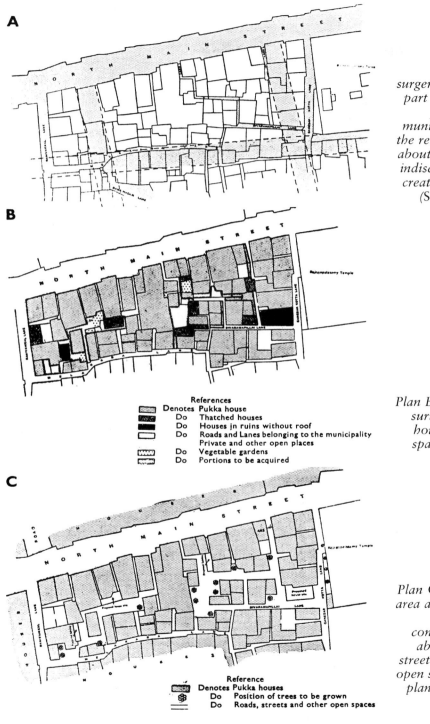

Geddes' 'conservative surgery' approach applied to part of Tanjore Fort, India. Plan A shows the municipality's proposals for the relief of congestion ('cost about Rs 30,000'), requiring indiscriminate demolition to create wide, straight streets. (Source: Tyrwhitt, 1947)

References

	Denotes	Pukka house
	Do	Thatched houses
	Do	Houses in ruins without roof
	Do	Roads and Lanes belonging to the municipality
		Private and other open places
	Do	Vegetable gardens
	Do	Portions to be acquired

Plan B is Geddes' 'diagnostic survey', identifying ruined houses, gardens and open spaces. (Source: Tyrwhitt, 1947)

Reference

	Denotes	Pukka houses
	Do	Position of trees to be grown
	Do	Roads, streets and other open spaces

Plan C shows 'the congested area as it would appear after the application of conservative surgery. Cost about Rs 5,000'. The old street pattern has been kept, open spaces created and trees planted. (Source: Tyrwhitt, 1947) delivered in the manner of officious amateur policemen. (Tyrwhitt, 1947, p. 22).

His Tanjore report of 1915 gives an example of how 'Conservative Surgery' might work:

first it shows that the new streets prove not to be really required since, by simply enlarging the existing lanes, ample communications already exist; secondly that, with the addition of some vacant lots and the removal of a few of the most dilapidated and insanitary houses, these lanes can be greatly improved and every house brought within reach of fresh air as well as of material sanitation – a point on which the more pretentious method constantly fails, as is evident on every plan. The estimated cost of the engineer's gridiron is, in this town, some 30,000 rupees, merely for the portion selected as a start, whereas, by Conservative Surgery, the total expense for this typical scheme (including necessary outlays on roads and drains) is officially estimated at only 5000 rupees. (Tyrwhitt, 1947, pp. 40–41)

Geddes was more aware of the relationship between Indian social practices and the urban landscape than British colonial officials had ever been. He wanted to encourage the revival of customs and traditions which promoted a clean environment. In Indore he was allowed to be Maharajah for a day, burning 'the Giant of Dirt and the Rat of Plague' on a bonfire before fireworks. He defended the Indian system of water tanks, which sanitary officials wanted to infill for anti-malaria measures.

Associated with Geddes for much of his Indian work was the architect-planner, H.V. Lanchester, who had a successful London practice. He first came to India on the planning committee for New Delhi, and returned for several months during most of the years between 1912 and 1937. His practice kept offices in several Indian cities, and he was Town Planning Adviser to the government of Madras in 1915–16. Outside India he undertook planning consultancies in Colombo, Burma and Zanzibar.[11]

As they became less welcome to British officialdom in India, Geddes and Lanchester took themselves off on consultancies for the rulers of the princely states. After 1857 the two-fifths of Indian territory which remained in princely states had been brought under 'indirect rule'. The princes' authority was reinforced, but British 'resident commissioners' urged them to be both traditional and modern rulers, rooted in the past yet participants in the creation of a new India. Town planning was supposed to be one of the benefits that British civilization could confer upon less developed peoples, and the Maharajahs of the princely states were the agents to transmit the new idea.

The Maharajah of Baroda, one of only five Indian princes entitled to a 21-gun salute on ceremonial occasions, was a particular enthusiast. His capital of Baroda at the 1921 census had a population of under a hundred thousand (tiny by comparison with the cities of Bombay and Calcutta), but rose to prominence as the capital of the Gaikwad dynasty, who were particular friends of the British. The Maharajah's wealth was based upon land revenue, but he promoted industrial development and investment, as well as championing a revival of Hindu cultural life and providing his people with public buildings, parks and tanks. This was the first head of a princely state to offer a consultancy to Geddes, in 1916. His role was to be a kind of trouble-shooter, spending a few days walking around and going through planning offices, then producing a report on the issues and opportunities. Geddes got many commissions of this type, and earned more money from them than he had in his life before, writing between 1915 and 1919 a total of fifty reports on Indian cities. The influence of Geddes upon the Maharajah of Baroda was reflected in the latter's words when he visited London and addressed the Town Planning Institute in 1920:

The peace, happiness and contentment of the people greatly depended upon health, and the health of the people greatly depended upon the conditions under which they lived and the way in which the towns were planned. The provision of fine avenues, roads and tree-planted streets was of great importance, for they could not but have an elevating

influence on the moral and social sense of the people
. . . After learning from Europe, they in India were
now gradually taking up the work of improving their
towns, and were doing as much as their financial
conditions would allow. For several years he had
had a landscape architect from England lay out his
gardens and also gardens for the public. When they
were first laid out the public hardly valued them, but
now one found in the evenings and on Saturdays and
Sundays people flocking to these places to hear the
music provided for their benefit. It was not hard to
imagine what influence this must have on the minds
of the people, and especially the younger generation
who might otherwise misuse their leisure.[12]

More usually the Maharajahs deployed the
new ideas on town planning and garden cities
for the benefit of their families and the
traditional elites. In Pune, for instance, an
upper-class garden suburb was developed by
the Deccan Gymkhana on a 38-acre site as a
kind of riding and country club. A hundred
'cottages' were owned by hereditary life
members of the Gymkhana, with swimming
pool, wrestling arena and sporting facilities.
Even a progressive ruler like the Maharajah of
Baroda, however, was reluctant to share power
with the rising political class of elected
politicians, and the princely states were swept
aside when India became independent.[13]

The new town planning approach in India
was also applied in the new company town of
Jamshedpur, developed by the Tata Iron and
Steel Company. The Parsi family of Tata
largely created Indian heavy industry, and by
1945 its family empire was estimated to be
worth £54 million and to be employing 120,000
people. In 1907 the company located a new
works at Jamshedpur. The location was chosen
to be equidistant from the sources of iron ore,
coal and fluxes, on a main railway, near a river
and with good access to Calcutta (155 miles
away). During the First World War the
company acquired nearly 16,000 acres with
8000 workers, and war production demanded a
further expansion of the town to 100,000
population.

The original town had been laid out by a
Pittsburgh engineer as a gridiron. In 1919 the
British administration in India seconded one of
its best civil engineers, F.C. Temple, to produce
a town extension scheme on garden city lines.
The Indian workers, however, wanted more
money, not a garden city, and went on strike,
so Geddes was brought in to advise. In his view
what was needed, rather than western-style
town planning, was a reinterpretation and
evaluation of indigenous customs, and the
physical urban forms they produced, to
make a new modern environment rooted in
eastern culture. Eventually the expansion of
Jamshedpur followed the contemporary
western fashion of a hexagonal layout
(advocated by Barry Parker). The concession
to local culture was in the use of clusters of
'group housing', accommodating twelve
families around a central space, instead of the
western suburban style of open layout.[14]

A 'GESTURE IN THE SPIRIT OF COLONIAL PATERNALISM': BRITAIN IN THE MIDDLE EAST

British influence in the eastern Mediterranean
grew as the Ottoman empire declined. In an
attempt at modernizing the Ottoman state
apparatus, in 1839 the Sultan had signed the
Tanzimat (or reorganization) Charter, which
separated public administration from religious
law, and allowed state intervention in private
property rights. New western-style local
government authorities were empowered to
provide infrastructure, roads, public open
space and town expansion schemes
(Yerolympos, 1993, p. 236). In the early
twentieth century, town planning was one of
the new modernizing ideas, and Egypt, Greece
and Palestine all received a dose of British
town planning expertise at this time.

Kitchener had already planned the new town of Khartoum in 1898 as a symbol of the Anglo-Egyptian condominium over the Sudan. In 1906 a Scottish civil engineer, William McLean, became its Municipal Engineer, with the job of providing more amenities for the whites: roads, surface water drainage, steam tramways, sewerage and water supply. Since no drawings survived (if such had existed) of Kitchener's town plan, McLean supervised the first systematic survey of the built-up area of Khartoum. He presented his paper and exhibition to the RIBA Town Planning Conference in London in 1910, under Kitchener's sponsorship. His new plan for the town extension was approved in 1912, and endorsed by the Governor-General, Wingate, with the words: 'This plan was prepared by Mr. McLean under the personal direction of Lord Kitchener.' This was the beginning of McLean's later career in town planning, and he published several articles on the planning of Khartoum.[15]

From the Sudan McLean moved to Egypt, on Kitchener's recommendation. The British declared a protectorate over Egypt in 1914, to guarantee Anglo-French interests during the First World War, and needed to demonstrate that western expertise could improve on the Ottoman Tanzimat. A form of Western-style representative local government was created, and McLean was appointed to the Ministry of the Interior, with the title of 'Engineer-in-Chief, Section of Municipalities and Commissions'. He was responsible for the protection of the town water supplies in Egypt during the First World War. His urban renewal projects for some fifty towns included Alexandria, where he proposed a Beaux-Arts style of grand public buildings. He later embarked upon an ambitious 'National and Regional Development Planning Scheme for Egypt', but little of this survived his retirement from Egypt in 1926.

As well as Egypt and the Sudan, British town planners found themselves in demand in Greece, when the collapse of the Ottoman

empire at the end of the First World War forced mass movements of population. The Greek Liberal Government of 1917–20, faced with the task of replanning settlements in Eastern Macedonia destroyed by the occupying Bulgarians in 1916–18, used British planners. J.W. Mawson, the son of the leading landscape architect and planner, had been in Greece since 1918 advising on housing and town planning, and in 1919 was appointed head of the reconstruction service. He recruited British and other European architects to prepare town plans, but in 1920 the Greek Liberal Government fell and the foreign advisers left.[16]

An even more complex situation arose in Palestine, where Britain acquired a League of Nations mandate after 1918. A succession of planners grappled with the challenges of the Holy Land, where the Mandate demand for the safeguarding of the Arabs' interests came into conflict with the guarantee of a Jewish national home under the Balfour Declaration, and with securing British interests in the region. As one of them, Clifford Holliday, wrote:

Almost anything written about Palestine whether it be of momentary interest, historical associations or some Utopian future dream, excites the interest of politicians, religious adherents, shrewd business developers and a host of ordinary folk. (JTPI, Vol. 24, 1937–38, p. 202).

Sir Herbert Samuel, the first High Commissioner, Liberal politician and Zionist supporter, favoured the new planning as a way of introducing modern methods of administration, and a Town Planning Ordinance was passed in 1921. During the thirty turbulent years of the Mandate, until the state of Israel was formed in 1948, the British deployed a succession of town planners in an attempt to manage the intercommunal tensions. Hyman (1994) has identified their different styles: McLean the civil engineer and imperial planner, Geddes the sociologist, Ashbee the

City walls of Jerusalem. Kaiser Wilhelm had a hole knocked in the walls to allow him to enter by car, while General Allenby entered on foot as a pilgrim, 'a gesture in the spirit of paternalism'. (Source: *The author, photo taken in 1992*)

arts and crafts enthusiast and lover of traditional crafts (the most pro-Arab and anti-Zionist), and Holliday the professional 'with a newly fashioned box of tools'. Others included Austen Harrison, who combined the posts of Government Architect and Town Planning Adviser (1923–27), and Howard Kendall (1935–48).

The first issue facing the town planners was how to preserve or conserve the unique Holy City of Jerusalem. General Allenby chose to enter Jerusalem in December 1917, not as a conqueror, but on foot as a pilgrim, through the Old Jaffa Gate. This was in deliberate symbolic contrast with the Kaiser Wilhelm's visit of 1898, when a breach was made in the city walls to allow him to enter by motor car. To Lawrence of Arabia, Allenby's humble gesture was 'the supreme moment of the War',

but it was also intended as a 'gesture in the spirit of colonial paternalism' (Fuchs, 1992).

The British attempted to create a Preservation Trust for Jerusalem on the lines of the National Trust. This proved to be incompatible with Article 2 of the League of Nations Mandate requiring the development of self-governing institutions, and was opposed by the municipal council. But the Holy City continued to attract the attention of British town planners, resulting in 'a layering process by which one plan was superimposed on another, each one providing new elements of information and control' (Crawford, 1985, p. 188).

The first planner to address the special problems of Jerusalem was McLean, who was 'borrowed' from Egypt for a few months between March and August 1918. In the words of the Governor, Storrs, his task was 'not to

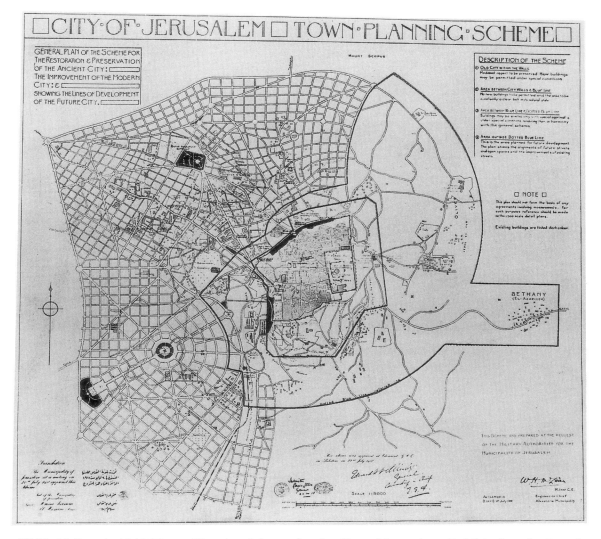

W.H. McLean's 1918 Town Planning Scheme for the City of Jerusalem. Exhibited at the Royal Academy, it was criticized as unimaginative and based on inadequate survey work (which McLean admitted), but had to be prepared in only a few weeks. (Source: McLean, 1930)

plan so much as to bring out regulations which will at any rate preserve the unique character and tradition of Jerusalem'. He was the author of the famous building proclamation of 8 April 1918, which imposed tight control over the demolition, erection, alteration, or repair of any building within a radius of 2500 metres of the Damascus Gate. It was followed by other public notices forbidding the use of stucco and corrugated iron within the old city, and prohibiting the display of advertisements. Later regulations were to require that buildings be of local stone.

Less successful was McLean's planning

scheme for the city outside the walls, which followed an unimaginative grid form, too European and unsympathetic to the spirit of the place. He proposed streets up to 150 feet wide, with large blocks of 200 × 100 metres (100 × 100 for residential, 75 × 100 for industrial). The Zionists complained that his scheme ignored the planned Hebrew University, and operated against their interests. The plan was severely criticized by Lanchester (doubtless encouraged by Geddes) when it was exhibited at the Royal Academy, London, in 1919: he called it 'lacking in even superficial study of the site and conditions' (quoted in Meller, 1990, p. 276). Eventually it was quietly forgotten, only one of its monumental avenues, King George V Street, being actually built.

The next planner to try his hand at the old city of Jerusalem was Patrick Geddes, who was invited to revise the McLean plan. Enthused by the challenge of forging a new Jerusalem, he went on endless perambulations of the city by day and night, describing it as 'by far the most important Sacred Park in the world'. He came up with three objectives for its planning:

To strengthen and emphasise the methods put forward by McLean for preserving the Old City; to encourage the archaeological excavations of the Old City of David as an essential activity for the regeneration of civic spirit; and to insist that new suburbs were laid out with more concern for contours of the land and the most economical (and more beautiful) grouping of houses. (Meller, 1990, p. 276)

He proposed a large parkland to the south and east, and a road system more sensitive to the contours of the site than McLean's. His work in Jerusalem soon ended, however, because his Zionist sympathies were unacceptable to British officials.

The third British planner to work there was C.R. Ashbee, a disciple of William Morris in the arts and crafts movement. He was Civic Adviser to the City of Jerusalem between 1919 and 1922, and for a time professional adviser to the Town Planning Commission. His contribution was to plan the park system outside the walls, and the rampart walk, and to introduce elementary zoning. He personally supervised conservation and repair work in the old City. He found old craftsmen capable of making the right tiles to repair the damaged Dome of the Rock, and persuaded them to set up a kiln in the city, thus reviving a craft industry.

After Ashbee came Clifford Holliday. His plans for Jerusalem in 1926 and 1930 attempted to consolidate the town, renew the slums, and relocate the Jewish settlements outside the walls. After Holliday came Howard Kendall, who prepared probably the most thorough plan for the city in the Mandate period, in 1944. When they departed, the British could claim, with some justification, that:

Whoever takes over the control of Jerusalem will have no cause to complain of Britain's guardianship of the city, or of the care and justness of her servants.[17]

Apart from Jerusalem, the main task of British colonial planning in Mandate Palestine was managing the successive waves of Jewish immigration. Zionism offered the British a settler population with energy and expertise, and so Palestine came to resemble Kenya during the interwar period, with a continuing conflict between settler and native rights. A hundred thousand hectares passed into Jewish hands (by 1930) and the Arabs reacted with an uprising. The Colonial Secretary, Lord Passfield, then attempted unsuccessfully to restrict Jewish immigration, but refugees from Nazi Germany soon after more than doubled the Jewish population in Palestine, from 172,000 in 1931 to 384,000 in 1936.

The Zionist Organization, after an early emphasis on rural settlement, was receptive both to the garden city idea, and to modern German planning, and prepared plans for low-density settlements in a garden city style. It commissioned Geddes in 1919 through the recommendation of Dr M.D. Eder, as one who 'knows how to maintain what is traditional and

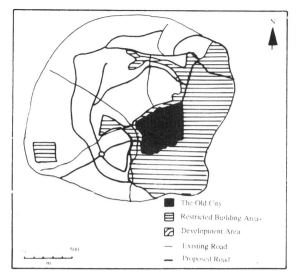

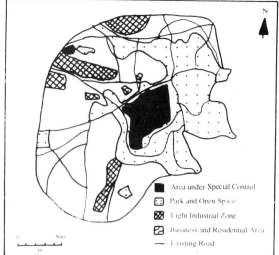

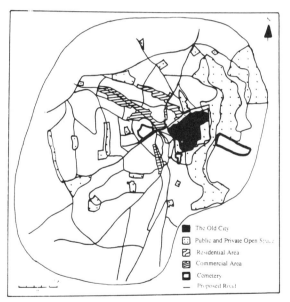

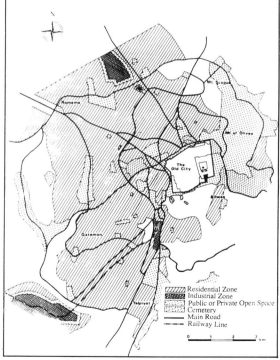

Later plans of Jerusalem during the British mandate in Palestine (1918–48) by successive British town planners. Top left: Geddes, 1919; Top right: Ashbee, 1922: Bottom left: Holliday, 1930; Bottom right: Kendall, 1944. Crawford (1985) called this 'a layering process by which one plan was superimposed on another'. (Source: Efrat, 1993)

Low-density garden suburb housing in Tel Aviv. Patrick Geddes planned several such layouts in the 1920s as consultant to the Zionist Organization. (Source: The author, photo taken in 1992)

beautiful in the past whilst combining it with all the necessary requirements in the way of sanitation and hygiene and modern requirements'. He proposed garden villages for the Carmel, consistent with his theories of the symbiosis of man and nature. His plan for Haifa, however, while prepared in co-operation with the military governor, Stanton, was considered by the Mandate administration to be too grandiose. He stayed only a year in 1919–20, and was replaced by the German architect-planner Richard Kauffmann as the main Zionist planner in Palestine. Geddes' plan for the northern extension of Tel Aviv, approved by the Jaffa Town Planning Commission in 1925, was his last commission, at the age of 70, and it is still evident in the street patterns of Tel Aviv. He advocated low-density houses with gardens in the garden village style, thinking of the Dutch in Colombo, 'who brought their gardening interests, skills and tastes with them to Ceylon', and this

proved influential upon the later Israeli planning style.[18]

The longest serving British planner in the Mandate period, however, was Clifford Holliday, who held various posts between 1922 and 1935, and undertook numerous town planning schemes for the Zionists. A former star pupil of Abercrombie from Liverpool University, he worked with him on the Haifa plan after 1930. Between them they opposed (albeit unsuccessfully) the demands of the oil industry for a large land allocation to the Iraq Petroleum Company, which deprived the town of access to the sea-shore. Holliday showed a certain disdain for what he saw as the amateurism of his predecessors and placed much emphasis upon the correct planning method. He was succeeded as full-time Town Planning Adviser by Howard Kendall, who stayed until the end of the Mandate in 1948, and prepared, not only a new Jerusalem plan, but also regional plans for the West Bank.[19]

THE TOWN PLANNING MISSIONARY: CHARLES COMPTON READE (1880–1933)

Geddes' place in the town planners' pantheon is secure, yet he was not the most active of the

first generation of self-styled town planners operating in the British Empire. This was

Reade, who deserves to be rescued from relative obscurity.[20] He worked in no fewer than five colonies after 1910 (New Zealand, South Australia, Malaya, Northern Rhodesia and South Africa), as well as maintaining strong connections with the British town planning movement. He was a founder associate of the Town Planning Institute, and became a full member in 1925.

Even more than Geddes, Reade could claim the title of town planning missionary. He even applied it to himself, in a lecture to the Town Planning Institute in 1926, claiming his inspiration from Raffles and Light:

There never was a time in the history of the whole (town planning) movement when the need for enlightened missionary effort throughout the civilised world was greater . . . The example of great pioneers like Sir Stamford Raffles at Singapore and Colonel Light in Adelaide was always an inspiration to those who laboured overseas for the spread of Town Planning knowledge and practice. (*JTPI* 1926, Vol. 11, pp. 10–12)

Although he was born and raised in New Zealand and called himself a colonial, Reade belonged to the English landed gentry, and indeed could be the only town planner in *Burke's Landed Gentry*. The family, from the

Charles Compton Reade (1880–1933), 'the town planning missionary'. He promoted town planning in New Zealand, South Australia, Malaya, Northern Rhodesia and South Africa, usually frustrated by 'a distinct hostility towards Town Planning in local official quarters'. (Source: Freestone, 1989)

village of Ipsden, Oxfordshire, had provided several lords lieutenant of the county. The ingredients of Reade's life can be seen in his family pedigree: public service, social reform, evangelicalism, and writing. His great uncle was Charles Reade, a successful Victorian author of novels and plays exposing social abuses. A cousin was William Winwood Reade ('traveller, novelist and controversialist', according to the DNB), who wrote the best-selling *The Martyrdom of Man*. The introduction to that book, a polemical attack on Christianity, referred to the author's 'longing to achieve something which should cause him to be remembered after his death', which seems a reasonable description of Charles C. Reade. His grandfather, E.A. Reade, was a servant of the East India Company who distinguished himself in the defence of Agra during the Indian Mutiny, and served on the Survey of India. His father, Lawrence Edward Reade, was a lawyer who emigrated to New Zealand and became the mayor of the town of Invercargill, on the South Island.[21]

As a young man Reade came to Britain, perhaps looking for a cause to espouse. Between 1906 and 1909 he worked on a London 'society' journal, and wrote a book on the new town planning movement (Reade, 1909) Returning for a time to New Zealand, in 1911 he was editor of the Auckland *Weekly Graphic and New Zealand Mail*, and lobbied unsuccessfully for town planning legislation. Back in England in 1912, he busied himself in the Garden Cities and Town Planning Association as secretary and editor of its journal, *Garden Cities and Town Planning*.

In 1914 Reade accompanied another planning propagandist, Davidge, on a successful lecture tour of Australia and New Zealand, and stayed on in Australia as the first government town planner in South Australia. His appointment, by the then Labour administration (from 1915 to 1920), reflected that government's continuing involvement in urban development, and he plunged into his work with energy and enthusiasm. He organized conferences and exhibitions in Adelaide and Brisbane, and recommended the creation of an outer ring of parklands for Adelaide, to relieve the monotony of suburban subdivisions. His main achievement in South Australia was the planning of the Mitcham Garden Suburb, later renamed Colonel Light Gardens – 'Charles Reade's Antipodean Hampstead'.

Reade clearly admired the life and work of Colonel William Light, and researched his career and the history of park belts in Australia and New Zealand. He sought to adapt the concept to accommodate recent urban growth, and seems to have identified closely with Light's tribulations, writing that:

Light's achievement was all the more remarkable in the face of the bitter opposition, and personal obloquy he suffered at the hands of those who owed everything to his brilliant skill and ability in selecting the site and planning the first great city of the reform era in Australia. (quoted in Hutchings, 1990)

He fought to get planning legislation in South Australia for an American-style planning commission but it was passed only in a much weakened form, because of landlord opposition. When he subsequently resigned his post, he described his own experience in similar terms to that of Light:

That decent people cannot attempt to do decent work for the good of Australia without personal malice and misrepresentation to hinder them is a disgrace to the democracy of this country. (quoted in DAustB)

In 1921, frustrated by his political battles, Reade left South Australia for a better paid job in the Federated Malay States. He was invited by the High Commissioner, and his salary rose handsomely to £2000 per year (plus expenses), from the £700 he had been paid in Australia. Initially on a short-term contract, he was confirmed in the post of government town planner on a permanent and pensionable basis in 1925.

The government of the Federated States at the time was enjoying a good income from

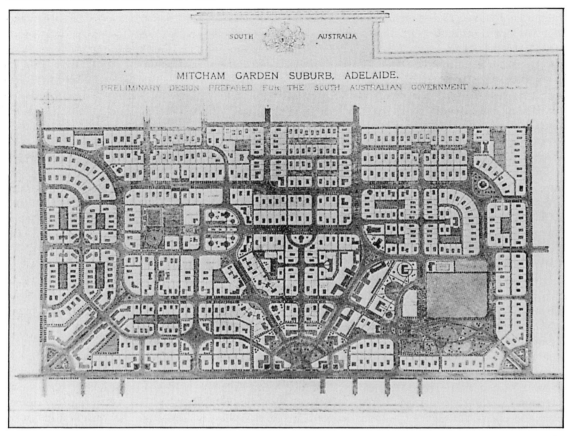

Charles Reade's plan for the Mitcham Garden Suburb (Adelaide) in 1919. Renamed Colonel Light Gardens, this is perhaps his most complete and best preserved development, modelled on Hampstead Garden Suburb. He left South Australia shortly after. (Source: Hutchings and Bunker, 1986)

export duties on tin and rubber, and was willing to embark on 'social experiments' under pressure from the dynamic Chinese business community. The capital, Kuala Lumpur, grew from 18,000 inhabitants in 1890 to 95,000 by 1926. As early as 1912 members of the Federal Council had been pressing for town planning:

the need of control over private ownership, the relation between over-crowding and crime, open-space and health, the disastrous consequences of neglect to lay out streets, etc., beforehand . . . The

Government is an all-powerful and benevolent one. Every Resident is a Socialist in his own State. (E. MacFadyen in 1915, quoted in Goh, 1988*b*, p. 7)

A Town Improvement Act was passed in 1917, and needed a specialist to implement it, hence Reade's appointment.

Reade set to work with his usual vigour. He organized a Town Planning and Housing Exhibition on the Geddes model, comprising forty panels of plans, photos, diagrams, posters, etc. illustrating the early days of civilization down to modern cities. He gave lectures, with slides of Letchworth, Hampstead and Port Sunlight, in the main towns. He wrote several articles about his work in Malaya, so that planning circles in Britain in the 1920s were better informed about developments in Malaya than any other colony. Unfortunately few of his schemes have survived the destruction of records in the Second World War, but his work was warmly endorsed by the government:

Anybody who has taken the trouble to study the work of Mr. Reade since he has been in this country cannot fail to be impressed with the extremely valuable result that he has achieved, in the face of opposition that sometimes has not been altogether reasonable. I have lived long enough in this country, and, particularly, long enough in Kuala Lumpur, to see the appalling waste of money and waste of efforts both public and private that we have suffered from, through lack of legislation and coordinated efforts in the direction of economic and sound town planning. (Acting Chief Secretary in 1923, quoted in Goh 1988b, p. 9)

He visited the Philippines to see the work of Daniel Burnham (the father of American planning), and applied the planning of the Americans' hill station at Baguio to a similar resort in the Cameron Highlands. His services were loaned to the British North Borneo Company to advise on the development of the ports of Jesselton (now Kota Kinabalu) and Sandakan. On another occasion he co-operated with E.P. Richards in preparing planning legislation for Singapore.

But once again Reade's job ended in frustration. He described himself as 'endeavouring to apply strictly scientific, and consequently really practical (sic) methods, to the planning of not only the cities (though that is his chief task), but also to the road system throughout the country, the straightening of streams in the cities, sanitary measures in city and country alike, as well as the more detailed working out of plans for the country as a whole' (GCTP, Vol. 19, 1929, p. 25). In this last phrase can be

seen the beginnings of his downfall, for his ambition over-reached him. He was criticized for being dictatorial, and for his wide road reservations, which were perhaps based upon his upbringing in Invercargill, a town of wide streets (Hargreaves, 1992). His 1923 Town Planning Act was seen as too much centralist, and was diminished in 1927 by a new Act. This decentralized planning under a Town Planning Superintendent, a newly created post for which Reade was passed over in 1928. The job was taken instead by P. Jones Williams, who had worked for local authorities in Bradford and South Wales. Reade felt his position had been made untenable, and he resigned.

He returned to London in 1930, and did not have to wait long for re-employment. He was well known in London planning circles, and the new Colonial Secretary, Lord Passfield (the former Sidney Webb), soon invited him to go out to Northern Rhodesia. There the rapid growth of mining towns in the Copper Belt had led to a Town Planning Ordinance in 1929 'to cope with problems of population and traffic density', modelled on legislation in the Cape Province and Kenya. A former Director of Medical and Sanitary Services, Northern Nigeria, D. Alexander, had been sent to advise on the selection and layout of the new townships, and his advice was that 'We need a town planner'.

In October 1930 Reade arrived in Northern Rhodesia in an advisory capacity, and by April 1931 his title was Director of Planning and Development. He set about preparing plans for Livingstone and Ndola and recruited an assistant (R.D. Jones of Pwlheli). Reade's progress note sent to the Town Planning Institute conveys some of his enthusiasm:

Various schemes are rapidly being formulated and Government and private works co-ordinated therewith. The T.P. Ordinance, a useful but defective measure, is being replaced by more up-to-date provisions and the Government has approved a scheme for departmental organisation and staff for the whole Territory.

At the time Professor Adshead was in Northern Rhodesia, having been commissioned to plan a 'Capital City and Government Centre', and the site of Lusaka was chosen in July 1931. Adshead planned for a European population of 5000, 1000 African police, and 'ample provision' (estimated at 4000) for other Africans, mostly domestic servants. He applied garden city thinking to create a 'generous gracious city' with landscaping, open space and wide streets.

Following Adshead's return to Britain, it was not to be Reade's crowning achievement to implement the plan for Lusaka. The Adshead proposals were refined into a working document, from which the capital was actually developed, but this was done by P.J. Bowling, instead of Reade, in July 1933. It assumed a larger projected European population of 20,000, and was further increased to 125,000 in the post-war Jellicoe plan.[22]

In circumstances that are unclear Reade's appointment had already been terminated in 1932. He could persuade neither the mining companies to accept general plans, nor the administration to incorporate subdivision control in the ordinance.

Once again, Reade was not long out of work. From London he was appointed Chief Town Planning Officer for the newly formed Witwatersrand Joint Town Planning Committee in July 1933, at a salary of £2000 a year. Visiting Johannesburg in January 1933 he had spoken of the opportunity to create 'a great city stretching from one end of the reef to the other' (quoted in Mabin, 1993, p. 50). He sailed in September and arrived in Johannesburg on 16 October and attended a meeting of the joint town planning committee. Then, inexplicably, on October 28 1933, he shot himself in a Johannesburg hotel.

Why did Reade take his own life? The local paper referred to recurrent malaria (often blamed for suicides) and depression. His obituary in the JTPI offers some clues:

Charles Reade was a man of delightful personality with a strong sense of humour and a rich fund of anecdotes. He did great work in unsettled districts, under trying conditions, and often against a distinct hostility towards Town Planning in local official quarters.

Perhaps he was tired of travelling, starting yet another new job, and fighting the political battles. He came from a family tradition of telling people what to do, but all too often they were reluctant to listen. A clue is given by the comment of a member of the South Australian Legislative council on him:

When a visitor to your home calls your paintings oleographs, your silver spoons brass, and your dog a mongrel, he is hardly the man you would desire to meet again. (quoted in Tregenza, 1986, p. 51)

Perhaps he wanted to spend more time with his growing family in England, but could only get a job in the colonies. He was a supporter of racial harmony, but found himself confronted with the discriminatory practices of South African mining capitalism. The tide was running against his style of planning and the Great Depression made prospects more difficult. He had money troubles, and left only a modest estate.

Perhaps the best summary of Reade's career is Tregenza's entry in the Australian Dictionary of Biography:

Whatever motivated Reade in his last hours, there is no doubt about the consistency of his faith and practice as a town planner for the preceding quarter of a century. For him, town planning was an art and a science which could immeasurably improve the quality of life for people of all races. In the days before academic courses in the subject he made himself an expert by the on-site study of existing examples of planning, by discussion with fellow pioneers and by omnivorous reading. It was characteristic of his thoroughness that in his Australian years he ordered from a London agency reports on town planning cut from world newspapers. A skilled photographer, journalist and speaker and a witty raconteur, he had an exceptional capacity to arouse enthusiasm for his cause among diverse people. He also proved a patient and skilled negotiator in framing legislation and devising town planning schemes. If he was denied the opportunity to plan on a large scale and to reform sub-standard housing, it was not because his ideas were faulty, but rather that he had to work within societies lacking democratic constitutions.

THE GARDEN CITY MEETS INDIRECT RULE: ALBERT THOMPSON IN AFRICA

A lesser figure than Geddes or Reade, but nevertheless the main British town planner operating in sub-Saharan Africa in the 1920s, was Albert Thompson, who spent some years each in South Africa and Nigeria.

Albert J. Thompson (1878–1940) trained in the architectural practice of Raymond Unwin and Barry Parker, and worked on the planning of Letchworth and Hampstead Garden Suburb. He started his own professional practice in London in 1914, and after military service in the First World War (rising to the rank of Major) designed the Swanpool Garden Suburb of Lincoln with the firm of Hennell & James. In 1920 he went to South Africa, on behalf of Hennell & James (then working on Welwyn Garden City), and probably on Unwin's recommendation, to design the Pinelands Garden Suburb of Cape Town and the Durban North Estate.[23]

Pinelands was a private township modelled closely on Letchworth, developed by a board of trustees (the Garden Cities Trust) on an 800-acre site granted by the Union government. It was promoted by Richard Stuttaford, a member of the Union government, who had visited Letchworth and met Ebenezer Howard, and believed that better housing (for the whites) through the garden city approach would improve health after the ravages of the influenza epidemic. Thompson designed the town with a close resemblance to Letchworth, and similar garden city approaches were followed in later new towns, such as Welkom and Vanderbijlpark.

Pinelands has been described as the first Garden City of South Africa. It is a first step in that direction and a trying-out on a small scale in South Africa of those principles upon which such great and inspiring achievements have been reached by the European and American nations in the building and re-building of cities. (Muller, 1993, pp. 6–7)

It was also one of the first whites-only housing developments, preceding the Group Areas Act by thirty years, so has its place in the history of apartheid planning.

After seven years in South Africa Thompson left in 1927 to take up a post as Town Planning Officer in the Nigerian Lands and Survey Department, at a salary of £1400 a year (with £240 duty pay). He was recommended by the consulting engineers for the Lagos drainage project, Howard Humphreys and Sons, who had also worked in South Africa.

The Nigerian government at the time was spending heavily on capital projects (water, electricity, hospitals), including housing for its European and African employees. A committee for town planning had been formed in 1922, following criticisms of the lack of foresight in planning new layouts. The Director of Public Works, for instance, accused the Kano and Zaria Townships of being:

devoid of any features of interest or aesthetic merit . . . I am aware that the Government gives no weight to aesthetic considerations, but in this matter I think it should be remembered that we are now laying the foundations of what may be the big cities of the future. (quoted in Home, 1983)

The new committee saw its objective as developing Nigeria's towns along 'modern lines . . . emulating the principles and practice of Town Planning followed elsewhere'. It concentrated most of its efforts on the planning of Enugu, the new railway and mining town in

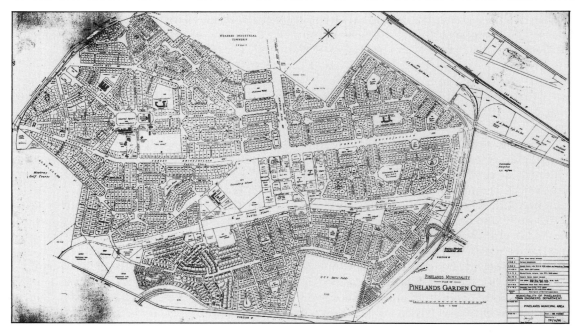

Albert Thompson's plan for Pinelands Garden City (Cape Town), which he designed between 1920 and 1924. The first self-contained garden city in South Africa, it became a model for segregated white low-density housing areas. There were only three entrances into the estate, which was surrounded by wide tree-planted roads, golf courses and other 'buffer strips'. The Central Square (top left) *bears close resemblance's to the central area of Letchworth Garden City, on which Thompson had worked.* (Source: *1970 Plan, Municipality of Pinelands Town Engineer's Department)*

Eastern Nigeria, but quickly encountered the opposition of Northern Nigerian officials to any central direction from Lagos. The Lieutenant Governor of the North managed to sabotage the initiative by appointing his own Town Planning Committee in 1924. A similar committee then had to be created for the Southern Provinces, and the central committee was disbanded, followed by the disbanding of the Northern and Southern Committees in 1927. In that year a memorandum on town planning principles was prepared by the Directors of Public Works and Medical Services.

Meanwhile attention had shifted to the rapid growth of the capital, Lagos, and its problems of plague. To cope with the acute shortage of housing for the African staff in the colonial administration a housing estate was begun at Yaba in 1926, and following an outbreak of plague detailed proposals were prepared for improving the drainage system of Lagos Island. In 1928 the Lagos Executive Development Board came into existence, with a fund of £200,000 to undertake swamp reclamation, slum clearance, market planning and the development of suburban estates. As with most other such bodies, the powers were not conferred on the Lagos Town Council, on the grounds that it was not a suitable organization for controlling development, especially where government grants were involved.

Thompson's appointment dated from January 1928, and his first task was redesigning the Yaba housing estate, where it was claimed that he achieved savings of 25 acres on the original land allocation. He was given a qualified assistant, R.B. Walker (with a Diploma in Town Planning and Civic Architecture from University College, London), who took up his post in December 1928, and another assistant, C.L. Waide, was appointed in 1930.

For a few years Thompson's little team was able to plan, not only for Lagos, but for other fast-growing towns in Southern Nigeria. (In Northern Nigeria fifty-one new layouts were approved between 1928 and 1931, but these were designed by the Surveys Department without using professional town planners, doubtless because of the old North-South rivalry.) Four priority towns were identified: Warri, Sapele, Benin and Onitsha. Thompson prepared a report on Enugu in 1928 which attempted to economize on road layouts, and planned a new industrial estate for coal-related processes.

Resistance was soon encountered from the local administrators who felt that the planners showed insufficient awareness of local conditions. One example was Walker's visit to Sapele in 1930. His 22-page preliminary report attacked the 'unreal zoning' of the township which segregated the native from European settlement by a building-free zone, ignoring all topography and isolating the wholesale trade area from its retail market in the native town. He proposed various rearrangements, including moving the market, but his layout, in the words of the Resident of the Province, 'commended itself to no section of the community and was disapproved in March 1931. A useful by-product has been a survey of the township which should enable the present mass of temporary occupation leases to be replaced by simple leases' (quoted in Home 1983).

After five years in Nigeria, in 1932 both Thompson and Walker were made redundant, part of a general cutting of expenditure undertaken by the new Governor, Cameron. The work of town planning was carried on by their assistant, C.L. Waide, who combined the posts of Secretary to the Lagos Executive Development Board and Town Planning Officer.

Thompson and Walker returned to England and set up a practice together at Brighton, where Thompson became secretary to the local architects' society. He died suddenly on 16 May 1940. According to his obituary notice, 'he had a fervent enthusiasm for all that makes for improvement in civic development and housing conditions.'

CONCLUSION: TOWN PLANNING 'A TENTATIVE EXPERIMENT'?

By the early 1930s the first generation of town planners active in the colonies had gone. Richards left Singapore in frustration in 1924, McLean retired from Egypt in 1926, and Thompson and Walker were 'retrenched' from Nigeria in 1932. Geddes died in 1932 and Reade in 1933. Town planning had seemingly failed to achieve the high ambitions which Geddes and Reade had entertained for it. The Great Depression made the year 1931 an *annus terribilis*, when 'men and women all over the world were seriously contemplating and frankly discussing the possibility that the Western system of society might break down and cease to work' (Arnold Toynbee, quoted in Cherry, 1974). In that year the Madras Town Planning Officer, Reginald Dann, commented gloomily about the prospects for town planning:

Town planning has not become general nor has it established itself in the minds of the Government or the people as an important administrative function.

It is still regarded as a tentative experiment or a luxury suitable for times of prosperity instead of an insurance against waste and the application of ordinary common-sense to City development. (GCTP, vol. 21, 1931, p. 150)

A reduced role was now being advocated for planning as a cost-saving exercise (which was how Thompson had justified his work in Nigeria). A leading planning consultant of the day, Thomas Adams, was claiming planning 'as a means of promoting economy, and the advisability of confining attention at the present time to those town planning projects or regulations that will result in saving rather than adding to public expenditure'.[24] In Britain the local authority town planner could be seen as:

one of the most pathetic figures in public life today . . . who labours unhonoured and unsung, anonymous almost as a dead dog, under the title of Temporary Town Planning Assistant to the Borough Engineer of This or the County Surveyor of That. (Jeremiah Barebones, a pseudonym, in 1936, quoted in Cherry, 1974, p. 112)

Yet this was also the decade in which the 'The Age of Planning had dawned' (Auster, 1989, p. 207). The Soviet centrally planned economy seemed to offer a model for the future, in which society could be seen as an industrial system, managed efficiently and rationally by the same kind of men who were running individual industrial enterprises. There could be an apparently easy transition from national economic management to local physical planning, through public works programmes and the regional survey movement. The Conservative politician, Harold Macmillan, put the case for planning in 1933:

Planning is forced upon us . . . not for idealistic reasons but because the old mechanism which served us when markets were expanding naturally and spontaneously is no longer adequate when the tendency is in the opposite direction. (quoted in Cherry, 1974, p. 108)

A new approach to city and regional planning was emerging, for which, once again,

Geddes provided the ideas. Towards the end of his life he believed that the concentration of power in metropolitan cities was a decisive factor encouraging governments to wage war, and peace could be ensured by provincial cities forming friendly cultural links: regional renewal and co-operation as the 'third alternative' to war or revolution', a prescient foreshadowing of European Community regional policy fifty years later (Meller, 1990, p. 326). McLean after his retirement from Egypt took up the regional planning approach in his book of 1930. In the year of the New Deal, the Town Planning Institute quoted an American commentator (Joseph Crane of Chicago):

Which one of the world-cities will win the race to reconstruct itself in scale with twentieth century ideals of what a great city should be? . . . Whatever the ultimate outcome of our groping for the perfect type of machine-age living, we are all passionately engaged now in the building and rebuilding of the existing big cities. The die is cast, the forces are gathering, the direction which each city takes will emerge within the next five years, and the final results will be known in a few brief decades. (JTPI, Vol. 19 (1932–33), p. 60)

NOTES

1. This is quoted in Mirams (1919–20), p. 56. Bogle (1929) has a similar definition, which is quoted in Meller (1990).
2. Quoted in Meller (1990), footnote 109, p. 235. He was giving consent for his son to fight in the War (in which he was killed in 1917).
Patrick Geddes (1854–1932) was a University professor whose sociological work on conservation in Edinburgh brought him into planning. His colonial work included Ireland (1911–14), India (1914–29) and Palestine (1919–29). He is the subject of several biographies, particularly Kitchen (1975) and Meller (1990). There is also a short study by Meller in Cherry (ed.) (1981).
3. The author wishes to thank Hilda Matthews, his research assistant in 1988, for assembling a thorough portfolio of the colonial

material in these journals, from which much of this and the following chapter is drawn.

4. Irving (1981) is the main study, but see also Gupta (1981), pp. 176–183, Hussey (1953) for Lutyens' role, Metcalf (1989), chapter 7, and Salkield (1924). There are short accounts in Hall (1988), pp. 183–192, Kostof (1991), Morris (1983), pp. 76–80, and Vale (1992), pp. 88–97.

5. Captain G.S.C. Swinton (1858–1937) was a former Army officer who had been a conservative London County Councillor since 1901, and resigned from the post of chairman to take up the post as chairman of the New Delhi Town-Planning Committee in 1912 (WWW).

6. Lutyens' antipathy to other planners is well documented. He seems to have stopped Lanchester getting work from the New Delhi Development Committee (Meller, 1990, p. 209). Lutyens was particularly dismissive of Geddes: 'He seems to have talked rot in an insulting way and I hear is going to tackle me! A crank who doesn't know his subject. He talks to a lot, gives himself away then loses his temper' (Lutyens in 1915, quoted in Kitchen, 1974, p. 255). According to Meller (1991), p. 236, 'He and Lutyens had an antipathy for each other which extended to their work and their views on the social evolution of the future'. Lutyens also had little time for the Viceroy himself, writing to his wife that 'if I am in the saddle, and the Viceroy wobbles, changes, and interferes in details – it is hardly worth while giving up best of one's life to this work' (quoted in Hussey, 1953, p. 285).

Sir Edwin Lutyens (1869–1944) is known as an architect rather than a town planner. As well as New Delhi, he designed the Cenotaph in London.

7. All the quotations on Pretoria are from Metcalf 1989, pp. 181–195.

Sir Herbert Baker (1862–1946), the close contemporary of Lutyens, worked in South Africa and New Delhi, and designed imperial buildings in Britain, such as Rhodes House in Oxford and India House in London.

8. For the planning of Canberra see Fischer (1984), Pegrum (1983), and Proudfoot (1991). There are short accounts in Freestone (1989), pp. 115–124, Hall (1988), pp. 192–196, and Vale (1992), pp. 73–88. Freestone and Hutchings (1993), p. 79, discusses the literature.

9. Geddes' work in India is thoroughly covered in Kitchen (1975), Meller (1990), chapters 7 and 8, and Tyrwhitt (1947). Hall (1988), pp. 244–8, and Kostof (1991), pp. 82–88, have short accounts.

10. John Sinclair, 1st Baron Pentland (1860–1925), was born and educated in Edinburgh, and served as an army officer until 1887. An early resident of Toynbee Hall, he became a progressive London County Councillor in 1889, and was a founder member of the London Playing Fields Society. Later a Liberal Member of Parliament, he was Secretary of State for Scotland 1905–9, and Governor of Madras 1912–19. DNB, WWW and Pentland (1928).

11. Henry Vaughan Lanchester (1863–1953) started in architectural practice in 1889, and was partner in the firm usually known as Lanchester and Lodge. He was editor of *The Builder* 1910–12, external examiner on the civic design diploma at Liverpool, president of the Town Planning Institute 1922–23, and author of *The Art of Town Planning* (1925). He first visited India in 1912, worked with Geddes there in 1915–16, and paid consultancy visits in 1919, 1920, 1921, 1922, 1925, 1927, 1929, 1932, 1934, 1935, and 1937 (his last visit). He also undertook colonial planning consultancies in Columbo (1920), Burma (1921), and Mombasa and Zanzibar (1922). He was Town Planning Adviser to the Government of Madras 1915–16. He planned a new town at Umrath for the Maharajah of Baroda (abandoned when the Maharajahs lost power), and town planning schemes for Delhi, Gwalior, Lucknow, Rangoon and Nagpur. For his life see RIBA biographical files, Burchell (1987), and Meller (1990).

12. Discussion on paper by Mawson, *JTPL*, Vol. 7 (1919–20). Sayajirao Gaikwad (1863–1939) ruled as Maharajah of Baroda 1875–1939, and was enough of a friend of the British to warrant an entry in DNB and WWW.

13. Reported in *JTPI*, Vol. 16 (1929–30), pp. 190–2. For Indirect Rule in the princely states, see Metcalf (1989), chapter 4, Jeffrey (1976), and Temple (1918), pp. 399–389 & 474–485.

14. Temple presented a paper on the planning of Jamshedpur at a meeting of the Town Planning Institute in 1928 (Temple, 1928). See also Dutt

(1959), Koenigsberger (1947) and Meller (1990), pp. 236–237 for Geddes' role. For the Tata family and Parsis, see Moorhouse (1983), p. 196, and Tindall (1982), pp. 94–104.

Frederick Charles Temple (1879–1957) was the grandson of a Lieutenant Governor of Sierra Leone (who died there in 1834), the son of one Archbishop of Canterbury and the brother of another. Educated at Rugby and Balliol College, Oxford, he was civil engineer to the Birmingham Elan Valley waterworks (1903–5), and then went to India, with the Military Works Services and the Public Works Department (1907–19). He became a member of the Town Planning Institute in 1920, and was the Chief Town Engineer of Jamshedpur (1919–24), and Administrator (1924–32). Aide-de-camp to the Viceroy of India (1931–36), he then retired from Indian service, and became a Regional Controller of the Ministry of Fuel and Power (1942–46) and Director of Opencast Coal Production (1947). He married the daughter of the Bishop of Calcutta (WWW).

15. William (later Sir William) Hanna McLean (1877–1967) qualified from Glasgow University with a degree in civil engineering in 1899. He spent his engineering pupillage on several major Glasgow infrastructure projects (sewers, the River Clyde bridge, dock works and valuations), and was resident engineer for various railway extensions on the west coast of Scotland 1900–6. He went to the Middle East as Municipal Engineer for Khartoum 1906–13, and became Engineer-in-Chief, Section of Municipalities and Commissions, Egyptian Ministry of Interior, 1913–26. Returning to Scotland on retirement in 1926, he took a Ph.D. from Glasgow with the title 'The Wider Application of the Principles of Town Planning (Regional, National and International Development Planning)', which was later published (McLean, 1930). He was Conservative MP for the Tradeston district of Glasgow 1931–35, a member of the Advisory Committee on Education in the Colonies 1932–38, and for thirty years 'honorary liaison officer' between the Colonial Office and the two Houses of Parliament. His life and work is the subject of a short article by Home (1990b), and his work in Jerusalem is examined in detail in Hyman (1994).

16. For the Macedonian episode, see Kafkoula (1992).

J.W. Mawson (1887–1966) was one of the first students to take the Diploma in Civic Design at Liverpool, and became a partner in his father's firm in Canada. He served with the Canadian forces in 1916–17, and then became housing and town planning adviser to the Greek Government in eastern Macedonia until 1920. He subsequently worked on the development of Moor Park (1922–24), and in 1928 became Director of Town Planning in New Zealand, where he settled. His obituary is in *JTPI*, Vol 52 (1966). For his better known father, Thomas Mawson, see Cherry, Jordan and Kafkoula (1993).

17. Quoted in Home (1990b). For the planning of Jerusalem, see Crawford (1985), Efrat (1993), Hyman (1994), Kark (1991), Kendall (1948), and Meller (1990).

C.R. Ashbee (1863–1942) was the founder of the Survey of London, as well as Civic Adviser in Palestine (WWW).

18. The letter from David Eder is quoted in Herbert and Sosnovsky (1993), p. 15. Eder was an early Freudian and the first practitioner of psychoanalysis in Britain, as well as being a member of the Zionist Commission. Geddes had sent him copies of his Indore Report, and Eder replied that 'there are certain similarities between our needs in Jerusalem and the great Indore City'. Geddes offered his services at £10 a day, or £300 per month, substantially less than he charged for his Indian consultancies. After 1920 he did not return to Palestine until 1925, although his son-in-law F.C. Mears visited regularly to advise on the Hebrew University of Jerusalem. See Meller (1990), pp. 263–82.

Richard Kauffmann (1887–1958). His obituary is in *JTPI*, Vol. 46, 1959–60, p. 128: 'full of culture, noble in his ways and always ready to give help'.

Colonel Edward Alexander Stanton (1867–1947) served in Egypt at Omdurman, was Governor of Khartoum 1900–8, and military governor of Haifa (the Phoenicia Division of Palestine) 1918–20 (WWW).

19. A. Clifford Holliday (1897–1960) trained at Liverpool, and worked as a town planner in Palestine 1922–35, Ceylon 1939–43, and Gibraltar 1944–47. He left Palestine with his

family in 1935, but maintained a private practice in Jerusalem until 1938. He was the chief architect of Stevenage New Town 1947–52, and in 1952 became the first Professor of Town and Country Planning at University of Manchester. WWW and obituary in *JTPI*, Vol. 46 (1959–60), p. 284.

Howard Kendall (1903–83) worked as a town planner, first in Malaya, then in Palestine 1935–48, and latterly in Jordan, Gibraltar, Zanzibar and Uganda. Unfortunately Hyman (1994) stops with Holliday, and says relatively little about Kendall, whose Jerusalem City Plan is reported in Kendall (1948).

20. There is no full biography of Reade, although there is an excellent short life by Tregenza in DAustB. His work in different colonies has been separately researched: South Australia in Freestone and Hutchings (1993), Garnaut (1995), Hutchings (1990), and Tregenza (1986), Malaya in Goh (1988*b*), and South Africa in Mabin (1993). Home (1990*a*) gives references for most of Reade's writings in the British town planning journals, of which Reade (1921*a* and *b*) are samples.

21. For Reade's family background, see entry on Reade of Ipsden in *Burke*, and entries in DNB. For his grandfather see Lawrence (1992), p. 42.

22. Alexander reference is in CO 795/30, 35260 and 35281 (PRO). For the planning of Lusaka, see Collins (1969) and (1980), and Williams (1986).

Stanley D. Adshead (1868–1946) was the first Professor in town planning at Liverpool University 1909–14, and Professor at University College London 1914–35. The Governor of Northern Rhodesia during the planning of Lusaka (1932–34) was Ronald Storrs (1881–1955), who had formerly sponsored planning as Governor of Jerusalem (1917–26).

23. Thompson's career is examined in Home (1974), (1983) and (1990). For Pinelands see Logan (1935–36) and Muller (1993). For Nigeria see also Urquhart (1977).

24. Reported in *JTPI* Vol. 18, 1931–22, p. 149. Tarmac-surfaced roads at the time were an expensive item of infrastructure, and could cost up to £20,000 p. mile (*JTPI*, Vol. 18, 1931–2, p. 311).

Thomas Adams (1871–1940) was the first town planner to make his living as a consultant, and divided his career between three countries: Britain (where he was active in the garden city movement and was first President of the Town Planning Institute), Canada, and the United States. From 1922 he operated a trans-Atlantic practice with F.L. Thompson and E. Maxwell Fry. See essay in Cherry (1980) and the biography by Simpson (1985).

7

'THIS NOVEL LEGISLATION': INSTITUTIONALIZING TOWN PLANNING (1900–1950)

Legislation of this nature is novel to Trinidad and it is not suggested that this bill is by any means complete or perfect, but, with the progress of time and experience, grounds will no doubt be found for its improvement . . . The main purpose of the bill is to improve conditions generally in Trinidad in order to make it a better and happier place to live in.
(Attorney-General of Trinidad and Tobago, 16 December 1938, quoted in Home, 1993b)

The strong personalities who first proselytized for town planning, particularly Geddes and Reade, failed to get their more extravagant ambitions realized, and had mostly passed on by the 1930s. Nevertheless, that was the decade which saw much of the governmental machinery for physical planning installed in many of the British colonies, setting a framework which has survived, for better and worse, into the post-colonial period.

The precursors of town planning legislation were the improvement boards, which followed the undemocratic model of the port trusts, and introduced British approaches to slum clearance into colonial cities. At the same time a series of planning acts, derived from English practice, provided a structure for managing town expansion, sometimes incorporating German land pooling and land readjustment techniques. Then the 1932 English Town and Country Planning Act provided a new model of comprehensive physical planning, which was attractive in many colonial situations because it appeared to offer land-use control over the whole territory. A new widened view of the planners' role coincided with the Second World War, incorporating the new concepts of regional planning, and development and welfare.

'OPENING UP THE CONGESTED AREAS': IMPROVEMENT BOARDS AND THEIR SUCCESSORS

Chapter 3 introduced the improvement trusts that were created in many colonial port-cities in response to the plague panic of the 1890s.

This mechanism for urban renewal was widely adopted in the British colonies, and became an institutional tradition in the post-colonial period, when new urban development authorities provided a centrally directed alternative to elected local government.

An early example of such an urban improvement body was the Dublin Wide Streets Commissioners (1757), which undertook large-scale urban renewal. The more immediate legislative origin was the English Towns Improvement Clauses Act of 1847 (a precursor of the 1848 Public Health Act), which provided for the creation of improvement trusts, separate from elected municipal councils. Slum clearance powers for the colonial improvement trusts were also based upon English legislation, such as the 1890 Housing Act and Kingsway Improvement Scheme Act, as well as upon similar German laws of 1893, 1911 and 1913. The legislation for Calcutta set out fairly typical aims for an improvement trust, as follows:

to make provision for the improvement and expansion of Calcutta by opening up congested areas, laying-out and altering of streets, providing open spaces for purposes of ventilation or recreation, demolishing or constructing buildings, acquiring land for the said purposes and for the re-housing of persons of the poorer and working classes displaced by the execution of improvement schemes and otherwise as hereinafter appearing.

The term 'trust' carried with it an implied association with the public good rather than profit-making. Later, with the growth of state institutions in the twentieth century it was supplanted by the terms 'board', 'corporation' or 'authority', although the functions remained similar. In Britain most such bodies were absorbed into multi-purpose elected local authorities, apart from the New Town Development Corporations (under the New Towns Act of 1945), and the later Urban Development Corporations (under the Local Government, Planning and Land Act of 1980). In the colonial situation their perceived advantage, of freedom from elected democratic control, ensured their survival into the post-colonial period, usually renamed, but with similar centrally controlled decision-making and lack of local democratic accountability.

The Bombay City Improvement Trust, already referred to, was the first such colonial body to be created, in 1898, as a direct response to the outbreak of plague. It was empowered to control development, make new streets, open out crowded localities, reclaim and drain land, and construct dwellings. It was also authorized to buy land and then re-sell it after laying out the scheme, but this proved unpopular with the owners because they did not benefit from the improvements. The Trust would acquire more land than was needed for the scheme so that it, rather than the former owners, would get the betterment: in one example, Church Gate Street was widened from 30 to 70 feet, giving the Trust a net profit of nearly £200,000 from the associated development, on an initial outlay of £64,000. Its autocratic powers to acquire and demolish any property simply by serving a notice, without compensation, were understandably resented by both landlords and tenants. Those displaced by slum clearance often chose not to move into the Improvement Trust chawls, but stayed around the demolished area in even more congested conditions. (Geddes successfully predicted, from his own experience of working with the Edinburgh Improvement Trust, that the outcome would be to make workers' housing too expensive.) By 1920 the Trust had demolished 24,428 dwellings, but built only 21,387 to replace them, so that, after considerable effort and expenditure, it was adding to the quantitative housing shortage rather than alleviating it, and was forced to resort to 'slum patching'. Such was its unpopularity for its demolition work, and lack of compensation to slum landlords, that in 1917 there was agitation (which the colonial officials resisted) to transfer it to the municipality. That still retained power over building by-laws and sanitary administration, including the declaration of rooms unfit for human habitation.[1]

It was a similar story with the Calcutta

Improvement Trust, of which it was said that 'there was no public body in Calcutta so intensely unpopular and so cordially disliked' (Ray, 1979, p. 71). Called by the Calcutta residents 'a scheme to gratify the white population of Calcutta', it was kept under tight official control. A British ICS official of autocratic style, C.H. Bompas, was appointed as chairman and 'supreme and undisputed master of the situation'. Its eleven-member Board comprised the chairman, six elected by the Calcutta Municipal Corporation and four others appointed by the administration. It was well resourced, with revenues derived from an additional stamp duty of 2 per cent, a passenger tax, an export duty on jute, a 2 per cent rate from the municipal corporation, and a Government grant, providing a total annual income of 20 lakhs.

Its programme of clearance started with a 21-acre area next to the business quarter which had a density of 333 people to the acre and only 5 per cent road coverage. Bompas showed his high-handed attitude to squatters, claiming that they were merely 'temporary immigrants to Calcutta, whose displacement would cause

Calcutta in 1942, showing the results of the Improvement Trust's approach. According to Patrick Geddes, 'When an engineer rushes into town planning he too often adopts the simple expedient of drawing straight thoroughfares on the drawing board across the town plan and then sawing them through the town, regardless of cost and consequence.' (Source: Tyrwhitt, 1947)

no great hardship'. The area was redeveloped at a profit to the trust, with 25 per cent road coverage and two-thirds site coverage.

By 1927 the Trust claimed to have improved 294 acres within the city, and developed about 950 acres of suburban housing and open space. The local criticism was that slum clearance only displaced people to adjacent areas. Even Bompas acknowledged that new tenement housing at economic rents had failed to help with the housing problems. He said that the temporary immigrants 'prefer to live in insanitary conditions near their work, rather than in more healthy and distant localities', implying that the housing problem derived from the preferences of the poor and lack of 'a public opinion appreciating decent standards of living'.[2]

The view of E.P. Richards, in his brief period as engineer to the Calcutta Trust, was that the 'first great act of improvement' should be 'a general system of main roads'. He compared Calcutta's road coverage adversely with European and American cities. These averaged 30 miles of roads and streets per square mile of land area, while Calcutta had only 7 miles, as well as a further 16 miles of narrow zig-zag lanes. Early reports by the trust were particularly keen to report the length and land area of roads being carved out of the dense urban mass: after ten years' operation the Trust prided itself on handing over to the Municipal Corporation 12.23 miles of roads, with an area of 374,419 square yards, while a further 19.73 miles were in progress. Another form of road improvement was the creation of 'back lanes', of not less than 15 foot width, between each block of back-to-backs, to provide for scavenging and nightsoil removal.

The Presidencies of Bombay and Calcutta seem to have been the first colonies to adopt the improvement trust approach, while the third Presidency, Madras, followed a different policy, as will be seen below. The Improvement Trust approach was then applied in the United Provinces and elsewhere in India, following the deaths of millions from plague. A sanitary conference passed recommendations about 'the great need of opening up the congested areas, improving the drainage, providing open spaces and facilitating communications'. Trusts were created in Hyderabad in 1914, Lucknow and Cawnpore in 1919, and Allahabad in 1920. The Indians remained sceptical of their value, the municipalities opposed them, and in the United Provinces the Swarajist Minister dealing with local government ordered an inquiry: 'This Committee succeeded in up-rooting the plants to see if they were growing and then declared that the growth was satisfactory' (*GCTP*, Vol. 26, pp. 167–168).

The most successful of the Trusts in the Indian interior seems to have been at Lucknow. There an enlightened indirect rule approach was followed by Commissioner Harcourt Butler in Oudh, keeping the old structures of society in being. Geddes had produced two reports for the city in 1916 and 1917, helped by Lanchester (who maintained a private office there into the 1920s). Geddes explored the city in the company of municipal administrators and Indian assistants, two of whom he put up for associate membership of the Town Planning Institute. He met with the temple authorities to help them develop their gardens, and designed a low-cost housing unit with an Indian assistant (A.C. Sinha, an engineering graduate of Manchester). The Geddes approach, of minimizing demolition, dealing individually with cases, and winning general confidence, proved successful, and was continued after his departure by an enlightened trust chairman, L.M. Jopling, working together with a Chief Engineer, J. Linton Bogle (a Liverpool planning graduate and friend of Abercrombie). An Indian non-official chairman was appointed to help keep in touch with public opinion. (The contrast is striking between this caring approach to the city and the brutal treatment meted out to it sixty years before, in the aftermath of the 1857 Mutiny.)

Lacking the population pressures of other Indian cities, Lucknow also had the advantage of owning most of the town's expansion land, either as trustee for government lands or by acquisition. It mapped the industrial and residential areas, reserved land for agriculture and forestry, and built new roads, a vegetable market, a public park made from derelict land, and flood embankments.[3]

In Delhi British colonial administrative control was so all-pervasive, especially combined with the new machinery for developing the new capital, that the British viewed the additional mechanism of an Improvement Trust as unnecessary. Goaded by the rising cost of living (brought on as much by the transfer of the capital as by the war), the Indian residents of Delhi organized a mass protest in 1919 (the Satyagraha incident), and pressed for improvements in their living conditions. In 1925 there was an attempt to introduce a Town Improvement Act (on the lines of the Punjab Act of 1922), which would have been mainly concerned with street improvements and the development of unoccupied areas, but it was turned down by the Chief Commissioner. He considered that the transfer of important municipal powers to the trust would be 'an expensive error'. As a result Delhi had to wait until 1937 before an improvement trust came into being (Gupta, 1981).

In Singapore Sir William Simpson's damning report on sanitary and housing conditions in 1907, and a subsequent Housing Commission report in 1918, had not succeeded in stirring the colonial administration into action. The 1918 Commission recommended setting up an improvement trust, with additional provisions for town planning schemes. E.P. Richards, the same who had been with the Calcutta Improvement Trust and had written the acclaimed planning report on the city, was appointed in 1920 to set up an embryonic trust in the municipality, and, with the assistance of Reade, produced a Town Improvement and Development Bill in 1923. This was found by the Government to be 'impracticable under existing conditions', and Richards left in frustration in 1924. Reade in 1928 described Singapore as

a striking example of planless modern city and regional growth undirected by any comprehensive general plan and comprehensive schemes of improvement and development. The outcome of that modern growth is much unnecessary disorder, congestion and difficulties for which remedial measures have long been overdue. (*GCTP*, Vol. 16, 1926, pp. 169–170)

The Singapore Improvement Trust was eventually created by an Act of 1927. Ten million Singapore dollars were set aside as an initial fund, and it was empowered to raise an improvement rate, undertake improvement schemes, and control land subdivision. Zoning remained a municipal responsibility, and there was no provision for comprehensive planning (a draft ordinance which would have added these powers being lost during the Japanese wartime occupation in 1942). In the years before the Second World War the Trust, following Simpson's recommendations, carved backlanes through some eight hundred shophouse blocks, a form of rehabilitation later abandoned in favour of more comprehensive renewal.

An exception to the improvement trust model was Hong Kong, always the most *laissez faire* of colonial ports. It preferred the mechanism of a Housing Committee, which cleared ten acres of the worst slums, and passed legislation to control insanitary dwellings, which was based upon the Glasgow Building Act of 1900. The philosophy of colonial administrators in Hong Kong was well expressed by Margery Perham in her biography of Lugard, writing of the period between 1907 and 1912, when he was the Governor:

Hong Kong existed for trade: full social services meant heavy taxation and if trade were heavily taxed it would go elsewhere. The Chinese labourers came to get good money in conditions of freedom and safety: to tax or nag these labourers beyond an essential minimum would make the Colony unattractive to them. As one of the British officials said in Council, the choice in Hong Kong was between wealth or health.[4]

Lugard, her hero, blocked proposals for a new municipal corporation, which had been recommended by a commission on public health, although he did prohibit the practice of spitting in and out of doors.

From its beginning in India the improvement trust idea spread around the empire in the wake of the plague and the First World War, notably to Colombo, Rangoon, and Lagos. The Sydney Harbour Trust, the first *ad hoc* authority created in New South Wales (1901–35), from the reconstruction of wharfs expanded its activities into city improvement and worker housing. The trust model was continued with later development boards, such as the Kingston Urban Development Corporation (created in 1968 to act as a developer in the public interest), and the Dacca Improvement Trust (created in 1956).[5]

EARLY TOWN PLANNING LEGISLATION (1915–1935)

Within a few years of the creation of the early improvement trusts, the continuing problems of rapid urban growth, and the example of new town planning instruments in Britain and Germany, led to further legislation in the colonies, to control urban expansion and provide for slum clearance and renewal. Early acts were passed in Bombay (1915), Madras and Palestine (1920), Malaya (1923), and South Africa after 1927. Such attempts to formalize planning arrangements through legislation were usually found in colonies with strong settler activity and potential for intercommunal conflict, where the activities of professional planners in the colonies tended to be concentrated.

As with the improvement trusts, it was Bombay which led the way. In its enthusiasm for municipal affairs it can be compared with another second city, Birmingham, which was the home of much early town planning activity. As Bombay's population grew rapidly (from 776,000 in 1901 to 1,176,000 in 1921), it became apparent that the Improvement Trust approach was quite inadequate for the scale of the problem. The Bombay Town Planning Act of 1915 was acclaimed as 'a sincere attempt to embody in one measure all that was best from every other Town Planning Act extant'. It drew upon the British Housing and Town Planning Act of 1909, but was claimed to be 'more vigorous and direct' (comment by Pepler in Mirams, 1919–20, p. 60). Trying to learn the lesson of the unpopular financial provisions in the Improvement Trust legislation, it sought to introduce a betterment approach, which distributed the cost of development schemes over the land improved, with a fair profit to the owners and a tax on betterment. (The Bombay Presidency was already operating an infrastructure charge system, whereby roads and railways were paid for by a special rate levied on districts to be served.)

Land pooling and redistribution was introduced by Section 12 of the Bombay Act. Derived from the German Lex Adickes, it stimulated a long discussion at the Town Planning Institute in London in 1920, because such provisions did not exist in Britain. With the consent of the landowners, a public authority could combine their interests, and give them one or more plots to be held under common ownership, in 'the spirit of true cooperation'. An owner could pool his irregular plot and receive a better one, and continue cultivating until ready to develop or sell. The Act thus sought to encourage onto the market large areas of development land which without co-operative action would have stayed as agricultural land.

While land redistribution was not an instrument familiar to British planning, the town planning scheme was. The Bombay Act also empowered municipalities or appointed committees to prepare town planning schemes, under procedures similar to the English 1909 Act, and used an 'arbitrator' to define boundaries, assess values and prepare the final scheme. The powers over a planning scheme were wider than in Britain, and comprised:

(a) the construction, diversion, alteration and stopping up of streets, roads and communications;
(b) the construction, alteration and removal of buildings, bridges and other structures;
(c) the plotting out of land as building sites whether such land is intended to be used for building purposes in the immediate future or not;
(d) the allotment or reservation of land for roads, open spaces, gardens, recreation grounds, schools, markets and public purposes of all kinds;
(e) drainage inclusive of sewerage and of surface drainage and sewage disposal;
(f) lighting;
(g) water supply;
(h) the preservation of objects of historical interest or natural beauty and of buildings actually used for religious purposes or regarded by the public with special religious veneration;
(i) the imposition of conditions and restrictions in regard to the open space to be maintained about buildings, the number, height and character of buildings allowed in specified areas and the purposes to which buildings or specified areas may or may not be appropriated;
(j) the suspension of other regulations
(k) any other matter.

While the Bombay Act contained many new approaches, implementation was slow, because of the problems of finding suitable valuers, and the lack of comparable values. It was originally applied to Salsette Island, then to all municipalities, and the most active official to work on it was A.E. Mirams, the Bombay Presidency's town planner. He toured its smaller towns and villages, giving lectures illustrated by slides which he had sent from the Garden Cities and Town Planning Association in England, and was arbitrator for some sixty land pooling schemes. The plots were demarcated on the ground with limewash lines and number plates fixed in the ground.[6]

In the Madras Presidency, Geddes' influence persuaded the colonial administration not to follow the example of Bombay and Calcutta. He opposed improvement trusts as a mechanism for urban renewal, and Madras chose instead to bring both town improvement and town extension schemes under municipal control through a town planning officer, Geddes' ally, Lord Pentland, the Governor, wrote to Unwin in London about a suitable candidate, and on Unwin's recommendation Lanchester was appointed in 1915. He followed the Geddes approach with a meticulous survey report on Madras, including maps of the occupational structure and health conditions (such as plague black spots, infant mortality), and it was acclaimed by the Town Planning Institute as 'the conspicuous example of good survey and planning in single-handed combination' (*JTPI*, 1920–21, Vol. 7, p. 127).

A few years later, in 1920, the Madras Town Planning Act was passed. This sought to improve upon the Bombay Act with such features as recovering half of the betterment as a first charge on the property, and including within the scope of planning schemes the 'construction of houses for the poorer and working classes' (which elsewhere was an Improvement Trust responsibility). Following the English Housing and Town Planning Act of 1919, it made planning schemes compulsory for every municipality over 40,000 population. The next year Lanchester, who was busy elsewhere, was succeeded as Town Planning Officer by Reginald Dann (again on Unwin's recommendation), who held the post until his retirement (and death shortly afterwards).[7]

While Bombay and Madras were the first colonies to legislate on planning, the British took a lively interest in town planning in Palestine from the beginning of the Mandate period in 1918.[8] It was sponsored by Samuel (the first High Commissioner) and Attorney-

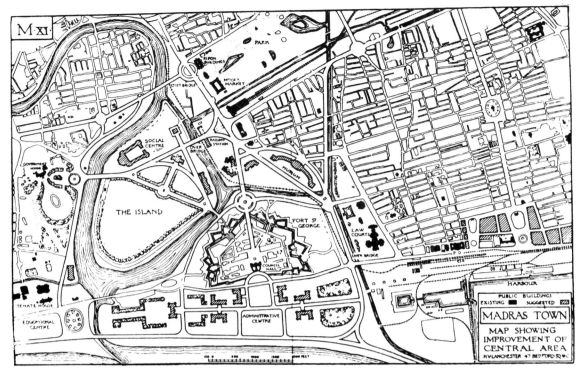

Lanchester's planning scheme for the improvement of Madras central area (1916). His proposals followed the Geddes approach of 'more studied and conservative lines' rather than wholesale clearances. (Source: Lanchester, 1925)

General Bentwich. Both were committed to the Balfour Declaration, and saw planning as the latest method of colonial administration (perhaps because neither of them were products of the career colonial service, which always remained sceptical). A Town Planning Act was passed in 1921, its purpose being stated in the explanatory note which accompanied it:

The principle is now established that a Government should control the growth and laying out of the towns and should see that they develop in a healthy and orderly way.

A Central Building and Town Planning Commission, together with local commissions, were created, all with appointed rather than elected, members so that the mandate administration could adjust the balance between officials, professionals and local representatives. The powers in the Act, which were based upon the Bombay Act and the English Act of 1909, included reparcellation, historic building preservation, and the expropriation of land for roads without compensation. Any area could be made a Town Planning Area, and a municipality could create its own local commission, and have planning and building control powers transferred to it.

The next stage in planning in Mandate Palestine was disappointing. As Hyman (1944, p. 703) says, 'After the fanfare of legislation, an embarrassing silence.' The 1921 Ordinance implied too much central control, and the colonial administrators did not understand it. Major projects like the Haifa Bay reclamation were undertaken without consulting the town planners. The status of the head of the Town Planning Central Commission was gradually reduced, being first the Chief Secretary himself, then the Legal Secretary, then the Head of the Department of Health. Then a new Ordinance was passed in 1936, which replaced the central Commission with three district commissions (each with five members, all government officials), and made the District Commissioners the top planning functionaries. This was a process of decentralization and downgrading similar to that which had taken place in Malaya a few years earlier.

Town planning in Palestine was thus firmly relegated to a local process for the approval of new housing developments, which were proliferating under the pressure of Zionist immigration. The population of Tel Aviv grew from 300 in 1910 to 150,000 in 1937, and in 1934–35 it was reported that the Commission considered nearly four hundred planning schemes and 250 'subjects relating to town planning'. British administration encouraged Zionist planning (e.g. the development of Tel Aviv, Nethanya and Haifa), and the Zionists used the new technical planning arguments to fight unwelcome government decisions.

In Malaya Charles Reade's dynamic presence between 1921 and 1929 resulted in unusually comprehensive and wide-ranging legislation, but the colonial administration subsequently cut it down in scope, as it did in Palestine.[9] Under the indirect rule system developed in the Malay States, the powers of traditional rulers had been strengthened under the influence of British colonial advisers (Residents), while in the tin-mining towns and rubber plantations immigrant Chinese and Indian labour was kept largely segregated from the indigenous Malay population. Towns were administered by sanitary and town boards, with appointed members and technical staff provided by the colonial administration.

Reade arrived from South Australia in 1921, and in the Town Planning Act of 1923, which he drafted, drew upon his wide knowledge of the subject. Its particularly comprehensive provisions incorporated development control, town improvement, building regulations, and sale and leasing of land, administered by a Town Planning Committee appointed by the Resident. The Government Town Planner was an *ex officio* member, and empowered with the committee to prepare a 'General Town Plan', with use zoning. No land could be sold without a certificate of conformity with the plan, there was provision for land redistribution, and standards for road widths were specified in the legislation.

Reade's Act was passed by a legislative council which probably did not grasp the implications, and within a few years his autocratic methods provoked a reaction. In 1927 a new Act was passed, following a review by a Select Committee of the Legislative Council, and transferred the powers of the local planning authority to the Sanitary Board. There was no provision for the town planner to be an *ex officio* member, only an adviser. The planning department was decentralized to offices set up in Ipoh, Kuala Lumpur and Seremban, each under a Town Planning Superintendant. This 'transformed town planning from a comprehensive exercise of land management and planning into an exercise of demarcation of communication lines and land use zones and nothing more' (Goh, 1988a, p. 10). Following this effective destruction of his powers, Reade gave up his position and returned to Britain (see p. 161). the 1927 Act was subsequently incorporated as Part IX of the Sanitary Board Enactment 1929. It remained in force, and was extended to unfederated states, until the Town & Country Planning Act of 1976 introduced the structure plan system and other provisions of the English Town & Country Planning Act of 1971.

Another colony where town planning was expected to help manage inter-ethnic relations was South Africa, where the dynamic growth of mining and white settlement, and active physical segregation by race, were both powerful influences upon the institutionalization of town planning, as has been explored in chapter 5. There was a close relationship between the segregation of South African cities and the early development of town planning, resulting in the country being already highly segregated before the implementation of the Group Areas Act by the Nationalist Government after 1948.

Reconstruction in Transvaal after the Anglo-Boer War included a Townships Board to guide land subdivision (the legislation was sponsored by Smuts), but public powers of racial zoning remained weak. A Transvaal Town Planning Association was created in 1919 and lobbied for legislation, the City Engineer of Johannesburg being particularly active. In 1925 it was decided that each province should promulgate its own legislation, rather than the Union government undertaking it centrally. A Town Planning Commission for the Transvaal in 1929 was followed by an Ordinance in 1931. Other provinces also passed town planning ordinances, for instance the Cape in 1927 and Natal in 1934, but only in Transvaal were these obligatory rather than discretionary. The Cape legislation included a 50 per cent betterment levy, but there were no such provisions in Transvaal and Natal (except

a set-off for increased value from a scheme). The ordinances were primarily concerned with local planning schemes and township approval procedures, with a bias toward control of suburban development rather than renewal. Town planning and landscape began to be included in university architecture courses at Cape Town and Johannesburg.

In the important mining area of the Witwatersrand and Pretoria the mechanism of a Joint Town Planning Committee was established. After the sudden death of its first planner, Charles Reade, in 1933, the London firm of Adams, Thompson and Fry were engaged as consultants from 1935 to 1939. Thompson was the partner responsible, spending two months a year in South Africa, until succeeded by P.J. Bowling. There were conflicts between the committee and provincial and local authorities who wanted more control, and the joint committee rarely met. Major infrastructure projects were deferred, and only in 1946 was the first of the Transvaal planning schemes approved. Nevertheless the Joint Town Planning Committee was a powerful influence upon South African planning, because of its conception of the planner's remit, the definition of the issues, the understanding of public-private sector relationships, the method of procedure and the style of the product in the form of the scheme'.[10]

THE COLONIAL OFFICE PROMOTES TOWN PLANNING: THE INFLUENCE OF THE ENGLISH TOWN PLANNING ACT OF 1932

For a period of two years, from June 1929 until the fall of the Labour government in July 1931, town planning had a friend in the Colonial Secretary – the Fabian Socialist, Sidney Webb (newly ennobled as Lord Passfield). His period of office was marked by difficulties in Kenya (where the white settlers were pressing to take land from the native reserves), nationalist pressures in India and Egypt, and ethnic tensions in Palestine (where there were anti-

Zionist riots by the Arabs in 1929). Passfield believed that planning had a contribution to make, and had a 'great respect for the individual whom he believed to be an expert'.[11] He issued a circular to his colonial governors and administrators which is worth quoting in full:

1. I have the honour to inform you that I have recently been giving consideration to the question of town and regional planning in the Colonies.

2. I think it may safely be said that careful planning of this nature, bearing in mind the probable development over a long period is essential to the fullest and healthiest development of which any particular area is capable. Town and regional planning in the proper sense is not a matter of new projects which would not otherwise have been undertaken; but should rather be regarded as an orderly and scientific method of controlling work already in progress or inevitable in the future, in a manner which secures the best and most far-reaching economical results from current expenditure as it takes place. Nothing is more expensive than haphazard or narrowly conceived development which will later involve the costly undoing of earlier mistakes.

3. Moreover, planning is more effective the earlier the stage at which it is applied. It is therefore important that advice should be secured and considered before and not after expensive projects for docks, railways stations, bridges, road developments, etc., are worked out.

4. Fortunately, the necessary technical personnel for giving this advice is now available; and there should be no difficulty in obtaining qualified men when they are required. Definite sources have been established and are rapidly producing trained men in increasing numbers. These sources are those such as are provided by the Diploma in Town Planning of the London and Liverpool Universities, and the examination recently instituted by the Town Planning Institute.

5. I therefore request that you will give your sympathetic consideration to the subject, particularly with regard to the desirability of appointing a Regional Planning Officer in all cases where any considerable development of residential, commercial, industrial, or transport conditions can be foreseen. If such an officer is appointed, he should be given an opportunity of scrutinizing and commenting on plans for important projects at an early stage of their examination.

6. It is, of course, open for consideration in the light of local circumstances whether town and regional planning is of sufficient importance in any Colony for the work to be regarded as a matter for the normal and continuous activity of Government, requiring the creation of a permanent planning organization, or whether it would be sufficient to

appoint a trained man on a temporary agreement to examine a particular problem. In most cases the latter will probably be the best course to adopt. (quoted in *JTPI*, Vol. 17 (1930–31), pp. 29–30)

Passfield's circular was followed within a few years by the introduction into much colonial legislation of a version of the English Town and Country Planning Act of 1932. This Act, which was passed with cross-party Parliamentary support, extended local authority planning control from urban areas to cover all land. Interim powers covered the period until the local authority had prepared a scheme. Betterment was recovered at 75 per cent, but the provisions were largely ineffective because local authorities made extravagant and unreal zoning allocations to avoid claims for compensation. Development not in accordance with a scheme was liable to be demolished without compensation (Cherry, 1974, p. 98).

Such a comprehensive approach to planning had its attractions to colonial administrations, or at least to the Colonial Office, which was concerned with wider issues of development and welfare, and saw an expanded role for the 'planner' beyond simple land-use regulation. This perhaps reflected the views of Charles Reade, who had known Webb for over twenty years, and was back in London after his time in the Federated Malay States. The regional planning movement was advocating a co-ordinated approach to development planning, including strategies for infrastructure (basically concerned with road and rail networks). As the engineer McLean's book on regional planning saw things, the problems of colonial development were essentially physical rather than political or economic.[12] The Colonial Office experimented with a 'forward policy' of social improvement after the Colonial Development Act of 1929, and formed a separate section in 1938 responsible for labour, health, education, and housing.

Much colonial planning legislation was passed in the 1930s and 1940s, closely modelled on the 1932 Act, and with housing and slum clearance provisions also based upon British legislation. These laws were enacted for individual territories, notably in the West Indies and West Africa in the wartime years and immediately after, as part of the new programmes of colonial development and welfare. The first was in Trinidad in 1938 (see pp. 184–187), following serious riots and critical findings by the Forster Commission, sent to investigate. The situation in Trinidad was soon followed by similar disturbances in Barbados and Jamaica, inconveniencing the British government at a time when it was preparing for war with Germany. Within months of the Forster Commission, a more important Royal Commission under Lord Moyne was touring the Caribbean in Moyne's private yacht, investigating social conditions in Barbados, British Guiana, British Honduras, Jamaica, the Leeward Islands, Trinidad and Tobago, and the Windward Islands. Its report, submitted at the end of 1939, was so politically embarrassing that the government withheld publication until 1945, when victory in the Second World War was assured. Moyne found 'a pressing need for large expenditure on social services and development which not even the least poor West Indian colonies can hope to undertake from their own resources'.[13]

Under the shadow of impending world war, the Forster Commission in Trinidad spent much time investigating whether the Trinidad riots might have been instigated by foreign agents, such was the British government's initial insensitivity to the real social grievances, and was relieved to find that bad social conditions had not undermined loyalty towards Britain. In May 1940 (at one of the darkest times of the war for Britain), the Colonial Secretary moved the creation of a Colonial Development and Welfare Fund in Parliament with these words:

At this critical hour let the world mark the passage of the Colonial Development and Welfare Bill through the British Parliament as a sign of our faith in ultimate victory . . . (We) must not default on our colonial obligations, we must not let slip the experienced skill of our guiding hand.

Initially the fund received the modest sum of £5 million, and implementation was slow. A policy memorandum in 1943 acknowledged the need for 'new capital developments of the character of social improvements, e.g. slum clearing, extensive replanning of urban areas, etc.' In 1944 governors were circulated a paper on the subject 'General Aspects of the Housing Problem in the Colonial Empire'.[14]

The West Indies became 'the testbed for the new development initiative', and were the subject of a 'running debate within the organization between those committed to serving the war effort and those whose principal sense of obligation was to maintain good relations with, and social and political order in, the West Indian colonies' (Lee and Petter, 1987, p. 177). A Comptroller for Development and Welfare in the West Indies, Sir Frank Stockdale, was appointed in 1940 and became an influential figure in colonial development planning. A post of Colonial Office Adviser in Planning and Architecture was approved in 1942, and offered to Holford, but was not filled.[15]

Housing was not seen as a particularly high priority, and indeed appeared only fifteenth on the list of project headings in the Colonial Office's first circular on the development and welfare programme, under the title 'Housing and Land Settlement (including reclamation of land and drainage schemes)'. 'Town planning' was not specifically mentioned at all. In the West Indies, however, housing and planning were given much more emphasis. Moyne, like Forster, had made a number of recommendations in the area: a balanced policy between rural and urban housing, more powers for slum clearance and compulsory purchase, better housing on the estates, and control over the siting of new housing. A town planning adviser, R.J. Gardner-Medwin, was appointed for the West Indies in 1944, and Stockdale's final report in 1945 incorporated his work, with

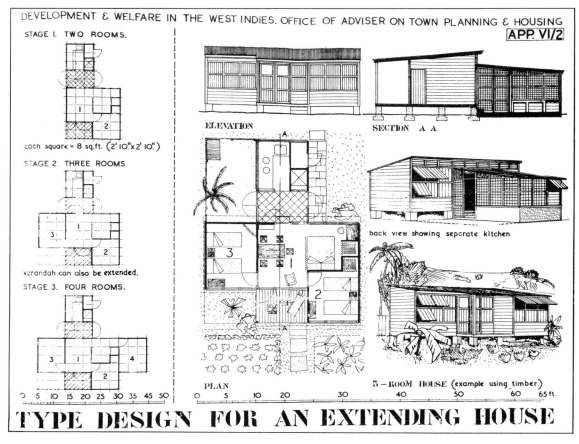

DEVELOPMENT & WELFARE IN THE WEST INDIES. OFFICE OF ADVISER ON TOWN PLANNING & HOUSING

APP. VI/2

STAGE I. TWO ROOMS.

each square = 8 sq.ft. (2'10"x2'10".)

STAGE 2. THREE ROOMS.

verandah can also be extended.

STAGE 3. FOUR ROOMS.

ELEVATION

SECTION A A

back view showing separate kitchen

PLAN

5 - ROOM HOUSE (example using timber.)

TYPE DESIGN FOR AN EXTENDING HOUSE

Gardner-Medwin's specimen design for an extending house. The housing programme in the West Indies was intended as a 'test-bed' for the new Development and Welfare programme after 1940. (Source: Housing in the West Indies, 1945)

specimen layouts, house plans, and minimum space standards. Among the various recommendations on town planning were that local authorities should be authorized to prepare schemes under central government approval. Density zoning was to be applied to prevent overcrowding, being seen as more flexible than control of house lot sizes through health or building regulations. Gardner-Medwin advocated planned neighbourhoods of 500–1500 families, 'as a working unit in providing sites and buildings for schools, community centres, play centres, health centres, shops etc'.[16]

On the subject of legislation Stockdale's report found that the Trinidad planning ordinance, 'having been found generally suitable for West Indian conditions, might well be taken as a basis' for similar legislation elsewhere. Planning was subsequently enacted in St. Lucia (1945), St. Vincent, Grenada, Dominica and British Guiana (1946), British Honduras (1947), and St. Kitts and Antigua (1948). By 1950 a Colonial Office memorandum on development and welfare in the West Indies said:

Housing is now generally recognized as a problem of government and the ancient legacy of employer responsibility for housing is fast disappearing. The legislative and administrative advances which have been made in recent years should ensure that future development is sound and well founded. (quoted in Home, 1993*b*)

The West Indian model was also transferred across the Atlantic, to the British West African colonies, where Maxwell Fry was Town Planning Adviser to the Resident Minister between 1943 and 1945. Legislation based upon the Trinidad Ordinance was passed for the four British West African colonies of Nigeria, the Gold Coast, Sierra Leone and the Gambia in 1945–46. It was viewed at the time by colonial administrators as:

a comparatively simple document prepared on a policy of expediency in an endeavour to give legal status to town planning at the earliest possible moment. Expert advice was therefore confined to essentials . . . It is fully recognized that a further Ordinance may be necessary in the not too distant future (*although in most cases this never happened –* author).[17]

Similar legislation followed in Nyasaland (1948), Uganda (1948 and 1951), Fiji, Aden, Sarawak, Seychelles and Mauritius. In the Far East, Hong Kong and Malaya had already incorporated the 1932 English Act in their legislation in 1939. The African legislation modified the West Indian model of planning schemes and interim control, in favour of a two-tier system of preliminary and final plans, and the Nigerian ordinance also provided for a property rate to fund planning. The type of planning authority varied: the Gold Coast, Sierra Leone and Uganda used an appointed central board, while in Nigeria and Nyasaland a separate planning authority was appointed for each planning area.

So the model of the 1932 Act and the 1938 Trinidad Ordinance came to be transferred to most of Britain's smaller colonies. The success of the legislation was, however, limited in the early years. In 1953 a colonial official involved with it, Stevens, sounded a cautionary note:

Thus the 1932 Act has left its mark in all corners of the world: in the Americas, Africa, the Middle and the Far East. Unfortunately, in many of the territories this legislation has been enacted far in advance of capacity to provide either finance or personnel for its execution . . . A more flexible system based on day-to-day consideration of development on its own merits in relation to a broad development plan is the ideal, but it would entail an organization at all levels in Government which is beyond the present financial and technical resources of most Colonies. (Stevens, 1953, p. 34)

Among the reasons for under-implementation were the geographical dispersal of the colonies, lack of resources and information, local opposition to a programme imposed from the centre, and the effects of inflation upon government spending programmes. A sceptical Colonial Office official wrote in 1949, commenting on the task of preparing 10-year development plans:

Whatever views I may hold about planning, I think the most I can hope for in the West Indies is a rather rough and ready measure of visible and probable resources, coupled with projects and scales of expenditure and resulting recurrent commitments, the whole being subject to frequent revision. (quoted in Home, 1993*b*)

In Nigeria Maxwell Fry prepared a report on planning in 1944 which advised concentrating efforts on three areas: village planning, the improvement of communications, and development of young and growing towns to prepare them 'for the impact of Western civilisation'. Writing in December 1944, he was concerned particularly with the return of soldiers after the war, and how to prevent African rural-urban migration ('the drift to the towns'). Development and welfare projects, included in the first Nigerian 10-year development plan, were 'not intended to cover merely the expansion and re-designing of big towns but will extend to all parts of the country, where the need for reconstruction and the provision of more modern facilities and amenities is a matter of extreme urgency' (quoted in Home, 1974, p. 238). Village reconstruction proved the most popular type of development project, and its share of the financial allocation for planning projects increased from a tenth to a third during the plan period. Fry himself put particular effort into village planning, preparing with his wife an illustrated booklet, *Village Housing in the Tropics*, which aimed to improve the quality of village life.

Town planning in Nigeria was placed in the hands of local planning authorities, operating separately from local or native authorities. Of the twenty-two authorities gazetted between 1946 and 1956, none was created in the North, for reasons of traditional indirect rule philosophy, its Chief Commissioner arguing that planning powers should be vested in the Native Authorities. In Southern Nigeria the experiment was not entirely a success, since nine authorities had been revoked by 1956,

while a further six were inactive. The most successful ones were in townships in the East and Mid-West, where property rating already existed and there was an established local government tradition. As the Resident wrote of a layout prepared for Enugu in 1952:

It is an extraordinary sensation to drive through open farm land carved out into squares with tarred roads, cement drains, filled plots and concrete floors for market stalls, but houses are now appearing as the building season advances. (quoted in Home, 1974, p. 247)

Much of the town planning vote remained unused, because of the shortage of qualified planners, and the fears of administrators about over-bureaucratic procedures. Many adminis-. trators believed that there would be onerous conditions on schemes, as discussed in greater detail in Home (1974), pp. 236–258. Within a few years policy moved away from the idea of separate local planning authorities to incorporate planning powers in general local government legislation, following the British model.

'We want Amenities': The Case of the Trinidad and Tobago Town and Regional Planning Ordinance of 1938[18]

The first of the new-style planning acts in the colonies was passed in Trinidad. It resulted from political pressure placed upon the British government by the riots of 1937, which were a major event in the history both of decolonization and Trinidad (Fryer, 1988, chapter 15). The passing and implementation of the ordinance makes an illuminating case study of the new legislation in practice at this period.

Trinidad had suffered from neglect throughout its colonial history. Its population composition and distribution could hardly have been less planned. Successive waves of African freed slaves and Indian migrant labourers left the plantations and settled either in the towns or on unclaimed rural land. In the nineteenth century some enlightened colonial governors

had planned resettlement villages, but there was no consistent or sustained programme. As sugar estates failed because of changing economic conditions, they were subdivided into agricultural smallholdings or residential plots. These were typically elongated strips up to half an acre in extent, and had minimal roads, drains or other services. Rapid population growth was not matched by economic growth or housing provision, with the result that by the 1930s Trinidad was suffering extreme unemployment, poverty, malnutrition, disease and bad housing. The Great Depression followed a century of underinvestment, both public and private, dating back to the emancipation of the slaves in 1834.

The crown colony administration was uncaring, and the discovery of oil in the south of the island brought little improvement in living standards. The Trinidadians expressed their criticism of colonialism in a rich tradition of festivals, street carnival and calypso singing, which sometimes spilled over into riots. As a 1920 calypso put it,

Class legislation is the order of this land.
We are ruled with the iron hand.
Britain boasts of democracy
Brotherly love and fraternity
But British colonists have been ruled
In perpetual misery – sans humanité.
(quoted in Liverpool, 1990)

In June 1937 Trinidad experienced mass political action, a general strike and rioting in which two policemen and twelve others were killed. This expressed 'the pent-up grievances and resentments of workers whose economic situation had deteriorated over the preceding years and who had no legitimate channels for the peaceful resolution of industrial problems' (Brereton, 1981).

The British government was shocked into appointing a Commission of Inquiry (the Forster Commission), which reported in January 1938. Appalled by the housing conditions, it recommended replacing barrack housing 'within three years' by family accommodation, and, while not referring directly to town planning, urged the government to provide, 'either from Crown lands or by acquisition, land for village development, the village to be planned and to be provided with roads, drains and water', and 'a general programme dealing with village housing and sanitary conditions'.[19] These recommendations led directly to the 1938 Trinidad Town and Regional Planning Ordinance.

A new governor, Sir Hubert Young, was appointed in response to the riots. He had a reputation for toughness in dealing with labour disputes, having succeeded in crushing a miners' strike in the Northern Rhodesian copperbelt, but also vigorously supported the need for new housing and planning legislation. Soon after his arrival in the colony he was writing to the Colonial Secretary:

It is quite clear to me that some form of town planning and housing authority will have to be set up . . . I am accordingly having two orders drafted, one for town planning and one for housing, but providing for the formation of one authority to deal with both.

The colony was now drawing increased revenue from rapidly growing oil extraction, and Young volunteered those revenues to service a loan of £1.5 million for housing renewal. Reginald Walker, one of the few town planners at the time with both colonial experience (in Nigeria) and practical knowledge of recent British legislation, was appointed town planning consultant. He drafted the new legislation, which he derived from the English 1932 Act and the similar Irish Free State Act of 1934.[20]

So it came about that, at the Legislative Council meeting of 16 December 1938, the Attorney-General of Trinidad and Tobago moved the second reading of 'An Ordinance to make provision for the orderly and progressive development of land, cities, towns and other areas whether urban or rural, to preserve and improve the amenities thereof, and for other matters connected herewith' (Cap. 37, no. 4).

It provided powers for the preparation, approval, revocation and modification of planning schemes (including regional schemes), and interim development control powers. Schemes were to deal with six specified matters: roads, buildings, amenities, public services, transport and miscellaneous. Compensation and betterment provisions allowed claims for injurious affection, and a betterment levy was set at 50 per cent of the increased value of land produced by planning. Powers relating to land pooling and redistribution were included, recognizing, in the words of the Attorney-General, that:

In many parts of Trinidad land has been so intensively subdivided into irregular shapes without any regard to future road requirements, topography, &c., that particularly troublesome conditions have been created from a planning point of view.[21]

The new Ordinance was expected to lead to the extension of planning control over the whole island (which eventually occurred with the 1969 Act), although in his speech the Attorney-General acknowledged that:

This is a very long-range objective at this initial stage of the introduction of the subject here in Trinidad, but the whole trend of planning practice and legislation in other countries during the past 20 years, as a result of experience and the pressure of constantly changing conditions, has been towards this widened basis as the really only satisfactory foundation.

Three members of the Council spoke in support. An Indian member, Mr. Teelucksingh, was particularly fulsome in his praise, seizing upon the prospect that 'amenities' were going to be provided:

I was very pleased to hear one of the big words, the 'amenities' of the district, used by the Honourable Attorney-General. I know, as he said, it is a very good word and carries something that will meet the approval and the spirit of us all. That is exactly what we want.

Another member, Mr. Wharton, took a more limited, aesthetic view, hoping that the new legislation would result in tighter control over the use of galvanized iron as roofing material.

A housing ordinance was passed at the same time. The powers of both ordinances were to be implemented by a combined Planning and Housing Commission, rather than conferring on the local authorities. The official explanation was that they lacked the technical resources and the problems were wider than local authority boundaries, but in reality the colonial administration distrusted the 'delinquent' Port of Spain Council. As the Forster Commission put it:

It is in our view inevitable that powers of slum clearance, vested in a City Corporation composed in sufficient part of persons, who are owners of or who have interests in insanitary property, to create opposition to schemes for its demolition, will not be effectively carried out; and that in such circumstances slum clearance is doomed to failure and the public interest must suffer. (Forster, 1938, paragraph 139)

The implementation of Trinidad's new planning and housing legislation was soon overtaken by the demands of the Second World War. The first serious problem experienced was finding qualified staff. Walker left in the summer of 1939, and Young and the Colonial Office sought for the post of chairman of the new Planning and Housing Commission 'a person of considerable tact and tenacity with good judgment in the weighing up and reconciling of the views of different parties and achieving both harmony and progress in the functioning of the Board'. A retired engineer with distinguished Indian experience, Sir Adrian Musto, was appointed in 1939, but returned to Britain on the outbreak of the Second World War after only a few weeks in post. He offered his comments on a replacement for Walker (whom he considered 'a tired man'):

I think it is essential that you should have a man able and willing to make responsible decisions and prepared to defend these against inevitable opposition from vested interests. Secondly, as about a third of the population is East Indian with its own special problems and idiosyncracies, I think the officer appointed should most preferably have Eastern experience, and personally, I think a man with experience of housing labour in India would be likely to give more satisfaction than any other. It was on both these points that I considered Walker was rather lacking. (quoted in Home 1993b)

After several months with neither chairman nor town planner for the new commission, Young lamented in a telegram to the Colonial Office that:

Hope deferred maketh the heart sick. It is now 18 months since my 5 year plan was framed (for housing renewal) and not one workman's home has been built although Government House has been completely renovated.[22]

In 1940 a local appointment was made, Robert Grinnell, an American engineer working in Tobago, who had experience on public utilities in Barcelona, but this did not last. A chartered town planner, M.F. Costello, was recruited on a three-year contract in 1947, but was made redundant within a year due to 'limitation of funds' and transferred to Guiana.[23] Only in the mid-1950s was a qualified town planner (R.J. Crooks) appointed on a long-term basis.

In 1942 the Attorney-General was complaining that 'The Commission is rather in the position of the "handy man" of the Colony' (quoted in Home, 1993b). Under its housing powers the new Commission demolished some of the worst barrack housing in Port-of-Spain, and built some five hundred houses between January and September 1940, but its activities soon slowed down because of the demands of the war effort and immediate post-war restrictions. By 1956 2175 families had been housed in new schemes in Port-of-Spain and San Fernando, particularly in the new township of Morvant, to the east of the capital. The travel writer Patrick Leigh Fermor described these in 1950 as 'trim white blocks of workers' flats, which are healthy but hideous' (Fermor, 1984, p. 150).

One early scheme for rehousing estate workers was sufficiently noteworthy to be the subject of a detailed report to the Colonial Office in 1950. At the Frederick Village Housing Settlement at Caroni, the sugar estate management granted 54 acres of land to the Commission in 1944, with the intention of rehousing workers from the estate barracks and two informal settlements known as Jumbie Piece and La Paille. Some 234 housing plots

were laid out, ranging in size from 5000 to 18,700 square feet, and were eventually taken up after some initial reluctance. An acre of land was reserved for community buildings, and simple land-use zoning was deployed (three different residential density zones, a zone for public services, and one for shops) (quoted in Home, 1993b).

During the Second World War road-building programmes were undertaken for the American air base at Chaguaramas and elsewhere. To restrain new buildings and accesses in a zone of 150 feet either side of the main highways, a Restriction of Ribbon Development Ordinance was passed in 1942. Administration of that ordinance, together with housing, absorbed more resources than did town planning, on which the Annual Reports were virtually silent throughout the 1940s and 1950s. In 1956, for instance, some seven hundred applications under the Restriction of Ribbon Development Ordinance were processed, and 2489 housing tenancies (a third of them at Morvant), but only two hundred building applications and twenty-four 'parcellations of land' under the planning legislation. It is not surprising that the Prime Minister in 1960 could refer to 'our Town Planning section which did so little Town Planning . . . the town planner of the country spent his time giving out Planning and Housing Commission houses and seeing what should be repaired, and what rentals people should pay'. Two planning schemes were declared in the 1950s, at Marabella and El Socorro (suburbs of San Fernando and Port-of-Spain respectively), but, even thirty years after the passing of the 1938 Ordinance, there was still little sign of practical implementation on any scale.

CONCLUSIONS

Town planning legislation on the British model was introduced in Trinidad and other British colonies as a response to political pressure, at a

time of crisis when the British government needed to ensure the loyalty of colonies in the Second World War. In the post-war world order, town planning played a part in the British attempt to stave off, or at least manage, the process of decolonization and constitutional change. It held out a promise of better living conditions ('colonial develoment and welfare'). But the resources, and indeed the political will, were always inadequate, so that achievements on the ground were few. As in Britain, colonial town planning, especially in the West Indies, was closely linked with housing issues, and with the change (which has proved to be temporary) from private to public sector as the main provider of shelter for the poor. Town planning legislation proved to be an inadequate technical response to massive pressure for social and political change, and was recognized by its creators at the time as a policy of expediency.

Not only was town planning inadequately resourced to deliver real improvements on the ground, but the relationship of 'town planning' to wider issues of 'development planning' or social welfare was confused, in the colonies as in Britain itself in the 1940s. During their short time in the West Indies or West Africa, architects and civic designers such as Walker, Gardner-Medwin and Fry prepared designs for buildings or estates, only some of which were destined to be built, and were confronted with impossible tasks of social control through the built environment. But the attractions of 'town planning' as an all-embracing state activity remained strong, for local politicians as well as colonial administrators. Eric Williams, moving the 1960 Town and Country Planning Ordinance, claimed that:

the time has come to put a stop to the differences between economic planning and physical planning.

Planning laid the foundations for a new government role in land management and land-use regulation, responding to the demands of population growth. A recurrent theme was the issue of political representation and control. Colonial administrators were reluctant to surrender control of the new planning agencies and powers, either to democratic representatives or to planning professionals. In the transition to independence the burdens of expectation could seem too great for the planning system to carry.

NOTES

1. There are short reports on the Bombay Trust in: *JTPI*, Vol. 9 (1922–23), pp. 94 and 99; and Vol. 10 (1923–24), pp. 195–97; in the *Town Planning Review*, Vol. 10 (1923–24), pp. 275–279; and Vol. 23 (1936–37), pp. 144–145; and *GCTP*, Vol. 14 (1924), p. 203; and vol. 17 (1927) p. 208. See also Burnett-Hurst (1925). For similar problems in English Victorian cities, see Wohl (1983).

2. For the Calcutta Trust's work, see Ray (1979), pp. 70–78. There is a report by Bompas in *GCTP*, Vol. 17 (1927), pp. 85–86. For Geddes' work on the Trust's Barra Bazar redevelopment, see Meller (1990), pp. 282–284. Cecil Henry Bompas (1868–1956) was educated at Westminster and Trinity College, Cambridge, and entered the Indian Civil Service in 1887 (WWW).

3. For Improvement Trusts in the United Provinces, see *GCTP*, Vol. 16 (1926), pp. 167–168. For Lucknow see *GCTP*, Vol. 17 (1927), pp. 84–85; Bogle (1929); Jeffrey (1978), p. 377; Jopling (1923); and Meller (1990), pp. 242–248.

Sir Spencer Harcourt Butler (1869–1938) was lieutenant-governor and governor of the United Provinces 1918–23, and subsequently governor of Burma 1923–27 (WWW).

4. Perham (1960), p. 312. For Hong Kong see also Bristow (1984), pp. 34–37.

5. For Singapore see Castells *et al.* (1990); Cross (1992); Fraser (1957); Webb (1923–4); and Yeoh (1991). Singapore already had a Dock Board (1905, renamed the Harbour Board in 1913), and such appointed boards remained a feature of the island's government after independence, with the Jurong Town Corporation created in 1968 and the Urban Redevelopment Authority in 1974. In 1920 the Rangoon Development Trust came into existence, benefitting from

a large urban estate which it developed in phased settlements. For Sydney see O'Flanagan (1989). For Kingston see Knight (1984).

6. The Bombay Act is described in *Town Planning Review*, Vol. 6 (1915–16), pp. 250–251; Meller (1990), p. 212; Mirams (1919–20); and *JTPI*, Vol. 10 (1923–24), pp. 195–196.

Albert E. Mirams (d. 1938?) was Consulting Engineer to the Government of Bombay, and was later Town Planning Adviser in Uganda (1928–29). In Meller's (perhaps too harsh) judgment, Mirams' work on the Act was 'an isolated effort and for all his enthusiasm, his activities were rather amateurish.' The origins and operation of the Bombay Act, and Mirams' work, justify further research, which I am not aware has yet been undertaken.

7. For town planning in Madras, see Davidge (1921); Lanchester (1916–17); Lewandowski (1975) and (1984); and Neild (1979).

Reginald Dann (1883–1939) was a landscape architect and director of the London office of Mawson & Sons at the time of his appointment as the first Director of Town Planning, Madras, in 1921. A Quaker from Ackworth, Yorkshire, he served in a firm of nurserymen for 15 years (Joseph Cheal & Son of Crawley), entering various planning and housing competitions, and joined Mawson's after the First World War. From 1932 he was also consulting architect to the Government of Madras. In a letter of 12 February 1939 to the Royal Institute of British Architects after his death, his widow, then living in Welwyn Garden City, expressed the opinion that 'the overwork from holding the dual posts resulted in the permanent undermining of his health'. She wrote of 'his particular genius for planning so that the environment is an integral part of the design, and his great care that planning should be economically efficient and suitable to local requirements' (RIBA biographical file).

8. The principal source on town planning in the Mandate period in Palestine is Hyman (1994). The 1921 Ordinance was reported briefly in *GCTP*, Vol. 11 (1921), p. 191, and the 1936 Ordinance in *JTPI*, Vol. 24 (1937–38), pp. 202–203.

9. On Malaya, there is a short account of the 1923 Act in *JTPI*, Vol. 10 (1923–24), pp. 202–

203, and articles and reports by Reade (1921). See also Goh (1988*a*) and Home (1989*a*).

10. See Mabin (1993). The Committee was responsible for Johannesburg, Pretoria, Randfontein, Krugersdorp, Roodepoort, Germiston, Boksburg, Benoni, Brakpan and Springs.

Francis Longstreth Thompson (1890–1973) graduated in engineering from London University, worked for the Port of London Authority and the Ministry of Health, and formed a partnership with Thomas Adams in 1922. He wrote a book on site planning (1923), was the half-brother of G.L. Pepler, and was President of the Town Planning Institute 1932–33. He represented his firm as consultant to the Witwatersrand, Pretoria and Johannesburg Joint Town Planning Committee 1935–39, and on the development of Cape Town in 1940 (Simpson, 1985).

Colonel Peter James Bowling (1889–1957), Thompson's assistant and an important figure in South African planning from 1935, trained as a Royal Engineer and rose to the rank of lieutenant colonel in the First World War. Town planning consultant to Chelmsford council, he became the Government Town Planning Engineer in Northern Rhodesia 1932–35, worked with the Witwatersrand Committee 1935–40, and remained afterwards in South Africa.

With the importance of reconstruction in South Africa after the end of *apartheid*, we are fortunate in having a substantial recent literature on its planning history. The South African Planning History Group published papers from its first workshop, held in Johannesburg in 1992, in *Planning History*, Vol. 15, No. 2 (1993). The full proceedings of its second symposium, held at Pietermaritzburg are in South African Planning History 1993. A third symposium was held at Pretoria in 1994. See also Lemon (1990), Mabin (1991) and (1993); Mandy (1984); Maylam (1990); Muller (1993); Robinson (1990). For short contemporary reports, see the *JTPI*, Vol. 16 (1929–30), pp. 218–219, Vol. 18 (1931–32), pp. 310–311, and Vol. 22 (1935–36), pp. 199–201.

The development of planning legislation in other settler colonies of central and East Africa has been less studied. Kenya passed an ordinance in 1930, based upon English practice, with sub-division control, joint schemes, land pooling and readjustment. See *JTPI*, Vol. 17 (1930–31), pp. 30–32, and Vol. 18 (1931–32), pp. 147–149.

11. Cole (1974), pp. 201–218. See also Webb (1978).

Sidney Webb, 1st Baron Passfield (1859–1947), was a Fabian Socialist writer and Labour politician.

12. After his retirement from Egypt in 1926, McLean took up regional planning, writing a Ph.D. thesis which was published (McLean, 1930). It placed much emphasis on transport infrastructure in the colonies, including a world-wide network of airship routes which became redundant within a year when a series of disasters revealed the dangers of airship travel. See Home, 1990*b*, and also Home (1974) for transport developments in one colony (Nigeria) at this time.

13. Quoted in *Housing in the West Indies* (1945), Introduction.

Lord Moyne (1880–1944), a member of the Guinness family, described in the DNB as 'states-man and traveller', had a particular interest in working-class housing, through the Guinness Trust, and chaired a Departmental Committee on Housing in 1933. He was later Colonial Secretary, and was assassinated by Zionist extremists in Cairo in 1944.

14. For the 1943 memorandum (the Caine Memorandum), see Lee and Petter (1982), p. 172. Malcolm Macdonald's speech in the House of Commons, 21 May 1940, is quoted in CO 1042/67 (PRO).

15. Sir Frank Stockdale (1883–1949), formerly a lecturer in agriculture in the West Indies, British Guiana and Mauritius, was Comptroller of Development and Welfare from 1940–45, and adviser on development planning at the Colonial Office from 1945–48 (appointed 'at the highest possible salary'). WWW.

16. The circular (1 June 1940) is in CO 1042/67. See also Housing in the West Indies (1945), paragraphs 28, 34, 66.

Robert Joseph Gardner-Medwin, RIBA, FRTPI (1907–95), was educated in architecture and civic design at Liverpool and Harvard Universities. He combined practice with teaching at the Architectural Association before joining the Royal Engineers in 1940. Town Planning Adviser in the West Indies 1944–47, he returned to Liverpool as Professor of Architecture in 1952. WWW.

17. Memorandum by H.L. Ford on draft Nigerian Town & Country Planning Ordinance, August 1945, in CSO 26/43607 (NNA). For Nigerian legislation see Home (1983) and Ola (1977).

E. Maxwell Fry, CBE, BArch, FRIBA, FRTPI (1899–1987), the eminent architect and town planner, was trained at Liverpool and practised with Gropius 1934–36. A partner in the firm of Adams, Thompson and Fry, he was Town Planning Adviser in West Africa 1943–45, and worked with Le Corbusier on Chandigarh 1951–54. WWW. His 1944 report on planning in Nigeria is in CSO 26/41722 (NNA).

18. This is a revised version of Home (1993*b*). For government land policy in Trinidad, see Blouet (1977) and Smith (1914). For the social background see Brereton (1981); Campbell (1988); Jackson (1988); Johnson (1969); and Thomas (1987).

19. Forster (1938), especially paragraphs 117–139, 281 (xvi), 126, 280 (vi), and 283 (xix).

The chairman, John Forster, later Lord Forster of Harraby (1888–1972), was a barrister special-izing in labour relations who chaired various inquiries into industrial disputes, including one in Northern Rhodesia in 1940. WWW.

20. Sir Hubert Young (1885–1950) was Governor from 1938 to 1942. He had formerly served with T.E. Lawrence in Arabia, and as Governor of Northern Rhodesia from 1934 to 1938 (WWW).

Reginald Beckwith Walker (1896–?) qualified with a Diploma in Town Planning and Civil Architecture from University of London, and, after working for Adshead and as Town Planning Assistant at Norwich, was Assistant Town Planning Officer in Nigeria 1928–31. Made redundant from Nigeria, Walker went into partnership in Brighton with his former boss, Albert Thompson, from which he was appointed town planning consultant in Trinidad 1937–39, at a salary of £1800. See Home (1974) and (1993*b*). His sailing for Trinidad was reported in *JTPI*, Vol. 23 (1936–37), p. 215.

21. This and following quotations come from

the 1938 Trinidad and Tobago Hansard, pp. 625–654.

22. Young to Colonial Office 12 February 1940 (and Musto comment) in CO 295/616/70459 (PRO), quoted in Home (1993b).

Sir Arnold Musto (1883–1977) was a graduate engineer who worked on the Rotherhithe Tunnel and then on major canal and irrigation projects for the Indian Public Works Department for 25 years, before retirement and a knighthood in 1932. On his return from Trinidad he served as a Regional Transport Commissioner from 1940 to 1953. WWW.

23. Colonial Office Annual Report for Trinidad and Tobago 1949. M.F. Costello, MRIAI, AMTPI, became the planning officer to the Central Housing and Planning Authority, British Guiana, and prepared a draft planning scheme in 1950.

8

'WHAT KIND OF COUNTRY DO YOU WANT?' THE TRANSITION TO INDEPENDENCE

What kind of country do you want? Every person has ideas about these important questions, and this is how it should be, because they affect everyone intimately. People have widely different needs and expectations but there are certain essentials that are basic to all: the house you live in, the job you do and the availability of money for food, clothing, etc., the form and quality of transportation, where and how you spend your leisure time, children's schooling. All these factors can be summed up in the phrase THE QUALITY OF LIFE. Basically this is why planning is essential – TO IMPROVE AND MAINTAIN THE QUALITY OF LIFE.

(Town and Country Planning Division, Government of Trinidad and Tobago, *You and Planning c.* 1973)

Such sentiments, expressed by the town planners of Trinidad, may now seem naive and patronizing, but at the time they represented a new approach to managing public opinion by the political classes of the post-colonial nation states. Physical planning was seen as one of the tools with which to negotiate a better living environment, and thereby deliver the promise of independent nationhood. After the end of the Second World War the British progressively lost political control over the colonies and withdrew from them. There was a more or less planned devolution to local political leaders and constitutional reforms, which happened to coincide with a massive growth and redistribution of populations. The years after 1945 saw unprecedented efforts by governments in the countries emerging from colonialism, to redevelop villages and create new towns, driven by population pressures and migration which have often continued down to the present day. In the politics of decolonization and independence, planning and state intervention assumed an important role.

STATE CONTROL OF POPULATIONS:
COMPOUNDS, CAMPS AND RESETTLEMENT VILLAGES

The control of populations is as much as a feature of colonialism as racial discrimination, and British colonial expansion is full of stories of control of built environments. The wide

'What kind of country do you want?' This illustration, from a public relations leaflet by the Town Planning Department of Trinidad and Tobago (about 1973), is interesting for the body language displayed: 'the planner' (male) leaning in an almost intimidatory way over the apprehensive 'public' (female). About this time the planners failed to get approval for the wholesale redevelopment of the informal settlement in East Port of Spain. (Source: Trinidad and Tobago Town Planning Department, c. 1973)

You Can Take Part

By exchanging your ideas with the planners

Independence ('Merdeka') Day celebrations in Kuala Lumpur, Malaysia. The girl guides are assembled on the 'padang', with the colonial Law Courts in the right foreground and the Elizabethan-style Selangor Golf Club in the background. (Source: The author, photo taken in 1985)

streets of colonial cities had a defensive as well as public health function, in the tradition of Haussmann in Paris. A governor of New South Wales in the era of the Chartists rejected public squares and parks because of the opportunity they accorded for public gatherings and demonstrations. It is said that a police chief in the Caribbean rejected the installation of sewers because they offered hiding places for escaped slaves, while the building regulations of Jamaica were also designed to help catch fugitives from justice.

In this coercive tradition the twentieth century can be characterized as the century of the camp. Coercive authority, both of the state and private business, made camps to accommodate many groups of people: the military and militia, internees and evacuees, estate and construction workers, refugees and persecuted minorities. In the design of these new settlements the British Empire developed a particular expertise. It needed to isolate and control unwanted or particular social groups in largely self-sufficient, state-run encampments, which were kept separate from the rest of society under a special disciplinary regime.

Classifying and segregating social groups became an important element in European political and social theory during the fifty years which followed the end of the French Revolutionary Wars in 1815. Utilitarian ideas included the classification, segregation and control of minority groups. Its father figure, Jeremy Bentham, devised the famous *panopticon* (cited by Foucault as a paradigm of disciplinary technology), which subjected prisoners to solitary confinement under an all-seeing central supervision. His ideas were applied to the isolation of groups such as criminals and lunatics for special institutional treatment in purpose-designed buildings and settlements. Ebenezer Howard after 1900 continued the utilitarian tradition of classification and segregation. His plans for a system of garden cities would have located in a green belt special institutions for various groups ('inebriates', 'waifs', the insane, epileptics, convalescents, the blind), thus isolating 'those people which the eugenists wanted to exclude from further propagation' (Voigt, 1989).

New industrialized building technologies and materials also became more available during the nineteenth century for specialized and temporary buildings. Among such innovations were the machine sawing of timber, mass production of wirecut nails, cast-iron building

frames, and barbed wire. Balloon-frame timber buildings in the 1830s became a revolutionary method of fast construction, which helped to open up the American West for settlement (Rempel, 1980, pp. 121–123).

Aldershot military barracks can claim to be the first of the new type of camp. It began as a summer-only tented camp in 1853, but soon the authorities were experimenting with semi-permanent wooden barrack huts, often with verandas incorporated from Indian practice. Similar wooden barracks were erected in the Crimea for the winter siege of Sebastopol in 1854–55, and were soon adapted for the use of civilian construction workers on the canals and railways (Brice, 1984). The adaptation of the barrack building form for accommodating civilian workers across the empire has been discussed in chapter 4, and the evolution of the military camp into the cantonment in chapter 5.

The two world wars led to many variations of the camp idea, as millions of troops and workers had to be organized and accommodated in temporary facilities. In Britain standard designs for 'hutments' were devised: a barrack hut of 60 ft × 20 ft for one sergeant and 24 men, with dining hut, cookhouse, bathhouse, 'regimental institute', officers' and sergeants' messes, and drying hut for clothing. Handbooks were written on camps 'for speedy erection in invaded countries'. In the Russian empire, both under the Tsars and (after 1917) the Bolsheviks, the Siberian forced labour camps (where an estimated 15 million people died in the Stalinist period alone) anticipated the Nazi camps in many details. During the Great Depression in the United States migrants in search of work were accommodated in labour camps in California. By the Second World War the need for camps of all sorts (holiday camps, evacuation camps, school camps) was reflected in a special issue of the *Architects' Journal*, edited by Gordon Stephenson. This estimated that between two and eight million people would need to be moved from urban to rural areas in Britain in the event of war.[1]

The process of colonial expansion provided important models which were later adapted and used for the Nazi camps. The so-called 'concentration camps' were apparently first devised to control hostile populations during the colonial wars of the late nineteenth century: the Spanish in the Cuban insurrection of 1895, the Americans in the Philippines in 1898, and the British in the South African War (1900–1902). The idea of 'concentration camps' to control whole populations seems thus to have appeared at the turn of the twentieth century, and, as the coercive power of the state grew with two world wars, was applied in many situations, including the machinery of the Holocaust.

It was General Kitchener who authorized the creation of 'concentration camps' in South Africa to isolate the families of Boer commandos, and thus cut off a source of food, supplies and comfort. Bad water and inadequate sanitatory arrangements killed about thirty thousand Afrikaner women and children in these much-hated camps, and there were uncounted deaths in similar camps for the black Africans. The early tented camps were soon replaced by semi-permanent buildings erected by the Boers themselves, 'burgher tradesmen and labourers'. These buildings were light weight because of the costs of transport, and living accommodation was provided in rows of four-room huts, 14 feet square, and built of sun-dried brick.[2]

South Africa provided another model for population control in the closed compounds created by De Beers after 1885 (see pp. 00), which were soon adapted for state-sponsored forced labour camps elsewhere in Africa. Early in the history of South African mining, the mining interests obtained the agreement of the Cape government for state control of migrant labour, after a Government Commission in 1876. Mining compounds in both South Africa and the Belgian Congo were designed on the 'fan' principle radiating fanwise from the central compound offices, so that the compound manager could survey the whole area from his office window. This was a precise architectural realization of Bentham's panoptical design for maximizing surveillance. The French colony of Madagascar between 1925 and 1930 formed so-called 'pioneer camps', in which 8000–10,000 Africans each year were 'trained in European work disciplines'. Such camps were condemned as inhumane by the International Labour Organization, but nevertheless survived in South Africa, where the fan design became from the late 1940s the industry standard.

In the South African mining camps, experimental chambers subjected new mine recruits to heat tests to assess their tolerance to high underground temperatures, a ritual of debasement that demonstrated the power of the mining industry over its African subjects (Foucault's 'sovereign power'). The initial medical examination was another ritual of debasement, selecting labour according to three classifications: those immediately acceptable, those detained for further scrutiny, and those rejected. This was a precursor of medical practice in Nazi camps.[3]

The South African War of 1899–1902 exposed some of the weaknesses of the British empire which had apparently dominated the world for a century. Over the succeeding fifty years the British had to give up what Matthew Arnold had called the 'too heavy burden' of Empire (quoted in Morris, 1983, p. 222). In India the growth of political violence was symbolized by the attempted assassination of Governor-General Hardinge with a bomb at his state entry into the new capital of Delhi in 1912. Other successful and attempted assassinations followed over the years, including the shooting of Lord Moyne by the Stern gang in Cairo in 1944, the only British cabinet minister to be assassinated this century. The insensitive demolition activities of sanitary engineers in some Indian cities resulted in communal riots.

A minor improvement scheme in Kanpur, for instance, led to serious rioting in 1914, and made the British more sensitive to the social and political costs of intervention in the Indian social order. From this time the British found themselves having to control increasingly hostile populations in many colonies, notably in Palestine and Malaya.

In Palestine the British tried to manage growing Arab-Jewish ethnic conflict. The response included the brutal physical destruction of the old city of Jaffa, an episode

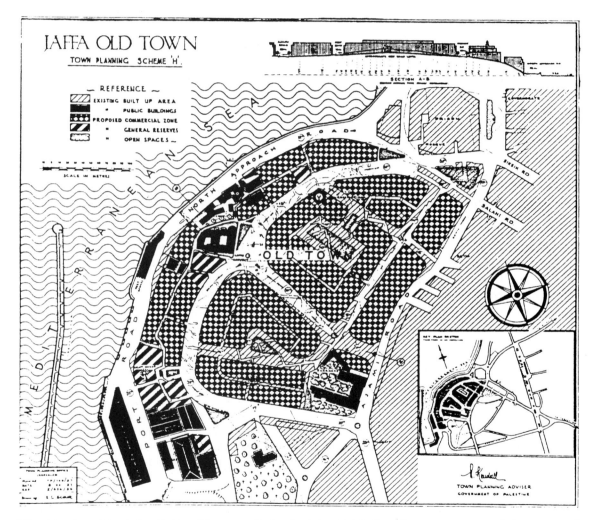

The 'Anchor Plan' for Jaffa old town (Palestine) in 1936–37. This was prepared by Howard Kendall, Town Planning Adviser to the Mandate administration, in an unconvincing attempt to legitimize large-scale demolition as a 'means of reducing a recalcitrant urban area'. (Source: Gavish, 1989)

reminiscent of the treatment meted out to north Indian cities after the Mutiny of 1857. The circumstances were that in April 1936 the Arab community went on strike, aiming to force the British government to stop Jewish immigration, and the old city, with its maze of streets and sewers, was barricaded and turned into a 'no go' area for the British. After several weeks of violence the British authorities decided on drastic action. They dropped thousands of leaflets in Arabic on the city from a light bomber, announcing that a major demolition of houses was being undertaken 'for the improvement of the old city'. Royal Engineer demolition squads then blew up many houses in a row from east to west in one day (17 June 1936), leaving an open strip, between 10 and 30 yards wide, clear through the old city. A few days later further demolitions cut another swathe through the old city from north to south. Although a British court later ruled that the government had misled the public and concealed its security motives, the operation was successful in quelling the revolt.

Soon afterwards the Town Planning Adviser, Howard Kendall, not long in post as Holliday's successor, was ordered to produce an *ex post facto* justification for the demolitions. His town planning scheme became known as the 'Anchor Plan', after the shape of the new street plan. It gave a semblance of legitimacy to an exercise which the British reported as 'a good illustration of a means of reducing a recalcitrant urban area by the most human means'. The British suppressed publicity to the incident, and the story was only uncovered from two aerial photographs found by accident in 1967 when the Jewish forces occupied the city. In the words of an Israeli historian, the operation was:

a punitive action carried out in accordance with special emergency regulations, as no other way was found to subdue the rebel leaders. The government evidently attempted to minimise publicity about the method they had selected for a 'face-lifting' of

Jaffa's old city. The operation did damage to an Arab city and an Arab populace, and it is reasonable to suppose that if the campaign had been directed against the Jews, it would not have been silenced, and effaced from the national memory. (Gavish, 1989, p. 318)

In Malaya the British also had to control ethnic conflict when they returned in 1945 after the Japanese occupation. They found a highly unstable situation, with widespread Communist sympathies among the Chinese minority population (mostly descended from indentured labourers). Some half a million people, mostly Chinese, were squatting on some 70,000 acres of abandoned rubber estates, public and other land, raising food and surviving as best they could. Since Malaya was at the time the biggest single repository of their overseas investment, the British had to suppress Communist insurgency, and rehousing was a key part of the approach. In 1946 a government committee on housing estimated that 30,000 new houses were needed, and a housing trust was created.

During the so-called Malayan 'Emergency' of 1948–56, the Briggs Plan made 'resettlement villages' the answer to Communist insurgency, following Kitchener's approach in South Africa.[4] The colonial government's emergency powers included resettlement and restrictions on movement. Those who refused settlement could be forcibly repatriated to China, then in the aftermath of a brutal civil war, where their prospects were, to say the least, highly uncertain. People were compulsorily regrouped in defensible camps, enclosed by a barbed wire fence, with one or two controlled entrances. The main aim was to control the estate workers, and prevent food and supplies passing to the Communist insurgents. Eventually over half a million people, mostly Chinese plantation workers, were forcibly resettled in 480 such villages, often with an enforced change of occupation. These villages were usually small, with populations of 100–1000, and only 12 had more than 5000 inhabitants. Small holdings of about three acres were allotted under

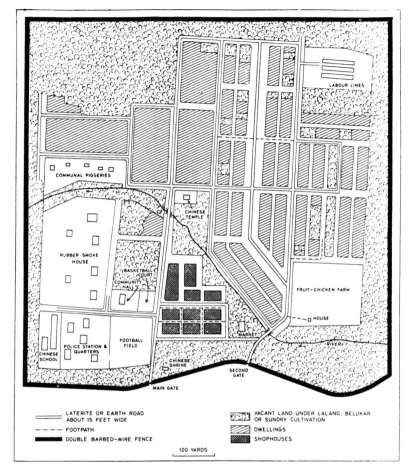

A typical 'New Village' in Malaya (about 1953). During the anti-Communist 'Emergency' period, the Town Planning Department laid out camps, surrounded by barbed wire, where half a million Chinese were forcibly resettled. Most of the settlements have continued to exist to the present day. (Source: Nyce, 1973)

LATERITE OR EARTH ROAD ABOUT 15 FEET WIDE
FOOTPATH
DOUBLE BARBED-WIRE FENCE
VACANT LAND UNDER LALANG, BELUKAR OR SUNDRY CULTIVATION
DWELLINGS
SHOPHOUSES

100 YARDS

the 'aided self-help' principle (a precursor of sites-and-services schemes): the government supplied the sites and basic construction materials (walls, posts and roofs), while the settlers were expected to find their own materials and labour to complete the houses.

The resettlement programme caused the rapid growth of the Town Planning Department (founded under very different circumstances, and with very different aims in mind, by Charles Reade in the 1920s), and it became an advisory department within the Ministry of the Interior and Justice. The new villages were sited on the main roads or on hill sites, and laid out on a simple grid with 'only elementary principles of layout design', because of the need for quick implementation and the lack of available trained staff. The villages were controlled under the Town Board Enactment (with its regulations relating to nuisance, street selling etc.), and funded mainly from a property rate, with about a third contributed by central government in a so-called 'balancing grant'. The standard of facilities was intended to be similar to surrounding areas, which was described as 'a matter of policy in order to prevent envy' from the indigenous Malays (Hamzah, 1966).

Forced resettlement was successful in bringing to an end the Emergency, and was followed by the granting of independence to Malaya in 1957. The constitutional arrangements guaranteed the indigenous Malays political dominance, and led in turn to the secession of the predominantly Chinese Singapore in 1965. Resettlement was claimed as a social revolution which 'expedited the process towards the establishment of compact communities different from the traditional fragmented or open type of settlement':

The policy of resettlement has opened up a long vista of favourable openings for physical, economic and social development. Living in compact communities offers high advantages especially for lower income groups because it shows economical use of time and energy for personal and social affairs. (Hamzah, 1966, p. 69)

The model was afterward used by the Malaysian government for rural repopulation, and was attempted unsuccessfully by the Americans in South Vietnam.

Such new settlements might have been crudely planned in the first instance as a temporary expedient, but had a tendency to become permanent. Colonial planners at an Town Planning Summer School in 1958, considering the planning of temporary townships for construction workers, recommended that 'All temporary townships should be planned so that they may well form the basis of permanent development' (TCPSS, 1958 pp. 168–170).

An example of the transformations that a temporary camp could experience comes from Palestine. The settlement of Rosh Ha'ayin lies between Tel Aviv and Jerusalem in Israel, at

Low-income housing estate in Batu Pahat, Malaysia. The serried ranks of rowhouses continue a colonial tradition. (Source: The author, photo taken in 1985)

the junction of two important roads. It was originally a British army camp during the Mandate period, and was used for a short time during the Arab-Israeli war of 1948 by Arab irregular troops. After the establishment of the state of Israel, it became a home for six thousand Yemeni Jews, brought to Israel in Operation Magic Carpet in 1949–50. The Jewish Agency installed public services, and the settlement became self-governing in 1954. After a period of slow growth, it was re-discovered by the Israeli planners in the late 1980s, when its locational advantages, of cheap housing land and accessibility to both Tel Aviv and Jerusalem, transformed it into a town scheduled for rapid expansion. As an Israeli planner said of it, 'If you want to make something permanent, make it temporary'.[5]

The Lure of Physical Planning

Apart from the use of planning techniques to control hostile populations, the two decades after the Second World War saw the active export of British planning. This was driven by the Commonwealth Development and Welfare programme, and the Attlee government's policy of developing local democracy in the colonies. The new planners, barely recognized as a profession, were expected to address immense challenges of post-war reconstruction, and compensate for decades of neglect by colonial administrations. In 1947 there were some fifty architects and planners working in colonial administrations (King, 1990), and the numbers grew rapidly until by 1959, when the Town Planning Institute received its royal charter, of the membership of 2600, 450 were working overseas. In 1948 a Colonial Liaison Unit was created at the Building Research Station, near London, which published *Colonial Building Notes* 1950–58 (subsequently renamed *Overseas Building Notes*). Overseas branches and affiliates of the Town Planning Institute proliferated in the colonies at this time: in Malaya, Central Africa, New Zealand, Australia, South Africa, and India (Cherry, 1974, pp. 236–237).

The planning consultant most active in the colonies during the immediate post-war period was Patrick Abercrombie. After his work on the development plan for London he received a knighthood in 1945 and retired from his position as Professor at University College London in 1946. Having already worked with his former student Holliday on the planning of Haifa in the 1930s, and on the design of the University of Ceylon in 1940, after his official retirement he embarked upon a busy few years of overseas work, travelling usually by flying boat for consultancy visits of a few weeks. In 1948 he worked on a plan for Colombo, and proposed a regional plan for decentralization and regrouping in satellite towns. He undertook other short planning consultancies in Malta, Hong Kong, and Cyprus, and was working on proposals for Ethiopia until shortly before his death.[6]

Other town planning consultants from Britain were invited to assist with post-war planning and reconstruction in the colonies. Abercrombie's successor at both Liverpool and London, Holford, undertook plans in his native South Africa for Pretoria, Pietermaritzburg, Cape Town and Johannesburg. These were generally not implemented, however, because the post-1948 Afrikaner Nationalist Government was not interested in the views of the British-trained consultant (Muller, 1994). Pepler, after his retirement from government planning in Britain, worked for some years on the master plan for Singapore. Another consultant was Max Lock, who, having done pioneering work on social surveys and planning in Middlesbrough and elsewhere, worked on the expansion of the capital created by Lugard for Northern Nigeria, Kaduna, in the period around Nigerian independence in 1960.

An increasing number of overseas students came to study town planning in Britain in 1950s, and an overseas section of the Town and Country Planning Summer School was started in 1957 (Cherry, 1974, pp. 172–173, and TCPSS, 1957 and subsequent years). This Summer School expressed much interest in the content and organization of training for planners to work in the former and remaining colonies. In 1961 it was lamenting the shortage of planners in proportion to populations in different countries and continents, claiming that the United Kingdom had a ratio of 1:17,000, Australia and Canada 1:100,000, but for India the ratio was only 1:750,000, for Pakistan 1:1,000,000, and for Nigeria 1:2,500,000 (TCPSS, 1961, p. 151).

In the midst of all the enthusiasm for physical planning, linked to the colonies becoming independent countries, there was a considerable confusion over what the precise role of the planner was or should be. This was expressed in a concern over the lack of research, or an adequate theoretical basis for the new profession.[7] The 1959 Overseas Summer School, for instance, was unable to establish a clear focus for planning, and this confusion was expressed when in 1959 its four invited outside lecturers addressed such disparate topics as Ekistics (then a fashionable planning concept, the lecture being delivered by its proponent, Doxiadis), regional economic planning, the relationship between food, health and population, and the place of photogrammetry (TCPSS, 1959). Delegates at the Overseas Summer School regularly expressed their concern over questions such as the appropriate administrative structure for planning, where in the government structure it should be located, and how it should be financed. Linked to this, and particularly important in the period of transfer of political power to new democracies, was how to involve the public in planning decisions, a process

called 'public relations' in the days before public participation became the more recognized term.

One of the leading advocates of town planning in the colonies at this time, P.M.D. Stevens, argued for a particularly wide-ranging definition of town planning. To him it was no less than 'the co-ordination of all economic activities, whether public or private, connected with the development of land in the best interests of the territory as a whole' (quoted in TCPSS, 1957, p. 108). At the same time, perhaps carrying forward the Indirect Rule prejudices of Temple and Lugard, the British colonial planners recognized that planning was 'an anathema in the mind of the African' (TCPSS, 1957, p. 124).

In 1967 Otto Koenigsberger argued at the Overseas Summer School that planning methods devised in Europe were unsuited to the rapid urban growth being experienced by the developing countries. Traditional survey methods were too slow, development control procedures were less relevant than in Britain because of the relative lack of private developers, and planning in Britain was a local government function, usually separated from the responsibility for executing development. He advocated instead a pragmatic 'action planning' approach, which later became the identifying theme of the Development Planning Unit which he founded at University College London. This emphasized immediate practical action on the ground, the involvement of local people in the process, an acceptance rather than rejection of new-comers into urban areas, and a knowledge of the different land tenure concepts in developing countries.[8]

By the time the 'winds of change' had blown away most of Britain's colonial possessions, a new view of the role of the planner was being expressed, which was 'to arbitrate, to adjudge the claims of the various factions, to settle priorities' (David Eversley, quoted in Cherry, 1974, p. 230). Even if the overall spirit and purpose of planning, and its practical political limits within the newly-emerging nation states, were unclear, it did at least offer a number of policy tools which could be deployed to varied political ends.

One of these was the attempt to prevent the flood of migrants to the towns through planned dispersal policies. Colonial administrators had long been disturbed at the implications of rapid urbanization and rural-urban migration, particularly in Africa. They often viewed it with undisguised disgust and alarm, as British officials in Nigeria expressed in their provincial annual reports:

The acquisition of a smattering of book-learning inspires the average youth with contempt for the humdrum agricultural life, and, in the search for employment, he is inevitably attracted to the largest town . . .

The problem of juvenile delinquency continues to present a growing problem and hordes of homeless children and young hooligans infest the larger markets and towns . . . Lack of parental discipline and the ease with which children can leave their homes and live on their wits are the main causes of the problem. (1946 and 1948, quoted in Home, 1974, p. 156)

To restrict the flow of migrants to the towns, controls over labour movement were attempted, following in the tradition of indentured labour regulation. The pass laws in South Africa were the most notorious example, but elsewhere migration was also discouraged. In Nigeria, for instance, employment in the timber port of Sapele was only available to those who could prove residence for at least three years.

In South Africa the idea of planned de-centralization was borrowed from British planning practice. English-speaking Natal drew upon the famous British Barlow Report on industrial decentralization in its formation of a Town and Regional Planning Commission, which applied racial segregation during the *apartheid* period. Along with Green Belts or 'buffer strips' as physical separation measures, the decentralization argument was deployed to justify racial segregation measures. Conservative-minded social anthropologists supported controls over migration, and gave aid and comfort to the advocates of *apartheid* in South and Central Africa. Audrey Richards, for instance, speaking at the Over-seas Summer School in 1958, disagreed with 'the view that the African flocked into the towns in a light-hearted manner to satisfy a sense of adventure which he no longer enjoyed through participation in tribal warfare'. She supported the planners' policy of 'attempts to halt the drift to the towns by providing attract-ive stopping places a few miles outside the boundaries', the later notorious locations or townships. She also defended tribal zoning within the towns, which, while 'a retrograde step as a permanent arrangement', she saw as offering 'some kind of breathing space in the race towards industrial life and the obliteration of all the old traditional rules'.[9]

Israel offers another example of the use of planning tools and techniques to manage ethnic relations and control ethnic groups. During the Mandate period, the newly appointed British town planner, Howard Kendall, prepared outline regional plans for Samaria and Jerusalem, and concerned himself with village development, in accordance with the Colonial Office policy of Development and Welfare. After the end of the Mandate the Palestine Town Planning Ordinance of 1936 was incorporated into Jordanian Law (No. 79 of 1966) in an even more centralized adminis-trative form, and his plans were taken over.

The political uses of Kendall's physical plans were exploited after the Arab-Israeli War of 1967, when half of the land area of the West Bank, conquered from Jordan by force of arms, was expropriated by the Israeli govern-ment and prohibited for use by Arabs. A network of new towns and villages was built for exclusive use by Israeli citizens of Jewish faith. In this new land-use regime, the old Mandate plans of Kendall were not replaced, nor were fresh amendments approved. The Israeli government instead made use of the Kendall plans to restrict Arab development outside existing towns or villages, refusing building permits because they did not comply, even though the regional plan accompanying the map could not be found, and had apparently never been approved. Kendall's original plans had been very general, with villages shown by diagrammatic symbols rather than by site-specific boundaries. Although these were presumably intended to allow local flexibility, in practice they were strictly interpreted. With the high birth rates in the Palestinian population, the population targets of the plans were all exceeded, but the planning authorities continued to prohibit the building of more than one house on an unsubdivided plot, and to interpret strictly the zonings for nature reserve and agriculture. The Arab community was not consulted in revisions to the plan, which were placed on deposit in 1982 to define Jewish settlements (12–15 per annum were proposed), and to provide 'a cloak of legal respectability' for Zionist settlement policies. Arabs who could not prove ownership of land (difficult to do with only a third of titles being registered) were denied the legal status to object to the plans. Thus laws and development plans originally prepared under the British Mandate were used to restrict Arab development, and to create opportunities for Israeli colonization. In the words of the main critic of these policies, Anthony Coon:

. . . many will feel a sense of revulsion, previously reserved for the achievements of planning in South Africa, that these efforts are being directed so uncompromisingly towards establishing the advantage of the dominant racial group.[10]

As well as decentralization and regional plans, another planning tool which was attractive to post-war colonial administrations was the master plan. In pre- and post-independence Singapore this became firmly embedded in the centralized governmental system. The neglect of housing conditions in the first part of the century was followed by the deep humiliation of defeat and occupation by the Japanese between 1942 and 1945. The post-war colonial authorities certainly needed to try harder than before, especially against the background of the Malayan Emergency. A determined attempt at master planning and decentralized development sought to persuade the population of a better life to come, and the expiry of 99-year leases (granted by the former East India Company) gave new opportunities for large-scale urban renewal and new town development. A Master Plan was prepared in 1950–56 by a team led by Pepler. After Singapore became independent in 1965, physical and economic planning became a high-profile state activity, and the new government created an Urban Redevelopment Authority, the Jurong New Town Corporation and other state development bodies. The five-year master plans, together with the earlier master plan and a long-range 'Concept Plan' adopted in 1971, have, it has been claimed, 'provided the driving force for the systematic transformation of the city from its largely entrepot role into a modern financial, trading and tourist centre'.[11]

NEW TOWNS AND HOUSING AFTER 1945

The biggest impact of colonialism upon urban form during the period of decolonization can be seen in the programmes of mass housing, new towns and new capitals, informed by the Western-driven international movement in architecture and planning. An estimated 25–30 million dwellings were destroyed world-wide between the years 1936 and 1946 (Crane and Paxton, 1951), and this was followed by massive forced redistributions of population through partitions and wars of decolonization, and rapid population and urban growth. The full range of such activities is beyond the scope of this book, but examples of colonial government responses to the pressure of the time are the housing programmes of Hong Kong and Singapore, the new town programmes of India and Israel, and the new capitals developed in sub-Saharan Africa.

For the city-states of Hong Kong and Singapore, both now acclaimed as successful models of free enterprise capitalism, a key factor in economic development has been the public house building initiated in the late colonial period:

in one of the most striking paradoxes of urban policy in the world, the two market economies with the highest rates of economic growth in the last twenty-five years are also those with the largest public housing programs in the capitalist world, in terms of the proportion of the population directly housed by the government.[12]

For Hong Kong the end of Japanese occupation in 1945 was followed by the return of former residents and a new flood of refugees from the upheavals of the Chinese civil war. A tenth of the housing stock was destroyed and another tenth damaged during the war. Its population, in 1945 estimated at 1 million, returned to the prewar figure of 1.6 million by 1946, and by 1956 was 2.5 million, in spite of the introduction of immigration restrictions in 1950. The rapid population growth continued, until by 1986 the population reached 5.5 million. Of this increase, about one million represented new immigration, and the rest comprised returning prewar residents and natural increase. The squatter population rose rapidly from 30,000 to 300,000 between 1947 and 1949, many of them Hong Kong residents forced out of housing by landlords seeking higher rents. The largest of the squatter camps, at Shek Kip Mei, on the northern outskirts of Kowloon, held 80,000 people at its peak. Occasional riots and costly building collapses were followed on Christmas Eve, 1953, by a disastrous fire which made 50,000 homeless at Shek Kep Mei.

Hong Kong had been among the least planned of British port cities, and the post-war authorities remained reluctant planners. Abercrombie's preliminary outline plan, prepared during a short visit in 1948, was largely ignored:

Official Hong Kong policy – 'Build now, plan later' – has proved to be the whole negation of his teaching both in theory and results . . . a vast slum on the border of China in the face of decades of professional and academic protest. If the Isle of Wight had been so treated by Asians, Britain would have risen in resentment long since . . . The condition of Wanchai and the Western District of Victoria is a lasting and unmerited smear on British planning expertise. (Davis, 1965)

Faced with the Shek Kip Mei housing crisis, the colonial government made the utilitarian calculation that it was cheaper to build a sixty-storey resettlement block than pay relief to 50,000 people for two weeks. Such a house-building programme would have the additional benefits of controlling fire and health hazards, and possible threats to public order. So between 1954 and 1964 resettlement estates were built for over 600,000 people, in the form of PWD (Public Works Department) Mark I and II blocks. The designs show the influence of earlier Improvement Board chawls in India, with low space standards and high densities. Rents were kept low enough to provoke the accusation that resettled squatters had become a privileged section of the community. This low-cost housing was deployed by the colonial government as 'a means of squatter control, devised in order to free land needed for permanent development and to reduce the risk of fires in squatter camps' (Dwyer, 1971, p. 46).

After the priority programme of squatter resettlement, the Hong Kong Government then embarked upon the development of industrial satellite towns. In 1957 Kwun Tong was the first, followed by Tsuen Wan, Kwai Chung, Shatin and Castle Point, where river estuaries and shallow waters were suitable for reclamation. A massive decentralization to new towns in the New Territories was started, following the earlier British planning principles of Barlow and Abercrombie, self-containment and balanced development. Thus Hong Kong belatedly adopted a planned approach, one based upon private rather than public development, with the Government New Territory Development Department assembling the land and infrastructure. New towns received a major boost when Governor MacLehose announced a 10-year public housing programme from 1972, aiming to improve quality and space standards. Between the end of the Second World War and 1969 a total of 1.4 million public housing units were built, over a million of them on resettlement estates. By the end of 1970 1.6 million people out of 4 million were in public housing, representing 'one important element in an overall economic and social complex which had given rise to the highest rate of economic growth based upon industrialization in the whole of the developing world' (Castells *et al.*, 1990). By 1986 45 per cent of the Hong Kong population was in public housing, the building of which from the 1960s accounted for a high proportion (over a tenth) of total government expenditure. The policy was a major factor in socializing a largely immigrant population into the city and merging ethnic differences. Keeping the proportion of household consumption spent on housing to a guaranteed minimum greatly dampened demands for wage increases, and contributed to keeping Hong Kong's labour costs among the lowest in the developed world.

The other colonial port-city of the British Far East, Singapore, carried out a similar government-directed housing and new settlement programme. The traditional urban settlement pattern had created severe problems of overcrowding, housing shortage, social and ethnic segregation, and civil unrest based on racial and ideological differences. The postwar period saw rapid formation of slums and squatter settlements, the result of high birthrates and in-migration. The Housing Committee in 1947 reported densities of 2000 persons per hectare, with 100,000 people living in huts. The Singapore Improvement Trust,

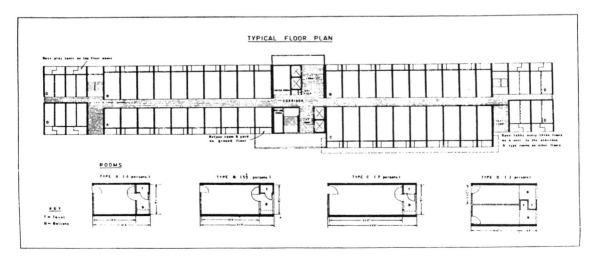

Mass resettlement housing in Hong Kong. This Mark VI design still shows the influence of the Indian chawl. (Source: Dwyer, 1971)

formed in a belated response to the housing problems, had only managed to build 2103 dwellings and shops in the period 1930–39, but improved its performance to 40,000 units in the period 1947–59. Unfortunately the population grew by 600,000 over the same period.

The Statutory Master Plan, approved in 1958, projected a population growth to two million by 1972, and embraced the planning concepts of decentralization and green belt. In 1962–63 a United Nations urban planning team stressed the need for an integrated approach to housing, urban renewal, industrial development and transport. After Singapore seceded from Malaya in 1965 the post-independence government continued the use of statutory boards, which had started with the Dock Board (1905, and from 1913 the Harbour Board) and the Improvement Trust (1927). In 1960 the Improvement Trust became the Housing and Development Board, which built half a million housing units in the following 25 years with the support of a strong land acquisition act. The Jurong Town Corporation was created in 1968 and the Urban Redevelopment Authority in 1974.

As a result of these authorities' programmes, fifteen new towns were built, and 86 per cent of the population now live in public sector housing. Such emphasis upon public housing and suburbanization has had the effect of breaking down the traditional spatial concentration of ethnic and Chinese dialect groups, and has resulted in the emergence of a clearer Singaporean social and cultural identity.

The new town idea, which was being implemented in Britain under the New Towns Act of 1945, was applied in many colonies, not only in Hong Kong and Singapore, but also in India, Israel, Malaysia and elsewhere. These were all states struggling with large-scale population growth and political upheaval. The political shocks transmitted by the new Communist regime in China after 1948, for instance, had their consequences for Hong Kong, Malaysia and Singapore. The partition of India and Pakistan led to massive forced population movements, while in Israel the Arab-Israeli wars and in-migration necessitated a government settlement policy. Usually these new town programmes were implemented by some form of public development corporation through public land ownership, and deployed the same concepts of a self-contained economic base, clustered housing to promote interaction and reduce sprawl, reliance upon public transport, and extensive public open spaces.

India accommodated some five million people in 118 new towns built between Independence in 1949 and 1981, in what has been probably the largest new town programme in the world. India had a tradition of new settlement creation (they are mentioned in Vedic scriptures), and the British had built thirty railway towns by 1941 (e.g. Karagpur and Manmad). Some of the post-Independence new towns were built to resettle refugees at partition (e.g. Faridabad, Nilokheri, Gandhidam and Asonekar). Others were new complexes for large-scale industry built under the Five Year Plans (e.g. Rourkela, Bhilai, Durgapur, Bokaro, and Nana Nangal). Others again were capital cities, notably Chandigarh, but also Bhubaneshwar and Gandhinagar, the capitals of Punjab, Orissa, and Gujarat respectively). Mostly these were towns each of less than 100,000 population, with ten over 100,000.

The usual method of implementation was through a Notified Area Committee, nominated by the State government, which formulated by-laws but had weaker revenue powers than municipal authorities. Finance came from federal or state government, with a subsidy for the public services and housing. The typical plan was a grid-iron with neighbourhood units. Among the problems encountered were lack of public facilities, and unplanned peripheral growth, in spite of attempts to prevent it through control ordinances.[13]

In Israel the rapid population growth during

the Mandate (for instance the doubling of Tel-Aviv's population between 1937 and 1950) was soon dwarfed by the arrival of Holocaust refugees and successive waves of immigrants fleeing persecution. The 650,000 inhabitants in 1948 grew to 2.4 million in 1962, of which 920,000 were post-1948 immigrants. The new country became an experimental laboratory for theories of settlement planning and techniques of prefabricated housing. Planning concepts of Christaller settlement hierarchies were borrowed from Germany, while Britain was an influence through the planning reports of Barlow, Abercrombie and Uthwatt, and concepts such as neighbourhood, garden suburbs and green belt. The governmental responsibility was shared between the Ministry of Interior (in charge of physical planning), the Ministry of Labour and Social Insurance (in charge of housing) and the Prime Minister's office (in charge of national planning). The national physical plan (1948–50) identified 24 zones and five types of settlement, and about forty new towns were established in the years up to 1964. Ten of these were created in the two years 1949 and 1950, mostly on the sites of existing settlements in the coastal plain of Israel which had been abandoned by the Arabs during the war of 1948–49. For primarily defensive reasons the immigrant population was dispersed around the country, and a third went to the southern part of the country, which included the Negev desert.

Initially, because of the past Zionist tradition of rural settlement, and also the influence of British garden city ideas, the new settlements were planned for low densities, with one-storey houses and large land plots intended for agriculture. Between 25 per cent and 40 per cent of private development land was reserved for open space, but this proved expensive to maintain and irrigate in an arid climate. The immigrants of the 1950s, more than those who had preceded them, came with large families and high proportions of children and elderly. Consequently there was a shift towards more compact development at higher densities, and small neighbourhood open spaces, designed for minimal maintenance and borrowing from local traditions of urban form.[14]

In Malaysia the new Federation came into existence in 1957 for a country that was still divided by inter-ethnic conflict, and recovering from the aftermath of the Emergency. When the new Federal Capital Territory at Kuala Lumpur was declared, a third of its population of 300,000 were squatters and refugees from the war. The British had already designated a new town at Petaling Jaya, outside Kuala Lumpur, in 1953, which was built on a former rubber plantation compulsorily purchased by the government. Its development was guided by a master plan for a land area of 3000 acres, projecting employment for 10,000 people, and 3200 houses were built in the first five years. Other new towns in the new Federation included Shah Alam, which was developed after 1967 as the new state capital of Selangor. New rural and urban settlements were created as part of a plan to urbanize the indigenous Malays, and to decentralize growth to the constituent states through a regional planning machinery. The intercommunal riots of 1969 led to creation of a New Economic Plan to increase the participation of the Malays in urban and economic development, with a new Urban Development Authority.[15]

The postwar period also saw the global spread of designed capitals, following the earlier examples of Imperial federation in New Delhi, Canberra, Pretoria and Ottawa. Sometimes these were purpose-made, as in the case of Lilongwe (the capital of Malawi, which was decreed to move from Zomba in 1965), Abuja (the capital of the Federation of Nigeria, where the decision to move from Lagos was made in 1975), Dodoma (the capital of Tanzania, designated in 1973) and Chandigarh. Sometimes they were, in the words of Max Lock, 'Pygmalion capitals . . . finding themselves called upon to wear a crown of Government and seeking to robe themselves fittingly by

Planned housing from the era of decolonization. Top: Concrete block family housing on a government residential area in Ibadan, Nigeria. (Source: The author, photo taken in 1965); Bottom: African Housing estate on the edge of Salisbury, Southern Rhodesia, next to an industrial estate, and segregated from white housing areas. (Source: The author, photo taken in 1965); Above right: 'Native' residential area at Vanderbijl Park in the 1940s. Within a conventional grid road layout the housing pretends to be grouped in 'the traditional kraal formation'. (Source: Van der Bijl, 1947)

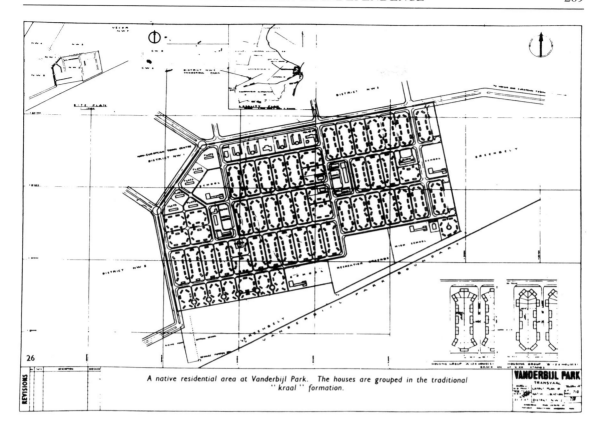

A native residential area at Vanderbijl Park. The houses are grouped in the traditional "kraal" formation.

large scale civic improvements and extension' (quoted in TCPSS, 1965, p. 141). Examples of that type were Amman (the capital of Jordan after the Nine Days War in 1967), Gaborone (the capital of Botswana after 1961, which replaced Mafeking in South Africa), and Dhaka (the capital of Bangladesh after 1971). Sometimes they were 'Siamese Twin' cities which combined the new and the old. This was the case with Old/New Delhi, and with Rawalpindi/Islamabad. (Islamabad, the new capital of Pakistan was planned by Doxiadis as a 'dynapolis', which would fan out in time from the original planned core.)[16]

Capital cities are not only the practical and symbolic focus of national administration, but, in states emerging from control by an external power, they represent a focus for efforts to promote a sense of national identity out of the ties of blood, race, language, region, religion or custom. A speaker at the first session of Parliament in the newly unified Italy in 1860 said 'We have made Italy, now we have to make Italians' (quoted in Vale, 1992, p. 45). Usually the new cities were planned by imported architect-planners of the Modern Movement, and often building them proved to be a great strain on the country's budget, so that the plans remained substantially unimplemented. The new capitals were expected to do too much. 'What the modern capital lacks in size and diversity of economic base, it is asked to make up for in sheer density of symbolism' (Vale, 1992, p. 15).

Of all the new capitals, Chandigarh probably received the most attention at the time. It was the first Modernist planned capital city, founded in 1951 after the partition of India and Pakistan. Capital of the new Punjab after the loss of Lahore to Pakistan, after 1966 it became the joint capital of the new states of Punjab and Haryana. It was first planned immediately after partition by the American architectural firm of Mayer, Whittlesey & Glass. The first architect was the young Pole, Matthew Nowicki, head of the School of Architecture at North Carolina State College, who was unfortunately soon killed in a plane crash. Subsequently Le Corbusier, then towards the end of his career, was brought in as part of a team (which included Maxwell Fry and Jane Drew) to develop the Mayer plan. The new city was planned in superblocks, which were originally of 300 × 450 square metres, proportions based on the Golden Section, but were later enlarged by Le Corbusier to 800 × 1200 square metres. Neighbourhoods were segregated into income groups, and the target population was 150,000 (later expanded to half a million) (Sarin, 1979).

Peter Hall describes the ironies of Le Corbusier's involvement. When he finally found a great patron towards the end of his life, it turned out to be 'a post-colonial government steeped in the autocratic traditions of the British Raj. He produced for them an exercise in the City Beautiful decked in the trappings of modern architecture . . . The relationship between streets and buildings is totally European, and is laid down without regard for the fierce north-Indian climate or for Indian ways of life' (Hall, 1988, p. 214). Maxwell Fry, however, defended the design, calling the venture 'no vainglorious national projection, but a sober necessity for a shattered State gathering its remnants to consider the future' (TCPSS, 1961, pp. 99–122).[17]

While these projects were planned and executed by the state, the tradition of private company towns also persisted, particularly to meet the needs of heavy industry and mining. The Tata Corporation's new town at Jamshedpur was an early colonial example (see p. 151). In South Africa company towns were developed at Welkom, Sosilburg, and Vanderbijl Park; racial residential segregation as well as garden city principles were applied in the period immediately before official *apartheid* in that country. Vanderbijl Park was developed after 1941, when steel was increasingly difficult to obtain from abroad because of the restrictions of the Second World War. It was planned for the South African Iron and Steel Industrial Corporation on 24,000 acres west of Vereeniging, Transvaal, for a target population of 200,000. Segregated into European and non-European townships, it included green belts or buffer strips, with the aim to 'encourage a high standard of living and promote a sense of citizenship, pride and enterprise'.[18]

One aspect of both new and old towns and cities in the post-colonial situation which demanded official attention was ethnic complexity, and choices over cultural segregation. Nicosia and Jerusalem were two capital cities where intercommunity antagonisms created international political problems, while the legacy of South African *apartheid* is only now slowly being disentangled. In some situations ethnic complexity was reduced after Independence through forced population transfers, while elsewhere less mutually antagonistic communities found that they could accommodate each other politically through a programme of multi-culturalism, as occurred in Malaysia after the riots of 1969.

'THE BIG MAN IS PLAYING SKULLDUGGY' (*sic*):
A CASE STUDY OF TRINIDAD AND TOBAGO

The changing view and role of physical planning in the transition from colonial to independent status can be seen in one of the smaller nation states. Trinidad and Tobago had already been the testing ground for the new-style town planning legislation based upon the 1932 English Town and Country Planning Act (see pp. 184–187) Its population grew more than tenfold in the century and a half before independence, and doubled between the time of the 1937 riots and Independence in 1962.[19]

The period either side of independence saw frequent re-organizations of government, and of the place of planning within it. When in 1956 the People's National Movement took control of the Legislative Council, it established a Planning Bureau under the Ministry of Finance for the first Five-Year Development Program 1958–62. In 1961 the United Nations Department of Economic and Social Affairs advised on the organization of the planning function. In 1963 the Planning and Housing Commission was split into the National Housing Authority and the Town and Country Planning Division, the latter under the Prime Minister's Office until 1967, when it was incorporated in the Ministry of Planning and Development (later the Ministry of Planning and Mobilization).

In 1960 a new Town and Country Planning Ordinance was passed, replacing the 1938 Ordinance, although it did not come into force until August 1969. It was based upon the British 1947 and subsequent legislation, and followed a visit by Desmond Heap, the leading British planning lawyer of the day.[20] Its full title was:

to make provision for the orderly and progressive development of land in both urban and rural areas and to preserve and impose the amenities thereof; for the grant of permission to develop land and for other powers of control over the use of land; to confer additional powers in respect of the acquisi-

tion and development of land for planning; and for purposes connected with the matters aforesaid.

Dr. Eric Williams, the Premier and Finance Minister, took it upon himself to propose the new planning bill, in 1960, reflecting the importance with which it was seen at the time. In his speech he listed some consequences of a lack of planning:

. . . the substitution of housing settlements, however badly needed, for what had hitherto been good agricultural land . . . the effects of the drainage for isolated buildings creating floods, soil erosion, silting and so on, and the traffic hazards in the streets that were never intended for the traffic that they now have to carry . . . the location of drive-in cinemas . . . the indiscriminate location of gasolene stations . . . Most of the Ministries here compete one with the other in respect of land. They want land for a Fire Station, . . . for a Police Station; the Minister of Health for a Hospital; the Minister of Education for a school; the Minister of Agriculture to plant pangola grass; the Minister of Housing to root up the pangola grass and substitute some houses etc. The only Minister, as I look around here who is completely neutral in this day-to-day conflict – competition for the use of land is the Premier. He requires no land at all.[21]

He expressed the high expectations associated with the concept of physical planning at that period:

For the first time through its own duly elected government the population of the Territory can take matters in its own hands and decide how, where and when all resources, land and people, are to be utilized for social and economic ends. This clearly casts physical planning and its technical and legal procedure in a very positive and politically dynamic mold.

The 1969 Ordinance added to the six planning topics listed under the 1938 Ordinance a seventh, 'Community Planning'. This reflected a new perception of government's responsibilities for social welfare, derived from the colonial development and welfare approach. Community planning was defined as:

1. Providing for the control of land by zoning or designating for specific uses,

2. Regulating layout of housing areas including density, spacing, grouping or orientation of houses in relation to roads, open spaces and other buildings, and

3. Determining the provision and siting of community facilities including shops, schools, churches, meeting halls, play centres and recreation grounds in relation to the number of siting of houses.

Elaborate physical planning standards and hierarchies were devised for community facilities – recreation grounds, for instance, were to provide 1 acre per 100 persons, minimum size 5 acres – but these aspirations were soon curtailed by political and financial realities.

The town planning section was slow to build up its staff. By 1973, a decade after Independence, there were sixteen qualified town planners in the country, of whom eleven were in government, to serve a population of a million. In its first serious test, an ambitious redevelopment in East Port of Spain, the planners failed to get the necessary compulsory purchases confirmed, which dealt a body blow to the whole planning idea. East Port of Spain was a large, old-established informal settlement of family plots and twisting paths, outside the formal gridiron layout of the colonial city. The evidence of the objectors to the compulsory purchase, as recorded *verbatim* in the proceedings of the public inquiry, give vivid and moving witness to the poor people's response to urban renewal:

The big man is playing skullduggy (*sic*) and we can't even plant a tomato in our backyard. (Mr. Tshali, 4 September 1974)

One of the gentlemen told me, after they pay me off, I will have to look for my own home . . . I

walked up and down, travelled east and west to get a bit of land to rent but I cannot. Nobody will rent land nowadays . . . a poor man cannot buy . . . I felt so sad, so thrown out of this world that I think, my Government do me that . . . I prefer to die than to live on the street. May God bless you. (Mr. Howell, 26 August 1974)

Do you know how many houses Town and Country Planning broke up? Do you know how many wives and children go astray through Town and Country Planning? Is this the protection in this modern day and age that Government should offer to the people who have sacrificed so much? The Government helps to break up homes. My children and wives are in Antigua, just because I can't build a house for them . . . My piece of land will blow up for the convenience of Town and Country Planning. (Mr. Samuel, 27 August 1974)

It would mean more hospitals, more gaols and more mental homes, because we may go out of our minds to know that our homes are broken down . . . You know when you fight hard and your dream comes true, from week to week in poverty, struggling to live in a house where stars are shining through the roof – you go to work and come to sleep and dream of the work you have to do tomorrow – God help you. You get a little house and you with your own eyes see it is smashed. You have to go back into the field and creep along. God alone can help you. (Mr. Simmons, 28 August 1974).

After this setback, the Director of Town and Country Planning lamented:

the complete lack of public, and at times official, understanding of the purposes of planning, which was viewed, not as a necessary function for regulating the use of the country's physical resources, but as an infringement of the individual right to the unfettered enjoyment of private property' (quoted in Home, 1993*b*, p. 406).

In spite of this setback, the new physical planning function of government should not be written off as a failure. A framework for regulating new development, albeit weak, was established, and it also allowed some opportunity for democratic involvement in government at the local level, through community participation.

PLOT LAYOUT
FIGURE 15

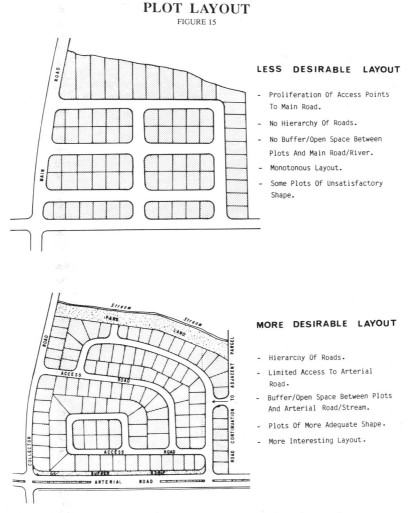

LESS DESIRABLE LAYOUT

- Proliferation Of Access Points
  To Main Road.
- No Hierarchy Of Roads.
- No Buffer/Open Space Between
  Plots And Main Road/River.
- Monotonous Layout.
- Some Plots Of Unsatisfactory
  Shape.

MORE DESIRABLE LAYOUT

- Hierarchy Of Roads.
- Limited Access To Arterial
  Road.
- Buffer/Open Space Between Plots
  And Arterial Road/Stream.
- Plots Of More Adequate Shape.
- More Interesting Layout.

Recommended housing layouts for Trinidad (about 1985). This shows the transition from the 'less desirable' style associated with civil engineers and cost saving to the more organic layouts associated with garden cities and town planning. (Source: Trinidad and Tobago Town Planning Department, c. 1985)

POST EMPIRE IN BRITAIN

While this book has been concerned predominantly with the forming of colonial cities outside Britain, one should not forget the impact of Britain's overseas expansion upon her own cities and people. Britain enjoyed vast wealth and trade surpluses from the Empire, from such sources as the 'Great Drain' of Bengal, the slave trade, and primary production from colonial mines and estates. This allowed the creation and maintenance of large family fortunes, great estates and their houses, and provided capital for investment in foreign wars, urban development and industrialization.[22] The industrialists' planned company towns of the nineteenth century, such as Bournville and Port Sunlight, usually were made possible by the profits from processing primary produce imported from the colonies.

One example of colonial connections in British urban development comes from the area of inner north-east London where the author lives. The De Beauvoir Estate was begun in the 1830s by a local speculative builder, who happened to be the grandfather of Cecil John Rhodes. He laid out a Georgian gridiron, with squares and circuses, closely resembling the nearly contemporary William Light plan for Adelaide. Rhodes, however, was thrown off the development after acrimonious legal proceedings in the House of Lords, and the estate was completed by the Benyon family. They had family seats at Culford (Suffolk), and Englefield (Berkshire), and derived much of their considerable fortune from the East India trade, especially trans-mitting silver bullion to China in the eighteenth century. A Benyon had been a governor of Madras, and many Benyons have been Members of Parliament down to the present day.[23]

Several of the building types and urban forms which are now a familiar part of the British scene derived from colonial experience. We can mention the chalet-bungalow, the garden city and the Green Belt concept. The import of the bungalow from India into Britain, and its enthusiastic adoption as a vacation home in the plotlands of southern England, has been well documented by Anthony King (1980, chapter 6, 1984, and 1990, chapter 6).

The low-density suburban housing promoted by the garden city movement drew upon the spacious layouts of the settler colonies of America and Australia, derived from the 'Grand Modell' of colonial settlement. While the intellectual tradition of the colonial town

planning model was submerged during the hey-day of colonial immigration, it re-emerged as an influence upon the Garden City movement. Ebenezer Howard, who drew upon many sources and had worked for a time in the American mid-west, was aware of the Wakefield approach through his reading of Mill's *Principles of Political Economy*, and involved himself in attempts to create a 'Home Colony' on Wakefieldian lines in the 1890s, some years before publishing his garden city ideas.[24]

The Green Belt, probably the best known and most successful British planning concept, has strong colonial roots in the model of the self-contained town surrounded by a park belt. Howard used a plan of Adelaide in his book, and Frederick Osborn sought to distinguish the terminologies:

Country Belt, Agricultural Belt, Rural Belt. These terms are synonymous. They describe a stretch of countryside around and between towns, separating each from the others, and predominantly permanent farmland and parkland, whether or not such land is in the ownership of a town authority.

Green Belt. Originally used by Unwin as a further synonym for Country Belt, this term has also been applied, thus far confusingly, to a narrow strip of parkland more or less encircling part of a built-up metropolitan or large urban area. Park Belt is a better name for such a strip. (1945 preface to Howard, 1965)

The concept of a 'green girdle', a quarter mile wide, at a 10-mile radius from the centre, was proposed in 1910 at the RIBA Town Planning Conference, and Unwin later recommended concentric rings of parkland for London (Miller, 1989).

Forms of government and control were experimented with in the colonies, and could then be brought back to Britain. Appointed executive agencies were used in the port cities of the Empire and then introduced into Britain. Port authorities were such an example, but more significant were the large-scale colonial improvement boards and trusts, which seem to have influenced the new towns, and later the urban development corporations after 1980. Urban reconstruction and regeneration could sometimes be considered too important to be left in the hands of democratically-elected local government, and experience of colonial administration was often seen as useful for running such enterprises, especially when decolonization was providing a timely supply of ex-officials needing new jobs.[25] Techniques of repression applied in the colonies could also be used at home. The army's anti-terrorist methods, for instance, learned in Kenya during Mau Mau, and in Cyprus during the Eoka emergency, were applied to the civilian population of Northern Ireland, with disastrous political consequences for many years.

It was not only administrators and the military who brought their colonial experience to Britain. The traditions of colonial migrant labour continued with the arrival in Britain of workers from the Caribbean. Previously relatively few people from the colonies had come to Britain to stay permanently, mainly the small communities of freed or fugitive slaves in ports such as Bristol, Liverpool, London and Cardiff, which continued over generations with some inter-breeding but relatively little integration or assimilation. In 1948 the 'Empire Windrush' brought the first Caribbean immigrants to meet the demand for labour in post-war Britain, 125,000 entering the country over the following ten years. The politics of decolonization brought further immigration, especially after the partition of India and Pakistan, and the Home Office estimated that nearly half a million people entered the country from the 'tropical Commonwealth' between 1955 and 1962, the year in which tighter immigration control was introduced. Further immigration followed when Asians were expelled from East Africa (Fryer, 1984; Rex, 1973).

As a result of these population movements, London is now one of the most culturally diverse cities in the world, as befits its history as the capital of the British Empire. According to the 1991 population census over half a million Londoners claimed a black ethnic affiliation, another half million were South Asian, and nearly 300,000 were Chinese or other Asian. Political and planning structures have moved slowly and uneasily to accommodate these 'ethnic minorities', in spite of a machinery of legislation against racial discrimination (Krishnarayan and Thomas, 1993). But then, in a phrase often used by black commentators to explain the consequences of the colonial relationship for Britain, 'we are here because you were there' (Merriman 1993, p. 5).

NOTES

1. *Architects Journal*, Vol. 90, No. 2321, 13 July 1939 (my thanks to Peter Inch for bringing this to my attention). The origins of the Soviet gulag system are discussed in Bunyan (1967) and Pipes (1990). See also entry on barracks in *Encyclopaedia Britannica* (1937 edition), Home (1933a), and Ringelman (1915).
2. Trollope (1903) is an account of these camps by one of their superintendants. For the Boer concentration camps see Martin (1957) and Pakenham (1982). For the camps for black Africans, see Warwick (1983), chapter 8.
3. For the Belgian Congo camps see Pearson and Mouchet (1923). For Madagascar see Wright (1987). For South African mining design see Butchart (1994) and Wasserfall (1990).
4. For resettlement villages in Malaya see Concannon (1951) and (1958) (he was the head of the Town Planning Department during the Emergency), Hamzah Sendut (1966), and Nyce (1973). Zasloff (1962–63) examines the attempted application of the approach to South Vietnam by the Americans.
5. Information on Rosh Hayim supplied by International Federation of Housing and Planning Congress, Jerusalem, 1992.
6. For Abercrombie, see chapter by Gerald Dix in Cherry (1981), and entries in WWW and DNB. Ling (1988), p. 216, refers briefly to his

work in Ceylon, and Bristow (1984), pp. 69–72, to that in Hong Kong. His colonial activities await more detailed research.

Sir Leslie Patrick Abercrombie (1879–1957) qualified as an architect and began an academic career, combined with professional practice, at Liverpool in 1909 as a research fellow and the first editor of *Town Planning Review*. He succeeded Adshead both as Professor of Civic Design at the University of Liverpool 1915–35, and then as Professor of Town Planning at University College London 1935–46. He won a competition for the planning of Dublin in 1914, and was President of the Town Planning Institute in 1925–26. His membership of the Barlow Commission (1937–40) made him an advocate of decentralization policies. His son Neil became Town Planning Commissioner for Tasmania.

7. Training for overseas planners was a re-current theme of discussions at the Town and Country Planning Summer Schools (1957, pp. 159–160, 1958, pp. 174–175, 1960, pp. 144–145, 1961, p. 151).

8. Otto Koenigsberger (b. 1911) was the son of a German local authority architect in Berlin. Unable to stay in Germany during the Nazi regime, he worked in India (on Jamshedpur) during the Second World War, and then on many consultancies in developing countries. As Professor of Tropical Architecture and Planning at the Bartlett School of Architecture, University College London, he founded the Development Planning Unit, which still carries forward his work.

9. Quoted in TCPSS (1958), pp. 133–137. For decentralization in South Africa see Geyer (1989).

Audrey Richards (1899–?) was a Cambridge-educated social anthropologist who held academic posts in London, Johannesburg, Kampala and Cambridge, wrote books on African social change, and advised the Colonial Office and research committees. WWW.

10. Article by Coon in *Planning Newspaper*, no. 945, 22 November 1991, pp. 14–15. Planning in Israel's West Bank in the period before the recent settlement is explored more fully in Coon (1990) and (1992), and also in Troen (1992) and Yiftachel (1992).

11. Eng (1992), p. 183. For post-war planning in Singapore see also Bristow (1992). For other examples of master plans, see Armstrong (1987).

Sir George Lionel Pepler (1882–1959) was Chief Town Inspector at the Ministry of Health 1919–41, Chief Technical Adviser at the Ministry of Town & Country Planning 1943–46, and town planning consultant in Singapore 1950–54 (WWW). Cherry (1981), p. 140.

12. Castells, Goh and Kwok (1990), p. 1. This book compares Hong Kong and Singapore, as does Phillips and Yeh (1987), Dwyer (1971) and Wang and Yeh (1987). Bristow (1989) deals with the Hong Kong new towns.

13. For Indian new towns see the thesis by Kumer (1981), and also Gupta (1964), Jacobson and Prakash (1967), Koenigsberger (1952), and Prakash (1972).

14. There is a substantial literature, some of it in Hebrew, on the post-1948 physical planning of Israel. See (in English) Abrams (1951), Baruth (1951), Efrat (1989) and (1994), TCPSS (1964), pp. 108–124, and Troen (1988) and (1992).

15. For post-war Malaysian new towns see Bruton (1982) and (1985) on regional planning, Concannon (1958) on the origins of Petaling Jaya, essay by Mohammed in Blair (1984), and Hamzah Sendut (1965).

16. Vale (1992) explores the relationship between built environment and political purpose in new capital cities. It contains both long and short case studies, and chapters are devoted to New Guinea, Sri Lanka, Kuwait, and Bangladesh. The book also contains full source references. For individual new capitals see: on Abuja, Moore (1984), Vale (1992), pp. 134–147, and essays in Blair (1984) and Galantay, Constandense and Ohba (1985); on Dodoma, Hayuma (1981), Vale (1992), pp. 147–160, and essays in Blair (1984) and Galantay, Constandense and Ohba (1985); on Gaborone, Best (1970); on Islamabad, Doxiadis (1965) and Vale (1992), pp. 128–132; on Lilongwe, Potts (1985).

17. For Chandigarh, see Evenson (1966), Hall (1988), pp. 212–15, Sarin (1979), and Vale (1992), pp. 105–114.

18. Van der Bijl (1947). The founder of Vanderbijl Park was an Afrikaner industrialist, Hendrik Johannes Van der Bijl (1887–1948) (DSAB).

19. This section on Trinidad draws upon the

author's field research. For more detail and full source references, see Home (1993*b*). Trinidad's population was 73,023 in 1844, 273,899 in 1901, 412,783 in 1931, and 827,957 in 1960.

20. Sir Desmond Heap (b. 1907) was Solicitor to the Corporation of the City of London 1947–73, and on the editorial board of the newly founded *Journal of Planning Law* from 1948. He was a member of the Colonial Office Housing and Town Planning Advisory Panel from 1953–65, and visited many developing countries to advise on planning law.

21. Quoted in *Review of Work Carried out by the Town and Country Planning Division 1969–74*, Government of Trinidad and Tobago, 1975. Also quoted in Home (1993*b*).

22. An introduction to these issues is given in Fryer (1988), especially Part I. See also King (1990), chapter 7, and Braudel (1984), pp. 575–584.

23. Information supplied by my neighbour, Charles Posner, who has been researching the Benyon family history.

24. For influences upon Howard, see particularly Beevers (1988) and Buder (1990).

25. At least seven new town managers were former colonial administrators of many years experience, and often had family connections with colonial service. G.J. Bryan (Londonderry) had served in Swaziland and the West Indies, A.M. Grier (Redditch) in West Africa, India and Borneo, W.S. Holley (Washington) in Malaysia, D. Kirby (Irvine) in Sierra Leone, R.W. Phelps (Central Lancashire) in Nigeria, and J.V. Rowley (Bracknell) in the Sudan (latterly as Governor of Darfur Province). M.W. Biggs (Hatfield and Welwyn) had military experience in East Africa. WWW.

CONCLUSIONS:
THE LEGACY OF COLONIAL
TOWN PLANNING

European empires of the nineteenth century were economy empires, cheaply obtained by taking advantage of new technologies, and, when the cost of keeping them rose a century later, quickly discarded. In the process, they unbalanced world relations, overturned ancient ways of life, and opened the way for a new global civilisation.

(Headrick, 1981, p. 209)

This judgment, based upon a study of the technological 'tools' with which Empire was acquired, helps us understand how the British colonial city has influenced the present-day cities of the Third World. The laying out of towns, using improved technologies of land measurement and engineering survey, was one such technological tool. Streets, blocks and subdivisions created the basic physical structure of many a present world city – 'Patterns in Perpetuity', to use the title of a study of Adelaide (Cheesman, 1986). Colonialism deployed many forms of urban built environment which have lasted, including the gridiron street plan, the 'fan' design of surveillance, devices for racial segregation, and low-density residential patterns.

The British Empire was acquired, of course, in order to serve British needs. After Britain became the so-called first modern industrial nation, the Empire provided its capitalists with cheap raw materials, land and labour. Colonial ports and cities were largely creatures of the Industrial Revolution, their very physical form made possible by the new machines for land surveying and infrastructure provision. New professions, particularly civil engineering and public health in the nineteenth century, shaped those cities, informed by Benthamite ideas of classifying and controlling society.

Colonial dominance was expressed in the management, control and use of land. Great tracts of land were expropriated, usually without compensation, and European legal concepts of private, corporate and state owner-ship were deployed to deny land rights to the colonized communities and peoples. Belatedly, the trusteeship or indirect rule approach to colonial management incorporated policies to preserve some measure of aboriginal or native land rights.

To preserve (as they saw it) their health and purity, as well as their status and dominance, the colonizers segregated themselves into exclusive, endogamous, and defensible enclaves. Racial segregation in the colonial city emerged from the same mania for classification and order that characterized utilitarianism and the new science of society in the early nineteenth century. Colonial urban form increasingly sought to enforce separation: white from black, migrant from native, traditional from modern, men from women and family. The most severe example of structural segregation was in South Africa, where the *apartheid* city was eventually to discover that the political and economic costs of segregation were too great to be sustainable.

Colonial authority sought to render the city open to its controlling gaze. Public spaces and wide streets were maintained, not particularly for any communal benefit, but to preserve colonial power through surveillance. The goal was to produce 'a sanitary/commercial/administrative space that was uniform, predictable, and manageable . . . a space for the symbolic representation of the authority of the colonial power and its paradigms of economy, health, and status' (Archer, 1994, pp. 22–23). The British colonizers had little interest in learning from other long-established urban cultures, and sometimes sanctioned a violent physical assault on such cultures, justifying their actions by a rhetoric concerned with issues of defence and public health. Later a strategy of preserving and sealing off such old cities and cultures was endorsed by the dual mandate doctrine.

While the colonial city was shaped by the forces of colonialism, it was occupied by many peoples, and continuously transformed by processes of conflict and negotiation between colonizers and colonized. The urban built environment was thus a complex, multi-coded space continually reinterpreted in everyday usage. An urban history from below, focusing attention at 'the interfaces where colonialist and coolie meet' (Yeoh, 1991, p. 24), is beginning to expose these dimensions.

In the early twentieth century the idea of town planning emerged as a new approach to managing the colonial city. It offered a 'toolbox' of techniques, packaged within a new professional and legislative structure. These included the following: land-use zoning, public authority control of urban expansion and urban renewal, financial provisions for landowners involved with the planning and development process (through compulsory purchase and betterment levies), the garden city or garden suburb model of low-density family housing, and policies of urban containment and decentralization.

Much was claimed for 'town planning' by its exponents at that time. Patrick Geddes thought that, by offering a better future through physical improvements for the urban masses, it could defuse political tensions and even save the Empire, and he tried to apply his remedies in Ireland, Palestine, and India. The concept of separating incompatible land uses through zoning had a particular appeal in the colonial situation, where different racial groups had to be managed and powerful capitalist forces were at work: racial and community zoning could be used to divide and partition urban space and thus maintain the dominance of the 'colonial masters'. Town planning also became part of the unsuccessful bribe offered by British colonialism in an attempt to hang on to power – a promise of 'amenities' incorporated in new legislation under the colonial development and welfare programme from the 1930s.

But within a matter of twenty years Britain's Empire was swept away. The high hopes for town planning as a modern approach to colonial management were not realized. In Malaya, for instance, the government planning department, created by the visionary Reade in the 1920s to bring a better life to the colonial community, was a generation later laying out resettlement villages to neutralize Chinese Communist insurgents – a situation that would have appalled him. In Trinidad the government's town planner was relegated to a housing management role, while in Palestine he was instructed to justify urban demolitions carried out for security reasons.

What legacy, then, has colonial planning

offered the teeming cities of the so-called developing world? The problems of these cities have their roots deep in the colonial situation, and colonial approaches survive in the policies of government and development agencies.

The public sector dominance of solutions to the pressures of urban growth continued a colonial tradition into the post-colonial period. The *ad hoc* agency (the improvement board or trust) has survived with new urban development agencies. A reluctance to allow local land-use planning and regulation to be controlled by democratically-elected local authorities has contributed to the situation whereby local government has become an administrative backwater in many countries, lacking both financial and technical capacity.

Another legacy is the use of urban space for conspicuous consumption and the maintenance of inequality. Racial segregation was replaced by social segregation, and the idea remained that low density equals high income (and *vice versa*). The garden city planners' preference for low-density development, often reflected in an administrative bias against high density schemes, has added to the inefficiencies and inequities created by the colonial city. The services by government – shelter, transport, water supply, and electric power – have tended to benefit a privileged minority rather than serve the majority.

Physical planning, which at the time of Independence appeared attractive as a means of taking an inventory of national resources, has become discredited, with resources for development proving finite and the planning ideology becoming associated with a centralizing state role. Nation states have abandoned attempts to control and direct settlement size and location, and to plan the physical form of cities, following the manifest failure of planners and their associated bureaucracies to order urban growth or improve conditions for most urban dwellers. It is still seen as a specialist, professional activity, the exclusive

preserve of a segment of the bureaucratic elite or foreign consultants. Its ideology, derived from the essentially liberal democratic context of metropolitan Europe, persists as an element in an expanding global culture diffused through the capitalist world economy.

Perhaps the most serious legacy of the colonial city is the failure to manage the tidal wave of urban growth and informal settlements. This book has tried to show that 'informal housing' has been a feature of colonial urban development from its outset, with patterns of informal settlement on the edge of the city which the colonial authorities had little interest in controlling or managing. Land policies which sought to exclude, or limit the involvement of, the indigenous communities in urban life, helped to create so-called 'squatter' settlements on the outskirts.

Recently has come the slow recognition that it is beyond the power of many nation states to restrain urban-rural migration, or even to provide the shelter, infrastructure, and services needed by their rapidly growing urban populations. With this has come a belated reappraisal of the respective roles and contribution of the public and private sectors. There has been a dramatic shift, for instance, from the traditionally negative view of Third World housing as slums and squatter settlements, to a positive one which recognizes the value of 'self-help' housing as a flexible and participative approach to shelter provision.

Colonial systems, like socialist ones, centralized political choices and technical expertise. The perceived inefficiencies of segregationist policies, new concepts of human rights and democracy, the recognition that the state cannot meet all needs and the professionals do not know everything, and the increasing irrelevancy of the concept of the Third World are all new elements influencing the post-colonial city, and eliciting more flexible approaches. The colonial city, like the socialist city, at last is being overtaken by history.

BIBLIOGRAPHY

Aalen, F.H.A. (1989) Lord Meath, city improvement and social imperialism. *Planning Perspectives*, **4**(2), pp. 127–152.

Abdul Sattar (1965) Historical Development of Cantonments and their Effect on Urban Growth in West Pakistan. M.Sc. Thesis, University of Engineering & Technology, Lahore, Pakistan.

Abrams, C. (1951) Israel's greatest problem. *Town and Country Planning*, **19**, pp. 504–508.

Abu-Lughod, J. (1980) *Rabat: Urban Apartheid in Morocco*. Princeton: Princeton University Press.

Abu-Lughod, J.L. (1987) The Islamic City – historic myth, Islamic essence, and contemporary relevance. *International Journal of Middle East Studies*, **19**, pp. 155–176.

Akbar, J. (1988) *Crisis in the Built Environment: The Case of the Muslim City*. Singapore: Concept Media.

Alexander, L. (1983) European planning ideology in Tanzania. *Habitat International*, **7**(1/2), pp. 17–36.

Alford, R.G. (1900) Tropical sanitation, with special reference to Hong Kong. *PICE*, **141**, pp. 262–268.

Alleyne, W. and Fraser, H. (1988) *The Barbados-Carolina Connection*. Kingston: Macmillan Caribbean.

Alleyne, W. and Sheppard, J. (1990) *The Barbados Garrison and Its Buildings*. Kingston: Macmillan Caribbean.

Amos, F.J.C. (1984) Low-cost development authorities. *Cities*, **1**(4), pp. 404–413.

Anderson, G. (1991) *The Call of the Ancestors*. Washington: AMAR.

Anthony, C. (1976) The big house and the slave quarters. *Landscape*, **20**(3), pp. 8–19, and **21**(1), pp. 9–15.

Archer, J. (1994) City of Palaces, City of Lesions: Empire, Improvement, and Environmental Medicine in Early 19th-Century Calcutta. IPHS Conference Paper, Hong Kong.

Armstrong, A. (1987) Master plans for Dar-es-Salaam, Tanzania. *Habitat International*, **11**(2), pp. 133–145.

Arnold, D. (ed.) (1988) *Imperial Medicine and Indigenous Societies*. Manchester: Manchester University Press.

Ashton, P. (1992) The accidental city: writing the history of planning in Sydney. *Planning History*, **14**(3), pp. 30–33.

Auster, M. (1989) Construction of the planning idea: Britain, the USA, and Australia 1919–1939. *Planning Perspectives*, **4**(2), pp. 224–250.

Baine, Rodney M. and De Vorsey, L. (1989) The provenance and historical accuracy of 'A View of Savannah as is Stood the 29th of March, 1734'. *Georgia Historical Quarterly*, **73**(4), pp. 784–813.

Ballhatchet, K. and Harrison, J. (eds.) (1980) *The City in South Asia: Premodern and Modern*. London: Curzon.

Bannister, T.C. (1961) Oglethorpe's sources for the Savannah plan. *Journal of the Society of Architectural Historians*, May.

Bardon, J. (1982) *Belfast: An Illustrated History*. Dundonald: Blackstaff Press.

Barley, N. (1993) *The Duke of Puddle Dock: In the Footsteps of Stamford Raffles*. London: Penguin.

Baruth, K.H. (1951) *The Physical Planning of Israel*. Jerusalem: Legal and Technical Press.

Basu, D.K. (ed.) (1985) *The Rise and Growth of the Colonial Port Cities in Asia*. Berkeley, California: California University Press.

Batey, P. (1993) Town planning education: As it was then. *The Planner*, April, pp. 25 and 33.

Baylen, J.O. and Grossman, N.J. (1979 and 1984) *Biographical Dictionary of Modern British Radicals*. Sussex: Harvester.

Beames, J. (1961) *Memoirs of a Bengal Civilian*. London: Chatto & Windus.

Beckles, H. and Shepherd, V. (eds.) (1991) *Caribbean Slave Society and Economy: A Student Reader*. Kingston: Macmillan Caribbean.

Beevers, R. (1988) *The Garden City Utopia: A Critical Biography of Ebenezer Howard*. London: Macmillan.

Begde, P.V. (1982) *Forts and Palaces of India*. New Delhi: Sagar Publications.

Bell, C. and R. (1969) *City Fathers: The Early History of Town Planning in Britain*. London: Cresset.

Bell, L.P. (1964) A new theory on the Plan of Savannah, Georgia. *Georgia Historical Quarterly*, **48**, pp. 147–165.

Benevolo, L. (1967) *The Origins of Modern Town Planning*. London: Routledge.

Best, A.C.G. (1970) Gaborone: Problems and prospects of a new capital. *Geographical Review*, **69**, pp. 1–14.

Betjeman, J. (1988) *Collected Poems*. London: John Murray.

Blainey, G. (1993) *The Rush That Never Ended*. Melbourne: Melbourne University Press.

Blair, T.L. (ed.) (1984) *Urban Innovation Abroad: Problem Cities in search of Solutions*. New York: Plenum.

Blouet, B.W. (1977) Land policies in Trinidad 1838–50. *Journal of Caribbean History*, **9**, pp. 43–59.

Blussé, L. (1985) An insane administration and an unsanitary town. The Dutch East India Company and Batavia (1619–1799), in Ross and Telkamp (eds.).

Bogle, J.M.L. (1929) *Town Planning: India*. Bombay: Oxford University Press.

Boyd. R. (1952) *Australia's Home: Its Origins, Builders and Occupiers*. Melbourne: Melbourne University Press.

Braudel, F. (1984) *Civilization and Capitalism 15th–18th Century*. Vol. 3: *The Perspective of the World*. London: Collins (translation).

Brereton, B. (1979) *Race Relations in Colonial Trinidad 1860–1900*. Cambridge: Cambridge University Press.

Brereton, B. (1981) *A History of Modern Trinidad 1783–1862*. London: Heinemann.

Brice, M.H. (1984) *Stronghold: A History of Military Architecture*. London: Batsford.

Bridenbaugh, C. (1938) *Cities in the Wilderness: The First Century of Urban Life in America 1625–1742*. New York.

Brine, J. (1993) Diagrams of utilitarianism: The panopticon and the city of Adelaide, in Freestone (ed.) (1993), pp. 11–17.

Bristow, R. (1984) *Land-use Planning in Hong Kong: History, Policies and Procedures*. Hong Kong: Oxford University Press.

Bristow, M.R. (1989) *The Hong Kong New Towns: A Selective Review*. Hong Kong: Oxford University Press.

Bristow, R. (1992) *The Origins of the Singapore Land-Use Planning System*. Occasional Paper 32, Dept. of Planning and Landscape, University of Manchester.

Brown, L. (1933) *The First Earl of Shaftesbury*. New York.

Bruce, W.D. (1895) The Kidderpur Docks, Calcutta. *PICE*, **121**, pp. 88–151.

Bruton, M. (1982) The Malaysian planning system. *Third World Planning Review*, **4**(4), pp. 315–334.

Bruton, M. (1985) Peninsular Malaysia: Conflict between economic and social goals. *Cities*, **2**(2), pp. 124–139.

Buder, S. (1990) *Visionaries and Planners: The Garden City Movement and the Modern Community*. New York: Oxford University Press.

Bunker, R. and Hutchings, A. (eds.) (1986) *With Conscious Purpose*. Adelaide: Wakefield.

Bunyan, J. (1967) *The Origin of Forced Labour in the Soviet Union 1917–1921*. Baltimore, Md.

Burchell, J. (1987) *The History of Lancaster and Lodge*. Macclesfield, Cheshire: McMillan Martin.

Burnett-Hurst, A.R. (1925) *Labour and Housing in Bombay*. London: King and Sons.

Burrow, J.W. (1966) *Evolution and Society: A Study in Victorian Social Theory*. Cambridge: Cambridge University Press.

Butchart, A. (1994) The Industrial Panopticon: Mining and the Medical Construction of Migrant African Labour in South Africa.

London: Institute of Commonwealth Studies seminar paper.

Butt, M.R. (1990) *Manual of Cantonment Laws.* Lahore: Mansoor Book House.

Campbell, P.C. (1923) *Chinese Coolie Emigration to Countries within the British Empire* (Reprinted 1971.) London: Frank Cass & Co.

Campbell, S. (1988) Carnival, calypso and class struggle in 19th century Trinidad. *History Workshop*, **26**, pp. 1–27.

Cangi, C.M. (1993) Civilizing the people of South-east Asia: Sir Stamford Raffles' town plan for Singapore, 1819–23. *Planning Perspectives*, **8**(2), pp. 166–187.

Cannon, M. (1991) *Old Melbourne Town Before the Gold Rush.* Melbourne: Loch Haven.

Cannon, M. (1993) *Melbourne After the Gold Rush.* Melbourne: Loch Haven.

Castells, M., Goh, L. and Kwok, R. Y-W. (1990) *The Shek Kip Mei Syndrome: Economic Development and Public Housing in Hong Kong and Singapore.* London: Pion.

Catanach, I.J. (1988) Plague and the tensions of empire: India 1896–1918, in Arnold (ed.) pp. 194–172.

Chadwick, G.F. (1966) *The Park and The Town: Public Landscape in the 19th and 20th Centuries.* London: Architectural Press.

Chakrabarty, D. (1981) Communal riots and labour: Bengal's jute mill-hands in the 1890s. *Past and Present*, No. 91, pp. 140–169.

Chakrabarty, D. (1983) On deifying and defying authority: Managers and workers in the jute mills of Bengal *c.* 1890–1940. *Past & Present*, No. 100, pp. 124–146.

Chan Sieg (1984) *The Squares: An Introduction to Savannah.* Norfolk, Va.: Donning.

Cheesman, R. (1986) *Patterns in Perpetuity.* Adelaide: Thornton House.

Cherry, G.E. (1974) *The Evolution of British Town Planning.* Leighton Buzzard, Bedfordshire: Leonard Hill.

Cherry, G.E. (ed.) (1980) *Shaping an Urban World.* London: Mansell.

Cherry, G.E. (ed.) (1981) *Pioneers in British Planning.* London: Architectural Press.

Cherry, G.E., Jordan, H. and Kafkoula, K. (1993) Gardens, civic art and town planning: the work of Thomas H. Mawson (1861–1933). *Planning Perspectives*, **8**(3), pp. 307–332.

Chitale, L.M. (1928) Housing problems in India. *Garden Cities and Town Planning*, **18**, pp. 114–116.

Chitale, L.M. (1937–38) Problems of Madras City. *JTPI*, **24**, pp. 364–366.

Chokor, B.A. (1993) External European influences and indigenous social values in urban development and planning in the Third World: the case of Ibadan, Nigeria. *Planning Perspectives*, **8**(3), pp. 283–306.

Christopher, A.J. (1977) Early settlement and the cadastral framework, in Kay and Smout (eds.), pp. 14–25.

Christopher, A.J. (1988) *The British Empire at Its Zenith.* London: Croom Helm.

Christopher, A.J. (1992) Urban segregation levels in the British overseas Empire and its successors, in the twentieth century. *Transactions of Institute of British Geographers*, **17**, pp. 95–107.

Church, L.F. (1932) *Oglethorpe: A Study of Philanthropy in England and Georgia.* London.

Clarke, C.G. (1975) *Kingston, Jamaica: Urban Development and Social Change, 1692–1962.* Berkeley: University of California Press.

Clarke, C., Ley, D. and Peach, C. (1984) *Geography and Ethnic Pluralism.* London: Allen & Unwin.

Clarke, C.G. (1985) A Caribbean Creole capital: Kingston, Jamaica (1692–1938), in Ross and Telkamp (eds.), pp. 153–170.

Cobban, J.L. (1992) Exporting planning: the work of Thomas Karsten in colonial Indonesia. *Planning Perspectives*, **7**(3), pp. 327–344.

Cockrill, J.W. (1916–17) Presidential Address. *JTPI*, **3**, pp. 2–3.

Cole, M. (ed.) (1974) *The Webbs and Their Work.* London: Harvester.

Coleman, K. (1976) *Colonial Georgia: A History.* New York: Scribner.

Colley, L. (1992) *Britons: Forging the Nation 1707–1837.* Yale: Yale University Press.

Collins, J. (1969) Lusaka: The Myth of the Garden City. Zambian Urban Studies No. 2, Institute for Social Research, University of Zambia.

Collins, J. (1980) Lusaka: Urban planning in a British colony 1931–64, in Cherry (ed.)

Colman, J. (1993) The Liverpool connection and

Australian planning and design practice 1945–1985, in Freestone (ed.) pp. 59–69.

Concannon, T.A.L. (1951) Town planning in Malaya. *JTPI*, **38**(2), pp. 32–33.

Concannon, T.A.L. (1958) Town planning in the Malaya Federation. *Town and Country Planning*, August, pp. 301–307.

Condon, J.K. (1900) *The Bombay Plague*. Bombay: Educational Society.

Connah, G. (1988) *Of the Hut I Builded: The Archaeology of Australia's History*. Cambridge: Cambridge University Press.

Coode, Sir J. (1890) British Colonies as fields for the employment of the Civil Engineer, – past – present – and future. *PICE*, **99**, pp. 1–39.

Coon, A.G. (1990) Development plans in the West Bank. *GeoJournal*, **21**(4), pp. 363–373.

Coon, A.G. (1992) *Town Planning Under Military Occupation: An Examination of the Law and Practice of Town Planning in the Occupied West Bank*. Aldershot: Darmouth.

Cosgrove, D. and Daniels, S. (1988) *The Iconography of Landscape: Essays on the Symbolic Representation, Design, and Use of Past Environments*. Cambridge: Cambridge University Press.

Crane, J.L. and Paxton, E.T. (1951) The worldwide housing problem. *Town Planning Review*, **22**, pp. 17–43.

Craton, M. (1978) *Searching for the Invisible Man*. Ithaca, New York.

Craven, W.F. (1949) *The Southern Colonies in the Seventeenth Century 1607–1689*. Louisiana: Louisiana State University Press.

Crawford, A. (1985) *C.R. Ashbee: Architect, Designer and Romantic Socialist*. Yale: Yale University Press.

Cullingworth Report (1969) *Council Housing Purposes, Procedures and Priorities. 9th Report of the Housing Management Sub-Committee of the Central Housing Committee*. London: HMSO.

Curl, J.S. (1986) *The Londonderry Plantation 1609–1914*. Chichester: Phillimore.

Curtin, P.D. (1985) Medical knowledge and urban planning in tropical Africa. *American Historical Review*, **90**(3), pp. 594–613.

Curtin, P.D. (1989) *Death By Migration: Europe's Encounter with the Tropical World in the 19th Century*. Cambridge: Cambridge University Press.

Daly, W.M. (1986) *Empire on the Nile: The Anglo-Egyptian Sudan 1898–1934*. Cambridge: Cambridge University Press.

Daunton, Martin J. (1983) *House and Home in the Victorian City: Working Class Housing 1850–1914*. London: Arnold.

Daunton, M.J. (ed.) (1990) *Housing the Workers: A Comparative History 1850–1914* London: Pinter (Leicester University Press).

Davenport, T.R.H. (1970) The triumph of Colonel Stallard: The Transformation of the Natives (Urban Areas) Act between 1923 and 1937. *South African Historical Journal*, No. 2.

Davidge, W.R. (1921) The Madras Town Planning Act. *Town Planning Review*, **11**, pp. 160–161.

Davies, P. (1985) *Spendours of the Raj: British Architecture in India, 1660–1947*. London: John Murray.

Davis, D.B. (1984) *Slavery and Human Progress*. New York: Oxford University Press.

Davis, S.G. (1965) *Land Use Problems in Hong Kong*. Hong Kong: Hong Kong University Press.

Davison, G. (1978) *The Rise and Fall of Marvellous Melbourne*. Melbourne: Melbourne University Press.

De Beer, E.S. (1976) *The Correspondence of John Locke*, Vol. 1. Oxford: Clarendon.

Denoon, D. (1988) Temperate medicine and settler capitalism: on the reception of western medical ideas, in MacLeod and Lewis (eds.), pp. 121–138.

Dobbin, C. (1972) *Urban leadership in western India: Politics and Communities in Bombay City 1840–1885*. London: Oxford University Press.

Dodwell, H.H. (ed.) (1914) *Cambridge History of the British Empire*. Cambridge: Cambridge University Press.

Doebele, W.A. (1987) The evolution of concepts of urban land tenure in developing countries. *Habitat International*, **11**(1), pp. 7–22.

Dossal, M. (1989) Limits of colonial urban planning: a study of mid-nineteenth century Bombay. *International Journal of Urban & Regional Research*, **13**(1), pp. 19–31.

Doxiadis, C.A. (1965) Islamabad: The creation

of a new capital. *Town Planning Review*, **36**, pp. 1–37.

Drake, M.F. (1993) Centralised control: Historical overview of a planning pre-occupation. *Planning History*, **15**(2), pp. 44–48.

Drew, P. (1992) *Veranda: Embracing Place*. Australia: Angus & Robertson.

Dubow, S. (1989) *Racial Segregation and the Origins of Apartheid in South Africa 1919–36*. Oxford: Macmillan.

Dumett, R.E. (1968) The campaign against malaria and the expansion of scientific, medical and sanitary services in British West Africa, 1898–1910. *African Historical Studies*, **I**, pp. 153–197.

Dutt, A.K. (1959) Critique of town plans of Jamshedpur. *National Geographical Journal of India*, **5**(4), pp. 205–211.

Dutt, B. (1925) *Town-Planning in Ancient India*. Calcutta: Thacker Spink.

Dutton, G. (1960) *Founder of a City*. Adelaide: Rigby.

Dwyer, D.J. (1971) *Asian Urbanization: A Hong Kong Casebook*. Hong Kong: Hong Kong University Press.

Edney, M. (1990) Mapping and Empire: British Trigonometric Surveys in India and the European Concept of Systematic Survey 1799–1843. PhD Thesis, University of Wisconsin-Madison.

Edwards, N. (1990) *The Singapore House and Residential Life 1819–1939*. Singapore: Oxford University Press.

Efrat, E. (1989) *The New Towns of Israel (1948–1988)*. Munich: Minerva.

Efrat, E. (1993) British town planning perspectives of Jerusalem in transition. *Planning Perspectives*, **8**, pp. 377–393.

Efrat, E. (1994) New development towns of Israel (1948–93). *Cities*, **11**(4), pp. 247–252.

Elder, D. (1984) Introduction to *William Light's Brief Journal and Australian Diaries*. Adelaide: Wakefield Press.

Eldridge, H.W. (ed.) (1975) *World Capitals: Toward Guided Urbanization*. Garden City, N.Y.: Anchor Press.

Eng, Teo Siew (1992) Planning principles in pre- and post-independence Singapore. *Town Planning Review*, **63**(2), pp. 163–185.

Ettinger, A.A. (1936) *James Edward Oglethorpe: Imperial Idealist*. Oxford: Oxford University Press.

Evans, F.D. (1915) Engineering Operations for the Prevention of Malaria. *PICE*, **200**, pp. 2–61.

Evans, F.D., and Pirie, G.J. (1939) *Selection of Sites for Towns and Government Residential Areas*. Lagos: Government Printer.

Evenson, N. (1966) *Chandigarh*. Berkeley: University of California Press.

Evenson, N. (1989) *The Indian Metropolis: A View Toward the West*. Yale: Yale University Press.

Fermor, P.L. (1984) *The Traveller's Tree*. London: Penguin (first published 1950).

Finer, S.E. (1972) The transmission of Benthamite ideas 1820–1850, in Sutherland, G. (ed.) *Studies in the Growth of Nineteenth-Century Government*. London: Routledge.

Finney, C. (1993) *Paradise Revealed: Natural History in nineteenth-century Australia*. Melbourne: Museum of Victoria.

Fischer, K. (1984) *Canberra: Myths and Models*. Hamburg: Institute of Asian Affairs.

Fitzgerald, R. (1982) *A History of Queensland from the dreaming to 1915*. St. Lucia, Queensland: University of Queensland Press.

Fitzgerald, S. (1992) *Sydney 1842–1922*. Sydney: Hale and Iremonger.

Forster Commission (1938) *Trinidad and Tobago Disturbances 1937: Report of Commission*. Command 5641. London: HMSO.

Foster, W.C. (1985) *Sir Thomas Livingston Mitchell and His World 1792–1855*. Sydney: Institute of Surveyors.

Foucault, M. (1980) *Power Knowledge*. New York.

Fraser, J.M. (1957) The work of the Singapore Improvement Trust. *JTPI*, pp. 190–196.

Fraser, W.J. (1989) *Charleston! Charleston! The History of the Southern City*. Charleston: University of South Carolina Press.

Freestone, R. (1983) John Sulman and 'the laying out of towns'. *Planning History Bulletin*, **5**(1), pp. 18–23.

Freestone, R. (1986) Canberra as a garden city 1901–1930. *Journal of Australian Studies*, **19**, pp. 3–20.

Freestone, R. (1989) *Model Communities: The*

Garden City Movement in Australia. Melbourne: Thomas Nelson.

Freestone, R. (1993) *The Australian Planner*. Proceedings of the Planning History Conference, May 1993. Environmental Planning and Management Series, School of Town Planning, University of New South Wales, Sydney.

Freestone, R. and Hutchings, A. (1993) Planning history in Australia: the state of the art. *Planning Perspectives*, **8**(1), pp. 72–91.

Friedmann, J. (1986) The world city hypothesis. *Development and Change*, **17**, pp. 69–83.

Frost, L.E., and Jones, E.L. (1989) The fire gap and the greater durability of nineteenth century cities. *Planning Perspectives*, **4**, pp. 333–347.

Fry, E.M. and Drew, J.B. (1947) *Village Housing in the Tropics*. Lagos: Government of Nigeria.

Fryer, P. (1984) *Staying: The History of Black People in Britain*. London: Pluto.

Fryer, P. (1984) *Staying Power: The History of Black People in Britain*, London: Pluto.

Fuchs, R. (1992) Austen St. Barbe Harrison – A British Architect in the Holy Land. DSc Thesis, Haifa Technion (in Hebrew).

Furedy, C. (1982) Whose responsibility? Dilemmas of Calcutta's bustee policy in the nineteenth century. *South Asia*, NS **5**, pp. 38–39.

Fuschtman, J. (1986) Statutory Planning As a Form of Social Control: The Evolution of Town Planning Law in Mandatory Palestine and Israel 1917–1980. PhD Thesis, University College London.

Galantay, E.Y. Constandense, A.K. and Ohba, T. (eds.) (1985) *New Towns World-Wide*. The Hague: IFHP.

Garnaut, C. (1995) Of passion, publicity and planning: Charles Reade and the Mitcham Garden Suburb. *Australian Planner*, **32** (3), pp. 181–189.

Garvan, A. (1951) *Architecture and Town Planning in Colonial Connecticut*. New Haven.

Gaskell, S.M. (1987) *Model Housing from the Great Exhibition to the Festival of Britain*. London: Mansell.

Gavish, D. (1989) Aerial perspective of past landscapes, in Kark (ed.), pp. 308–319.

Geyer, H.S. (1989) Apartheid in South Africa and industrial deconcentration in the PWV

area. *Planning Perspectives*, **4**(3), pp. 251–269.

Ghosh, M., Dutta, A.K. and Ray, B. (1972) *Calcutta: A Study in Urban Growth Dynamics*. Calcutta: Mukhopadhyay.

Gillespie, R. (1985) *Colonial Ulster: The Settlement of East Ulster 1600–1641*. Cork: Cork University Press.

Gilpin, J. (1992) International perspectives on railway townsite development in Western Canada 1877–1914. *Planning Perspectives*, 7, pp. 247–262.

Goh Ban Lee (1988*a*) The foundation of urban planning in George Town and Adelaide. *Kajian Malaysia*, **6**, pp. 44–67.

Goh Ban Lee (1988*b*) Import of Urban Planning into Malaysia. *Planning History*, **10**(1), pp. 7–12.

Golany, G. (1973) *New Towns Planning and Development – World Wide Bibliography*. Washington, DC: Urban Land Institute.

Golany, G. (1984) Validity of New Town Principles for the Developing Countries, in Blair (ed.), pp. 376–395.

Graicer, I. (1989) Social architecture in Palestine: Conceptions in working-class housing, 1920–1958, in Kark (ed.), pp. 287–307.

Greig, D. (1987) *The Reluctant colonists: Netherlanders abroad in the 17th and 18th Centuries*. The Netherlands: Van Gorcum.

Grierson, A.E.P. (1928) *Influence of Parks and Gardens and Open Spaces in Civic Development*. Allahabad: Government Press.

Gupta, N. (1971) Military security and urban development: A case study of Delhi 1857–1912. *Modern Asian Studies*, **5**(1), pp. 61–77.

Gupta, N. (1981) *Delhi Between Two Empires 1803–1931: Society, Government, and Urban Growth*. Delhi: Oxford University Press.

Gupta, S. (1993) Theory and practice of town planning in Calcutta, 1817 to 1912: An appraisal. *Indian Economic and Social History Review*, **30**(1), pp. 29–55.

Gupta, S.C. (1964) New towns in India – a socio-economic experiment. *Journal of Institute of Town Planners India*, **38**, pp. 4–5.

Haley, K.H.D. (1986) *The First Earl of Shaftesbury*. New York: Oxford University Press.

Hall, P. (1988) *Cities of Tomorrow*. Oxford: Blackwell.

Hall-Jones, J. (1992) *John Turnbull Thomson, First Surveyor-General of New Zealand*. Dunedin, NZ: John McIndoe.

Hamer, D.A. (1990) *New Towns in the New World*. New York: Columbia University Press.

Hamzah Sendut (1965) The Structure of Kuala Lumpur. *Town Planning Review*, **36**, pp. 127–138.

Hamzah Sendut (1966) Planning resettlement villages in Malaya. *Planning Outlook*, **1**, pp. 58–70.

Hancock, T.H.H. (1986) *Coleman's Singapore*. Kuala Lumpur. Malaysian Branch of the Royal Asiatic Society.

Hardy, D. (1989) War, planning and social change: the example of the garden city campaign, 1914–1918. *Planning Perspectives*, **4**(2), pp. 207–223.

Hardy, D. (1991) *From Garden Cities to New Towns: Campaigning for town and country planning 1899–1946*. London: E. & F.N. Spon.

Hargreaves, R.P. (1992) Street Widths in Victorian New Zealand. *Planning History*, **14**(1), pp. 29–32.

Harrison, B. (1985) *Holding the Fort: Melaka under two flags 1795–1845*. Kuala Lumpur: Malaysian Branch of the Royal Asiatic Society.

Haswell, C.W. (1921) Town-planning and housing in Cairo. *GCTP*, **11**, pp. 256–258.

Hayuma, A.M. (1981) Dodoma: The planning and building of the new capital city of Tanzania. *Habitat International*, **5**(5/6), pp. 653–680.

Headrick, D. (1981) *The Tools of Empire: Technology and European Imperialism in the Nineteenth Century*. New York: Oxford University Press.

Heiden, C.N. van der (1990) Town planning in the Dutch Indies. *Planning Perspectives*, **5**(1), pp. 63–84.

Henderson, J.W. (1958) Lagos, Nigeria: The work of the Lagos Executive Development Board. *JTPI*, **44**, pp. 114–118.

Herbert, G. (1989) Crossroads: imperial priorities and regional perspectives in the planning of Haifa 1918–1939. *Planning Perspectives*, **4**(3), pp. 333–347.

Herbert, G. and Sosnowski, S. (1993) *Bauhaus on the Carmel and the Crossroads of Empire: Architecture and planning in Haifa during the British Mandate*. Jerusalem: Yad Izhak Ben-Zvi.

Hetherington, P. (1978) *British Paternalism and Africa 1920–1940* London: Frank Cass.

Hietala, M. (1987) *Services and Urbanization at the turn of the century*. Helsinki: SHS.

Higman, B.W. (1973) Household structure and fertility on Jamaican slave plantations: A nineteenth-century example. *Population Studies*, **27** (Part 3), pp. 527–550.

Hinde, G.W. (1971) *New Zealand Torrens System Centennial Essays*. Wellington.

Holliday, A.C. (1921) Restrictions governing city development: II, Zoning-use districts. *Town Planning Review*, **9**, pp. 217–238.

Holmes, R. (1993) *Dr. Johnson and Mr. Savage*. London: Hodder and Stoughton.

Home, R.K. (1974) *The Influence of Colonial Government upon Nigerian Urbanisation*. PhD Thesis, University of London.

Home, R.K. (1976) Urban growth and urban government: Contradictions in the colonial political economy, in Williams, G. (ed.) *Nigeria: Economy and Society*. London: Rex Collings.

Home, R.K. (1982) *City of Blood Revisited*. London: Rex Collings.

Home, R.K. (1983) Town planning, segregation and indirect rule in colonial Nigeria. *Third World Planning Review*, **5**(2), pp. 165–175.

Home, R.K. (1986) Urban development boards in Nigeria: the case of Kano. *Cities*, **3**(3), pp. 228–236.

Home, R.K. (1989*a*) Colonial town planning in Malaysia, Singapore and Hong Kong. *Planning History*, **11** pp. 8–11.

Home, R.K. (1989*b*) *Planning Use Classes: A Guide to the 1987 Order*, 2nd ed. Oxford: Blackwell.

Home, R.K. (1990*a*) Town planning and garden cities in the British colonial empire 1910–1940. *Planning Perspectives*, **5**, pp. 23–37.

Home, R.K. (1990*b*) British colonial town planning in the Middle East: The work of W.H. McLean. *Planning History*, **12**(1), pp. 4–9.

Home, R.K. (1991) Green belts and the origins of Adelaide's parklands. *Planning History*, **13**(1), pp. 24–28.

Home, R.K. (1993*a*) Barrack camps for

unwanted people: a neglected planning tradition. *Planning History*, **15**(1), pp. 14–21.

Home, R.K. (1993*b*) Transferring British planning law to the colonies: The case of the 1938 Trinidad Town and Regional Planning Ordinance. *Third World Planning Review*, **15**(4), pp. 397–410.

Housing in the West Indies (1945) *Development & Welfare Bulletin*, No. 13. Barbados: Government Printer.

Howard, E. (1965) *Garden Cities of To-morrow*. London: Faber.

Hoyles, M. (1991) *The Story of Gardening*. London: Journeyman.

Hudson, N., and McEwan, P. (1986) *That's Our House: A History of Housing in Victoria*. Melbourne: Ministry of Housing.

Hume, J.C. (1986) Colonialism and sanitary medicine: the development of preventive health policy in the Punjab, 1860 to 1900. *Modern Asian Studies*, **20**(4), pp. 703–724.

Hunter, R.J. (1971) Towns in the Ulster Plantation. *Studia Hibernica*, **11**, pp. 40–79.

Hussey, C. (1953) *Life of Sir Edwin Lutyens*. London: Country Life.

Hutchins, F. (1967) *The Illusion of Permanence*. Princeton: Princeton University Press.

Hutchings, A. (1987) Light's Adelaide Plan – A South American connection? *South Australian Geographical Journal*, pp. 60–63.

Hutchings, A. (1990) The Colonel Light Garden Suburb in South Australia: The continuing influence of the garden city tradition. *Planning History*, **12**, pp. 15–20.

Hutchings, A. and Bunker, R. (1986) *With Conscious Purpose: A History of Town Planning in South Australia*. Adelaide: Wakefield Press.

Huttenback, R.A. (1976) *Racism and Empire: White Settlers and Colored Immigrants in the British Self-Governing Colonies, 1830–1910*. Ithaca: Cornell University Press.

Hyde, F.E. (1947) Utilitarian town planning 1825–45. *Town Planning Review*, Summer.

Hyman, B. (1994) British Planners in Palestine 1918–1936. PhD Thesis, University of London.

Illick, J.E. (1976) *Colonial Pennsylvania: A History*. New York: Schribner.

Irving, R. (1981) *Indian Summer: Lutyens, Baker and Imperial Delhi*. New Haven: Yale University Press.

Irving, R. (ed.) (1985) *The History and Design of the Australian House*. Melbourne: Oxford University Press.

Jackson, P. (1988) Street life: the politics of Carnival. *Environment and Planning D: Society and Space*, **6**(2), pp. 213–227.

Jackson, P. (1989) *Maps of Meaning: An Introduction to Cultural Geography*. London: Unwin Hyman.

Jacobson, L. and Prakash, V. (1967) Urbanization and regional planning in India. *Urban Affairs Quarterly*, **11**(3), pp. 36–65.

Jeans, D.N. (1965) Town Planning in New South Wales 1829–1842. *Australian Planning Institute Journal*, **3**(6), pp. 188–196.

Jeans, D.N. (1981) Official town-founding procedures in New South Wales, 1828–1842. *Journal of Royal Australian Historical Society*, **67**, pp. 227–237.

Jeffrey, R. (ed.) (1978) *People, Princes and Paramount Power: Society and Politics in the Indian Princely States*. Delhi: Oxford University Press.

Johnson, D.L. and Langmead, D. (1986) *The Adelaide City Plan: Fiction and Fact*. Adelaide: Wakefield Press.

Johnson, H.B.D. (1969) *Crown Colony Government in Trinidad 1870–1897*. PhD Thesis, University of Oxford.

Johnson, H. (1977) The West Indies and the conversion of the British official classes to the development idea. *Journal of Commonwealth and Comparative Politics*, **15**, pp. 55–83.

Jones, A. (1989) *Backsight: A History of Surveying in Colonial Tasmania*. Sydney: Institute of Surveyors of Australia.

Jopling, L.M. (1923) Town planning in Lucknow. *Town Planning Review*, **10**, pp. 25–36.

Kafkoula, K. (1992) The replanning of the destroyed villages of Eastern Macedonia after World War I: The influence of the Garden City tradition on an emergency programme. *Planning History*, **14**(2), pp. 4–10.

Kain, R.J.P. and Baigent, E. (1992) *The Cadastral Map in the Service of the State: A History of Property Mapping*. Chicago: University of Chicago Press.

Kanyeihamba, G.W. (1980) The impact of received law in urban planning and development in Anglophonic Africa. *International*

Journal of Urban and Regional Research, **4**(2), pp. 239–266.

Kanyeihamba, G.W. and McAuslan, J.P.W. (1978) *Urban Legal Problems in East Africa*. Uppsala: Scandinavian Institute of African Studies.

Kark, R. (ed.) (1989) *The Land That Became Israel: Studies in Historical Geography*. New Haven: Yale University Press.

Kark, R. (1991) *Jerusalem Neighbourhoods: Planning and By-Laws (1855–1930)*. Jerusalem: Mount Scopus Publications.

Kay, G. and Smout, M.A.H. (eds.) (1977) *Salisbury: a Geographical Survey of the Capital of Rhodesia*. London: Hodder and Stoughton.

Kearle, J. (1951) Planning in Israel. *Town and Country Planning*, **19**, pp. 182–185.

Kendall, H. (1948) Jerusalem City Plan. *Town and Country Planning*, **16/17**, pp. 104–107.

Kendall, H. and Baruth, K.H. (1950) *Village Development in Palestine*. London: Crown Agents.

Kennedy, D. (1981) Climatic theories and culture in colonial Kenya and Rhodesia. *Journal of Imperial and Commonwealth History*, **10**, pp. 50–66.

King, A.D. (1976) *Colonial Urban Development*. London: Routledge and Kegan Paul.

King, A.D. (ed.) (1980) *Buildings and Society: Essays on the Social: Essays on the Social Development of the Built Environment*. London: Routledge.

King, A.D. (1982) Town Planning. A note on the origins and use of the term. *Planning History Bulletin*, **4**(2), pp. 15–17.

King, A.D. (1984) *The Bungalow: A Product of Several Cultures*. London: Routledge.

King, A.D. (1990) *Urbanism, Colonialism and the World-Economy*. London: Routledge.

Kiple, K.F. (ed.) (1993) *Cambridge World History of Human Disease*. Cambridge: Cambridge University Press.

Kirk, J.B. (1931) *Public Health Practice in the Tropics*. London: Churchill.

Kitchen, P. (1975) *A Most Unsettling Person*. London: Gollancz.

Klein, I. (1986) Urban development and death: Bombay City, 1870–1914. *Modern Asian Studies*, **20**(4), pp. 725–754.

Knight, G. (1984) Kingston, Jamaica: Strategies for managing urban growth and development, in Blair (ed.), pp. 39–63.

Koenigsberger, O.H. (1947) *Jamshedpur Development Plan*. Tata Iron and Steel (privately printed).

Koenigsberger, O.H. (1952) New towns in India. *Town Planning Review*, **23**, pp. 95–131.

Koh-Lim Wen Gin (1989) Conservation of historic districts, Singapore. *Planews* (Singapore Institute of Planners) **12**(1), pp. 15–22.

Kooiman, D. (1985) Bombay: from fishing village to colonial port city (1662–1947), in Ross and Telkamp (eds.), pp. 207–230.

Konvitz, J.V. (1978) *Cities and the Sea: Port City Planning in Early Modern Europe*. Baltimore: Johns Hopkins University Press.

Kostof, S. (1991) *The City Shaped*. London: Thames and Hudson.

Krishnarayan, V. and Thomas, H. (1993) *Ethnic Minorities and the Planning System*. London: Royal Town Planning Institute.

Kulkarni, L.M. (1979) Cantonment towns of India. *Ekistics*, **46**(277), pp. 214–220.

Kumer, D. (1981) British and Indian post-war New Towns: A Comparative Analysis. MSc Thesis, Department of Architecture, University of Edinburgh.

Labaree, L.W. (ed.) (1935) *Royal Instructions to British Colonial Governors 1670–1776*, 2 volumes. New York: Appleton.

Lanchester, H.V. (1914) Calcutta Improvement Trust: Precis of Mr. E.P. Richards' Report on the City of Calcutta. *Town Planning Review*, **5**, pp. 115–30 and 214–24.

Lanchester, H.V. (1916–17) Town planning in Southern India. *JTPI*, **3**, pp. 90–115.

Lanchester, H.V. (1925) *The Art of Town Planning*. London: Chapman & Hall.

Larson, M.S. (1977) *The Rise of Professionalism: A Sociological Analysis*. Berkeley: University of California Press.

Lawrence, J. (1990) *Lawrence of Lucknow: A Biography* London: Hodder and Stoughton.

Lee, J.M. and Petter, M. (1982) *The Colonial Office, War and Development Policy 1939–1945*. London: Maurice Temple Smith.

Lee, K.L. (1988) *The Singapore House 1819–1942*. Singapore: Times Editions.

Lemaine, G. *et al.* (eds.) (1976) *Perspectives on*

the Emergence of Scientific Disciplines. The Hague: Mouton.

Lemon, A. (ed.) (1990) *Homes Apart: South Africa's Divided Cities*. London: Paul Chapman.

Lemon, J.T. (1984) Spatial order: Houshold in local communities and regions in Greene, J.P. and Pole, J.R. (eds.) *Colonial British America: Essays in the New History of the Early Modern Era*. Baltimore: Johns Hopkins University Press.

Lewandowski, S.J. (1975) Urban growth and municipal development in the colonial city of Madras, 1869–1900. *Journal of Asian Studies*, **34**, February.

Lewandowski, S.J. (1984) Urban planning in the Asian port city: Madras, an overview 1920–1970. *South Asia*.

Lewis, J.N. (1983) *Ajoupa: Architecture of the Caribbean and Its Amerindian Origins*. Washington: American Institute of Architects.

Lewis, M. (1993) Darling and anti-Darling in the Plan of Melbourne, in Freestone (ed.), pp. 40–50.

Lim, J.S.H. (1993) The 'Shophouse Rafflesia': An outline of its Malaysian pedigree and its subsequent diffusion in Asia. *JMBRAS*, **66** (Part 1), pp. 47–67.

Ling, A. (1988) *Urban and Regional Planning and Development in the Commonwealth*. Sleaford: Howell Publications.

Lines, J.D. (1992) *Australia on Paper: The Story of Australian Mapping*. Box Hill, Victoria: Fortune Publications.

Lines, W.J. (1991) *Taming the Great South Land: A History of the Conquest of Nature in Australia*. St. Leonard's, New South Wales: Allen and Unwin.

Lip, E. (1984) *Chinese Geomancy: A Layman's Guide to Feng Shui* Singapore: Times Life International.

Liverpool, H.U.L. (1990) *Kaiso and Society*. Diego Martin, Trinidad: Juba.

Lloyd-Jones, R. (1990) The first Kondratieff: The long wave and the British industrial revolution. *Journal of Interdisciplinary History*, **22**(4), pp. 581–605.

Logan, J.W.P. (1935–36) Garden cities for Africa: Pinelands, a venture at Cape Town. *Town and Country Planning*, **4**, pp. 26–28.

Logan, T. (1976) The Americanization of German Zoning. *Journal of The American Institute of Planners*, **42**, pp. 377–385.

London, C.W. (1987) British Architecture in Victorian Bombay. DPhil, University of Oxford.

Lorimer, D.A. (1978) *Colour, Class and the Victorians*. Leicester: Leicester University Press.

Losty, J.P. (1990) *Calcutta: City of Palaces*. London: Arnold, British Library.

Lugard, F.D. (1919) *Revision of Instructions to Political Officers on Subjects Chiefly Political and Administrative 1913–1918*. London: Waterlow & Sons.

Lugard, Lord (1965) *The Dual Mandate in British Tropical Africa*. London: Frank Cass (reprint).

Lumsden, M. (1982) *The Barbados-American Connection*. Kingston: Macmillan Caribbean.

Lyons, M. (1985) From 'death camps' to cordon sanitaire: the development of sleeping sickness policy in the Uele district of the Belgian Congo, 1901–1914. *Journal of African History*, **26**, pp. 69–91.

Mabin, A. (1986) Labour, capital, class struggle and the origins of residential segregation in Kimberley, 1880–1920. *Journal of Historical Geography*, **12**(1), pp. 4–26.

Mabin, A. (1991) Origins of segregatory urban planning in South Africa, c. 1900–1940. *Planning History*, **13**(3), pp. 8–16.

Mabin, A. (1992) Comprehensive Segregation: The orgins of the Group Areas Act and its planning apparatuses. *Journal of Southern African Studies*, **18**(2), pp. 405–29.

Mabin, A. (1993) The Witwatersrand Joint Town Planning Committee 1932–1940: Of rigour and mortis. *Planning History*, **15**(2), pp. 49–54.

Mabin, A. (1993) Towards new planning legislation for South Africa. Proceedings of Second International Conference on Planning Law in Africa. Department of Local Government, Windhoek.

Mabin, A. and Smit, D. (1992) *Reconstructing South Africa's Cities 1900–2000: A Prospectus (Or, A Cautionary Tale)*. Occasional Paper No. 3, Programme for Planning Research, University of Witwatersrand, Johannesburg, South Africa.

Mabogunje, A.L. (1968) *Urbanisation in Nigeria*. London.

McAuslan, J.P.W.B. (1985) *Urban Land and Shelter for the Poor*. London: Earthscan.

McCoubrey, H. (1988) The English model of planning legislation in developing countries. *Third World Planning Review*, **10**(4), pp. 371–387.

McDaniel, G. (1982) *Hearth and Home: Preserving a People's Culture*. Philadelphia: Temple University Press.

McGee, T.G. (1967) *The South-East Asian City*. London: Bell.

McLean, W.H. (1917) Local government and town development in Egypt. *Town Planning Review*, **8**(2), pp. 83–97.

McLean, W.H. (1924–25) Notes on a proposed general scheme of national and regional development planning in Egypt. *JTPI*, **21**, pp. 149–152.

McLean, W.H. (1930) *Regional and Town Planning*. Glasgow: Crosby Lockwood.

MacLeod, R. and Lewis, M. (eds.) (1988) *Disease, Medicine, and Empire: Perspectives on Western Medicine and the experience of European expansion*. London: Routledge.

McParland, E. (1972) The Wide Streets Commissioners: Their importance for Dublin architecture in the late 18th–early 19th century. *Quarterly Bulletin of the Irish Georgian Society*, **15**(1), pp. 1–31.

Macpherson, K.L. (1987) *A Wilderness of Marshes, The Origins of Public Health in Shanghai, 1843–1893*. Hong Kong: Oxford University Press.

Mahabir, D.J. (1942) Twenty-five years after. *The Observer*, **1**(12), pp. 8–9.

Mahabir, N.K. (1985) *The Still Cry: Personal Accounts of East Indians in Trinidad and Tobago during indentureship 1845–1917*. Trinidad: Calaloux Publications.

Maharaj, B. (1992) The Group Areas Act in Durban: Central-Local State Relations. PhD Thesis, University of Natal.

Mahboub Bey, S. (1934–35) Cairo: Some notes on its history, characteristics and town plan. *JTPI*, **21** pp. 288–302.

Mandy, N. (1984) *A City Divided: Johannesburg and Soweto*. Johannesburg: Macmillan.

Marks, S. and Andersson, N. (1988) Typhus and social control: South Africa: 1917–1950, in MacLeod and Lewis (eds.), pp. 257–283.

Marks, S. and Trapido, S. (1979) Lord Milner and the South African State. *History Workshop*, No. 8, pp. 50–80.

Markus, T.A. (1993) *Building and Power: Freedom and Control in the Origin of Modern Building Types*. London: Routledge.

Marshall, P.J. (1985) Eighteenth-century Calcutta, in Ross and Telkamp (eds.), pp. 87–104.

Martin, C.A. (1957) *The Concentration Camps, 1900–1902*. Cape Town: Howards Timmins.

Maslen, T.J. (1830) *The Friend of Australia*. London.

Maslen, T.J. (1843) *Suggestions for the Improvement of Our Towns and Houses*. London: Smith, Elder & Co.

Maylam, P. (1990) The rise and decline of urban apartheid in South Africa. *African Affairs*, **89**, pp. 57–84.

Mayne, A.J.C. (1982) *Fever, Squalor and Vice: Sanitation and Social Policy in Victorian Sydney*. St. Lucia, Australia: University of Queensland Press.

Maxon, R.M. (1980) *John Ainsworth and the Making of Kenya*. Lanham, Maryland: University Press of America.

Mehta, V.C. (1937–38) Town planning: Past with the present. *JTPI*, **24**, pp. 386–392.

Meir, I.A. (1992) Urban space evolution in the desert – the case of Beer Sheva. *Building and Environment*, **27**(1), pp. 1-11.

Meller, H. (1990) *Patrick Geddes: Social Evolutionist and City Planner*. London: Routledge.

Merriman, N. (ed.) (1993) *The Peopling of London: Fifteen Thousand Years of Settlement from Overseas*. London: Museum of London.

Metcalf, T.R. (1989) *An Imperial Vision: Indian Architecture and Britain's Raj*. London: Faber & Faber.

Michie, J.L. (1990) *Richmond Hill Plantation 1800–1868: The Discovery of Antebellum Life on a Waccamaw Rice Plantation*. Spartanburg, SC: Reprint Co.

Miller, M. (1989 The elusive green background: Raymond Unwin and the Greater London Regional Plan. *Planning Perspectives*, **4**(1), pp. 15–44.

Mirams, A.E. (1919–20) Town planning in

Bombay under the Bombay Town Planning Act 1915. *JTPI*, **6**, pp. 43–62.

Mirams, A.E. (1931–32) Town planning in Uganda. *JTPI*, **18**, p. 26.

Mitchell, T. (1989) *Colonising Egypt*. Cairo: American University of Cairo.

Mohammed bin Haji Abdul Rahman (1984) New Towns in Malaysia: Problems, Failures and Achievements, in Blair (ed.), pp. 313–345.

Montgomery, R. (1717) *A Discourse Concerning the Designed Establishment of a New Colony to the South of Carolina, in the Most Delightful Country of the Universe*. London.

Moody, T.W. (1939) *The Londonderry Plantation 1609–41: The City of London and the Plantation in Ulster*. Belfast.

Moore, J. (1984) The political history of Nigeria's new capital. *Journal of Urban History*, **22**(1), pp. 167–175.

Moorhouse, G. (1970) *Calcutta*. London.

Moorhouse, G. (1984) *India Britannica*. London: Paladin Press.

Morris, A.E.W. (1979) *History of Urban Form Before the Industrial Revolution*. London: Godwin.

Morris, J. (with Winchester, S.) (1983) *Stones of Empire: The Buildings of the Raj*. Oxford: Oxford University Press.

Morris, J. (1988) *Hong Kong*. London: Viking.

Morse, J. (1794) *The American Geography, or a view of the present position of the United States of America*. London.

Muller, J. (1993) Parallel paths: The origins of planning education and the planning profession in South Africa. *Planning History*, **15**(2), pp. 5–11.

Muller, J. (1994) The Imperial Imprint: British influences on South African Planning. Proceedings of Sixth International Planning History Conference. Hong Kong: Centre for Urban Planning & Environmental Management.

Muller, J. (1995) Influence and experience: Albert Thompson and South Africa's garden city. *Planning History*, **17**(3), pp. 14–21.

Murray, D.J. (1965) *The West Indies and the Development of Colonial Government 1801–1834*. Oxford: Clarendon.

Mutale, E. (1993) Managing Rapid Urban Growth, with Particular Reference to Lusaka, Zambia. MSc Thesis, University of East London.

Napier, (1853) *Defects, Civil and Military, of the Indian Government*, 2nd ed. London: Westerton.

Neild, S.M. (1979) Colonial urbanism: The development of Madras City in the eighteenth and nineteenth centuries. *Modern Asian Studies*, **13**(2), pp. 217–246.

Nicolson, I.F. (1969) *The Administration of Nigeria 1900–1960: Men, Methods and Myths*. Oxford: Oxford University Press.

Nishiyama, Y. (1988) Why Taiwan-Type cul-de-sac failed in Kaohsiung? Proceedings of Third International Planning History Conference, Tokyo.

Norberg-Schultz, C. (1980) *Genius Loci: Towards a Phenomenology of Architecture*. London: Academy Editions.

Nyce, R. (1973) *Chinese New Villages in Malaysia: A Community Study*. Kuala Lumpur: Malaysian Sociological Research Institute.

Oberlander, H.P. (1962) *A Report on the Establishment and Organization of Planning for Urban and Regional Development in Trinidad and Tobago*. New York: United Nations Technical Assistance Programme.

Obudho, R.A. and El-Shakhs, S. (eds.) (1979) *The Development of Urban Systems in Africa*. New York: Praeger.

O'Flanagan, N. (1989) *The Sydney Harbour Trust: The Early Years* Canberra: Australian National University.

Okpala, D.C.I. (1987) Received concepts and theories in African urbanisation studies and urban management strategies. *Urban Studies*, Vol. 24, No. 2, pp. 137–150.

Ola, C.S. (1977) *Town and Country Planning Law in Nigeria*. Ibadan: Oxford University Press.

Oldenburg, V.T. (1984) *The Making of Colonial Lucknow 1856–1877*. Princeton: Princeton University Press.

Oliver, P. (1987) *Dwellings: The House Across the World*. Oxford: Phaidon.

Olsen, D.J. (1964) *Town Planning in London*. New Haven: Yale University Press.

Olsen, D.J. (1974) Victorian London: specialization, segregation and privacy. *Victorian Studies*, **17**, pp. 265–278.

Orde Brown, G.St.J. (1941) *Report on Labour Conditions in West Africa*. Command 6277. London: HMSO.

Osunsade, F.L. (1965) *The Colonial Development and Welfare Scheme and the First Plan Period in Nigeria*. MSc Thesis, University of Ibadan.

Oxford (1914) *Oxford Survey of the British Empire*. Oxford: Oxford University Press.

Pakenham, T. (1982) *The Boer War*. London: Macdonald.

Parnell, S. (1988) Racial segregation in Johannesburg: The Slums Act 1934–39. *South African Geographical Journal*, **70**(2), pp. 112–126.

Parnell, S. (1993) Creating Racial Privilege: Public Health and Town Planning Legislation 1910–1920. Proceedings of the Symposium on South African Planning History. Pietermaritzburg: Planning History Study Group.

Patterson, O. (1982) *Slavery and Social Death*. Cambridge, Mass: Harvard University Press.

Pearson, H.F. (1969) Lt. Jackson's Plan of Singapore. *JMBRAS*, Vol. 42, No. 1, pp. 161–165.

Pearson, A. and Mouchet, R. (1923) *Practical Hygiene of Native Compounds in Tropical Africa*. London: Baillère Tindall and Cox.

Pegrum, R. (1983) *The Bush Capital: How Australia Chose Canberra as its Capital City*. Sydney: Hale & Iremonger.

Pentland, Lady (1928) *The Rt. Hon. John Sinclair, Lord Pentland, GCSI: A Memoir*. London: Methuen.

Perham, M. (1956) *Lugard: The Years of Adventure 1858–1898*. London: Collins.

Perham, M. (1960) *Lugard: The Years of Authority 1898–1945*. London: Collins.

Perry, E. (1930) Housing conditions in Cape Town and Cape Province. *GCTP*, **20**, pp. 270–275.

Phimister, I.R. (1987) African labour conditions and health in the Southern Rhodesian mining industry, 1898–1953, in Phimister and Van Onselen, C. (eds.) *Studies in the History of African Mine Labour in Colonial Zimbabwe*.

Phillips, D., and Yeh, A.G.O. (eds.) (1987) *New Towns in East and South-East Asia: Planning and Development*. Oxford: Oxford University Press.

Pike, D. (1951–52) The utopian dreams of Adelaide's founders. *Proceedings of the Royal Geographical Society of South Australia*, **53**, pp. 65–77.

Pike, D. (1957) *Paradise of Dissent*. Melbourne: Melbourne University Press.

Pim, A. (1946) *Colonial Agricultural Production*. London.

Pipes, R. (1990) *The Russian Revolution 1899–1919*. London: Collins Harvill.

Plamenatz, J. (1966) *The English Utilitarians*. Oxford: Basil Blackwell.

Pooley, C.G. (ed.) (1992) *Housing Strategies in Europe, 1880–1930*. Leicester: Leicester University Press.

Posel, D. (1991) *The Making of Apartheid, 1948–1961: Conflict and Compromise*. Oxford: Oxford University Press.

Potts, D. (1985) Capital relocation in Africa: The case of Lilongwe in Malawi. *Geographical Journal*, **151**(2), pp. 182–196.

Powell, R. and Tracy, E. (1989) The urban morphology of Little India – meaning and values in urban form. *Journal of Singapore Institute of Planners*, **12**(1), pp. 23–35.

Power, G. (1983) Apartheid Baltimore style: The residential segregation ordinance of 1910–1913. *Maryland Law Review*, **42**, pp. 296–301.

Prakash, V. (1972) *New Towns in India*. Princeton: Princeton University Press.

Price, A.G. (1924) *The Foundation and Settlement of South Australia 1829–1845*. Adelaide: F.W. Preece.

Proudfoot, P. (1991) Canberra: the triumph of the Garden City. *Journal of the Royal Australian Historical Society*, **77**(1), pp. 20–39.

Rabinow, Paul (ed.) (1986) *The Foucault Reader*. London: Penguin.

Rainger, R. (1980) Philanthropy and science in the 1830s: The British and Foreign Aborigines' Protection Society. *Man*, **15**, pp. 702–717.

Rakodi, C. (1986) Colonial urban planning in Northern Rhodesia and its legacy. *Third World Planning Review*, **8**(3), pp. 193–218.

Ramasubban, R. (1988) Imperial health in British India, 1857–1900, in MacLeod and Lewis (eds.), pp. 38–60.

Ramphele, M. (1993) *A Bed Called Home: Life in the Migrant Labour Hostels of Cape Town*: New Zealand: Gordon and Gotch.

Rand, B. (1914) *Percival and Berkeley*. Cambridge: Cambridge University Press.

Rapoport, A. (1982) *The Meaning of the Built Environment*. Beverley Hills: Sage.

Rasmussen, S.E. (1937) *London: The Unique City*. London: Jonathan Cape.

Ratcliffe, B.M. (1990) Cities and environmental decline: elites and the sewage problems in Paris from the mid-eighteenth to the mid-nineteenth century. *Planning Perspectives*, **5** (2), pp. 189–222.

Ravetz, A (1988) Women in planning history: Theories and applications. *Planning History*, **10**(1), pp. 23–25.

Ray, R. (1979) *Urban Roots of Indian Nationalism: Pressure Groups and Conflict of Interests in Calcutta City Politics, 1875–1939*. New Delhi, Vikas.

Reade, C.C. (1909) *The Revolution of Britain: A Book for Colonials*. New Zealand: Gordon and Gotch.

Reade, C.C. (1921*a*) Town planning in Malaya. *Town Planning Review*, **9**(3).

Reade, C.C. (1921*b*) Town planning legislation in South Australia: A retrospect. *Town Planning Review*, **9**, pp. 153–161.

Redfield, R. and Singer, M.B. (1954) The cultural role of cities. *Economic Development and Cultural Change*, **3**, pp. 53–73.

Reece, T.R. (1963) *Colonial Georgia: A Study in British Imperial Policy in the Eighteenth Century*. Athens: University of Georgia.

Rempel, J.I. (1980) *Building With Wood, and Other Aspects of Nineteenth-Century Buildings in Central Canada*, 2nd ed. Toronto: University of Toronto Press.

Reps, J.W. (1965) *The Making of Urban America*. Princeton: Princeton University Press.

Reps, J.W. (1979) *Cities of the American West: A History of Frontier Urban Planning*. Princeton: Princeton University Press.

Reps, J.W. (1984) C2 + L2 = S2? Another look at the origins of Savannah's town plan, in Jackson, Harvey, H. and Spalding, Phinizy (eds.) *Forty Years of Diversity*: Essays on Colonial Georgia. Athens, Georgia: University of Georgia Press.

Rex, J. (1973) *Race, Colonialism and the City*. London: Routledge and Kegan Paul.

Reynolds, H. (1982) *The Other Side of the Frontier: Aboriginal resistance to the European invasion of Australia*. Ringwood, Victoria: Penguin.

Reynolds, H. (1992) *The Law of the Land*, 2nd ed. Ringwood, Victoria: Penguin.

RIBA (Royal Institute of British Architects) (1911) *Transactions of RIBA Town Planning Conference, London 10–15 October 1910*. London: RIBA.

Ringelman, M. (1915) *Temporary Structures in Invaded Countries*. Paris: Bulletin de la Société d'Encouragement pour l'industrie Nationale.

Roach, H.B. (1968) The Planning of Philadelphia: A seventeenth-century real estate development. *Pennsylvania Magazine of History and Biography*, *92*, pp. 3–47 and 143–194.

Roberts, A. (1994) *Eminent Churchillians*. London: Weidenfeld and Nicholson.

Robinson, J.B. (1990) The Power of Apartheid; Territoriality and State Power in South African Cities, Port Elizabeth, 1923–72. PhD Thesis, Cambridge University.

Robinson, P.S. (1984) *The Plantation of Ulster: British Settlement in an Irish Landscape 1600–1670*. Dublin: Gill and Macmillan.

Robison, E.C. (1992) A British proposal for American settlement: Granville Sharp's plan for a town and township. *Planning History*, **14**(3), pp. 23–27.

Roebuck, J.A. (1835) *Pamphlets for the People*. London: Charles Ely.

Ross, R. and Telkamp, G.J. (eds.) (1985) *Colonial Cities*. Netherlands: Martinus Nijhoff.

Russell, A.G. (1944) *Colour, Race and Empire*. London: Victor Gollancz.

Said, E. (1979) *Orientalism*. New York: Vintage Books.

Salkield, T. (1924) Delhi, the imperial city and capital of India. *GCTP*, **14**, pp. 5–10.

Sandes, E.W.S. (1933) *The Military Engineer in India*. Chatham: Institute of Royal Engineers.

Sarin, M. (1979) *Urban Planning in the Third World: The Chandigarh Experience*. London: Mansell.

Saunders, K. (ed.) (1984) *Indentured Labour in the British Empire 1834–1920*. London: Croom Helm.

Selby, I. (1928) Robert Hoddle and the Planning

of Melbourne. *Victorian History Magazine*, **13**(2), pp. 54–64.

Sharon, A. (1954–55) Collective settlements in Israel. *Town Planning Review*, **25**, pp. 255–270.

Sharp, S. (1788) *A Short Sketch of Temporary Regulations (until better shall be proposed) for the Intended Settlement on the Grain Coast of Africa, near Sierra Leone*, 3rd ed. London: H. Baldwin.

Sharp, G. (1794) *A General Plan for Laying Out Towns and Townships on the New-Acquired Lands in the East Indies, America or Elsewhere*. London.

Shelton, A. (1914) Land tenure and values in Hong Kong. *Professional Notes of The Surveyors' Institution*, **20**, pp. 109–129.

Silver, C. (1991) The racial origins of zoning: southern cities from 1910–40. *Planning Perspectives*, **6**, pp. 189–205.

Simon, D. (1989) Colonial cities, postcolonial Africa and the world economy: a reinterpretation. *International Journal of Urban and Regional Research*, Vol. 13.

Simon, D. (1992) *Cities, Capital and Development: African Cities in the World Economy*. London: Belhaven.

Simons, A. and Lapham, S. (eds.) (1970) *The Early Architecture of Charleston*. Columbus, SC: University of South Carolina Press.

Simpson, M. (1985) *Thomas Adams and the Modern Planning Movement: Britain, Canada and the United States 1900–1940* London: Mansell.

Simpson, W.R.C. (1907) *Report on the Sanitary Conditions of Singapore*. London: Waterlow.

Simpson, W.J.R. (1908) *The Principles of Hygiene As Applied to Tropical and Sub-Tropical Climates*. London: John Bale & Sons.

Simpson, W.J.R. (1916) *The Maintenance of Health in the Tropics*, 2nd ed. London: John Bale.

Singapore (1928) Town Planning in Singapore. *JTPI*, 81–3.

Smith, D.M. (ed.) (1992) *The Apartheid City and Beyond*. London: Routledge.

Smith, J. (1985) *Slavery and Rice Culture in Low Country Georgia 1750–1860*. Knoxville: University of Tennessee Press.

Smith, J.L. (1914) Hints on land settlement

surveys in the West Indies. *Professional Notes of the Surveyors Institution*, **20**, pp. 129–137.

Smithers, A.J. (1991) *Honourable Conquest: An Account of the Enduring Work of the Royal Engineers throughout the Empire*. London: Leo Cooper.

Soderlund, J.R. (ed.) (1983) *William Penn and the Founding of Pennsylvania 1680–1684: A Documentary History*. Philadelphia: University of Pennsylvania Press.

Sosin, J.M. (1980) *English America and the Restoration Monarchy of Charles II*. Lincoln: University of Nebraska Press.

South African Planning History (1993). Proceedings of Symposium held at Pietermaritzburg, 6–7 September. Planning History Study Group.

Southworth, H. (1991) Strangling South African cities: resistance to group areas in Durban during the 1950s. *International Journal of African Historical Studies*, **24**(1), pp. 1–34.

Sparkes, A. (1990) *The Mind of South Africa: The Story of the Rise and Fall of Apartheid*. London: Heinemann.

Spitzer, L. (1986) The mosquito and segregation in Sierra Leone. *Canadian Journal of African Studies*, **11**, pp. 49–61.

Spodek, H. (1989) From Gandhi to violence: Ahmedabad's 1985 riots in historical perspective. *Modern Asian Studies*, **23**(4), pp. 765–795.

Statham, P. (ed.) (1989) *The Origins of Australian Capital Cities*. Melbourne: Cambridge University Press.

Stelter, G. (1984) The classical ideal: Cultural and urban form in eighteenth century Britain and America. *Journal of Urban History*, **10**, pp. 351–382.

Stevens, P.M.D. (1953) Planning legislation in the colonies. *Town and Country Planning*, **23**, pp. 119–123.

Stokes, E. (1959) *The English Utilitarians in India*. London: Basil Blackwell.

Sulman, J. (1921) *An Introduction to the Study of Town Planning in Australia*. Sydney: Government Printer.

Sutcliffe, A. (1981) *Towards the Planned City*. Oxford: Blackwell.

Swanson, M.W. (1977) The sanitation syndrome: Bubonic plague and urban native policy in the

Cape Colony, 1900–1909. *Journal of African History*, **13**(3), pp. 387–410.

Swilling, M., Humphries, R. and Shubane, K. (1991) *Apartheid City in Transition*. Oxford: Oxford University Press.

Taylor, B.B. (1979) Planning Discontinuity: Modern colonial cities in Morocco. *Lotus International*, **36**, pp. 52–66.

TCPSS (1957) Proceedings of Town and Country Planning Summer School, Oxford.

TCPSS (1958) Proceedings of Town and Country Planning Summer School, Bangor.

TCPSS (1959) Proceedings of Town and Country Planning Summer School, Southampton.

TCPSS (1960) Proceedings of Town and Country Planning Summer School, Saint Andrews.

TCPSS (1961) Proceedings of Town and Country Planning Summer School, Reading.

TCPSS (1964) Proceedings of Town and Country Planning Summer School, Exeter.

TCPSS (1965) Proceedings of Town and Country Planning Summer School, Saint Andrews.

TCPSS (1967) Proceedings of Town and Country Planning Summer School, Queen's University Belfast.

Temple, C.L. (1918) *Native Races and Their Rulers*. London: Frank Cass (reprinted 1968).

Temple, F.C. (1928) Jamshedpur: The birth and first twenty years of an industrial town in India. *JTPI*, **14**, pp. 265–286.

Thomas, N. (1990) Sanitation and seeing: The creation of state power in early colonial Fiji. *Comparative Studies in Society and History*, **32**, pp. 149–170.

Thomas, R. (ed.) (1987) *The Trinidad Labour Riots of 1937: Perspectives Fifty Years Later*. St. Augustine: University of West Indies.

Thompson, E.P. (1967) Time, work discipline and industrial capitalism. *Past and Present*, No. 38, pp. 56–97.

Thompson, E.T. (1975) *Plantation Societies, Race Relations and the South: The Regimentation of Populations*. Durham, NC: University of North Carolina.

Thompson, F.L. (1923) *Site Planning in Practice*. London: H. Frowde.

Throup, D. (1987) *Economic and Social Origins of Mau Mau 1945–53*. London: James Currey.

Tikasingh, G.I.M. (1973) The Establishment of the Indians in Trinidad 1870–1900. PhD Thesis, University of West Indies.

Tindall, G. (1982) *City of Gold: The Biography of Bombay*. London: Temple Smith.

Tinker, H. (1974) *A New System of Slavery: The Export of Indian Labour Overseas 1830–1920*. Oxford: Oxford University Press.

Torstendahl, R. and Burrage, M. (eds.) (1990) *The Formation of Professions: Knowledge, State and Strategy*. London: Sage.

Tregenza, J. (1986) Charles Reade: Town planning missionary, in Bunker and Hutchings (eds.).

Tregenza, J. (1989) Colonel Light's Theberton Cottage and his legacy to Maria Gandy. *Journal of Historical Society of South Australia*, **17**, pp. 5–24.

Trietsch, D. (1923) Garden cities for Palestine. *GCTP*, **13**, pp. 11–13.

Trinidad and Tobago (n.d., c. 1973) *You and planning*. Port of Spain: Town and Country Planning Division.

Trinidad and Tobago (n.d., c. 1984) *Guide to Developers and Applicants for Planning Permission*. Port of Spain: Ministry of Planning and Mobilization.

Troen, S.I. (1988) The transformation of Zionist planning policy: From agricultural settlements to an urban network. *Planning Perspectives*, **3**(1), pp. 3–23.

Troen, S.I. (1992) Spearheads of the Zionist frontier: Historical perspectives on post-1967 settlement planning in Judea and Samaria. *Planning Perspectives*, **7**(1), pp. 81–100.

Troen, S.I. (1995) New departures in Zionist planning: The development town, in Troen, S.I. and Lucas, N. (eds.) *Israel: The First Decade of Independence*. New York: New York State University Press.

Trollope, H.C. (1903) Work done in the Orange River Colony Refugee Camps. **153**, pp. 312–318.

Trzebinski, E. (1985) *The Kenya Pioneers*. London: Heinemann.

Turnbull, C.M. (1972) *The Straits Settlements 1826–1867*. Oxford: Oxford University Press.

Turrell, R. (1984) Kimberley's model compounds. *Journal of African History*, **25**, pp. 59–75.

Turrell, R. (1987) *Capital and Labour on the*

Kimberley Diamond Fields, 1871–1900. Cambridge: Cambridge University Press.

Tyrwhitt, J. (1947) *Patrick Geddes in India.* London: Lund Humphries.

Urquhart, A.W. (1977) *Planned Urban Landscapes of Northern Nigeria.* Zaria: Ahmadu Bello University Press.

Vale, L.J. (1992) *Architecture, Power and National Identity.* New Haven and London: Yale University Press.

Van der Bijl, H.J. (1947) The creation and planning of Vanderbijl Park. *Town and Country Planning*, **15**, pp. 64–68.

Van Heyningen, E.B. (1989) Agents of Empire: The medical profession in the Cape Colony. *Medical History*, **33**(4), pp. 450–471.

Van Tonder, D. (1993) Boycotts, unrest and the Western Areas Removal Scheme, 1949–1952. *Journal of Urban History*, **20**(1), pp. 19–53.

Vance, J. (1977) *This Scene of Man: The Role and Structure of the City in the Geography of Western Civilization.* New York.

Vlach, J.M. (1976) The Shotgun House: An African American legacy. *Pioneer America*, **8**(1), pp. 47–56, **8**(2), pp. 57–76.

Voigt, W. (1989) The garden city as eugenic utopia. *Planning Perspectives*, **4**, pp. 295–312.

Walvin, J. (1992) *Black Ivory: A History of British Slavery.* London: Harper Collins.

Warren, J.F. (1986) *Rickshaw Coolie: A People's History of Singapore 1880–1940.* Singapore: Oxford University Press.

Wang, L.H., and Yeh, A.G.O. (1987) Public housing-led new town development: Hong Kong and Singapore. *Third World Planning Review*, **9**(1), pp. 41–64.

Ward, S.V. (ed.) (1992) *The Garden City – Past, Present and Future* London: Spon.

Warwick, P. (1983) *Black People and the South African War 1899–1902.* Cambridge: Cambridge University Press.

Wasserfall, J. (1990) Early Mine and Railway Housing in South Africa. PhD Thesis, University of Cambridge.

Watson, C.M. (1914) *History of the Corps of Royal Engineers.* Chatham: Institute of Royal Engineers (reprinted 1954).

Watson, I.B. (1980) Fortifications and the 'idea' of force in early English EIC relations with India. *Past and Present*, No. 88 pp. 70–87.

Watson, I.B. and Potter, R.B. (1993) Housing and housing policy in Barbados: The relevance of the chattel house. *Third World Planning Review*, **15**(4), pp. 373–395.

Watts, S.J. and Watts, S.J. (1986) Morphology, planning and cultural values: a case study of Ilorin, Nigeria. *Third World Planning Review*, **8**(3), pp. 237–249.

Webb, C.M. (1923–24) The development of Rangoon. *Town Planning Review*, **10**, pp. 37–42.

Webb, S. & B. (1978) *The Letters of Sidney and Beatrice Webb*, Vol. 3 (Mackenzie, N. (ed.)). Cambridge: Cambridge University Press.

Weinreb, B., and Hibbert, C. (1983) *The London Encyclopeadia.* London: Macmillan.

Weir, R.M. (1983) *Colonial South Carolina: A History.* New York: Millwood.

Wekwete, K.H. (1988) Development of urban planning in Zimbabwe: An overview. *Cities*, **5**(1), pp. 57–71.

Wells, R.V. (1975) *The Population of the British Colonies in America before 1776. A Survey of Census Data.* Princeton: Princeton University Press.

Welsh, D. (1971) *The Roots of Segregation: Native Policy in Colonial Natal 1845–1910.* Cape Town: Oxford University Press.

Western, J. (1984) *Outcast Cape Town.* Cape Town: David Philip.

Wigglesworth, M. (1982) Planning Legislation as a Necessary Charade, in *Planning Legislation: Proceedings of a Seminar in Cyprus.* London: Commonwealth Association of Planners, pp. 133–142.

Williams, E. (1962) *History of the People of Trinidad and Tobago.* Port of Spain: PNM Publishing.

Williams, G.J. (ed.) (1986) *Lusaka and Its Environs.* Lusaka: Zambian Geographical Association.

Williams, M. (1966) The parkland towns of Australia and New Zealand. *Geographical Review*, **56**(1), pp. 67–89.

Williams, M. (1974) *The Making of the South Australian Landscape.* London: Academic Press.

Wilson, E.G. (1976) *The Loyal Blacks.* New York: Capricorn Books.

Wilson, E.G. (1972) *Migrant Labour in South Africa*. Johannesburg: South African Council of Churches.

Winchester, S. (1985) *Outposts*. London: Hodder and Stoughton.

Wohl, A.S. (1983) *Endangered Lives: Public Health in Victorian Britain*. London: Dent.

Wood, D. (1968) *Trinidad in Transition: The Years After Slavery*. London: Oxford University Press.

Wood, J.D. (1982) Grand design on the fringes of Empire: new towns for British North America. *Canadian Geographer*, **26**, pp. 243–255.

Wood, J.S. (1991) 'Build, therefore, your new world': The New England village as settlement ideal. *Annals of Association of American Geographers*, **81**(1).

Worboys, M. (1988) Manson, Ross and colonial medical policy: tropical medicine in London and Liverpool 1899–1911, in MacLeod and Lewis (eds.), pp. 21–37.

Wright, G. (1987) Tradition in the service of modernity: Architecture and urbanism in French colonial policy 1900–1930. *Journal of Modern History*, No. 59, pp. 291–316.

Wright, M. (1982) *Lord Leverhulme's Unknown Venture: The Lever Chair and the Beginnings of Town and Regional Planning, 1908–1948*. London: Hutchinson.

Wright, R. (1989) *The Bureaucrats' Domain: Space and the Public Interest in Victoria 1836–1884*. Melbourne: Oxford University Press.

Yeoh, B.S. (1991) Municipal Control, Asiatic Agency and the Urban Built Environment in Colonial Singapore 1880–1929. DPhil, Thesis, University of Oxford.

Yerolympos, A. (1993) A new city for a new state. City planning and the formation of national identity in the Balkans (1820s–1920s). *Planning Perspectives*, **8**(3), pp. 233–257.

Yitftachel, O. (1992) *Planning a Mixed Region in Israel: The Political Geography of Arab-Jewish relations in the Galilee*. Aldershot: Avebury.

Zasloff, J.J. (1962–63) Rural settlement in South Vietnam: The Agroville Program. *Pacific Affairs*, **35**, pp. 327–340.

GLOSSARY AND ABBREVIATIONS

Population and year of Independence of main British colonies (previous name in brackets where appropriate)

COUNTRY	INDEPENDENCE Year	POPULATION (1986, millions)
Australia	1931	15.7
Bangladesh (East Pakistan)	1972	98.6
Botswana (Bechuanaland)	1966	1.1
Canada	1931	25.4
Cyprus	1960	0.7
Fiji	1970	0.7
Gambia, The	1965	0.8
Ghana (Gold Coast)	1957	13.6
Guyana (British Guiana)	1966	0.8
Hong Kong	1997	5.5
India	1947	750.9
Israel	1948	4.1
Jamaica	1962	2.3
Kenya	1963	20.3
Lesotho (Basutoland)	1966	1.5
Malawi (Nyasaland)	1964	6.8
Malaysia (Malaya)	1957	15.6
Mauritius	1968	1.0
New Zealand	1931	3.3
Nigeria	1960	96.2
Pakistan	1947	89.8
Papua New Guinea	1975	3.3
Sierra Leone	1961	3.6
Singapore	1965	2.6
Sri Lanka (Ceylon)	1948	15.8
Tanzania (Tanganyika/Zanzibar)	1961	21.7
Trinidad & Tobago	1962	1.2
Uganda	1962	15.5
Zambia (Northern Rhodesia)	1964	6.7
Zimbabwe (Southern Rhodesia)	1979	8.3

(*Source*: Ling, 1988)

Abbreviations

CUP	Cambridge University Press
DAmB	Dictionary of American Biography
DAustB	Dictionary of Australian Biography
DCanB	Dictionary of Canadian Biography
DNB	Dictionary of National Biography (United Kingdom)
DNZB	Dictionary of New Zealand Biography
DSAB	Dictionary of South African Biography
GCTP	Garden Cities and Town Planning
HMSO	Her Majesty's Stationery Office
JMBRAS	Journal of the Malaysian Branch of the Royal Asiatic Society
JTPI	Journal of Royal Town Planning Institute
NNA	Nigerian National Archives (Ibadan)
OUP	Oxford University Press
PICE	Proceedings of Institution of Civil Engineers
PRO	Public Record Office (Kew, London)
WWW	Who Was Who

Glossary of Foreign Terms

Charpoy (Hindi)	Bedstead of rope on a frame
Feng shui (Chinese)	Ancient Chinese science of placing and designing buildings
Godown (Malay)	Warehouse or store
Maidan (Arabic)	Open space near a town; esplanade or parade ground
Nabob (Urdu)	British official gathering great wealth in India (from Mogul title of deputy governor of a province)
Padang (Malay)	Parade ground
Plat (Middle English)	Flat piece of ground surveyed on a cadastre

INDEX